Structural Characterization Techniques

Structural Characterization Techniques

Advances and Applications in Clean Energy

edited by
Lorenzo Malavasi

PAN STANFORD PUBLISHING

Published by

Pan Stanford Publishing Pte. Ltd.
Penthouse Level, Suntec Tower 3
8 Temasek Boulevard
Singapore 038988

Email: editorial@panstanford.com
Web: www.panstanford.com

British Library Cataloguing-in-Publication Data
A catalogue record for this book is available from the British Library.

Structural Characterization Techniques: Advances and Applications in Clean Energy

ISBN 978-981-4669-34-4 (Hardcover)
ISBN 978-981-4669-35-1 (eBook)

Printed in the USA

Contents

Preface

A major worldwide challenge is the development of cleaner, sustainable sources of energy to deal with the environmental threat of global warming and the finite nature of fossil fuel reserves. Promising energy conversion and storage technologies, including fuel cells and lithium batteries, are being developed to help cut carbon dioxide emissions. The performance of these energy systems depends crucially on the properties of their component materials, thus requiring the development of innovative materials chemistry strategies to synthesize and characterize such materials.

The effective performance of materials developed for clean energy applications is strongly related to their physico-chemical properties and, as a consequence, the correlation between these properties and the materials' crystal structure is a central topic in modern materials chemistry. Materials are getting as well more complex from a chemical point of view along with the development of new synthetic strategies, and thus the study of the correlation between their structure and properties requires the application of advanced techniques in order to unveil all the key aspects affecting the materials' performance. In addition, a more accurate description of the processes involved in several materials of interest for clean energy applications requires their structural investigation by means of *in situ* and *in operando* conditions in order to provide a more realistic picture of their function.

In this book, we collected several examples that cover most of the advanced characterization tools that are nowadays used to characterize the crystal structure of complex materials of interest for energy conversion and storage technologies. State-of-the-art spectroscopic, crystallographic, and modeling strategies are provided with reference to materials for oxide ion and protons solid-oxide fuel cells, lithium batteries, and hydrogen storage materials. Such collection of examples given by authoritative scientists in the field of materials chemistry will help the reader get a comprehensive overview of advanced structural characterization techniques in the field of materials for clean energy applications.

Lorenzo Malavasi

1.2 Architecture and Operation Principle of Solid Oxide Fuel Cells

Electrochemical energy conversion and storage devices like batteries, fuel cells, electrolyzers, supercapacitors, and photo-electrochemical cells have in common that they have an electronically conducting anode and cathode separated by an ion-conducting electrolyte. Specific for the SOFC is its high operation temperature of up to 1000°C, which is necessary to activate the oxygen ion conductivity of the electrolyte, typically gadolinium cerium oxide, or yttrium stabilized zircon oxide. The SOFC has the great advantage that it can convert hydrocarbon fuels such as natural gas or biomass gas into electricity, whereas alternative fuel cell concepts typically require cleaner and fuels such as high purity hydrogen.

The extremely high operation temperatures of SOFC are very demanding and require ceramic materials for most of their components. Readily existing large-scale SOFC systems are based on tubular electrode architecture. For the mid-scale and small scale, planar architectures are being used. For a review on SOFC, see reference [1].

Standard SOFC cathodes are made from porous ceramics with perovskite structure of the ABO_3-type, specifically $La_{1-x}Sr_xMnO_3$ with a high oxygen catalytic activity and electronic and ionic conductivity at the operation temperature.

Standard anodes are based on porous gadolinium cerium oxide with dispersed nickel nanoparticles. For electrolytes see [2], for example.

Tubular SOFC systems have been well established for large-scale power plants for many decades. The tubular architecture is less suited for systems for medium and small scale. Instead, flat electrode-electrolyte assemblies are used for latter technology and stacked as repeating units together, with Cr-containing metallic interconnector plates in between.

1.3 Neutron Tomography on SOFC Stacks

As has been shown in Fig. 1.1, the cell assemblies in SOFC are stacked together as repeating units in series in order to match the required cell voltage. A particular mechanical pressure must be applied in order to maintain proper fuel and exhaust gas transport, sealing, and electric contacting between metallic interconnects and ceramic parts. In general, thermal cycling and the mechanical pressure may over time incur cracking of ceramic SOFC components. However, checking for such potential cracks by disassembling the stack may also cause cracking, and it is hard to tell whether cracks observed after disassembling are caused by the disassembling itself or by the thermal cycling during SOFC operation.

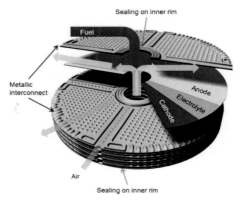

Figure 1.1   Design of the SOFC stack in the Galileo system by Hexis AG. Courtesy Swiss Electric Research (http://www.swisselectric-research.ch/de/sof-ch-esc.html).

It is therefore of interest to have a non-destructive analytical technique to look into the SOFC stack without the necessity to disassemble it. Neutron tomography is such method particularly because it allows for the imaging of a complete cell stack. Neutron tomography has been applied for a long time to polymer electrolyte fuel cells and has been pioneered at the Paul Scherrer Institute by the Laboratory for Electrochemistry and the NEUTRA beamline at the SINQ Swiss Spallation Neutron Source [3]. The particular merit that neutron tomography has in this respect is due to the pronounced sensitivity of neutrons to protons or hydrogen containing materials such as water. Water management is an important issue in PEM fuel cells and can be mapped with ease with neutron tomography [4].

The neutron radiography and tomography images shown in Fig. 1.2 allow in general the identification of structural inhomogeneity in the sub-millimeter size range down to say 80 μm. Recent improvements in instrumentation may allow for even better spatial resolution. For neutron tomography, the object under investigation is placed on a table which is in the neutron optical path between neutron source and neutron detector.

Figure 1.2   Neutron tomography images of a SOFC stack, recorded at NEUTRA beamline at the Swiss Spallation Neutron Source SINQ. The stack was provided by Dr. Josef Sfeir (HEXIS AG). Beamtime and technical support were provided by Dr. Eberhard Lehmann, Peter Vontobel, and George Necola (SINQ, PSI).

The object, in this case the SOFC stack, is then irradiated until a particular number of neutron counts are measured by the neutron detector. Then the table with the SOFC stack is rotated by several degrees, and another neutron image is recorded. Then the table with the SOFC stack is rotated again, and so on. In the subsequent computational neutron image analysis, the corresponding projection of the stack image is being accounted and corrected for. In the end, a stack of neutron images represents basically a three-dimensional voxel dataset that represents the structure of the SOFC stack with a spatial resolution in the sub-millimeter range.

To the best of the author's knowledge, there have not yet been any systematic neutron tomography studies on SOFC stacks so far, whereas there are many studies on PEM fuel cells [5]. One reason for this is that water and humidity play an important functional role in PEM fuel cells.

For the hydrogen in this water, the neutrons constitute an excellent analytical probe. However, in view of the increasing interest in the thermo-mechanical behavior of SOFC components, neutron radiography and tomography as non-destructive methods for structure determination may also become a method of interest.

1.4 Microstructure Investigation with Small-Angle X-Ray Scattering

We saw in the previous section how imaging by neutron radiography and tomography as a non-destructive analytical tool might assist for example in the diagnostics of fracture evolution in SOFC stacks. The limited spatial resolution of neutron tomography and radiography puts a limit on the structural analyses of SOFC and its components. Progress in tomography technology of course may in future push these limits further, which holds also for any other analytical technique.

Fuel cell components are chemically and structurally highly complex and heterogeneous. For example, the presence of porosity in electrodes and their absence in solid electrolytes are critical for their functionality. Typically, engineers employ imaging and microscopy techniques in order to study structural details.

An alternative method for microstructure characterization is small-angle scattering with x-rays (SAXS). SAXS has been known to materials scientists for a long time and can provide quantitative information on the topological structure parameters of ordered and disordered media such as particle size, pore size distributions, porosity, internal surface area, fractal dimensions. By default, SAXS is a 3D method and non-destructive. For a book with the basic principles and applications of SAXS, we refer the reader to the book *Small Angle X-ray Scattering* (eds. Glatter and Kratky) [6]. Small-angle neutron scattering (SANS) follows in analogy the principles of SAXS and is often used in polymer sciences and basically applicable to PEM-FC membranes, for example. A review about the use of SAXS for ceramic materials can be found in [7].

The Fourier nature of the x-rays scattered in the reciprocal space warrants that the aforementioned structure parameters are measured with high statistical significance and confidence—without need for complicated stereological considerations and laborious computational formalisms. Recent advancements in synchrotron instrumentation allow measuring pore space and its conjugated objects with sizes ranging from 1 nm to several microns (Ultra-SAXS, USAXS) and to map the structure parameters of complicated cell assemblies in steps of 10 μm [8]. Because the x-ray energies at synchrotron centers are tunable, they can be employed for chemical contrast variation and thus for separation of scattering signals by different chemical constituents in the material (Anomalous SAXS: ASAXS). According to the Bragg equation $n\lambda = 2\,d\sin(2\Theta/2)$, the diffractogram shifts towards smaller Bragg angles when shorter wavelengths λ are applied.

Small-angle scattering can be observed in a conventional x-ray or neutron diffraction experiment, when the diffracted or scattered intensity increases when we approach the "(000)" Bragg reflection at near 0 angle. SAXS and SANS is diffuse scattering, and the intensity may increase by several orders of magnitude in a very small angular range. Typically, scattering curves are then represented in a double logarithmic (log-log) plot. The diffraction (scattering) angle 2Θ is transformed into the momentum transfer k-vector. Alternative symbols for the momentum transfer are q and Q, for example: $k = 4\,\pi\sin\Theta/\lambda$. This is a meaningful transformation, because the scattering angle 2Θ is renormalized by the wavelength λ, so that when SAXS is carried out with different wavelengths λ (and this is necessary for ASAXS), the shift of scattering curves is lifted and the scattering curves can be easily compared. This holds not only for small-angle scattering, but also for wide-angle scattering and Bragg diffraction.

1.4.1 SAXS on Supercapacitor Electrodes

Figure 1.3 shows SAXS curves obtained from three different processed porous glassy carbon specimen, which were tested for the use in supercapacitor electrodes [9]. We divert here for a short period from the SOFC topic for the ease of explanation of the methodology. Glassy carbon is a highly porous material and a very good standard material for calibration of SAXS intensities. For the q-range 0.0002 Å^{-1} to 0.02 Å^{-1} we find a steep decay of SAXS intensity with a power law which is characteristic for a particular fractal dimension of the pore space.

The intensity plateau in the intermediate range 0.03 Å^{-1} to 0.2 Å^{-1} can be fitted with a structure function for spheres (micropores), convoluted with a log normal size distribution. The bow intensity for $q > 0.4$ represents another plateau which, too, can be fitted with a sphere structure factor and a log normal distribution (here macropores). The complete analysis procedure is exercised in ref. [10]. Small-angle scattering can also be made with neutrons as probes (small-angle neutron scattering, SANS). Similar experiments and observation were made with electrochemically oxidized and reduced glassy carbon with SANS [11].

Glassy carbon is a two-phase material, and the two phases are the solid carbon matrix and the open pores in this matrix. From the SAXS point of view, this is a relatively simple model system because it contains only carbon as a chemical elements and in the pores a low concentration of air or other gas, or vacuum.

Actual electrode assemblies such as in SOFC or batteries are more complex, and it can be difficult to distinguish pores from particles that contain different chemical elements. But this information is necessary for a full structural analysis.

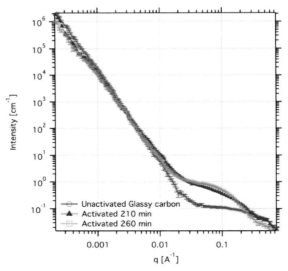

Figure 1.3   SAXS curves of three different samples of glassy carbon in log-log representation. The bottom curve was recorded from an unactivated (open circle) glassy carbon sheet of 60 μm thickness, which has small and closed micropores. After thermal oxidation (activation) in a furnace in air for 210 min (filled triangles) and 260 min (open square), the pores become open and enlarged. The enlargement manifests in the increase of SAXS intensity of the plateau range.

1.4.2 SAXS on SOFC Electrode Assemblies

We have employed SAXS to quantify the pore space and surface areas as a function of position within electrodes and electrolyte of a SOFC assembly as shown in Fig. 1.4. The primary structure parameters are determined over a length scale from nanometers to micrometers in one single USAXS measurement with 20 µm spatial resolution normal to the electrode.

Figure 1.4 shows the optical micrograph of a fracture cross section of a SOFC electrode assembly, i.e., cathode, electrolyte, and anode with a total thickness of around 200 µm.

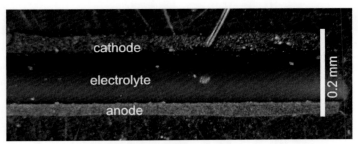

Figure 1.4 Optical micrograph of ceramic SOFC assembly highlighting cathode, electrolyte, and anode. The total thickness is around 200 µm.

Visual inspection of the morphology of the assembly shows that cathode, electrolyte, and anode have apparently different levels of porosity.

The further magnified region of anode and electrolyte in Fig. 1.6 shows the microstructure with a spatial resolution of roughly 1 µm. The electron optical contrast in the electron micrograph gives already some account of the chemical heterogeneity of the anode, which is the highly porous and electronically non-conducting CGO matrix (bright) with dispersed Ni aggregates (grey) at its surface and the surrounding open pores (black).

Figure 1.5a shows a polished piece of such assembly embedded in a metal ring with phenolic resin prepared for SAXS. The magnified electron micrograph on the right side of Fig. 1.5b shows two large (black) cavities in the cathode layer, which are not of interest in this study. The black contrast in the cathode and in the anode is indicative to the pores through which oxygen, fuel gas and reaction products can flow during SOFC operation. The bright regions in the assembly represent the not well electronically conducting materials such as the ion-conducting electrolyte in the center and the cerium gadolinium oxide (CGO) that is admixed in the anode.

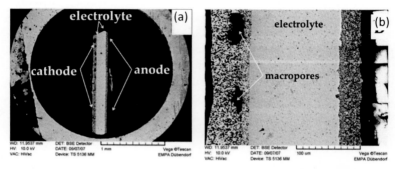

Figure 1.5   Electron micrographs of SOFC assembly embedded in resin and thinned for further analyses. Shown are two magnifications with size bar 1 mm (a) and 100 μm (b).

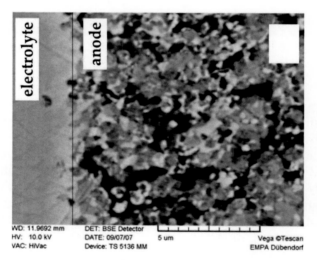

Figure 1.6   Electron micrograph of SOFC assembly embedded in resin highlighting the interface region of anode and electrolyte.

Closer inspection of the SOFC images would show that the assembly is actually made of more layers than just those which are immediately visible. The particles, grains, and pores that consti-tute the components of the assembly are arranged in an irregular network which cannot be quantified in a straightforward procedure. The primary structure parameters are the particle sizes and pore sizes, and, more specific their respective size distributions. Directly linked with these are the surface areas and porosities. Of particular interest with respect to electrochemical reactions are the triple phase boundaries where gases get in contact and can react with the surfaces of electrochemically active species and where charge transfer can occur. Thus, in addition of the topological inhomogeneity we have to consider also an interconnected chemical heterogeneity which extends from the micrometer range to the molecular size scale of nanometer and below [12].

Figure 1.7 shows in an oversimplified schematic how such thin cell assembly is then mounted at the SAXS instrument between synchrotron x-ray source and x-ray detector. The SOFC sample is measured in the transmission mode, which means the x-ray beam must penetrate the entire sample. Because the x-ray beam is attenuated by the sample in a Lambert–Beer-type exponential decay of the x-ray intensity, the sample must be thin enough so as to allow for a sufficient x-ray transmission:

$$I = I_0 \exp(-\mu d)$$

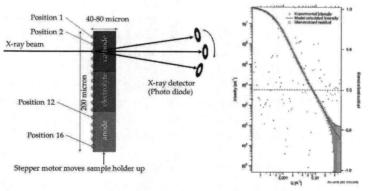

Figure 1.7 (Left) The schematic explains the position of x-ray beam and sample position. The sample is moved by a stepper motor vertical to one particular position, then exposed to the x-ray beam for one USAXS scan, and then moved to the next sample position for the subsequent USAXS scan, and so on. (Right) USAXS scattering curve recorded from a cathode position in the SOFC assembly shown in Fig. 1.5. The black solid line is a least square fit to a model assuming sphere-like objects.

The optimum sample thickness *d* in scattering and spectroscopy experiments is typically 1 scattering length, or slightly below that value. The scattering length depends on the densities and linear absorption coefficients μ of the components in the sample. In the experiment presented here, the SOFC assembly had to be thinned to below 80 μm in order to warrant sufficient transmission at the Ce K-shell absorption edge. Figure 1.7 shows the schematic where the sample is moved by a stepper motor across the x-ray beam into position 3, the x-ray beam coming from the left.

The sample scatters the incoming beam to the right, and a photo diode (x-ray detector) is step-by-step moved in a rotation while the intensity is recorded. The range of small-angle scattering is typically from slightly above 0° (forward scattering) to half of the angle where the first Bragg reflection would occur, often around 5° to 10°. In analogy to x-ray diffraction, we obtain a small-angle scattering pattern with scattered x-ray intensity plotted versus the scattering angle. So to speak we are recording in SAXS the (000) Bragg reflection. The right panel in Fig. 1.7 shows such USAXS curve recorded from the cathode of the SOFC assembly.

The scattered x-ray intensity decays in a very small angular range over several orders of magnitude. The ordinate has been transformed from the technical quantity 2θ [°] to the physically more reasonable k-vector (reciprocal space vector): $k = 4\pi \sin\theta/\lambda$. X-ray diffraction and also SAXS is traditionally done with laboratory based x-ray tubes with characteristic x-ray radiation from a metal target, such as Cu Kα with λ = 1.54056 Å wavelength. When the wavelength is changed such as by changing the target metal or by tuning the x-ray energy at a synchrotron, Bragg's law shows that also the diffractogram or the SAXS curve will shift on the 2θ axis: $n\lambda = 2 d \sin\theta$. It thus becomes difficult to compare diffractograms or SAXS curves obtained with different wavelengths—unless the 2Q angle is transformed to the k vector. We will see in this section and also later in the section about XRD that changing the x-ray wavelength allows taking advantage of the anomalous scattering properties of materials, and thus obtain element specific diffraction and scattering data by x-ray contrast variation (resonant x-ray scattering). This is very important for the study of complex materials.

The SAXS intensity profile in Fig. 1.7 basically represents the curvature of the (000) Bragg reflection and can be modeled mathematically as follows:

$$\frac{d\Sigma}{d\Omega}(k) = \Delta n_f^2 N \int_{R=0}^{\infty} V^2(R)S(k,R)P(R)dR,$$

where $d\Sigma/d\Omega$ is the experimental measured scattering cross section which can be obtained in absolute electrostatic units with a calibrated sample and is measured as cm^2/cm^3, i.e., like a surface area within a particular probed volume. N is the number of objects in the probed volume with the x-ray scattering contrast Δn_f. The argument of the integral contains the volume of the objects with radius R and the structure factor $S(k, R)$, which describes how the geometry of the probed object will influence the scattering pattern. For objects (pores or particles) with spherical geometry, the structure factor reads

$$S(Q,R) = \left(3\frac{\sin(QR) - QR\cos(QR)}{(QR)^3}\right)^2$$

P is the size distribution, which is often—for practical reasons—considered a logarithmic normal distribution. Least square fit routines thus allow deriving the size distribution (Fig. 1.8) of particles or pores from the SAXS curves, which are then also the base forinternal surface areas and porosities. The mathematical theory of small-angle scattering allows for the derivation of many more quantities and properties from the SAXS curves, for which I refer the reader to the book of Glatter and Kratky [6], for example.

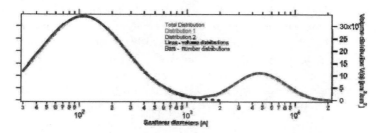

Figure 1.8   Bi-modal pore size distribution obtained from a USAXS curve recorded at cathode SOFC position.

A bi-modal size distribution at some SOFC cathode position is hence shown in Fig. 1.9 with modes at 100 and at 5000 Å. The SAXS instrument used in the study shown here is based on a Bonse–

Hart camera and able to record scattering signals at extremely small angles and thus perform ultra-small-angle x-ray scattering (USAXS). The sizes of objects that can be resolved with this instrument range from 1 nanometer to several micrometers. Hence, micropores, mesopores, and also the lower tail of macropores can be probed with USAXS.

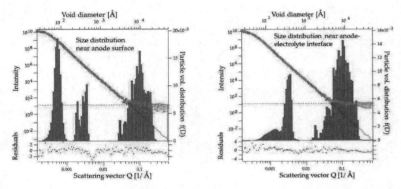

Figure 1.9 USAXS curves (green data points with error bars), and conjugated pore size distributions (vertical bars) in an anode SOFC assembly near the anode surface (left) and near the anode-electrolyte interface (right).

The USAXS instrument at UNICAT at the Advanced Photon Source has an x-ray beam with prismatic cross section of 5 μm × 1 mm. It is thus possible to direct the beam to particular positions on the sample. Figure 1.9 displays two USAXS curves and the derived size distributions from sample positions near the top of the anode surface and near the anode-electrolyte interface. Compared with the schematic in Fig. 1.7, this would correspond to sample positions 16 and 12, respectively. The left panel in Fig. 1.9 shows three size modes near the anode surface, the smallest one with maximum at 85 Å, the next one with 300 to 400 Å, and the largest one with 10,000 Å. The size distribution of the sample position in the anode near the anode-electrolyte interface looks different. The smallest size mode of 85 Å is here missing. Instead, we have a small and wide but well-defined mode at 190 Å as the new smallest resolved mode, and the two larger modes at 300 to 400 Å, and at 10,000 Å. We are thus able to resolve structural gradients of the pore size distribution in SOFC electrode assemblies with a finesse of 5 μm. This is of interest for the understanding of the industrial processing of SOFC assemblies and changes in the microstructure during operation.

SAXS is a matured method which allows quantitative determination of structure parameters. Figure 1.10 shows the diameter of objects such as pores in SOFC assemblies exposed to two different operation conditions, i.e., operated with gas containing sulfur (sulfur B), and gas that had passed through a sulfur filter stage (filter A). It shows mode, mean and median of pore sizes ranging from several hundred nanometers to around thousand nanometers. The samples were scanned across the entire assemblies so that depth-resolved size information is obtained [12].

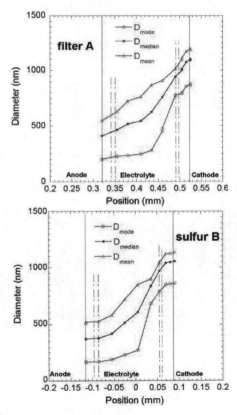

Figure 1.10 Variation of object diameter across the SOFC assembly thickness (the "Position (mm)" axis) for a SOFC stack operated with sulfur containing (sulfur B) and sulfur-filtered fuel (filter A) gas.

The advantage of SOFC technology is that they can be powered with low-cost natural gas, unlike polymer electrolyte membrane fuel cells, which require clean hydrogen—an expensive fuel. Unfortunately, natural gas contains sulfur compounds whichlike to interact with the nickel catalyst in the anode. This is a deleterious process called *"sulfur poisoning"* [13, 14].

1.4.3   Anomalous SAXS (ASAXS) on Lithium Battery Electrodes

We have shown here two examples for SAXS measurements that were performed *ex-situ*. It is possible to do SAXS experiments also *in-situ* or even *operando*. An example is shown below for lithium ion batteries.

The spectro-electrochemical cell necessary for *operando* experiments is built from one polypropylene disk and one stainless steel disk and has beryllium disks as x-ray windows. This cell has been used *operando* for ASAXS, anomalous x-ray diffraction and x-ray absorption spectroscopy (XAS) in the transmission mode with a thin lithium battery cell between the disks [15, 16].

Figure 1.11 shows the disassembled *in-situ* cell with metal lithium counter electrode and $LiMn_2O_4$ positive electrode (cathode). This cell is mounted at a diffractometer at a synchrotron beamline.

Figure 1.11   Left panel shows the polypropylene plate, with one BUNA O-ring on top and a lithium metal counter electrode in the center. The stainless steel plate on the right shows two more O-rings and the positive $LiMn_2O_4$ electrode (black disk) in the center. The right panel shows the assembled cell mounted at beamline 2-1 at Stanford Synchrotron Radiation Lightsource.

When studying the components of actual devices like batteries and fuel cells, we have to remind ourselves about the complex structural and chemical heterogeneity. SAXS beforehand is a method for microstructure analyses. To account for chemical heterogeneity, we can use a spectral trick by taking advantage of the anomalous scattering properties of all chemical elements when subject to x-ray scattering.

For this, we carry out the SAXS experiment with an x-ray energy that is close to an x-ray absorption threshold of a chemical element of interest. In this particular case here we are interested in the Mn of the battery cathode. We have thus recorded several SAXS scans but each one with a different x-ray energy (Fig. 1.12). Ranging from 6400 to 6600 eV, spanning the Mn K-shell pre-edge and the entire absorption range. Figure 1.13 shows the corresponding SAXS curves, where the anomalous scattering of the Mn causes an x-ray optical contrast which manifests in enhanced scattering intensity at large angles, i.e., at Q vectors larger than 0.08 1/Å.

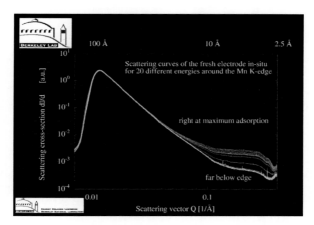

Figure 1.12 Anomalous small-angle x-ray scattering curves of a lithium battery cathode, recorded with x-rays energies ranging from 6500 to 6600 eV. Observe the enhanced small-angle scattering intensity for large Q, modulated by the anomalous, resonant x-ray scattering at the Mn K-edge.

X-ray energy dependent anomalous small-angle x-ray scattering (ASAXS) curves therefore bear—due to the scattering contrast— the structure information which can be assigned to the element Mn in the compound. For the quantitative analysis it is necessary to perform a weighted subtraction of either scattering curves. This is demonstrated in Fig. 1.13, where the ASAXS curves for 6400 and 6545 eV are shown, and their difference weighted by the scattering contrast for Mn, which is energy dependent. This formalism requires accurate information on the f' and f'' of Mn, which are determined from a XANES curve of Mn and its corresponding Fourier transform, with the use of the optical theorem. The weighted difference curve is then subject to further data reduction steps, including the Q^{-4} Porod fit, which is subtracted. The resulting curve shows two scattering shoulders, which we account for with a global Guinier fit with 2 Guinier exponentials. With a more advanced and computerized data analysis package, the entire 20 scattering curves can be used as input information for the data reduction and structure refinement. This constitutes a complex algebraic problem with an overestimated equation system.

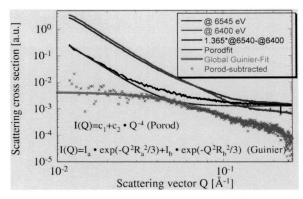

Figure 1.13 Anomalous small-angle x-ray scattering data from a LiMn$_2$O$_4$-based lithium cathode recorded during battery operation with 6545 eV (blue) and 6400 eV (red) x-ray energy. Black curve is the weighted difference which serves for Porod-fit subtraction. The result of this is the green data points, to which two Guinier ranges are fitted (orange solid line).

1.4.4 ASAXS on SOFC Electrodes with Micro X-Ray Beam

We have applied this methodology to the aforementioned three SOFC samples and conducted ASAXS at the Ni K-edge and Zr K-edge [17]. It is important here to realize that SAXS is typically a bulk-sensitive method done in x-ray transmission (unless SAXS is done in reflectometry on surfaces). To warrant sufficient transmitted X-ray intensity, the electrode assembly has to be sufficiently thin. Since the x-ray transmission depends on the x-ray energy via $\mu(E)$ and the sample thickness in the relation

$$I = I_0 \exp(-\mu d)$$

For resolving the Zr and Y K-edges we need x-ray energy of around 17 and 18 keV, which warrants a higher transmission than 8.3 keV, which is the position of the absorption edge of Ni. Hence, to make an ASAXS resonant for Ni, the sample has to be significantly thinner than for resonant Zr ASAXS. Once the sample thicknesses are adjusted for the experiment, the scattering contrast remains to be determined. Figure 1.14 shows the theoretical determined scattering contrast for the Ni phase vs. air (the void, the pore), the YSZ phase vs. air via the Zr atoms, and the YSZ vs. the LSM phase; here the contrast is based on the different electron densities of the Zr ion and the Mn ion. We have calculated the x-ray optical contrast for every x-ray energy that we used for the ASAXS scans.

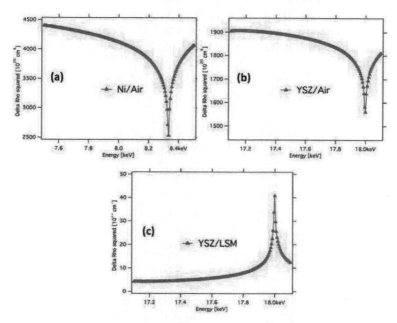

Figure 1.14 Real part of the calculated scattering contrast factor, $|\Delta\rho|2$, versus x-ray energy for (a) the Ni/void interface near the Ni x-ray absorption edge; (b) the YSZ/void interface and (c) the YSZ/LSM interface near the Zr x-ray absorption edge.

The actual detailed analysis of the AUSAXS data is very tedious and goes beyond the scope of this chapter. I want to mention here that major part of the analysis is the formulation of an algebraic tensor equation, including a set of rational constraints that come from the experimental conditions and the samples.

Here I have to express my gratitude to my highly appreciated colleagues Dr. Jan Ilavsky from APS Argonne Lab, who has built together with Dr. Pete R. Jemian a unique micro-beam AUSAXS end-station, including a complete software package based on Igor Pro macros which allows for excellent SAXS and SANS data acquisition, reduction, analysis and modeling [18].

And I have to express my gratitude to my highly appreciated colleague Andrew J. Allen from NIST in Gaithersburg, who did the entire data reduction, analysis, and interpretation. Going over the original paper [17] of this work, the reader may notice that the data structure of this spatially resolved μ-AUSAXS experiment is extremely complex.

I am not aware of a similar SAXS experiment with this extent of complexity. It therefore needed a lot of book keeping during data reduction and data analysis, plus many multiple re-iterations.

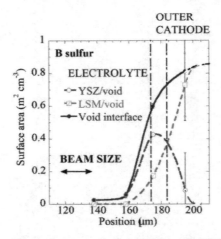

Figure 1.15 Specific surface areas of the YSZ/void, LSM/void, and total void interfaces versus position through the cathode side of sample B sulfur [17].

With the thus-obtained quantitative information, we can extract the standard SAXS structure parameters such as surface areas or volumes or particles sizes. Here, however, with respect to the relevant electrochemical interfaces, because we have taken advantage of the contrast variation which leads us to discriminate the surfaces and interfaces in the electrode assemblies (Fig. 1.15).

At this point, it is permissible to look back at the original problem of the study, this is, the sulfur poisoning of the SOFC. We had investigated samples that were exposed to different levels of sulfur concentration. With this information, Dr. Allen was able to sketch a simplistic graphical model (Fig. 1.16) which reflects the anticipated microstructural changes upon long-term sulfur exposure in SOFC [17].

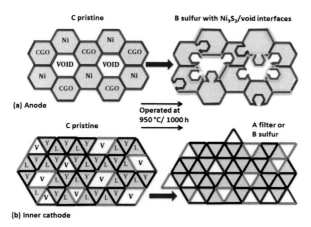

Figure 1.16 Simple schematics illustrating anticipated microstructure changes in the (a) anode and in the (b) inner cathode layer during SOFC operation. In the anode: Ni_3S_2 formation is highlighted by the colorful "glowing" Ni/void interface; for the phase boundaries: red = Ni/void, green = CGO/void, blue = Ni/CGO. In the cathode: L = LSM, Y = YSZ, V = voids; for boundaries: orange = LSM/void, purple = YSZ/void, black = YSZ/LSM. After [17].

1.5   X-Ray Diffraction with Contrast Variation

X-ray diffraction (XRD) is the most important method for obtaining the crystal structure and for crystal phase analysis. Its theory is part of every curriculum for inorganic chemistry and solid-state physics and crystallography in undergraduate studies at university. We therefore refer the reader to the following textbooks [19, 20].

We want to show some special and not so well-known applications of XRD for the cases where synchrotron radiation with tunable x-ray energies is possible. In the previous Section 1.4 we remember the *in-situ* ASAXS microstructure study on a lithium battery during operation. The same spectro-electrochemical cell with a comparable battery assembly was used to carry out XRD with contrast variation by recording diffractograms at two different x-ray energies around the manganese *K*-shell absorption edge around 6500 eV [21, 22]. Note that the cell components plus the components from the battery assembly, i.e., aluminum current collector, carbon black, graphite, polymer separator, lithium metal, liquid electrolyte, and beryllium windows add their signature to the entire diffractogram, in addition to the lithium manganite spinel, which was our component of interest in the battery study. The experiment is shown in ref. [21, 22].

In Fig. 4 in [21] is shown part of the diffractogram of the lithium manganese oxide battery electrode, specifically the [111] Bragg reflection range. The diffractograms were recorded at 6500 eV before the Mn K-edge and at 6538 eV, thus providing chemical contrast. Note, however, that these diffractograms were recorded during electrochemical cycling of the battery electrode. Changes in the diffractograms can thus be related to different state of charge which happened between the scan at 6500 and 6538 eV.

Some rare-earth transition metal oxides with perovskite structure are candidates for proton conducting ceramic electrolytes for intermediate temperature solid oxide fuel cells [23]. Specific examples are yttrium substituted barium cerium oxide (BCY) and barium zircon oxide (BZY). The Zr and Ce in $BaZrO_3$ and $BaCeO_3$ have the formal valence Zr^{4+} and Ce^{4+}, respectively. Substitution of the tetravalent Zr^{4+} with the trivalent Y^{3+} causes the material to become oxygen deficient, i.e., $BaZr_{x-1}Y_xO_{3-\delta}$. In the presence of ambient water vapor, the oxygen vacancies become filled with the oxygen ion from water molecules, forming an O-H hydroxyl group and releasing the second proton of the H_2O molecule into the lattice and thus maintain charge neutrality [24–26].

It is of interest to know how the oxygen vacancy, the Y-ion and the protons are related with each other in the crystal lattice. Therefore it is important to be able to distinguish the Zr from the Y ions in an XRD experiment. This is possible when the x-ray energies are selected so that they are resonantly scattered by the Zr or by the Y ions. The practical choice for the x-ray energies is the K-shell absorption energies of 16.9 and 17 keV for Y and Zr, respectively.

Figure 1.17 shows on the right side the x-ray diffractograms of $BaZr_{0.9}Y_{0.1}O_{2.95}$ recorded with x-ray energies at 16, 16.9, and 17 keV. The diffractograms recorded at 16 keV are particularly sensitive to Y. Here we notice two extra Bragg reflections, highlighted by the black rectangles.

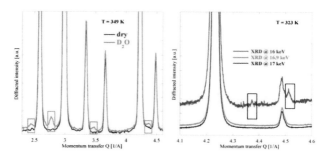

Figure 1.17   Neutron (left) and x-ray (right) diffractograms of 10% Y substituted barium zirconate: $BaZr_{0.9}Y_{0.1}O_{2.95}$. XRD was measured Y- and Zr-resonant with 3 x-ray energies at 16, 16.9, and 17 keV. For the ND, contrast enhancement is made with deuterated water D_2O. Reprinted from *Appl. Phys. Lett.*, **95**, 224103, 2009. Copyright AIP Publishing LLC 2009.

The Bragg reflections (300) and (221) coincide at $Q = 4.49$ Å^{-1}. At 16 keV, which is 1 keV below the Y absorption edge, this peak is split into two peaks at $Q = 4.49$ and 4.51 Å^{-1}, while at other energies such split is not discernible. This material is known to be composed of two isostructural phases, α and β, with similar lattice constants. Two non-equivalent peaks of each phase are coincident. Bragg reflections of the ABO_3 type cubic perovskites with one even and two odd indices have crystallographic structure factors proportional to fB+fO–fA, which is small for the main phase β in condition of normal scattering.

Therefore, anomalous factors in proximity to the x-ray absorption edge may have large effect on the intensity. This is different and possibly opposite for the secondary phase α. The observed splitting could originate from the shift and/or the splitting of any of the four component peaks, possible indicating, for example, that the secondary phase is not truly cubic. Hence, the Y atoms in this proton conductor electrolyte occupy distinct lattice positions, and hence likely form an ordered solid solution. The procedure for obtaining the structure from these resonant (anomalous) XRD is briefly exercised in [24].

Contrast variation can also be done with neutron methods, either by contrast matching media or like in the case here by using protonated and deuterated samples. The corresponding neutron diffraction (ND) data show extra peaks which originate from the deuterium located in the perovskite structure. The left panel in Fig. 1.11 shows the ND of dry and deuterated samples. The emerging extra peaks upon deuteration indicate that the deuterons occupy particular lattice positions [24].

1.6 Charge Carrier Dynamics Studies with Quasi-Elastic Neutron Scattering

Understanding the charge carrier dynamics is essential for all electric components, particularly for electrodes and (solid) electrolytes. Charge carriers in this respect are electrons, holes, polarons, ions, including protons. Latter play a role in fuel cells and electrolyzers where hydrogen and hydrocarbons are used as fuels, and where water is formed as reaction product. Since x-rays interact strongly with electrons, x-rays are unfortunately not a good probe for hydrogen, which contains as the lightest element one electron only. Neutrons are very good probes for hydrogen, protons, and other light elements. As far as the charge carrier dynamics is concerned, electroanalytic methods can provide very good information. Electrical (electrochemical) impedance spectroscopy (EIS) is a method of choice for electrochemists and engineers who study energy converters and storage devices.

The molecular scale interaction of protons with neutrons allows determination of these interactions directly with neutron scattering methods, which is an advantage over EIS. We learnt in Section 1.4 about the small-angle scattering, which in contrast to Bragg scattering a diffuse scattering method. We now turn to quasi elastic neutron scattering (QENS), which phenomenological is also a diffuse scattering method. The neutron scattering beamline for our QENS experiments is shown in Figure 1.18. A sharp peak in a scattering experiment is typically a manifestation of ordering in the probed structure, pretty much like the Bragg reflections in x-ray or neutron diffraction in a highly crystalline material. Deviation from this sharpness is a deviation from order; hence, a diffuse peak is a sign of partial disorder. This is why a sharp elastic neutron peak in a neutron experiment happens to show a broadening when the probed sample contains species in motion [25].

Figure 1.18 Neutron scattering beamline with time-of-flight neutron spectrometer "FOCUS" for cold neutrons at Swiss Spallation Neutron Source SINQ in Villigen [27].

Figure 1.19 shows a set of QENS spectra from $BaZr_{0.8}Y_{0.2}O_{3-d}$ (BZY20), which is a model proton conductor material for SOFC for operation at intermediate temperatures. The samples were ceramic slabs which had been exposed to saturated water vapor at 720 K in a furnace so as to "load" the samples with protons. The oxygen atoms from water vapor molecules fill engineered oxygen vacancies in the BZY, whereas the two hydrogen atoms (protons) form bonds with adjacent crystal oxygen ions.

For this measurement it was necessary to bring the sample into a furnace which could heat up to the desired temperatures. It was also necessary to encapsulate the sample in a platinum container to prevent degassing of the water vapor which was trapped in the samples. We built a cell with electric feedthroughs which permit to paint platinum contact electric terminals on the sample and thus also connect the samples with the impedance analyzer (Solartron 1260). Thus we were able to record impedance spectra and QENS spectra from the very same samples during heating (Fig. 1.20).

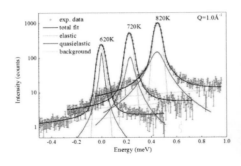

Figure 1.19 QENS spectra recorded from $BaZr_{0.8}Y_{0.2}O_{3-d}$ pellets at 620, 720 and 820 K. The spectra (data points with error bars) are deconvoluted into an elastic part with a Lorentzian shape, and a quasi-elastic part with a Gaussian shape. The photo on the right shows a sample holder inserted into a furnace in the neutron spectrometer, which holds electric terminals for the contacting of the proton conductor samples for the impedance analyzer.

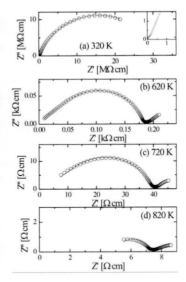

Figure 1.20 The photo on the left shows the impedance analyzer workstation (SI 1260) connected with the sample in the neutron spectrometer. Impedance spectra on the right were corrected for extensive inductivity signatures which originate from the long cables (4 meter!) between sample in the neutron detector and impedance analyzer.

The width $\Lambda(Q)$ of the quasi-elastic broadening accounts for the diffusivity D of the species which cause the broadening, in this case the protons. The incoherent neutron scattering cross section of protons is larger than that of oxygen, for example. The Chudley–Elliott model [27] for jump diffusion predicts quite well the proton diffusion of hydrated perovskites like BZY20 and reads as follows:

$$\Lambda(Q) = \frac{6\hbar D}{l^2}\left(1 - \frac{\sin(Ql)}{Ql}\right),$$

where Q is the scattering vector, D the diffusion coefficient and l is the jump length.

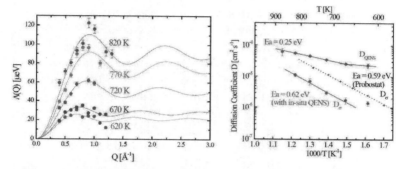

Figure 1.21 Width $\Lambda(Q)$ of the QENS spectra recorded at sample temperatures 620 to 820 K versus scattering vector Q in. The solid lines are least square fits to the Chudley–Elliott model (Equation 3).

Diffusion coefficient D and ionic conductivity σ are related via the Nernst–Einstein relation.

$$\sigma = \frac{e^2}{k_B T}\frac{[OH^\bullet]}{V}\cdot D$$

It is therefore possible to determine the proton conductivity at the molecular level from the QENS data and compare it with the conductivity obtained from impedance spectroscopy. Since we have recorded the impedance spectra and QENS spectra over different sample temperatures, we can plot them versus the reciprocal temperature in Arrhenius representation and thus determine the energy barrier which needs to be overcome in order to thermally activate the proton conductivity processes.

We have done this in the right panel in Fig. 1.21, which shows the diffusivities of BCY20 for various temperatures as obtained by QENS (top 6 data points in red color) and EIS (bottom 5 data points in blue color) from the same sample. The activation energy for the self-diffusion as obtained by QENS is only 0.25 eV, whereas the one obtained by EIS is 0.62 eV. Note also the overall higher diffusion coefficient for the data obtained from QENS. The data points on the dotted line in the middle are from a different type of BCY20 sample measured with EIS at Empa with a so-called ProboStat [28].

Visual inspection of the neutron spectra shows that the QENS broadening increases with increasing temperature. This is so-to-speak an experimental manifestation of the increasing "business" of the protons with increasing thermal activation. It is possible to suppress this effect by application of an external compressive strain on the crystal lattice of the proton conductor. This has been verified first with impedance spectroscopy [29, 30], when the semicircle indicative of bulk resistivity increased with applied pressure. This was confirmed also by QENS where a specifically designed high-pressure–high-temperature neutron scattering cell had to be built first [31].

We therefore learn that it is possible to derive the electric transport properties not only from electroanalytical methods, but also from scattering methods, in this particular case the proton conductivity from quasi-elastic neutron scattering. Moreover, it is possible to combine electroanalytical measurements such as impedance spectroscopy, directly with neutron scattering like QENS on the very same sample while for example heating it to different temperatures and thus determine activation energies for the charge transport. We obtain different activation energies and maybe even different trends for different temperature ranges, but we can rule effects that might originate from the different sample conditions when measured for EIS specific and QENS specific conditions. This gives us confidence that the differences in measured signals relate to differences in the resolved processes and thus brings us closer to qualitative and quantitative under-standing of the proton conductors.

1.7 Conductivity of SOFC Cathode Studied with Soft X-Ray Spectroscopy

1.7.1 Brief Introduction to Hard X-Ray Absorption Spectra

SOFC cathodes are typically manufactured from metal oxides with perovskite structure. A standard material is $La_{0.6}Sr_{0.4}MnO_3$ [32]. Their electronic conductivity is based on the superexchange and double exchange mechanism [33], where the oxygen anion plays a decisive role by mediating charge transport or spin transport. Consequently, the electronic structure of the oxygen intimate with the metal cations, specifically the B-site cations, should provide key information for the conductivity.

This is indeed the case and can be shown with x-ray absorption spectroscopy at the oxygen K-shell absorption threshold. Such XAS studies require tunable and monochromatized x-rays, which nowadays is typically available at synchrotron radiation centers [34].

The design of such synchrotron centers was done in a way that it favored an x-ray energy range which permits to measure particularly the K-shell absorption edges of 3d transition metals, virtually all of which are of technological relevance. Depending on the oxidation state of these metals in compounds, their absorption edge shifts on the x-ray energy axis with respect to the edges of the metal species, this is called *chemical shift*. This x-ray absorption near edge-structure (XANES) contains thus chemical information.

After calibration with x-ray spectra from reference compounds with known oxidation state for the metals, it is possible to assign the metal in the compound under investigation its oxidation state, the chemical valence.

Approximately 20 eV after their absorption edge, metal XAS spectra exhibit a region of intensity oscillations which originate from the scattering of the photoelectrons with their molecular environment. These extended x-ray absorption fine structure (EXAFS) oscillations carry structural geometric information about their short range ordering with next and next-to-next neighbors and thus can provide structural information which cannot so easy be measured with x-ray diffraction. For the basics of XAS, XANES, and EXAFS, we refer to the book of [35].

Knowledge of the oxidation state of metals in SOFC cathode materials is important for mathematical defect modeling in high-temperature solid-state electrochemistry [36]. Defects such as vacancies, interstitials etc. can be important charge carriers. Figure 1.22 shows the XANES spectra of $Pr_{1-x}Sr_xMn_{1-y}In_yO_{3-\delta}$, which was a SOFC cathode model compound in one PhD thesis at ETH Zürich [37].

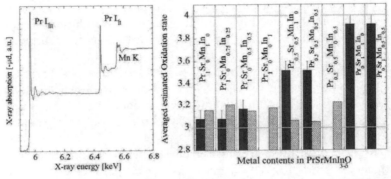

Figure 1.22 X-ray absorption spectrum of $PrMnO_{3-\delta}$ obtained at HASYLAB Hamburg, Germany, by Dr. Anke Hagen, Risoe National Laboratory. The right panel shows the averaged estimated oxidation states for the Mn and Pr in $PrSrMnInO_{3-\delta}$ compounds.

In that substitution study it was necessary to determine whether the Pr and Mn would change their oxidation states. The figure shows the average determined oxidation states of the Pr and Mn; Pr is virtually $Pr^{+3.2}$, whereas Mn ranges in this study from $Mn^{+3.1}$ to $Mn^{+3.9}$.

The EXAFS oscillations provide valuable information about the near range order of materials. This is particularly useful when long-range order is not existent or not available. EXAFS was thus developed for nanoparticles and glasses, where Bragg reflections are not possible because the coherence length of nanoparticles provides only very broad Bragg reflections, or where in glasses no coherence domain is possible. In such cases Bragg diffraction will fail, although the diffuse scattering of wide-angle x-ray scattering provides also near range order information.

However, the particular advantage of EXAFS is that it is by default applied to the absorption threshold energy of a particular chemical element under investigation, say, Ni in a nickel containing catalyst. Thus a chemical contrast is provided, which for x-ray diffraction is not by default the case. Notwithstanding that x-ray diffraction can be performed at synchrotrons with tunable x-ray energy and thus resonant. We have shown in Section 1.5 an application of resonant x-ray diffraction on ceramic proton conductors. An example of XANES and EXAFS is shown for the SOFC cathode model materials LaSrCo-oxide and LaSrFe-oxides in *J. Solid State Chem.* [38].

1.7.2   Metal L-Edges and Multiplet Simulation

The overwhelming majority of XAS studies has been performed and is still being performed on the metal absorption edges. Catalysis and mineralogy and geo-sciences in general are major fields where XAS has been applied, particularly for the 3d metal K-shell absorption thresholds, like Mn, Fe, Ni, Cr, Ti, Co. This is the energy range of say 4 to 12 keV. The design of first-generation synchrotrons was possibly based on the needs from these communities, i.e., predominantly the x-ray beamlines which allowed for such K-edge studies.

Over time there had been interest in the so called soft x-ray energy range because the important chemical elements like oxygen and carbon, also nitrogen, needed to be studied. These are relevant in organic compounds. The absorption energies are 285 and 520 eV. When the beamlines are designed to also cover the energy range up to say 1200 eV, then also the 3d metal L-edges can be measured.

The metal L-edges generally bear more information on the electronic structure than the corresponding K-edges [39]. For obtaining electronic structures, 3d metal L-edges have some advantages [40, 41] over K-edges, such as a diagnostic and theoretically interpretable [42, 43] spectroscopic multiplet originating from the interaction between the 2p hole and 3d electrons, a direct probe of the ligand-metal bonding orbital (3d+ ligands), a dipole-allowed 2p $\rightarrow$ 3d transition, plus a much better x-ray energy resolution.

In addition, the so-called L-edge sum rule analysis can be exploited for directly measuring the electric charge localized in certain elements [44]. L-edge spectroscopy is thus more sensitive to characterize metal centers inside various 3d transition metal complexes [45–48]. For an extensive review on the metal L-edges, see the textbook by de Groot and Kotani [49].

Figure 1.23 shows two iron NEXAFS spectra of La_{1-x} $Sr_xFe_{0.75}Ni_{0.25}O_{3-\delta}$ series (x = 0.0, 0.50) which were synthesized using solid-state reaction [50]. The parent compound, $LaFeO_3$, is an insulator. Substitution on the A-site with Sr forces the iron to form Fe^{4+} species, which causes the electronic conductivity. The Fe L edge is split into two multiplets by the spin-orbit splitting of the iron 2p core level. Each multiplet is additionally split into t_{2g} and e_g orbital by the crystal field. The crystal field parameter 10Dq was determined for iron $2p_{3/2}$ and $2p_{1/2}$ in the range of 1.55–1.75 eV and 1.67–1.85 eV, respectively.

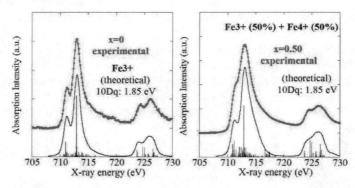

Figure 1.23 Fe L-edge NEXAFS spectra of $La_{1-x}Sr_xFe_{0.75}Ni_{0.25}O_{3-\delta}$ for x = 0 and x = 0.5, plus the multiplet simulation.

The energy difference between $2p_{3/2}$ and $2p_{1/2}$ calculated from Fe 2p spectra was in the range of 13.03–13.44 eV. The relative spectral weight of the L3 peak height, L3/(L3 + L2), is called the branching ratio and constitutes an integral measure for the oxidation state and spin state [46]. For our Ni and Sr substituted $LaFeO_3$ we found a positive relationship between electric conductivity and the intensity branching ratio L3/(L3 + L2).

1.7.3 Oxygen Ligand X-Ray Spectroscopy

The aforementioned Fe^{4+} species points to the relevance of O2p-type holes in the electronic structure. We thus investigated the soft x-ray absorption spectra of the samples were recorded also at the oxygen K edge [50]. The oxygen K edge spectra are used to characterize the unoccupied states which contain oxygen $2p$ character. The spectra reflect unoccupied 3d orbitals of iron/nickel due to the strong hybridization. The growing pre-peak at around 525 eV in the oxygen K edge spectra induced by the substitution of La^{3+} by Sr^{+2} shifts towards the Fermi level (E_F) depending on the relative Sr content. The sample with $x = 0.50$, which has the maximum spectral shift towards the Fermi level, has also the maximum conductivity.

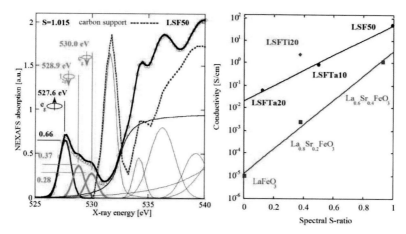

Figure 1.24 Oxygen NEXAFS spectrum of 50% Sr substituted $LaFeO_3$ with deconvoluted peaks. The right image shows the correlation of conductivity and spectral weight ratio S.

Figure 1.24 shows an oxygen K-edge spectrum of $La_{0.5}Sr_{0.5}FeO_3$. The large pre-peak at around 527 eV is the spectral indicator for the O2p hole which is formed by Sr^{2+} substitution, which converts part of the Fe^{3+} into Fe^{4+}, which is spectroscopically written as Fe 3d5$\underline{L}$, where $\underline{L}$ stands for the O2p ligand hole. The intensity next to this peak is attributed to the e_g-t_{2g} dublett from hybridized states. The e_g-to-t_{2g} band ratio is identified as a linear spectral indicator for conducting electron hole formation, whereas the t_{2g} band acts as a conductivity inhibitor by means of ferromagnetic double exchange coupling on the e_g electron [51]. We have made a systematic substitution study and found that the relative spectral weight of the hole peak scales exponentially with the conductivity

[52]. This quantitative correlation of transport properties and x-ray absorption spectra lets the complexity of substitution driven metal insulator transitions appear in a new light.

1.7.4   Photoemission and X-Ray Photoelectron Spectroscopy

We have seen that with the ligand spectra we can probe the valence band of electrode materials, for example. Typically, however, the valence band is probed with x-ray photoelectron spectroscopy (XPS). One issue that comes with XPS is that photoelectrons are used as probes. These electrons have only a very limited mean free path in solids [53], or, practically, spoken, a short escape depth. Typically it is few nanometers or even few Angstroms only deep of a sample which they can probe. This is not necessarily a disadvantage if you are interested in investigating the surface or a sub-surface of a sample. One just has to be aware of the probing depth when using neutron, x-ray, or electron spectroscopy methods.

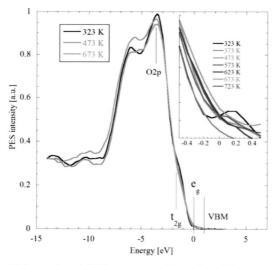

Figure 1.25   Valence band XPS spectra of $La_{0.9}Sr_{0.1}FeO_{3-\delta}$ recorded with 450 eV excitation energy at temperatures from 323 to 723 K.

We are now looking at a single crystal sample with stoichiometry $La_{0.9}Sr_{0.1}FeO_{3-\delta}$, which we have investigated with XPS under ultra-high vacuum of 10E-10 mbar with 450 eV excitation energy from a synchrotron storage ring (Advanced Light Source, Berkeley) [54]. Figure 1.25 shows the valence band spectra in the binding energy range from 0 to −15 eV. We have used a sample holder which could be heated during experiment, so that we could collect spectra when the sample was at temperatures as high as 723 K. Close inspection of the spectra shows that we can identify shoulders that can be associated with states with t_{2g} and e_g symmetry at −2 and 0 eV with respect to the valence band maximum (VBM), and the oxygen bonding peak at −3.5 eV.

The inset in Fig. 1.25 shows the magnified valence band range for seven temperatures ranging from 323 to 723 K. Since we notice spectral changes during annealing of the samples, we compare these changes along the changes of the conductivity during annealing in Fig. 1.26.

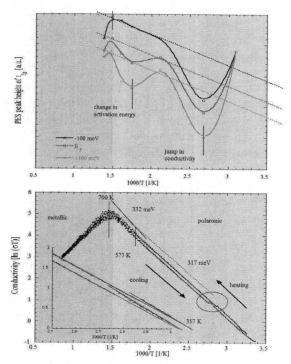

Figure 1.26   Comparison of peculiarities in the conductivity profile (bottom panel) during temperature change and corresponding changes in the photoemission intensity (top panel) of the valence band spectra near the Fermi energy.

The bottom panel in Fig. 1.26 shows the variation of the $La_{0.9}Sr_{0.1}FeO_{3-\delta}$ single crystal sample in the temperature range from 300 to 1250 K, plotted versus the reciprocal temperature in Arrhenius plot. The general conductivity profile is that for polaronic behavior from 300 to 700 K, and then metal type conductivity for $T > 700$ K. We notice peculiarities such as a small jump in the conductivity at around 357 K, and a change in the slope at around 573 K, and the change of sign in the slope at around 700 K. The top panel in Fig. 1.26 shows the photoemission intensity of the t_{2g} state in the valence band PEX spectra from Fig. 1.25, plotted also versus the reciprocal temperature. We clearly notice "dips" in the intensity at those temperatures where we have observed the aforementioned anomalies. This is a demonstration of how the electric charge transport properties change with temperature, such as in a SOFC, and how these can be correlated with changes in the valence band PES spectra.

The high temperatures in SOFC operation can trigger deleterious diffusion processes particularly when layers are very thin. To study this we made an annealing study [55] with a strained 175 nm thin film of $(La_{0.8}Sr_{0.2})_{0.95}Ni_{0.2}Fe_{0.8}O_{3-\delta}$ grown by pulsed laser deposition on $SrTiO_3$ (110). Reversible and irreversible discontinuities at around 573 and 823 K which we observe in the electric conductivity of this film are reflected by valence band changes as monitored in the PES (Fig. 1.27) and oxygen NEXAFS spectra. We observed an irreversible jump at 823 K and attributed this to the depletion of doped electron holes in connection with reduction of Fe^{3+} towards Fe^{2+}, as evidenced by oxygen and iron L-edge spectra (not shown here), and possibly of a chemical origin, whereas the reversible jump at 573 K was attributed to structural changes. From these two examples it becomes clear how well photoemission spectroscopy data correlate with the transport properties of metal oxides like mentioned here [56].

Certainly, it can be helpful when the spectroscopy data are supplemented by crystal structure data like from x-ray and neutron diffraction. The distances and angles between atoms measured with these methods allow for information on the overlap or orbitals which provide the charge transport [33]. Substitution of La by Sr in the $LaFeO_3$ parent compound causes hole doping and subsequent crossover from orthorhombic to rhombohedral, and then to cubic symmetry and crossover from Fe^{3+}-O^{2-}-Fe^{3+}

superexchange interaction to Fe^{3+}-O^{2-}-Fe^{4+} double exchange, with substantial increase of conductivity. These mechanisms depend on the superexchange angle, which approaches 180° with increasing Sr concentration, leading to an increase in overlap between the O (2p) and Fe/Ni (3d) orbitals. The enhanced charge transfer from O (2p) to Ni (3d) orbitals, so we found, suggests that the oxygen vacancies are predominantly created around Fe, and not around Ni [57].

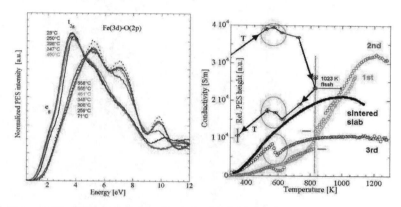

Figure 1.27   Valence band spectra during heating from 23 to 558°C and subsequent cooling to 71°C. Note the remarkable shift and relative spectra weight redistribution of the spectra between 450 and 558°C, revealing stark changes in the electronic structure of the film. Panel on the right compares the conductivity profiles (three curves with open symbols as first, second, and third annealing cycle from thin film; dark solid line from sintered slab with same composition for comparison). Note the conductivity dips at before 600 K, which correlate with PES height changes (curves with arrows).

We have recorded oxygen NEXAFS spectra from $LaFe_{3/4}Ni_{1/4}O_3$ *in-situ* for 300 K < *T* < 773 K. The spectra in Fig. 1.28 show in the pre-edge a small hole peak originating from Ni substitution. The relative spectral weight of this transition to the weight of the hybridized O(2p)–Fe(3d) transitions varies with temperatures and has a maximum at around 600 K. The characteristic energies of the thermal-activated spectral intensity and conductivity suggest that the concentration of charge transferred electrons from O(2p) to Ni(3d) increases and that the pre-edges account in part for the polaron-activated transport [58].

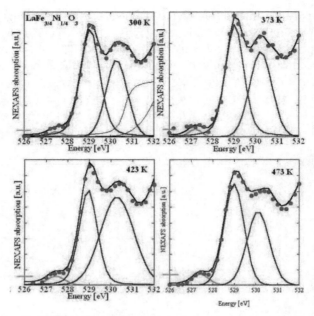

Figure 1.28 Oxygen NEXAFS spectra of $LaFe_{3/4}Ni_{1/4}O_3$ recorded at temperatures 300, 373, 423 and 473 K. The hole doping peak at around 527.5 eV is deconvoluted from the spectra by least square fitting of the characteristic well-known features of this class of materials. This allows for determination of the spectral weight of the hole peak.

We have plotted the conductivity and the relative spectral weight of this hole peak versus the reciprocal temperature in Arrhenius representation in Fig. 1.29. The slope of the conductivity with respect to the reciprocal absolute temperature can be interpreted as activation for conductivity, 1760 ± 15 meV. We interpret the thermal variation of the hole peak in the same spirit, notwithstanding that the assigned activation energy is here by a factor 2 smaller: 766 ± 444 meV. We do not yet know the reasons for this difference. Note that we did a similar approach with the proton conductivity obtained by EIS and by the width of the QENS broadening (Fig. 1.21 in Section 1.6).

With the experience we have now, we can sketch a band diagram for the density of states (DOS) of doped iron perovskites and the influence which temperature has on it. The occupied (PES) and unoccupied (NEXAFS) states are affected by annealing.

See the right panel in Fig. 1.29, which is inspired by the work of Wadati et al. [59].

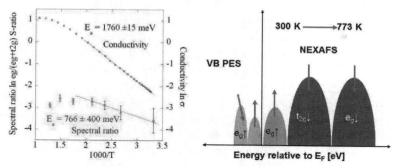

Figure 1.29 (Left) Comparison of conductivity and spectral weigh ratio for the e_g orbital hole peak in Arrhenius representation. (Right) Schematic for the DOS of LaSrFeNi-oxide for 300–773 K. The right bold arrow represents increasing T. Other bold arrows show whether a state increases or decreases, or whether it shifts along the energy axis.

Iron resonant valence band photoemission spectra of Sr substituted $LaFe_{0.75}Ni_{0.25}O_{3-\delta}$ have been recorded across the Fe 2p-3d absorption threshold to obtain Fe specific spectral information on the 3d projected partial density of states (Figure 1.30). Comparison with $La_{1-x}Sr_xFeO_3$ resonant VB PES literature data suggests that substitution of Fe by Ni forms electron holes which are mainly O2p character. Substitution of La by Sr increases the hole concentration to an extent that the e_g structure vanishes. The variation of the e_g and t_{2g} structures is paralleled by the changes in the electrical conductivity.

A general problem with valence band spectra is that they often contain peaks from hybridized states, and it is not beforehand possible to discriminate which orbital from which element is affected. The use of synchrotron radiation with energy tunable x-rays is an excellent way out of this dilemma, as we have registered already from the resonant (anomalous) SAXS and XRD experiments in the previous Sections. Tuning the excitation x-ray energy to an absorption threshold of a particular element in the compound under study allows for a chemical contrast enhancement. It is even possible to tune the x-ray energy to a particular spectroscopic feature and thus be resonant with particular orbital states.

We have performed resonant VB PES, and NEXAFS at OK edge and Fe $L_{2,3}$ edges on $La_{1-x}Sr_xFe_{0.75}Ni_{0.25}O_{3-\delta}$ (x = 0.0, 0.5, and 0.75). The spectral weight of occupied e_g and t_{2g} states of Fe is reduced upon electron hole doping up to 50% and then starts to increase which is parallel to changes in electrical conductivity. The spectral weight of the pre-peak in the oxygen NEXAFS spectra due to the p-type electron holes created on Ni 3d increases with increasing x. With respect to $La_{1-x}Sr_xFeO_3$, it is observed that the spectral weight transfers from below E_F to above it across the gap. However, here in $La_{1-x}Sr_xFe_{0.75}Ni_{0.25}O_{3-\delta}$ it is difficult to conclude this since the Ni 3d closer to E_F than Fe 3d and we do not consider any metal (Fe)-metal (Ni) electron hole transfer. For a more thorough discussion see [60, 61].

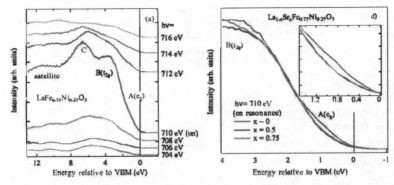

Figure 1.30 Resonant photoemission spectra of the valence band region of $LaFe_{0.75}Ni_{0.25}O_3$ recorded with x-ray energies from 704 to 716 eV. The spectrum at 710 eV shows resonant enhancement. The right panel shows the magnified region near the Fermi energy for three different Sr substitution levels x in $La_{1-x}Sr_xFe_{0.75}Ni_{0.25}O_3$.

At this point I want to make a general remark on soft x-ray spectroscopy experiments. They typically require a high vacuum or ultra-high vacuum environment in order to increase the detection signal strength. Any air or other gas will absorb too many x-ray photons which will be lost. Not to mention the electrons in XPS, which become lost in gas environment. Therefore, realistic fuel cell operation experiments which require that the electrodes are exposed to air and fuel gas conditions have historically not been possible for NEXAFS and XPS. Only since about one decade, x-ray and electron detectors and differential pumping technology has so much advanced that it is possible to expose a sample in a tiny volume which has local gas partial pressures of 1,000 Torr or more, while at the same time XPS and NEXAFS spectra can be recorded.

A pioneering study has been published few years ago by a consortium at the ELETTRA synchrotron in Italy. Specifically, a solid electrolyte-electrode assembly (SOFC cathodes with LSM catalyst and YSZ electrolyte) was equipped with electric terminals as current collectors and then heated up to 650°C under a controlled oxygen leak, while XPS spectra were recorded. The study was conducted at 650°C at a residual oxygen partial pressure of 10^{-6} mbar (using a controlled O_2 leak). Various bias settings were applied [62]. They explained that reduced manganese oxide species rapidly spread from the triple phase boundary over the electrolyte surface, "thereby providing high electronic conductivity in the zirconia surface scale and promoting the direct incorporation of oxygen from the gas into the electrolyte."

With very much improved instrumentation at the Advanced Light Source in Berkeley, it was possible few years later to determine some fundamental high-temperature electrochemical properties at even more realistic SOFC conditions [63].

1.7.5 Ambient Pressure XPS

Near Ambient pressure XPS (often misquoted as ambient pressure XPS) is a rapidly emerging analytical method for *in-situ* and for *operando* studies well suited for electrochemical and electrocatalytic studies, including batteries, supercapacitors, photoelectrochemical cells, SOFC, electrolyzers. As we have seen, the method has been used initially for SOFC related problems, particularly the cathode studies and solid electrolyte studies. I want to present here a study which was done on the ceramic proton conductors that I mentioned already in one of the previous sections on resonant XRD (Section 1.5) and quasi-elastic neutron scattering (QENS) (Section 1.6). QENS allows us to learn about the ionic charge carrier dynamics, specifically the protons in the ceramics.

The interaction of metal oxides with their ambient environment at elevated temperatures is of significant relevance for the functionality and operation of ceramic fuel cells, electrolyzers and gas sensors. Proton conductivity in metal oxides is a subtle transport process which is based on formation of oxygen vacancies by cation doping and substitution, and oxygen vacancy filling upon hydration in water vapor atmosphere.

To test this, we have studied the electric conductivity and electronic structure of the BaCeY-oxide proton conductor under realistic operation conditions from 373 to 593 K and water vapor pressures up to 200 mTorr *in-situ* by combining ambient pressure x-ray photoelectron spectroscopy and electrochemical impedance spectroscopy. We have therefore measured the electric conductivity and the XPS spectra from the same sample under the same conditions at the same time. The resonant VB PES element specific spectroscopic evidence that oxygen vacancies are filled by oxygen upon water exposure and partly oxidize Ce^{3+} and Y^{2+} towards Ce^{4+} and Y^{3+}.

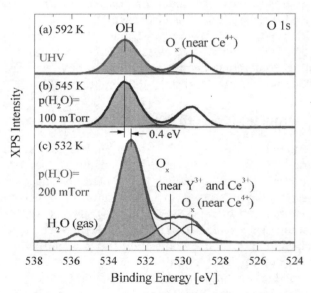

Figure 1.31 O 1s core level XPS for BCY20 at (592 to 532 K, temperature changes due to heat capacity of injected water vapor), in (a) UHV, and in water vapor with (b) $p(H_2O) = 100$ mTorr and (c) $p(H_2O) = 200$ mTorr. Photon energy = 700 eV. The spectra are normalized and aligned by the structural Ox oxygen peak (near Ce^{4+}).

Let me recall here, in the ceramic proton conductors, at low temperature the protons are structural components of the proton conductor crystal lattice. Specifically, a water molecule H_2O which enters the defect engineered oxygen deficient crystal lattice will fill an oxygen vacancy, and the two protons from the water molecule will form hydroxyl groups with adjacent oxygen ions of the lattice. In this case, the protons are not yet charge carriers because they are localized. At elevated temperature, they could engage in some sort of polaron-type behavior, still elastically bound to a vibrating crystal lattice. In the moment where a hydrogen bond breaks, or "melts," upon thermal activation, we would have a "free" charge carrier.

This bond breaking should be noticeable with x-ray spectroscopy [26]. Figure 1.31 shows the XPS oxygen core level spectra of $BaCe_{0.8}Y_{0.2}O_{3-\delta}$ under various temperature and water gas pressure conditions. It is often neglected that ambient air contains also humidity, water vapor. And it is often neglected that such humidity will react with metal oxides.

In ultra-high vacuum (UHV), at 592 K, the BCY20 exhibits a peak at 529.5 eV which originates from crystal lattice oxygen near a Ce^{4+} ion. The large peak at 533 eV is typically assigned to OH^-. Releasing water vapor into the UHV chamber cools down the sample temperature by about 50 to 545 K, while the sample is still being heated.

After 200 mTorr water vapor pressure, we notice the spectral signature of water gas at 535.5 eV, a large increase of the OH-species peak, but now slightly shifted by 0.4 eV towards lower binding energies, plus a new peak at about 531 eV which we assign to an oxygen ion in the crystal lattice, now in the proximity to Y^{3+} or Ce^{3+}.

It appears therefore that the H_2O ions from the water vapor enters the crystal lattice of oxygen deficient BCY20, forms hydroxyl groups and alters the local electronic structure near the metal central atoms Ce and Y in a way that they partially become reduced towards Y^{3+} and Ce^{3+}.

When we look at the corresponding valence band XPS spectra in Fig. 1.32, we notice that the spectra from the "dry," non-hydrated samples have a double peak structure at about 4.5 and 6.5 eV binding energy, labeled "A" and "B" in the Fig. 1.32. Upon exposure to water vapor in the XPS chamber, peak "A" decreases significantly in intensity and shows only a shoulder.

We have done this experiment in the resonant mode in order to assure that we can be specifically sensitive to the Ce and Y ions under resonance x-ray energies.

Same like observed in the oxygen core level spectra, it appears therefore that the oxygen ions from the water molecules fill the oxygen vacancies, which cause the peak "A" from the partially reduced Ce or Y metal atoms, and thus the intensity of this defect structure decreases. When we form the intensity differences by subtracting the wet spectrum from the dry spectrum, we should therefore have the spectra of the defect structures.

The right panel in Fig. 1.32 shows these difference spectra for the Ce $4p_{1/2}$ resonant excitation and for the Y $3p_{3/2}$ resonant excitation energies, 299 and 223 eV, respectively. It is interesting that the defect peak structures are separated at around 4.5 and 5 eV by about 0.5 eV [26].

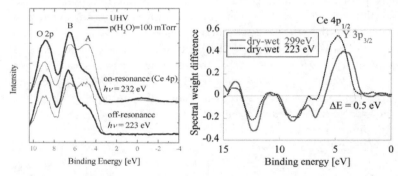

Figure 1.32 (Left) On- and off-resonance XPS spectra for dry and hydrated $BaCe_{0.8}Y_{0.2}O_{3-\delta}$ measured at ~537 K with $h\nu$ = 232 eV (Ce $4p_{1/2}$) and 223 eV, respectively. The spectra measured in water vapor are aligned to the spectrum obtained under UHV by shifting 0.6 eV to higher binding energy. (Right) Difference spectra from Y and Ce resonant XPS measurements under dry and wet condition show a chemical shift of 0.5 eV near the Fermi energy.

When we look at the impedance spectra recorded during the XPS experiments, we can follow the development of the proton conductivity during temperature change and water vapor exposure change. The experiment shown here took actually around 24 h. More than 100 impedance spectra were recorded, and over

1,000 (!) XPS spectra. The technical development of synchrotron instrumentation and accompanying electrochemistry data acquisition methods today puts the scientists in a position where they have to be more cautious with experiment planning and data management than the years before.

The impedance spectra in Fig. 1.33 are therefore only a small and prepared subset, showing how the semicircle radii decrease upon sample heating, revealing the increased conductivity.

What we learn from this combined impedance and XPS operando study is that he resonant valence band spectra of dry and hydrated samples show that oxygen ligand holes in the proximity of the Y dopant are by around 0.5 eV closer to the Fermi energy than the corresponding hole states from Ce. Both hole states become essentially depleted during hydration under water vapor, while the proton conductivity sets on and increases systematically. The charge redistribution between lattice oxygen, Ce, and Y when the proton conductor is heated in water vapor, provides insight in the complex mechanism for proton incorporation [26].

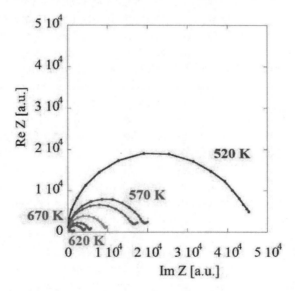

Figure 1.33 Electrochemical impedance spectra recorded operando under 150 mTorr water vapor pressure for 520 K < *T* < 670 K in the XPS chamber at the Advanced Light Source in Berkeley National Laboratory [26].

1.8 The Sulfur Chemistry of SOFC Anodes and Sulfur XAS

I want to conclude this Chapter with a Section about the sulfur chemistry in SOFC. In Section 1.5 I have said already that SOFC can be powered with natural gas, which, however, contains sulfur species which like to interact with the nickel in the anode. Literature studies show that typically Ni_xS_y compounds are named as reaction products. It is often Raman spectroscopy data [64] that point to this type of sulfidic compounds. From this it appears that this method leaves not much of a choice other than nickel-sulfur compounds. We therefore looked at a set of SOFC anodes which have been treated with different levels of sulfur compounds [65].

Two sets of SOFC electrode assemblies from different manufacturers were run under different operating conditions with different sulfur exposure, and then subjected to sulfur (1s) XAS. The sulfur K-edge is at around 2470 eV. This is in the x-ray energy range between hard x-rays and soft x-rays, recently referred to as "tender x-rays." Within the detection limits of the spectrometer, pristine fuel electrodes (anodes) show no traces of sulfur. The anodes operated with sulfur-containing natural gas and H_2S doped natural gas showed spectra, which were rich in sulfur structures. Two other electrodes run with sulfur-containing natural gas, one with a sulfur filter and the other without, showed an XAS spectrum with a very broad peak, covering the entire sulfur absorption range, and thus not allowing for identification of specific sulfur signatures.

These appear to be the first-ever reported sulfur XAS data on SOFC anodes, and the XAS technique shows promise to resolve some hitherto unsolved issues on sulfur poisoning of SOFC, particularly regarding the molecular speciation of the sulfur components [65].

We then tried to carry out an *operando* sulfur XAS study on SOFC anodes. We were not aware of any such previous study. Inspired by recent *in-situ* catalysis XAS work at the sulfur K-edge [67], we took a catalysis *in-situ* cell and equipped it with electric terminals so as to provide a high-temperature electrochemistry environment for the sample (Fig. 1.35) where we could polarize the SOFC anode (Ni cerium gadolinium oxide) and heat it in a hydrogen gas admixed with 5 ppm H_2S. The spectra were different depending on the temperature. Figure 1.36 shows the spectrum recorded at 450°C, deconvoluted into contributions from elemental sulfur on Ni, NiS, multi-SO_2 on Ni, Na_2SO_3, and $NiSO_4$ [13].

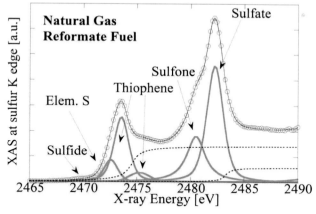

Figure 1.34 Sulfur x-ray absorption spectrum of a SOFC anode propelled with natural gas reformate fuel, which contains sulfur. The spectrum is deconvoluted with [66] into peaks which are assigned to sulfide, elemental sulfur, thiophene, sulfone, and sulfate.

Figure 1.35 Metal sample holder (upper panel) equipped with electric terminals, gas feedthroughs, thermocouples for *operando* high-temperature electrochemistry experiments with tender x-rays. Fuel/gas control panel provides SOFC-typical thermo-dynamic environment, mounted (lower left panel) at Phoenix beamline, Swiss Light Source. The lower right panel shows the *operando* cell in operation during XAS data collection.

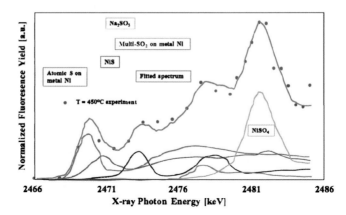

Figure 1.36 Experimental sulfur K-edge XANES spectrum of Ni CGO anode in 5 ppm H_2S mixed in H_2 in the working anode compartment at different temperatures (indicated in figure). Least square fitting results and model spectra used for fitting are shown as well. Digitally reproduced after [13].

1.9 Outlook

Synchrotron x-ray and neutron sources beamline technology are developing independently from electrochemistry. It depends to a wide extent on the synchrotron and neutron users how they want to use these publically available facilities for their particular experimental project purpose. In the recent 10–15 years, facilities have invested extra efforts to provide their users with a particular sample environment such as extreme temperatures, high magnetic fields, high pressure, and so on. More and more facilities are also prepared to provide simple or sophisticated electrochemical cells and the necessary data acquisition instruments on site, such as potentiostats and impedance analyzers. There are even facilities which run particular programs to serve a particular user community, including battery and fuel cell research. My recommendation for the researcher is to look out in the general scientific literature, not only energy and electrochemistry literature, and take inspiration from how other communities address particular problems. The Chapter shown here gives a number of examples which originated from literature that was not originally meant to solve battery and fuel cell problems.

Acknowledgments

Most of the material presented in this chapter is related to the work I have done with Empa on SOFC in the years 2005–2014. The funding for this work comes from a number of sources, specifically the EU FP6 Marie Curie Program project 042095 *HiTempEchem* and project no.: SES6-CT-2003-502612 *Real-SOFC*, which I have done with Dr. Peter Holtappels in the laboratory of Prof. Dr. Thomas Graule. I am grateful to Dr. Josef Sfeir of the HEXIS AG, who provided me with SOFC stacks and electrode assemblies. The neutron tomography work was done in collaboration with Dr. Eberhard Lehmann at SINQ, with support from Peter Vontobel and George Necola. The SAXS measurements were done at the APS UNICAT beamline with Dr. Jan Ilavsky, Dr. Pete R. Jemian and with Dr. Andrew J. Allen from NIST. The neutron diffraction and resonant XRD were performed by Dr. Vladimir Pomjakushin, SINQ, and Dr. Antonio Cervellino, Swiss Light Source. Dr. Alejandro Ovalle in my group synthesized the samples and conducted with Vladimir and Antonio the experiments, and they did the crystal structure modeling with Rietveld analyses. Alejandro did also the first QENS experiment combined with impedance spectroscopy at the FOCUS beamline, together with Dr. Jan P. Embs from SINQ. The QENS results shown here were obtained by Empa/ETH Zürich Physics PhD student Qianli "Lili" Chen in my group, who was funded by the Swiss National Science Foundation project *"Effect of lattice volume and imperfections on the proton-phonon coupling in proton conducting lanthanide transition metal oxides: High pressure and high temperature neutron and impedance studies"* http://p3.snf.ch/project-124812. I am grateful to my project co-PI Dr. Thierry Strässle and Prof. Joel Mesot, Lili's thesis advisor, both PSI, for their great support, and also Dr. Stuart Holdsworth for designing the high (p,T) neutron cell, and Dr. Gunnar Nurk (guest in my group from Tartu University) for taking the lead in the impedance scans during *in-situ* QENS. PhD student Selma Erat in my group synthesized many of the SOFC cathode samples shown here for NEXAFs measurements. She also ran the synchrotron scans, conductivity measurements and multiplet simulation. She was funded by the Swiss National Science Foundation project

"*Investigation of the driving forces of metal-insulator transitions in LaSrFeNi-oxides: Correlation crystallographic structure, electronic structure and transport,*" http://p3.snf.ch/project-116688. Most of the NEXAFS experiments were made beamline 9 at the Advanced Light Source in Berkeley with Prof. Bongjin Simon Mun, now at GIST in Korea, and Prof. Zhi Liu, now at SIMIT in Shanghai. Some of the data shown here were gathered at SSRL in Stanford (high-temperature thin film PES) and at BESSY in Berlin (high-temperature NEXAFS). Finally, I am very happy that Dr. Rudolf Struis from PSI made this first *operando* sulfur SOFC study possible. I am also grateful for funding by the Strategic Korean-Swiss Cooperative Program in Science and Technology which helped making the ambient pressure XPS with Simon Mun on the proton conductors at the ALS Berkeley.

The battery-related work was done in the years 1999–2001 when I was postdoctoral researcher with Prof. Elton J. Cairns at Berkeley National Laboratory. He had the affirmation that successful battery and fuel cell development would critically benefit from the new x-ray spectroscopy tools available at synchrotron centers. Prof. Cairns brought me in the group of Prof. Stephen P. Cramer, which paved the way to many new experiments and insights. Here I am grateful also to Dr. Uwe Bergmann, Dr. Pieter Glatzel, Dr. Tobias Funk and Dr. Weiwei Gu, and particularly Dr. Hongxin Wang for their kind advice and collaboration for my battery synchrotron studies. This work was supported by the Director, Office of Basic Energy Sciences, Chemical Sciences Division of the US Department of Energy, under Contract DE-AC03-76SF00098.

In Cairns' group I am grateful to support by Dr. Kathy Striebel, Dr. Mike Tucker, also Dr. Tom Richardson from LBNL MS Department, and for EETD's Susan Lauer and Charlotte Standish, who made sure that my trips to beamtimes in Stanford and Chicago went smooth. At this place I should disclose that summer student Shawn Shrout was very helpful for the operando battery at SSRL, and I am thankful for the assistance of ERULF students Bopamo Osaisai and Alison Fowlks with sample synthesis and beamline assistance at SSRL.

This work is based on experiments performed at the Swiss Spallation Neutron Source SINQ, Paul Scherrer Institute, Villigen, Switzerland. Use of the Stanford Synchrotron Radiation

Lightsource, SLAC National Accelerator Laboratory, is supported by the U.S. Department of Energy, Office of Science, Office of Basic Energy Sciences under Contract No. DE-AC02-76SF00515. The Advanced Light Source is supported by the Director, Office of Science, Office of Basic Energy Sciences, of the U.S. Department of Energy under Contract No. DE-AC02-05CH11231. I thank HZB for the allocation of synchrotron radiation beamtime at BESSY-II. I acknowledge the Paul Scherrer Institut, Villigen, Switzerland for provision of synchrotron radiation beamtime at beamline Phoenix of the SLS.

References

1. McIntosh, S. E., and Gorte, R. J. Direct hydrocarbon solid oxide fuel cells, *Chem. Rev.*, 2004, 104, 4845–4865.

2. Fergus, J. W. Electrolytes for solid oxide fuel cells, *J. Power Sources*, 2006, 162, 30–40.

3. Lehmann, E. H., Boillat, P., Scherrer, G., Frei, G. Fuel cell studies with neutrons at the PSI's neutron imaging facilities, *Nucl. Instrum. Methods Phys. Res. Sect. A*, 2009, 605, 123–126.

4. Geiger, A. B., Tsukada, A., Lehmann, E., Vontobel, P., Wokaun, A., Scherer, G. G., *In-situ* investigation of two-phase flow patterns in flow fields of PEFC's using neutron radiography, *Fuel Cells*, 2003, 2(2), 92–98.

5. Neutron Imaging Boillat, P., Scherer, G. G., in: Wang, H., Yuan, X. Z., Li, H. *Handbook of PEM Fuel Cell Durability*, vol 2: *PEM Fuel Cell Diagnostic Tools*, Taylor & Francis Group, LLC, Chapter 12, CRC (2011).

6. Small Angle X-ray Scattering (eds. Glatter & Kratky) [the book is now available for free at http://physchem.kfunigraz.ac.at/sm/ Service%5CGlatter_Kratky_SAXS_1982.zip.

7. Allen, A. J. Characterization of ceramics by X-ray and neutron small-angle scattering, *J. Amer. Ceram. Soc.*, 2005, 88(6), 1367–1381.

8. Long, G. G., Allen, A. J., Ilavsky, J., Jemian, P. R., Zschack, P. The ultra-small-angle x-ray scattering instrument on UNICAT at the APS (Pianetta, P., Arthur, J., Brennan, S., eds.), in: *Synchrotron Radiation Instrumentation*, Book Series: AIP Conference Proceedings, 2000, 521, pp. 183–187.

9. Braun, A., Bärtsch, M., Schnyder, B., Kötz, R., Haas, O., Haubold, H.-G., Goerigk, G. X-ray scattering and adsorption studies of thermally oxidized glassy carbon, *J. Non-Crystal. Solids*, 1999, 260(1–2), 1–14.

10. Braun, A., Seifert, S., Ilavsky, J. Highly porous activated glassy carbon film sandwich structure for electrochemical energy storage in ultracapacitor applications: Study of the porous film structure and gradient, *J. Mater. Res.*, 2010, 25(8), 1532–1540.

11. Braun, A., Kohlbrecher, J., Bärtsch, M., Schnyder, B., Kötz, R., Haas, O., Wokaun, A. Small-angle neutron scattering and cyclic voltammetry study on electrochemically oxidized and reduced pyrolytic carbon, *Electrochim. Acta*, 2004, 49, 1105–1112.

12. Multi-scale microstructure characterization of solid oxidefuel cell assemblies with ultra small-angle X-ray scattering, *Adv. Eng. Mater.*, 2009, 11(6), 495–501.

13. Nurk, G., Huthwelker, T., Braun, A., Ludwig, Chr., Lust, E., Struis, R. P. W. J. Redox dynamics of sulphur with Ni/GDC anode during SOFC operation at mid- and low-range temperatures: An operando S K-edge XANES study, *J. Power Sources*, 2013, 240, 448–457.

14. Braun, A., Janousch, M., Sfeir, J., Kiviaho, J., Noponen, M., Huggins, F. E., Smith, M. J., Steinberger-Wilckens, R., Holtappels, P., Graule, T. Molecular speciation of sulfur in solid oxide fuel cell anodes with x-ray absorption spectroscopy, *J. Power Sources*, 2008, 183(2), 564–570.

15. Braun, A., Seifert, S., Thiyagarajan, P., Cramer, S. P., Cairns, E. J. *In-situ* anomalous small angle X-ray scattering and absorption on an operating rechargeable lithium ion battery cell, *Electrochem. Commun.*, 2001, 3(3), 136–141.

16. Braun, A., Shrout, S., Fowlks, A. C., Osaisai, B. A., Seifert, S., Granlund, E., Cairns, E. J. Electrochemical *in-situ* reaction cell for X-ray scattering, diffraction and spectroscopy, *J. Synchrotron Radiat.*, 2003, 10, 320–325.

17. Allen, A. J., Ilavsky, J., Jemian, P. R., Braun, A. Evolution of electrochemical interfaces in solid oxide fuel cells (SOFC): A Ni and Zr resonant anomalous ultra-small-angle X-ray scattering study with elemental and spatial resolution across the cell assembly, *RSC Adv.*, 2014, 4, 4676–4690.

18. Ilavsky, J., Jemian, P.R. Irena: tool suite for modeling and analysis of small-angle Scattering. *J. Appl. Cryst.*, 2009, 42, 347.

19. Authier, A. *Dynamical Theory of X-Ray Diffraction*, Oxford University Press Academ. 2003, ISBN978-0-19-852892-0.

20. Waseda, Y., Matsubara, E., Shinoda, K., *X-Ray Diffraction Crystallography*, Verlag Springer, Berlin 2011, ISBN978-3-642-16634-1.

21. Braun, A., Shrout, S., Fowlks, A. C., Osaisai, B. A., Seifert, S., Granlund, E., Cairns, E. J. Electrochemical *in-situ* reaction cell for X-ray scattering, diffraction and spectroscopy, *J. Synchrotron Radiat.*, 2003, 10, 320–325.

22. Braun, A., Seifert, S., Thiyagarajan, P., Cramer, S. P., Cairns, E. J. *In-situ* anomalous small angle X-ray scattering and absorption on an operating rechargeable lithium ion battery cell, *Electrochem. Commun.*, 2001, 3(3), 136–141.

23. Fabbri, E., Pergolesi, D., Traversa, E. Electrode materials: A challenge for the exploitation of protonic solid oxide fuel cells, *Sci. Technol. Adv. Mater.*, 2010, 11, 044301.

24. Braun, A., Ovalle, A., Erat, S., Pomjakushin, V., Cervellino, A., Stolte, W., Graule, T. Yttrium and hydrogen superstructure and correlation of lattice expansion and proton conductivity in the $BaZr_{0.9}Y_{0.1}O_{2.95}$ proton conductor, 2009, *Appl. Phys. Lett.*, 95, 224103.

25. Braun, A., Duval, S., Embs, J. P., Juranyi, F., Ried, P., Holtappels, P., Hempelmann, R., Stimming, Th. Graule, U. Proton diffusivity in the $BaZr_{0.9}Y_{0.1}O_3$-delta proton conductor, *J. Appl. Electrochem.*, 2009, 39(4), 471–475.

26. Chen, Q., El Gabaly, F., Aksoy Akgul, F., Liu, Z., Mun, B. S., Yamaguchi, S., Braun, A. Observation of oxygen vacancy filling under water vapor in ceramic proton conductors in-situ with ambient pressure XPS, *Chem. Mater.*, 2013, 25(23), 4690–4696.

27. Blau, B., Clausen, K. N., Gvasaliya, S., Janoschek, M., Janssen, S., Keller, L., Roessli, B., Schefer, J., Tregenna-Piggott, P., Wagner, W., Zaharko, O. The swiss spallation neutron source SINQ at Paul Scherrer Institut, *Neutron News (Switzerland)*, 2009, 20(3), 5–8.

28. Chudley, C. T., Elliott, R. J. Neutron Scattering from a Liquid on a Jump Diffusion Model, *Proc. Phys. Soc.*, 1961, 77(2), 353–361.

29. Chen, Q., Banyte, J., Zhang, X., Embs, J. P., Braun, A. Proton diffusivity in spark plasma sintered $BaCe_{0.8}Y_{0.2}O_{3-\delta}$: In-situ combination of quasi-elastic neutron scattering and impedance spectroscopy, *Solid State Ionics*, 2013, 252, 2–6.

30. Chen, Q., Braun, A., Ovalle, A., Savaniu, C.-D., Graule, T., Bagdassarov, N. Hydrostatic pressure decreases the proton mobility in the hydrated $BaZr_{0.9}Y_{0.1}O_3$ proton conductor, *Appl. Phys. Lett.*, 2010, 97, 041902.

31. Chen, Q., Braun, A., Yoon, S., Bagdassarov, N., Graule, T. Effect of lattice volume and compressive strain on the conductivity of BaCeY-

oxide ceramic proton conductors, *J. Eur. Ceram. Soc.*, 2011, 31(14), 2657–2661.

32. Chen, Q., Holdsworth, S., Embs, J., Pomjakushin, V., Frick, B., Braun, A. High temperature high pressure cell for neutron scattering studies, *High Press. Res.*, 2012, 32(4), 471–481.

33. Jiang, S. P. Development of lanthanum strontium manganite perovskite cathode materials of solid oxide fuel cells: A review, *J. Mater. Sci.*, 2008, 43, 6799–6833.

34. Goodenough, J. B. Electronic and ionic transport properties and other physical aspects of perovskites, *Rep. Prog. Phys.*, 2004, 67, 1915–1993.

35. http://www.lightsources.org.

36. Koningsberger 1988, X-Ray Absorption: Principles, Applications, Techniques of EXAFS, SEXAFS and XANES–January 18, 1988 by D. C. Koningsberger (Editor), R. Prins (Editor) ISBN-13: 978-0471875475.

37. Poulsen, F. W. Method for calculating ionic and electronic defect concentrations in proton containing perovskites, *J. Solid State Chem.*, 1999, 143, 115–121.

38. Richter, J., Braun, A., Harvey, A. S., Holtappels, P., Graule, T., Gauckler, L. J. Valence changes of manganese and praseodymium in $Pr_{(1-x)}Sr_{(x)}Mn_{(1-y)}In_{(y)}O_{(3-\delta)}$ perovskites upon cation substitution as determined with XANES and ELNES, *Phys. B*, 2008, 403(1), 87–94.

39. Haas, O., Ludwig, C., Bergmann, U., Singh, R. N., Braun, A., Graule, T. X-ray absorption investigation of the valence state and electronic structure of $La_{1-x}Ca_xCoO_{3-\delta}$ in comparison with $La_{1-x}Sr_xCoO_{3-\delta}$ and $La_{1-x}Sr_xFeO_{3-\delta}$, *J. Sol. State Chem.*, 2011, 184(12), 3163–3171.

40. Wang, H. University of California Davis, personal communication 2013.

41. Cramer, S. P., et al., Soft x-ray spectroscopy of metalloproteins using fluorescence detection, *Nucl. Instrum. Methods Phys. Res. Section A*, 1992, 319(1–3), 285–289.

42. Cramer, S. P., et al., Bioinorganic applications of X-ray multiplets- The impact of Theo Thole's work, *J. Electron Spectrosc. Relat. Phenomena*, 1997, 86(1–3), 175–183.

43. Wang, H. X., et al., Iron L-edge X-ray absorption spectroscopy of myoglobin complexes and photolysis products. *J. Am. Chem. Soc.*, 1997, 119(21), 4921–4928.

44. de Groot, F. M. F., et al., 2p x-ray absorption of 3d transition-metal compounds-an atomic multiplet description including the crystal field, *Phys. Rev. B-Condensed Matter*, 1990, 42(9), 5459–5468.

45. Wang, H. X., et al., Integrated X-ray L absorption spectra. Counting holes in Ni complexes. *J. Phys. Chem. B*, 1998, 102(42), 8343–8346.

46. Wang, H. X., et al., Nickel L-edge soft X-ray spectroscopy of nickel-iron hydrogenases and model compounds–Evidence for high-spin nickel(II) in the active enzyme. *J. Am. Chem. Soc.*, 2000, 122(43), 10544–10552.

47. Wang, H. X., et al., L-edge X-ray absorption spectroscopy of some Ni enzymes: Probe of Ni electronic structure. *J. Electron Spectrosc. Relat. Phenomena*, 2001, 114, 855–863.

48. Ralston, C. Y., et al., Characterization of heterogeneous nickel sites in CO dehydrogenases from Clostridium thermoaceticum and Rhodospirillum rubrum by nickel L-edge X-ray spectroscopy, *J. Am. Chem. Soc.*, 2000, 122(43), 10553–10560.

49. George, S. D., et al., A quantitative description of the ground-state wave function of Cu-A by X-ray absorption spectroscopy: Comparison to plastocyanin and relevance to electron transfer, *J. Am. Chem. Soc.*, 2001, 123(24), 5757–5767.

50. de Groot, F. M. F., Kotani, A. *Core Level Spectroscopy of Solids* (CRC Press, New York 2008).

51. Erat, S., Braun, A., Ovalle, A., Piamonteze, C., Liu, Z., Graule, T., Gauckler, L. J. Correlation of O(1s) and Fe(2p) NEXAFS spectra and electrical conductivity of $La_{1-x}Sr_xFe_{0.75}Ni_{0.25}O_{3-\delta}$, *Appl. Phys. Lett.*, 2009, 95(17), 174108.

52. Braun, A., Bayraktar, D., Harvey, A. S., Beckel, D., Purton, J. A., Holtappels, P., Gauckler, L. J., Graule, T. Pre-edges in oxygen (1s) x-ray absorption spectra: A spectral indicator for electron hole depletion and transport blocking in iron perovskites, *Appl. Phys. Lett.*, 2009, 94, 202102.

53. Braun, A., Erat, S., Bayraktar, D., Harvey, A., Graule, T. Electronic origin of conductivity changes and isothermal expansion of Ta- and Ti-substituted $La_{1/2}Sr_{1/2}$Fe-oxide in oxidative and reducing atmosphere, *Chem. Mater.*, 2012, 24(8), 1529–1535.

54. Seah, M. P., Dench, W. A. Quantitative electron spectroscopy of surfaces: A standard data base for electron inelastic mean free paths in solids, *Surf. Interface Anal.*, 1979, 1(1), 2–11.

55. Braun, A., Richter, J., Harvey, A. S., Erat, S., Infortuna, A., Frei, A., Pomjakushina, E., Mun, B. S., Holtappels, P., Vogt, U., Conder, K., Gauckler, L. J., Graule, T. Electron hole–phonon interaction, correlation of structure, and conductivity in single crystal $La_{0.9}Sr_{0.1}FeO_3$, *Appl. Phys. Lett.*, 2008, 93, 262103.

56. Braun, A., Zhang, X., Sun, Y., Müller, U., Liu, Z., Erat, S., Ari, M., Grimmer, H., Mao, S. S., Graule, T. Correlation of high temperature X-ray photoemission valence band spectra and conductivity in strained LaSrFeNi-oxide on $SrTiO_3(110)$, *Appl. Phys. Lett.*, 2009, 95, 022107.

57. Braun, A., Erat, S., Mäder, R., Zhang, X., Sun, Y., Liu, Z., Bongjin, Mun, S., Ari, M., Grimmer, H., Pomjakushina, E., Mao, S. S., Conder, K., Gauckler, L. J., Graule, T. Quantitative correlation of bulk conductivity and surface representative valence band characteristics in iron perovskites for 300 K < T < 800 K: High temperature photoemission studies on single crystal monoliths and films, *J. Electron Spectrosc. Relat. Phenomena*, 2010, 181, 56–62.

58. Erat, S., Braun, A., Piamonteze, C., Liu, Z., Ovalle, A., Schindler, H., Graule, T., Gauckler, L. J. Entanglement of charge transfer, hole doping, exchange inter-action and octahedron tilting angle and their influence on the conductivity of $La_{1-x}Sr_xFe_{0.75}Ni_{0.25}O_3$: A combination of x-ray spectroscopy and diffraction, *J. Appl. Phys.*, 2010, 108, 124906.

59. Braun, A., Erat, S., Ariffin, A., Manzke, R., Wadati, H., Graule, T., Gauckler, L. J. High temperature oxygen NEXAFS valence band spectra and conductivity of $LaFe_{3/4}Ni_{1/4}O_3$ from 300 to 773 K, *Appl. Phys. Lett.*, 2011, 99, 202112.

60. Wadati, H., Chikamatsu, A., Hashimoto, R., Takizawa, M., Kumigashira, H., Fujimori, A., Oshima, M., Lippmaa, M., Kawasaki, M., Koinuma, H. Temperature-dependent soft x-ray photoemission and absorption studies of charge disproportionation in $La_{1-x}Sr_xFeO_3$, *J. Phys. Soc. Jpn*, 2006, 75(5), 054704.

61. Wadati, H., Kobayashi, D., Kumigashira, H., Okazaki, K., Mizokawa, T., Fujimori, A., Horiba, K., Oshima, M., Hamada, N., Lippmaa, M., Kawasaki, M., Koinuma, H. Hole-doping-induced changes in the electronic structure of $La_{1-x}Sr_xFeO_3$: Soft x-ray photoemission and absorption study of epitaxial thin films. *Phys. Rev. B*, 2005, 71, 035108.

62. Backhaus-Ricoult, M., Adib, K., St. Clair, T., Luerssen, B., Gregoratti, L., Barinov, A. In-situ study of operating SOFC LSM/YSZ cathodes under polarization by photoelectron microscopy, *Solid State Ionics*, 2008, 179, 891–895.

63. Zhang, C., Grass, M. E., McDaniel, A. H., DeCaluwe, S. C., El Gabaly, F., Liu, Z., McCarty, K. F., Farrow, R. L., Linne, M. A., Hussain, Z., Jackson, G. S., Bluhm, H., Eichhorn, B. W. Measuring fundamental properties in operating solid oxide electrochemical cells by using *in-situ* X-ray photoelectron spectroscopy, *Nat. Mater.*, 2010, 9, 944.

64. Dong, J., Cheng, Z., Zha, S., Liu, M.Identification of nickel sulfides on Ni–YSZ cermet exposed to H_2 fuel containing H_2S using Raman spectroscopy. *J. Power Sources*, 2006, 156, 461–465.

65. Dong, J., Cheng, Z., Zha, S., Liu, M. *J. Power Sources*, 2006, 156, 461–465.

66. Braun, A., Janousch, M., Sfeir, J., Kiviaho, J., Noponen, M., Huggins, F. E., Smith, M. J., Steinberger-Wilckens, R., Holtappels, P., Graule, T. Molecular speciation of sulfur in solid oxide fuel cell anodes with x-ray absorption spectroscopy, *J. Power Sources*, 2008, 183(2), 564–570.

67. Ressler, T. WinXAS: A program for X-ray absorption spectroscopy data analysis under MS-Windows, *J. Synchrotron Radiat.*, 1998, 5(2), 118–122.

68. Dathe, H., Jentys, A., Lercher, J. A. *In-situ* S k-edge X-ray absorption spectroscopy for understanding and developing Sox storage catalysts, *J. Phys. Chem. B*, 2005, 109, 21842–21846.

Chapter 2

In Situ Diffraction Approaches to Characterisation of Solid Oxide Fuel Cell Electrodes

Stephen J. Skinner

Department of Materials, Imperial College London, Exhibition Road, London, SW7 2AZ, UK

s.skinner@imperial.ac.uk

Solid oxide fuel cells offer an excellent solution to current challenges in energy generation. The electrodes are the key functional components and understanding the phase evolution, reactivity and stability under operating conditions is essential if these devices are to be commercially viable products. Diffraction techniques are powerful tools that provide detailed characterisation of the materials central to device development. *In-situ* measurements are vital in mimicking the operating conditions of cells and in aiding our understanding of the key mechanisms of device degradation and reactivity. Several aspects of the use of *in-situ* techniques will be outlined in this chapter, focusing on powder diffraction techniques.

Structural Characterization Techniques: Advances and Applications in Clean Energy
Edited by Lorenzo Malavasi
Copyright © 2016 Pan Stanford Publishing Pte. Ltd.
ISBN 978-981-4669-34-4 (Hardcover), 978-981-4669-35-1 (eBook)
www.panstanford.com

2.1 Introduction

Solid oxide fuel cells (SOFCs) offer an attractive solution to the current and future supply of efficient, low carbon energy with minimal emissions. The SOFC device has several advantages when compared with conventional combustion-based technologies, and also in comparison with alternative renewable technologies such as solar power, wind, wave, etc. Conventional power generation is limited by the thermodynamic considerations associated with the Carnot cycle, whilst many of the renewable technologies suffer from issues of intermittency. A solid oxide fuel cell is not a panacea for energy generation but will form a vital component of our future energy production landscape. To ensure that the technology is robust and with suitable extended operating lifetimes, it is essential that the structural chemistry of the materials used as the functional components of the cells is fully understood.

The SOFC will operate under a harsh environment, with the components, typically ceramics, experiencing elevated temperatures during both processing of the device and extended operation. Clearly under these conditions, reactivity between components is a significant concern as solid-state diffusion processes will be accelerated at high operating temperatures. It is the effect of these processes on the electrical properties of the device that is of concern, and indeed the *in-situ* determination of these degradation processes is of paramount importance. In this chapter, the use of diffraction techniques in the characterisation of SOFC electrodes will be discussed, along with the advent and challenges of combined electrochemical and structural measurements.

2.2 Requirements for SOFCs

SOFCs typically operate at temperatures in excess of 500°C and are based on a simple concept of an ionically conducting electrolyte separating a fuel electrode and an air electrode, as discussed in [1–6]. Porous electrodes, as single phases or composites, are in intimate contact with the electrolyte and with the current collector. Evidently there are several solid–solid interfaces and solid–gas interfaces. The key requirements for the individual components are that the air electrode is a mixed conducting oxide with oxygen reduction activity, whilst the fuel electrode is a cermet whose primary function is that of fuel oxidation. In terms of the materials used it is common for the air electrode to consist of a rare earth–based perovskite such as $La_{1-x}Sr_xMnO_{3-d}$ (LSM) whilst the fuel electrode is a Ni-yttria stabilised ZrO_2 (YSZ) composite. Each is closely matched in terms of their thermal properties to the electrolyte of choice; that of course depends on the operating temperature of the cell.

The fuel cell is expected to last for up to 60,000 h [7] without significant degradation in performance. To determine the extent of interaction between phases and of phase evolution in the electrodes, a key technique is powder diffraction. The application of diffraction techniques in the study of SOFC electrodes will form the rest of this chapter.

2.3 Structural Characterisation

The use of powder diffraction to characterise the crystal structure of materials is well documented [8, 9], and hence this section will focus on the specific challenges associated with SOFC electrodes.

In SOFCs there are a relatively small number of structure types that are commonly employed, as illustrated in Fig. 2.1. These are typically fluorite, AO_2, or perovskite, ABO_3, but increasingly layered oxides are of interest. Fluorite structured oxides are the conventional choice of material for electrolytes and composite anodes, whilst perovskites are the usual choice for cathodes, although exceptions do exist. Whilst the materials themselves evidently differ considerably in both composition and structure, the optimisation of the individual materials involves substitution with what can be quite low levels of cations of similar size and scattering power. Additionally the function of the materials relies on the presence of oxygen vacancies for ion transport in each of the components, and hence it can be challenging to fully determine the structural characteristics of each component. A combination of techniques is therefore required. Much of the existing characterisation of SOFC materials is carried out as *ex-situ* studies, focusing on post-mortem analysis, as highlighted in the following discussion.

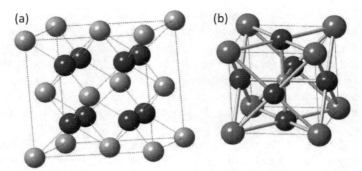

Figure 2.1   Fluorite structure as adopted by (a) CeO_2 and YSZ and (b) cubic perovskite, ABO_3.

2.4   Phase Evolution in Perovskite Cathodes

Common SOFC cathodes form in the solid solution space $La_{1-x}Sr_x$ (Co, Fe, Mn)$O_{3\pm\delta}$ and extensive work has been reported on the functional characteristics of these phases [3, 10–15]. An early example of the use of *ex-situ* characterisation is exemplified in Fig. 2.2, where the structural transition from rhombohedral to orthorhombic perovskite phase is determined as a function of B-site cation content for the $La_{1-x}Sr_xCo_{1-y}Fe_yO_3$ (LSCF) phase [16, 17]. These authors also note the effect of cation size on the phase stability of the rhombohedral phase, noting that a higher Sr content extends the stability field of this structure. Additionally in later work the same authors focus on the structural stability as a function of A cation content on the LSCF phase [17]. In this study it is apparent that as Sr content increases towards a value of $x = 0.8$ the rhombohedral distortion decreases until a point at $x = 0.8$, where a cubic phase is reported. Evidently this is a routine *ex-situ* study of single-phase electrode materials, but increasingly there is the requirement to investigate the stability of composite oxides, particularly as a function of temperature and/or time. In this case, the composites of interest are usually a Ni-electrolyte, where the electrolyte is either YSZ or Gd doped CeO_2 (GDC), as an anode material, or a cathode-electrolyte composite such as LSM-YSZ. In the case of LSM-YSZ, it is vital to be able to characterise any secondary phase formation that would be deleterious to device performance. For this system, it is well known that the phases that are likely to form are of the pyrochlore type, $La_2Zr_2O_7$, or perovskite, $SrZrO_3$ and are both ionically and electronically insulating [18, 19] and that a significant degradation in electrochemical performance is associated with the evolution of the pyrochlore phase. As shown in Fig. 2.3, in *ex-situ* diffraction data it is clear to see which phases have reacted. Of course this assumes that the reaction produces a phase that is above the detection limit of the diffraction technique. It is also likely that any subtle cation migration processes, or indeed reversible processes, would not be detected by conventional *ex-situ* X-ray powder diffraction. It is therefore clear that diffraction techniques are not standalone solutions for the characterisation of SOFC electrodes, but should be considered as one of a suite of techniques, including electrochemical and spectroscopic techniques that will provide a full characterisation of the electrode function. However to complement *ex-situ* X-ray diffraction studies the use of *in-situ* characterisation should be considered.

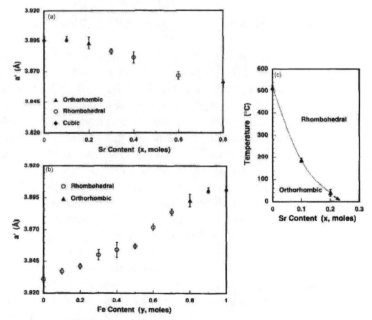

Figure 2.2   (a) Cube root of lattice volume for $La_{1-x}Sr_xCo_{0.2}Fe_{0.8}O_{3-\delta}$ vs. Sr content, (b) Cube root of lattice volume for $La_{0.8}Sr_{0.2}Co_{1-y}Fe_yO_{3-\delta}$ vs. Fe content and (c) Orthorhombic–rhombohedral phase transition temperature. From Tai et al., *Solid State Ionics*, 76, 1995, 259 and 273 [16, 17]. With permission.

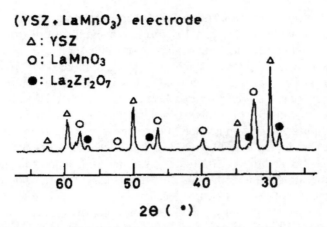

Figure 2.3   X-ray diffraction data of YSZ and LaMnO₃ reacted at 1200°C showing formation of La₂Zr₂O₇ pyrochlore phase. From Kenjo et al., *Solid State Ionics*, 57, 1992, 295 [18]. With permission.

2.5   *In-situ* Characterisation of SOFC Electrodes

It is only relatively recently that *in-situ* structural techniques have provided sufficient temporal resolution to be of use to researchers. The typical set-up involves using a standard X-ray diffractometer fitted with a stage capable of reaching temperatures of up to 2000°C under variable atmospheres. There are two main methods to achieve this: One is the use of a Pt heating strip for direct heating, and the second is to use radiative heating with the sample contained in a, typically, alumina sample holder. Of course these *in-situ* stages have the advantage of being able to control the atmosphere and hence measurements as a function of pO_2, pH_2 and pH_2O, directly relevant to SOFC operation are now possible. Additionally, to complement the use of X-ray diffraction, neutron diffraction is increasingly appealing for *in-situ* studies, particularly when there is a requirement to probe low atomic number species, such as oxygen.

As the operating temperature of solid oxide fuel cell electrodes is typically in the range of 500–1000°C, it is in this range that most *in-situ* studies are focussed. The most basic *in-situ* studies are of course simple phase evolution studies as a function of temperature and/or pO_2. An excellent example of this type of study is the work of Kuhn and Ozkan [20] in which the formation and stability of the LSCF6428 materials were investigated. In this study the decomposition of the LSCF phase under a 5% H_2/N_2 atmosphere was clearly identified as occurring at >850°C, as highlighted in Fig. 2.4. Further comprehensive unit cell parameter evolution data under air, 5% hydrogen and nitrogen are also presented, indicating the quantity of data that can readily be extracted from a simple, high quality diffraction study. These techniques can clearly be applied to cathodes, anodes and indeed composites to evaluate the long-term stability of the functional electrodes. Whilst the above study of an LSCF cathode focussed on phase evolution, it is clear that a full quantitative analysis would be of significantly greater value. Using the anode as an example in this case, Reyes-Rojas et al. [21] evaluated the Ni-YSZ anode material using *in-situ* XRD, following phase evolution, but also refining, using the Rietveld technique [22], the phase mixture (Fig. 2.5). Here the reduction rate was determined and changes in the cubic/tetragonal phase mixture reported. Further examples include developing an understanding of the oxidation of interconnect materials [23], and using *in-situ* diffraction techniques to probe kinetics [24].

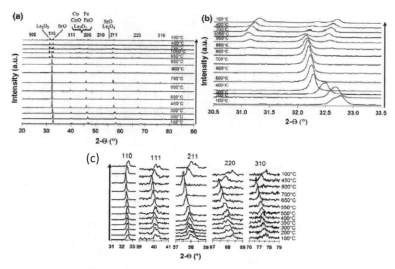

Figure 2.4   *In-situ* XRD data for $La_{0.6}Sr_{0.4}Co_{0.2}Fe_{0.8}O_{3-\delta}$ measured in (a) and (b) 5% H_2/N_2 and (c) air as a function of temperature. From Kuhn et al., *Catal. Lett.*, 121, 2008, 179 [20]. With permission.

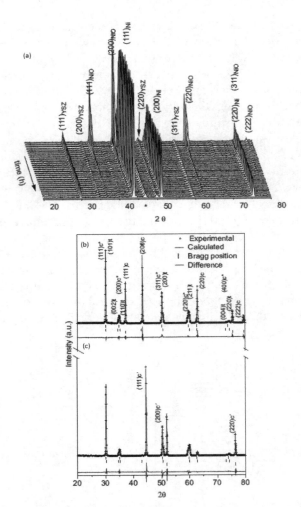

Figure 2.5   (a) *In-situ* XRD data of Ni-YSZ anodes during reduction,
(b) phase mixture before reduction fitted by Rietveld
refinement, and (c) phase mixture after reduction analysed
by Rietveld refinement.From Reyes-Rojas et al., *J. Phys.
D: Appl. Phys.*, 38, 2005, 2276 [21]. With permission.

Understanding of residual stress changes in SOFC electrodes
is essential when considering the durability and lifetime of devices.
As well as contributing to the phase understanding of materials,
X-ray techniques can also probe the residual stress changes in
materials. A recent example of this focuses on the segmented in

series design of SOFCs [25, 26] and investigates the residual stress induced by redox cycling of the cell, focussing on the electrolyte, Fig. 2.6. Additional studies by Malzbender et al. [27] characterise the effect of changes in the electrode through reduction mimicking operation on the stress in the electrolyte as a function of temperature. They find that cell curvature correlates well with the residual stress calculated from diffraction measurements, Fig. 2.7.

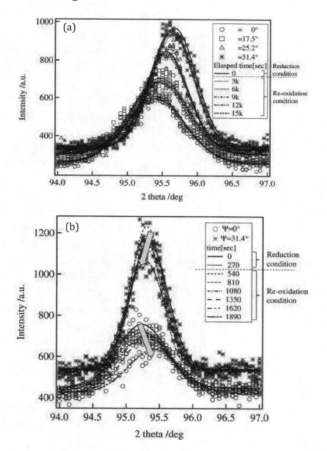

Figure 2.6   Evolution of peak position on moving from reducing to reoxidising conditions in (a) SIS type SOFC and (b) ASP type cell indicating residual stress induced through thermal cycling. From Somekawa et al., *J. Power Sources*, 221, 2013, 64 [26]. With permission.

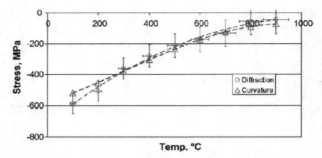

Figure 2.7 Comparison of experimentally determined residual stress from XRD with that calculated from thermal expansion. From Malzbender et al., *J. Power Sources*, 182, 2008, 594 [27]. With permission.

2.6 *In-situ* Synchrotron Diffraction Studies

Powder X-ray diffraction is clearly a valuable tool in the study of SOFC electrodes, but laboratory-based systems are unfortunately limited in their capability, and it is necessary to use higher resolution techniques, such as that provided by synchrotron radiation. The advent of third-generation synchrotron sources such as Diamond in the UK, ESRF and others, have led to the design and construction of very high resolution diffractometers. Evidently this does not address the issue of accessing information regarding low atomic number species, but the increased d-spacing resolution (I11 at Diamond achieves $\Delta d/d = 10^{-4}$ Å) allows phase evolution and minor phase impurities to be clearly distinguished. It is also feasible to collect data of sufficient quality with ms time resolution to allow full quantitative analysis of data sets. This increase in angular resolution has proven valuable in the field of composite electrodes, where the subtle lattice shifts associated with cation segregation can be extracted [28], as well as the potential to separate symmetry related systems, for example in the $La_2NiO_{4+\delta}$ system where the total oxygen content influences the mono- or biphasic nature of the electrode material.

The rapid data collection and high resolution offered by synchrotron techniques are supplemented by the energy ranges available, allowing users to tune the instrument, and by the monochromatic nature of the beam. Synchrotron radiation is of course also ideal for imaging and scattering experiments; techniques such as X-ray absorption spectroscopy provide an excellent complement to diffraction. Combined measurements providing diffraction and spectroscopy data, linking chemical changes with structural changes, are developing rapidly. For fuel cell electrodes, there is the additional requirement of determining electrochemistry under operating conditions. Increasingly these combined measurements with specially commissioned sample stages are being developed [29], but as yet no measurement of all three aspects has been possible. Structure and electrochemistry, structure and spectroscopy or spectroscopy and electrochemistry are possible, but to date no combination of all three has been reported.

2.7 Powder Neutron Diffraction

X-ray studies of SOFC electrode materials, whether by laboratory or synchrotron techniques will always lack the detailed information regarding low atomic number species. In studies of electrodes, typically oxide materials, a full structural analysis is often required and indeed the distribution and mobility of oxygen species within cathodes is essential to understanding phase evolution, durability and function. Many examples of the power of neutron diffraction are available [30–36] in which the structure and oxygen content of single-phase materials have been refined.

More recently the combination of Rietveld analysis with maximum entropy methods has proven valuable in visualising oxygen diffusion pathways through complex layered oxides such as those based on $Pr_2NiO_{4+\delta}$. Further validation of these studies has been recently provided through the use of atomistic simulation, in which a direct comparison of the nuclear density distribution maps, obtained from simulation and diffraction data have been compared and verified the proposed diffusion pathways [37–40]. One of the minor disadvantages of neutron techniques is the requirement to run samples under vacuum, but to a great extent careful design of sample environments have overcome these issues, allowing data collection at temperature in variable atmospheres. Recently *in-situ* conductivity cells have been developed for use with neutron diffractometers extending the capability of these instruments. Indeed combined impedance spectroscopy and structural measurements have been demonstrated in an electrolyte material [41], but the lack of spatial resolution of neutron diffraction techniques means that measurements of *in-operando* cells remains challenging.

The most recent and potentially revolutionary approach to analysis of diffraction data has been the introduction of total scattering methods for the analysis of diffuse scattering contributions to diffraction patterns [42, 43]. This technique can utilise laboratory X-ray, synchrotron and neutron diffraction data to provide a full understanding of the local structure as well as the traditional long-range structure represented by Bragg scattering. Changes in the local structure as a function of temperature, atmosphere and electrical load can all be readily probed, and through the implementation of Reverse Monte Carlo techniques robust structural models determined, as discussed in detail elsewhere in this text.

2.8 Conclusions

X-ray and neutron diffraction are a powerful combination of techniques that have the potential to provide key information *in-situ* and *in-operando* on the operation of fuel cell electrodes. From basic information on phase evolution, through residual stress evolution to local structure and diffusion pathways, a full understanding of all key processes in cell operation can be obtained. Further developments provide complementary electro-chemical data simultaneously. The evolution of these combined measurements, in combination with long duration experiments on functioning cells offer significant advantages to the research community involved in SOFC cell development.

References

1. Brett, D. J. L., Atkinson, A., Brandon, N. P., Skinner, S. J., Intermediate temperature solid oxide fuel cells. *Chem. Soc. Rev.*, 2008, **37**, 1568–1578.

2. Lashtabeg, A., Skinner, S. J., Solid oxide fuel cells: A challenge for materials chemists? *J. Mater. Chem.*, 2006, 16, 3161–3170.

3. Skinner, S. J., Recent advances in Perovskite-type materials for solid oxide fuel cell cathodes. *Int. J. Inorg. Mater.*, 2001, 3, 113–121.

4. Aguadero, A., Fawcett, L., Taub, S., Woolley, R., Wu, K. T., Xu, N., Kilner, J. A., Skinner, S. J., Materials development for intermediate-temperature solid oxide electrochemical devices. *J. Mater. Sci.,* 2012, 47, 3925–3948.

5. Atkinson, A., Barnett, S., Gorte, R. J., Irvine, J. T. S., McEvoy, A. J., Mogensen, M., Singhal, S. C., Vohs, J., Advanced anodes for high-temperature fuel cells. *Nat. Mater.,* 2004, 3, 17–27.

6. Steele, B. C. H., Materials for IT-SOFC stacks 35 years R&D: The inevitability of gradualness? *Solid State Ionics,* 2000, 134, 3–20.

7. *The Department of Energy Hydrogen and Fuel Cells Program Plan*; US DoE: Washington, USA, 2011.

8. Harris, K. D. M., Tremayne, M., Crystal structure determination from powder diffraction. *Chem. Mater.,* 1996, 8, 2554–2570.

9. Evans, J. S. O., Evans, I. R., Beyond classical applications of powder diffraction. *Chem. Soc. Rev.,* 2004, 33, 539–547.

10. Caneiro, A., Mogni, L., Grunbaum, N., Prado, F., Physicochemical properties of non-stoichiometric oxides. *J. Therm. Anal. Calorim.,* 2011, 103, 597–606.

11. De Souza, R. A., Kilner, J. A., Oxygen transport in $La_{1-x}Sr_xMn_{1-y}Co_yO_{3+/-\delta}$ perovskites: Part I. Oxygen tracer diffusion. *Solid State Ionics,* 1998, 106, 175–187.

12. De Souza, R. A., Kilner, J. A., Walker, J. F., A SIMS study of oxygen tracer diffusion and surface exchange in $La_{0.8}Sr_{0.2}MnO_{3+\delta}$. *Mater. Lett.,* 2000, 43, 43–52.

13. Godickemeier, M., Sasaki, K., Gauckler, L. J., Riess, I., Perovskite cathodes for solid oxide fuel cells based on ceria electrolytes. *Solid State Ionics,* 1996, 86–88, 691–701.

14. Huang, Y. Y., Vohs, J. M., Gorte, R. J., An examination of LSM-LSCo mixtures for use in SOFC cathodes. *J. Electrochem. Soc.,* 2006, 153, A951–A955.

15. Jiang, S. P., Development of lanthanum strontium manganite perovskite cathode materials of solid oxide fuel cells: A review. *J. Mater. Sci.,* 2008, 43, 6799–6833.

16. Tai, L. W., Nasrallah, M. M., Anderson, H. U., Sparlin, D. M., Sehlin, S. R., Structure and electrical properties of $La_{1-x}Sr_xCo_{1-y}Fe_yO_3$. I. The system $La_{0.8}Sr_{0.2}Co_{1-y}Fe_yO_3$. *Solid State Ionics,* 1995, 76, 259–271.

17. Tai, L. W., Nasrallah, M. M., Anderson, H. U., Sparlin, D. M., Sehlin, S. R., Structure and electrical properties of $La_{1-x}Sr_xCo_{1-y}Fe_yO_3$.

II. The system $La_{1-x}Sr_xCo_{0.2}Fe_{0.8}O_3$. *Solid State Ionics,* 1995, 76, 273–283.

18. Kenjo, T., Nishiya, M., $LaMnO_3$ air cathodes for HT SOFCs. *Solid State Ionics,* 1992, 57, 295–302.

19. Levy, C., Zhong, Y., Morel, C., Marlin, S., Thermodynamic stabilities of $La_2Zr_2O_7$ and $SrZrO_3$ in SOFC and their relationship with LSM synthesis process. *J. Electrochem. Soc.,* 2010, 157, B1597–B1601.

20. Kuhn, J. N., Ozkan, U. S., Effect of Co content upon the bulk structure of Sr and Co doped $LaFeO_3$. *Catal. Lett.,* 2008, 121, 179–188.

21. Reyes Rocha, A., Esparza-Ponce, H. E., Fuentes, L., Lopez-Ortiz, A., Keer, A., Reyes-Gasga, J., In-situ X-ray Rietveld analysis of Ni-YSZ solid oxide fuel cell anodes during NiO reduction in H_2. *J. Phys. D: Appl. Phys.,* 2005, 38, 2276–2282.

22. Rietveld, H. M., A profile refinement method for nuclear and magnetic structures. *J. Appl. Crystallogr.,* 1969, 2, 65–71.

23. Vargas, M. J. G., Lelait, L., Kolarik, V., Fietzek, H., Juez-Lorenzo, M. *The effect of water vapour on the oxidation of stainless steels studied by X ray diffraction*, In Mat. Sci. Forum, 2004, Eds. Steinmetz, P., Wright, I. G., Meier, G., Galerie, A., Pieraggi, B., Podor, R., Trans. Tech Pubs.: 2004, pp. 823–830.

24. Rupp, J. L. M., Scherrer, B., Gauckler, L. J. *Nucleation and grain growth kinetics of amorphous to nanocrystalline ceria solid solutions*, In Mats. Sci. Forum, 2007, Eds. Kang, S. J. L., Huh, M. Y., Hwang, N. M., Homma, H., Ushioda, K., Ikuhara, Y., 2007; pp. 1339–1344.

25. Fujita, K., Somekawa, T., Hatae, T., Matsuzaki, Y., Residual stress and redox cycling of segmented-in-series solid oxide fuel cells. *J. Power Sources,* 2011, 196, 9022–9026.

26. Somekawa, T., Fujita, K., Matsuzaki, Y., Residual stress change with time of a segmented-in-series solid oxide fuel cell using an *in-situ* X-ray stress measuring method. *J. Power Sources,* 2013, 221, 64–69.

27. Malzbender, J., Steinbrech, R. W., Singheiser, L., A review of advanced techniques for characterising SOFC behaviour. *Fuel Cells,* 2009, 9, 785–793.

28. Sayers, R., Parker, J. E., Tang, C. C., Skinner, S. J., *In-situ* compatibility studies of lanthanum nickelate with a ceria-based electrolyte for SOFC composite cathodes. *J. Mater. Chem.,* 2012, 22, 3536–3543.

29. Hagen, A., Traulsen, M. L., Kiebach, W.-R., Johansen, B. S., Spectro-electrochemical cell for *in-situ* studies of solid oxide fuel cells. *J. Synch. Rad.,* 2012, 19, 400–407.

30. Aguadero, A., Perez, M., Alonso, J. A., Daza, L., Neutron powder diffraction study of the influence of high oxygen pressure treatments on $La_2NiO_{4+\delta}$ and structural analysis of $La_2Ni_{1-x}Cu_xO_{4+\delta}$ ($0 \le x \le 1$). *J. Power Sources*, 2005, 151, 52–56.

31. Aguadero, A., Alonso, J. A., Fernandez-Diaz, M. T., Escudero, M. J., Daza, L., *In-situ* high temperature neutron powder diffraction study of $La_2Ni_{0.6}Cu_{0.4}O_{4+\delta}$ in air: Correlation with the electrical behaviour. *J. Power Sources*, 2007, 169, 17–24.

32. Aguadero, A., Alonso, J. A., Daza, L., Oxygen excess in $La_2CoO_{4+\delta}$: A neutron diffraction study. *Z. Natur. B*, 2008, 63, 615–622.

33. Alonso, J. A., Martinez-Lope, M. J., Aguadero, A., Daza, L., Neutron powder diffraction as a characterization tool of solid oxide fuel cell materials. *Prog. Solid State Chem.*, 2008, 36, 134–150.

34. Munnings, C. N., Sayers, R., Stuart, P. A., Skinner, S. J., Structural transformation and oxidation of $Sr_2MnO_{3.5+x}$ determined by in-situ neutron powder diffraction. *Solid State Sciences*, 2012, 14, 48–53.

35. Skinner, S. J., Characterisation of $La_2NiO_{4+\delta}$ using in-situ high temperature neutron powder diffraction. *Solid State Sci.*, 2003, 5, 419–426.

36. Skinner, S. J., Brooks, I. J. E., Munnings, C. N., Tetragonal $CeNbO_4$ at 1073 K in air and in vacuo. *Acta Crystallogr. C*, 2004, 60, I37–I39.

37. Yashima, M., Enoki, M., Wakita, T., Ali, R., Matsushita, Y., Izumi, F., Ishihara, T., Structural disorder and diffusional pathway of oxide ions in a doped Pr_2NiO_4-based mixed conductor. *J. Am. Chem. Soc.*, 2008, 130, 2762.

38. Yashima, M., Sirikanda, N., Ishihara, T., Crystal structure, diffusion path, and oxygen permeability of a Pr_2NiO_4-based mixed conductor $(Pr_{0.9}La_{0.1})_{(2)}(Ni_{0.74}Cu_{0.21}Ga_{0.05})O_{4+\delta}$. *J. Am. Chem. Soc.*, 2010, 132, 2385–2392.

39. Kushima, A., Parfitt, D., Chroneos, A., Yildiz, B., Kilner, J. A., Grimes, R. W., Interstitialcy diffusion of oxygen in tetragonal $La_2CoO_{4+\delta}$. *Phys. Chem. Chem. Phys.*, 2011, 13, 2242–2249.

40. Parfitt, D., Chroneos, A., Kilner, J. A., Grimes, R. W., Molecular dynamics study of oxygen diffusion in $Pr_2NiO_{4+\delta}$. *Phys. Chem. Chem. Phys.*, 2010, 12, 6834–6836.

41. Liu, J. J., Hull, S., Ahmed, I., Skinner, S. J., Application of combined neutron diffraction and impedance spectroscopy for in-situ structure and conductivity studies of $La_2Mo_2O_9$. *Nucl. Instr. Meth. B*, 2011, 269, 539–543.

42. Billinge, S. J. L., Nanostructure studied using the atomic pair distribution function. *Z. Kristallographie*, 2007, 17–26.

43. Billinge, S. J. L., Levin, I., The problem with determining atomic structure at the nanoscale. *Science,* 2007, 316, 561–565.

Chapter 3

Structural Characterisation of Oxide Ion Conductors

Ivana Radosavljević Evans

Department of Chemistry, Durham University, Durham DH1 3LE, UK

ivana.radosavljevic@durham.ac.uk

3.1 Introduction

Oxide ion conductors are technologically important materials, essential for applications, *inter alia*, in solid oxide fuel cells (SOFCs). The significance of crystallographic characterisation of oxide ion conductors is two-fold. Firstly, there is an intimate relationship between the structure of functional materials and their properties. Secondly, rational design of new and improved SOFC materials depends on the understanding of the mechanisms of ionic mobility; a full theoretical understanding of these mechanisms at atomic level, in turn, requires the knowledge of the crystal structure.

There are several factors which render accurate and precise crystallographic characterisation of oxide ion conductors a non-trivial, and often a very challenging, task. They can broadly be classified into four groups; those that stem from the composition; the form (single crystal vs. powder); the structure itself; and

Structural Characterization Techniques: Advances and Applications in Clean Energy
Edited by Lorenzo Malavasi
Copyright © 2016 Pan Stanford Publishing Pte. Ltd.
ISBN 978-981-4669-34-4 (Hardcover), 978-981-4669-35-1 (eBook)
www.panstanford.com

the behaviour of the materials studied. The fine details of the structure, and those particularly relevant for the properties, are often contained in the information about the oxygen atom arrangement in compounds which are typically ternary or higher mixed metal oxides. Most materials are synthesised and characterised in laboratories with X-ray diffraction instruments. The differences in the atomic scattering factors[1] mean that it is difficult to determine accurately the positions and other crystallographic parameters for oxygen atoms in the presence of heavy metals. This is exacerbated further by the fact that, due to incongruent melting or phase transitions, it is often very difficult or impossible to produce high-quality single crystals of target materials, so structural characterisation often relies on powder X-ray diffraction, at least initially. The use of neutron diffraction is very advantageous owing to the oxygen scattering length for neutrons being of the same order of magnitude as that for the relevant metals [1]. Many oxide ion conductors display subtle but complex superstructures, which means that their structures are closely related to and represent modifications of simpler structures with smaller unit cells and higher symmetry. The resulting inherent pseudo-symmetry can impede successful application of the traditional reciprocal space methods for structure solution (e.g. direct methods [2]). However, there are alternative approaches to structure solution, which can be applied successfully in these cases; such approaches include simulated annealing and charge flipping [3, 4]. These methods have been demonstrated to be robust and successful in solving a number of complex superstructure problems in different functional oxides [5–7]. An additional level of complexity arises if the superstructure observed is incommensurate, as has been recently shown for a number of oxide ion conductors [1, 2].

3.2 Structural Families of Oxide Ion Conductors

This chapter is not intended to provide a comprehensive coverage of all structure types exhibiting oxide ion conductivity. Instead, the focus will be on a narrow selection of specific representatives of structural families of oxide ion conductors. The examples chosen are of particular interest due to their crystallographic complexity, the combination of the characterisation methods employed, or the potential conceptual applicability of their structural features to the discovery of new ionic conductors. The fluorite-type oxide ion conductors, based on ZrO_2, CeO_2 and Bi_2O_3, are covered in detail in the chapter on PDF analysis and will not be covered here.

3.2.1 LaGaO₃-Based Materials

Oxide ion conductivity in materials based on lanthanum gallate $LaGaO_3$ was first reported by Feng and Goodenough, and Ishihara et al. in 1994 [8, 9]. These two groups reported high oxide conductivity, negligible electronic conductivity in a broad pO_2 range ($1-1 \times 10^{-20}$ atm) and an absence of proton conduction in La and Sr co-doped samples with composition $La_{1-x}Sr_xGa_{1-y}Mg_yO_{3-\delta}$ (commonly abbreviated as LSGM phases). LSGM materials belong to the perovskite structure type, ABO_3, which can be described as a network of corner-sharing BO_6 octahedra, with the larger A cation occupying a 12-coordinate site (Fig. 3.1a). Co-doping with Sr and Mg creates oxide ion vacancies both in the octahedral sublattice and on the 12-coordinate sites, and this can yield an optimum number and distribution of vacancies needed for high oxide ion conductivity.

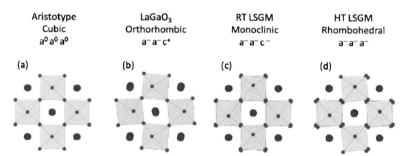

Aristotype	LaGaO₃	RT LSGM	HT LSGM
Cubic	Orthorhombic	Monoclinic	Rhombohedral
$a^0 a^0 a^0$	$a^- a^- c^+$	$a^- a^- c^-$	$a^- a^- a^-$
(a)	(b)	(c)	(d)

Figure 3.1 The evolution of the structural distortions in $La_{0.9}Sr_{0.1}Ga_{0.8}Mg_{0.2}O_{2.85}$ relative to the parent $LaGaO_3$ phase and the cubic perovskite aristotype. Large purple spheres represent the A cation, light blue octahedra and the small red spheres represent corner-sharing BO_6 octahedra.

At room temperature, the parent lanthanum gallate $LaGaO_3$ crystallises in orthorhombic space group Pbnm [10], arising from the cubic aristotype by tilts of the GaO_6 octahedra, such that the tilts of the successive octahedra along the c-crystallographic axis are in phase (Fig. 3.1b); this distortion can be represented as $a^-a^-c^+$ in the Glazer notation [11]. Slater et al. determined the crystal structure of $La_{0.9}Sr_{0.1}Ga_{0.8}Mg_{0.2}O_{2.85}$ by high-resolution neutron diffraction, and found it to be monoclinic (space group I2/a), although metrically very close to orthorhombic ($\beta = 90.0600(4)$ Å). Again, the structure distortion and symmetry lowering arise from octahedral tilts, which in the doped material are such that the successive units along the c-crystallographic axis tilt in an antiphase manner, i.e. $a^-a^-c^-$ (Fig. 3.1c) [12]. At temperatures associated with high oxide ion conductivity (>500°C), $La_{0.9}Sr_{0.1}Ga_{0.8}Mg_{0.2}O_{2.85}$ becomes rhombohedral ($a^-a^-a^-$), with further changes of the octahedral tilts relative to the room-temperature structure (Fig. 3.1d) [13].

Atomistic modelling studies by Khan et al. considered a range of doped $LaGaO_3$ compositions [14]. In the case of Sr- and Mg-doped $LaGaO_3$, the calculated binding energies for defect clusters suggested that the oxide vacancies tended to occupy positions around the Mg^{2+} substituent sites. This defect model agrees with the findings of Huang et al. [15] and Haavik et al. [16], based on conductivity measurements and the interpretation of the non-Arrhenius behaviour of LSGM. However, more recent multinuclear solid-state NMR experimental studies aided by DFT calculations carried out by Blanc et al. propose different models for local structure and defect chemistry of doped $LaGaO_3$ materials [17]. Firstly, their DFT calculations of the phase energetics in Mg-doped $LaGaO_3$ ($LaGa_{1-y}Mg_yO_{3-y/2}$, with $y = 0.0625, 0.125$ and 0.25) suggest a preference for a Ga-V_O-Ga configuration and find no tendency for the Mg-V_O pair formation. This is in contrast to the previously reported modelling results, which indicated a clear preference for vacancies to be located on sites adjacent to Mg dopants [14]. Blanc et al. sought evidence for vacancies in the first coordination sphere of Mg by ^{25}Mg solid-state NMR; however, they only observed Mg in six-fold coordination. They do, however, point out that it is n't possible to rule out the presence of (up to 30%) five-coordinate Mg sites, due to the detection limit of their experiment [17]. ^{71}Ga NMR, however, allowed direct experimental observation of both five- and six-coordinate Ga, clearly in line with the computational prediction that Ga-V_O-Ga configuration should be energetically favoured. Finally, in ^{17}O MAS NMR spectra, individual resonances were identified for the oxygen atoms around five-coordinate Ga, located on sites which are axial and equatorial relative to the Ga-V_O axis (Fig. 3.2). The ^{17}O chemical shifts thus show a clear sensitivity to the distortions of the local environment caused by the proximity of vacancies, and provide further support to the computationally predicted preference for the vacancies to be located on sites near Ga [17].

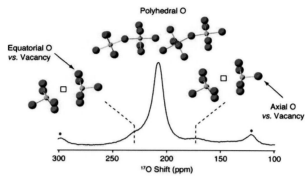

Figure 3.2 ^{17}O NMR provides direct evidence for the oxygen vacancies in LSGM to be located near Ga sites. Green, blue and red spheres represent Ga, Mg and O atoms, respectively, while the black square represents the oxygen vacancy, V_O. Reprinted with permission from Blanc, F., Middlemiss, D. S., Gan, Z. H., Grey, C. P., *J. Am. Chem. Soc.*, 2011, 133, 17662–17672. Copyright (2011) American Chemical Society.

3.2.2   La$_2$Mo$_2$O$_9$-Based Materials

High oxide ion conductivity ion La$_2$Mo$_2$O$_9$ was first reported by Lacorre et al. in 2000 [18]. At 580°C, the ionic conductivity of this material increases abruptly by almost two orders of magnitude and surpasses that of yttria- and calcia-stabilised zirconias. This change in properties is accompanied by a structural phase transition.

The crystal structure of the high-temperature β-La$_2$Mo$_2$O$_9$ form was solved and refined using powder neutron diffraction data [19]. β-La$_2$Mo$_2$O$_9$ crystallises in cubic space group $P2_13$, with a unit cell parameter a = 7.2351(1) Å and 5 atom in the asymmetric unit (1 La, 1 Mo and 3 O sites). While La and Mo form an ordered cation sublattice similar to that in b-SnWO$_4$, the oxygen sublattice is more complex. A fully occupied O1 position lies on the cubic three-fold axis, while the remaining two sites lie off the three-fold axis and are partially occupied: O(2) with a fractional occupancy of 0.78(2) and O(3) with 0.38(2). Both sites have large atomic displacement parameters (ADPs) at 670°C, with U_{equiv} values 0.097(5) and 0.24(2) Å^2 for O(2) and O(3), respectively [19].

Although electron diffraction carried out as part of this work suggested that the room-temperature structure of La$_2$Mo$_2$O$_9$ is a monoclinic 2 × 3 × 4 superstructure of the high-temperature cubic form, the structure remained unknown until single crystals suitable for X-ray structure analysis were obtained. The structure of α-La$_2$Mo$_2$O$_9$ was solved and refined by Evans et al. using laboratory single-crystal X-ray diffraction [20]. With unit cell parameters a = 14.325(3) Å, b = 21.482(4) Å, c = 28.585(6) Å, b = 90.40(3)°, V = 8796(3) Å^3 and space group $P2_1$, its asymmetric unit contains 312 atoms (48 La, 48 Mo and 216 O sites). All cation sites were located by direct methods; the oxygen atom positions were located using difference Fourier maps [21]. The Mo atoms in α-La$_2$Mo$_2$O$_9$ are found in three different coordination environments: 15 are four-coordinate, 15 five-coordinate and 18 six-coordinate, leading to a polyhedral representation depicted in Fig. 3.3a. This structural arrangement has clear implication on the oxide ion migration pathways in La$_2$Mo$_2$O$_9$, which can be inferred by comparing the structural models of the low- and high-temperature forms of the material.

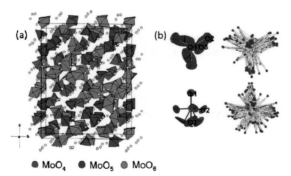

● MoO$_4$ ● MoO$_5$ ● MoO$_6$

Figure 3.3   (a) Polyhedral representation of α-La$_2$Mo$_2$O$_9$. (b) Dynamic disorder of oxygen atoms in the high-temperature β-La$_2$Mo$_2$O$_9$ compared to the static arrangement in α-La$_2$Mo$_2$O$_9$ (shown as the superposition of the 48 unique Mo atoms and their coordination spheres). Adapted with permission from Evans, I. R., Howard, J. A. K., Evans, J. S. O., *Chem. Mater.*, 2005, 17, 4074–4077. Copyright (2005) American Chemical Society.

A clear correlation between the dynamically disordered oxygen atoms in β-La$_2$Mo$_2$O$_9$ and the static oxygen atom distribution in room-temperature α-La$_2$Mo$_2$O$_9$ can be appreciated qualitatively from the positions and numbers of independent O atoms in α-La$_2$Mo$_2$O$_9$ relative to the shapes of oxygen atomic displacement parameters and site fractional occupancies in β-La$_2$Mo$_2$O$_9$, shown in Fig. 3.3b.

Furthermore, this relationship can be quantified by allocating the 216 unique oxygen atoms in the α structure into three groups, those that lie closest to each of the three crystallographic sites in the disordered β structure. There are 47, 116 and 53 oxygen atoms in α-La$_2$Mo$_2$O$_9$ that lie nearest to O1, O2 and O3 sites of β-La$_2$Mo$_2$O$_9$ respectively. Taking into account site multiplicities, this corresponds to effective site occupancies of 0.33, 0.81 and 0.37 in a simple cubic unit cell [20]. These values are remarkably close to the experimentally determined occupancies for β-La$_2$Mo$_2$O$_9$ of 0.33, 0.78(2) and 0.38(2) [19]. The key conclusion of this analysis is that the structure of the high-temperature highly conducting β-La$_2$Mo$_2$O$_9$ phase structurally corresponds to a time-averaged version of the room-temperature ordered α-La$_2$Mo$_2$O$_9$, and that an order-disorder phase transition leads to an abrupt increase of oxide ion conductivity. In the context of ionic conduction mechanisms, this strongly suggests that the ability of the Mo^{6+} cation to support variable coordination environment plays an essential role in providing low-energy migration pathways for oxide ion diffusion in La$_2$Mo$_2$O$_9$, and potentially in other oxide ion conductors [20].

Rietveld refinement of variable temperature laboratory powder X-ray diffraction data collected on heating and cooling between room temperature and 800°C was employed to extract the unit cell parameters of La$_2$Mo$_2$O$_9$. The results shown in Fig. 3.4 indicate that the phase transition between the α and the β forms of La$_2$Mo$_2$O$_9$ is accompanied by an abrupt and discontinuous change in unit cell volume, and by a hysteresis of about 15°. These features, together with the structures of the two forms discussed above, suggest that the α-to-β transformation in La$_2$Mo$_2$O$_9$ is a first-order order-disorder phase transition.

Atomic pair distribution function (PDF) analysis provides a means to directly probe local structure, by taking into account diffuse scattering, as well as the Bragg peaks. PDF analysis of time-of-flight neutron data collected on the two forms of $La_2Mo_2O_9$ was reported by Malavasi et al. [22]. This work confirmed that the structural phase transition corresponds to the onset of dynamic disorder of oxide ions, and that, although the average structure changes from monoclinic to cubic, the local structure remains monoclinic throughout the temperature range investigated.

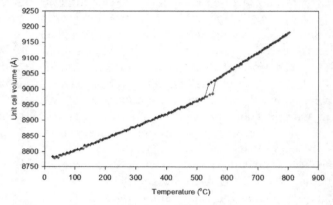

Figure 3.4 Variation of the unit cell volume of $La_2Mo_2O_9$ with temperature determined from a laboratory in-situ powder X-ray diffraction experiment. Red data points represent heating, blue data points represent cooling.

3.2.3 Apatite-Type Materials

Since the first reports of high oxide ion conductivity in apatite-type silicates by Nakayama et al. [23, 24], a large number of silicate and germanate materials have been reported to be good oxide ion conductors. Apatites adopt the general formula $A_{10}(MO_4)_6O_{2\pm\delta}$ (A = alkaline earth or rare earth cations, M = Si, Ge, P). The structures are typically hexagonal, and consist of isolated MO_4 tetrahedra and the A cations and oxide ions located in the channels along the crystallographic c-axis (Fig. 3.5).

Numerous studies have shown that the ionic conductivity of apatite-type oxides can be increased by introducing excess oxygen via A-site doping, implying an interstitial oxide ion conductivity mechanism in these materials. Another experimental observation which a good structural model should account for is that single crystal measurements indicate that, even though the conductivity is about an order of magnitude higher along the crystallographic *c*-axis, it is still appreciable in the perpendicular direction [25]. The key question which needs to be answered in order to elucidate the oxide ion migration pathways in apatites, both along and between the channels, is the precise location of the excess oxygen in the crystal structure. This has been an area of some controversy in the literature, especially for the silicate materials, the main issue being whether the excess oxygen atoms are located centrally in the channels or at the channel periphery.

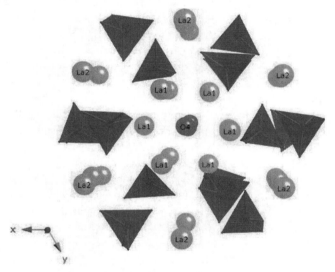

Figure 3.5   Representation of the apatite $A_{10}(MO_4)_6O_2$ structure type down the crystallographic *c*-axis. Blue polyhedra represent the MO_4 units, green spheres the large A cations and red spheres the oxygen atoms. Reprinted with permission from Jones, A., Slater, P. R., Islam, M. S., *Chem. Mater.*, 2008, 20, 5055–5060. Copyright (2008) American Chemical Society.

Different structural studies of germanate materials by a range of methods seem to have produced a fairly consistent picture. Powder neutron diffraction studies carried out by Pramana et al. [26] on composition $La_{10}(GeO_4)_6O_3$, which contains one extra oxygen atom per formula unit relative to the nominal apatite formula, located these interstitial oxygen atoms in the framework, within the channel walls. They reside between adjacent GeO_4 tetrahedra and tend to be closer to one Ge atom, whose coordination polyhedron is thus better described as GeO_5. This location of interstitial oxygen atoms readily accounts for the inter-channel diffusion. This model is consistent with subsequent PDF studies of a related composition, $La_{9.67}(GeO_4)_6O_{2.5}$, based on neutron total scattering, in which the excess oxygen was again found on the interstitial sites within the framework, and not in the channel along the *c*-axis [27]. In addition to these and numerous other neutron scattering based studies of apatite-type germanate oxide ion conductors, combined density functional theory (DFT) and experimental solid-state NMR can also be very powerful in resolving structural details in this type of material. Panchmatia et al. [28] carried out such a study on three apatite-type samples: $La_8Y_2(GeO_4)_6O_3$ (with one extra oxygen per formula unit), $La_8YCa(GeO_4)_6O_{2.5}$ (with half the amount of oxide ion interstitials relative to the first sample) and $La_{7.5}Ca_{2.5}(GeO_4)_6O_{1.75}$ (with no interstitials, oxygen-deficient relative to the nominal apatite formula). Due to the low natural abundance of the NMR-active ^{17}O species, the samples were enriched by hydrothermal treatment in the presence of ^{17}O-enriched water before carrying out the NMR experiments. A single resonance at a chemical shift of about 170 ppm was observed for the oxygen-poor sample, and this was assigned to the GeO_4 groups. In addition to this peak, a resonance at about 280 ppm was observed for the two oxygen-excess samples, and this was assigned to the GeO_5 units, whose formation was predicted by structure optimisations for these compositions [28]. This assignment was confirmed by DFT calculations carried out to predict the ^{17}O NMR spectrum for $La_8Y_2(GeO_4)_6O_3$. The simulated spectra showed a small chemical shift separation between the resonances corresponding to the GeO_4 tetrahedra in the framework and the GeO_5 units created by introducing interstitial oxygen atoms, thus corroborating the experimental results [28].

There is significantly less agreement in the literature about the precise location of interstitial oxygen atoms in silicate apatites, and the consequent implications for the mechanism of oxide ion mobility. The discrepancies of the results reported in the literature may suggest that the location of the interstitial oxygen atoms in silicate apatites depends on the exact sample composition, synthetic route and processing history. A more detailed survey of this topic can be found in the review by Orera and Slater and the references therein [29].

3.2.4   Melilite-Type Materials

The compounds belonging to the melilite structure type have a general formula AB_3O_7. In materials relevant to the topic of this article, the A cations rare- and alkaline-earths and the B cations are distributed over two unique crystallographic sites, each tetrahedrally coordinated by oxygen atoms. The BO_4 tetrahedra share corners to form B_3O_7 sheets in the (xy) plane, which are separated by layers of eight-coordinate A cations, Fig. 3.6. It is important to note that the corner-sharing patterns of the BO_4 tetrahedra centred on the two crystallographically unique sites which B cations occupy are different; one set of these tetrahedra share all corners (light green in Fig. 3.6), while the other set of the BO_4 groups share only three out of four corners (dark green in Fig. 3.6).

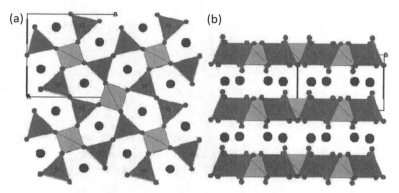

Figure 3.6   Representation of the melilite AB_3O_7 structure type down the crystallographic c-axis (a) and crystallographic a-axis (b). Green polyhedra represent the BO_4 units (light and dark green tetrahedra represent the two crystallographically independent units), purple spheres the A cations and red spheres the oxygen atoms.

Preparation, structure and properties of mixed metal oxides with formulae $La_{1+x}Sr_{1-x}Ga_3O_{7-\delta}$ (x = –0.15 to 0.60) were first reported by Rozumek et al., who found that the total conductivity in this series spanned four orders of magnitude, peaking at about 0.1 S/cm at 950°C for the composition with x = 0.60 [30, 31]. The oxygen atom transport numbers determined by emf measurements ranged between 0.80 and 0.95 above 600°C, suggesting predominantly ionic conduction. The samples were characterised by powder X-ray, neutron and electron diffraction. They crystallise in the melilite structure type described above, which, to a first approximation (*vide infra*), adopts tetragonal space group P-42$_1$m. Powder neutron diffraction was used to gain insight into any structural changes accompanying the change of composition from $x = 0$ (the parent compound LaSrGa$_3$O$_7$) to a La-rich composition with $x = 0.45$. A significant increase in diffuse scattering was observed in the pattern; however, no new crystallographic sites were found to be occupied, and the conclusion was that interstitial defects were not very likely [30, 31].

Kuang et al. subsequently prepared and characterised a closely related composition, La$_{1.54}$Sr$_{0.46}$Ga$_3$O$_{7.27}$ [32]. While the physical property measurements on this material agreed well with those reported by Rozumek et al., the structural characterisation results proved quite different. Powder neutron diffraction data were initially analysed by Rietveld refinement using the LaSrGa$_3$O$_7$ structural model. However, an inspection of the difference Fourier maps revealed residual nuclear density on an interstitial site located within the layers formed by corner-sharing GaO$_4$ tetrahedra, in the pentagonal channels running along the crystallographic c-axis. The fractional occupancy of this interstitial site refined to 0.136(5), leading to an oxygen excess of 0.27(1) per formula unit, in excellent agreement with the nominal composition and energy-dispersive spectroscopy (EDS) elemental analysis [32].

The size and shape of the anisotropic ADPs obtained from neutron diffraction data suggested likely average positional relaxations of ions around the interstitial oxygen defect. One of the two crystallographically unique Ga atoms, Ga(2), moves from its original position in the GaO$_4$ unit towards one of the faces of the tetrahedron, thus incorporating the interstitial O(4) site into its coordination sphere, i.e. giving rise to a GaO$_5$ trigonal bipyramid (Fig. 3.7).

Based on this structural model, the authors also used maximum entropy method (MEM) analysis of the ambient and high-temperature neutron diffraction data to explore different possible oxide ion migration pathways in La$_{1.54}$Sr$_{0.46}$Ga$_3$O$_{7.27}$ [32]. This work shows that, in a way similar to that previously demonstrated in La$_2$Mo$_2$O$_9$ [20], the ability of the Ga atoms to support flexible coordination environments enables the interstitial oxygen defect stabilisation in the structure, and provides pathways for oxide ion mobility in the material.

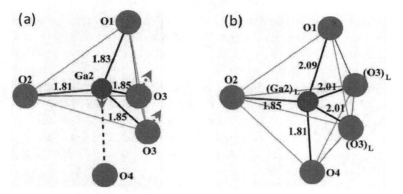

Figure 3.7   The change of the coordination environment of Ga(2) in the melilite-type oxide ion conductor $La_{1.54}Sr_{0.46}Ga_3O_{7.27}$, enabling the incorporation of interstitial oxygen atom O(4). The bond lengths shown are in the units of Å. Figure courtesy of X. Kuang.

Finally, it should be briefly pointed out that the true structure of the melilite-type solid electrolytes discussed here may be more complex. Many Si-containing melilites, both naturally occurring and synthetic, are known to be incommensurately modulated due to a misfit of the two structural building blocks, namely the layers formed by the corner-sharing tetrahedral units and the cations located between these layers. For example, single crystal X-ray structure analysis of natural melilite with composition $(Ca_{1.89}Sr_{0.01}Na_{0.08}K_{0.02})[(Mg_{0.92}Al_{0.08})(Si_{1.98}Al_{0.02})]O_7$, revealed a two-dimensional modulation of the basic $P-42_1m$ structure, with modulation vectors $q1 = 0.2815(3)(a^* + b^*)$ and $q2 = 0.2815(3)(-a^* + b^*)$ [33]. More recently, a similar characterisation approach was applied to a gallate with the melilite structure, and $CaNdGa_3O_7$ was also refined as a five-dimensional incommensurate structure, with modulation vectors $q1 = 0.2319(2)(a^* + b^*)$ and $q2 = 0.2319(2)(-a^* + b^*)$ [34]. Both displacive and occupational modulations were identified in the structure, and found to particularly affect the cations on the A site. As mentioned earlier, the A cations in the average melilite structure are described as eight-coordinate. However, in the modulated structure of

CaNdGa$_3$O$_7$, displacive modulations lead to deformations of the pentagonal rings shown in Fig. 3.6a, resulting in the A cations in the different regions of the crystal adopting six-, seven- and eight-fold coordination. Moreover, occupational modulation is also found for the A site over which the Ca and Nd cations are distributed. There appears to be a correlation between the two types of modulation, in that Ca-rich regions exhibit the highest degree of polyhedral distortion away from the ideal AO$_8$ coordination and the highest concentration of the AO$_6$ polyhedra [34]. This work provides a significant new insight into the degree of flexibility in the melilite structure type, with clear implications on the incorporation of the interstitial oxygen atoms and the resulting oxide ion conductivity in these materials.

3.3 Conclusions

This chapter focussed on four structural families of oxide ion conductors, highlighted the particularly challenging aspects of their structural characterisation and ways in which these challenges were addressed. The examples illustrate that it is often the understanding of the fine structural details, including small distortions from simpler higher-symmetry aristotypes, that are necessary to elucidate the behaviour of oxide ion conductors. They also reinforce the idea that multi-technique approaches and innovative data analysis or interpretation methods are vital in providing a full atomic-level insight into structural features and dynamical processes which enable and facilitate ionic conduction in solids.

References

1. *International Tables for Crystallography Volume B*, IUCr.

2. J. Karle and H. Hauptman, *Acta Crystallogr.*, 1950, **3**, 181–187.

3. G. Oszlanyi and A. Suto, *Acta Crystallogr. A*, 2004, **60**, 134–141.

4. G. Oszlanyi, A. Suto, M. Czugler, and L. Parkanyi, *J. Am. Chem. Soc.*, 2006, **128**, 8392–8393.

5. I. R. Evans, J. A. K. Howard, and J. S. O. Evans, *J. Mater. Chem.*, 2003, **13**, 2098–2103.

6. S. E. Lister, I. R. Evans, and J. S. O. Evans, *Inorg. Chem.*, 2009, **48**, 9271–9281.

7. S. E. Lister, I. R. Evans, J. A. K. Howard, A. Coelho, and J. S. O. Evans, *Chem. Commun.*, 2004, **22**, 2540–2541.

8. M. Feng and J. B. Goodenough, *Eur. J. Solid State Inorg. Chem.*, 1994, **31**, 663–672.

9. T. Ishihara, H. Matsuda, and Y. Takita, *J. Am. Chem. Soc.*, 1994, **116**, 3801–3803.

10. W. Marti, P. Fischer, F. Altorfer, H. J. Scheel, and M. Tadin, *J. Phys. Condensed Matter*, 1994, **6**, 127–135.

11. A. M. Glazer, *Acta Crystallogr. B*, 1972, **B28**, 3384–3392.

12. P. R. Slater, J. T. S. Irvine, T. Ishihara, and Y. Takita, *Solid State Ionics*, 1998, **107**, 319–323.

13. P. R. Slater, J. T. S. Irvine, T. Ishihara, and Y. Takita, *J. Solid State Chem.*, 1998, **139**, 135–143.

14. M. S. Khan, M. S. Islam, and D. R. Bates, *J. Phys. Chem. B*, 1998, **102**, 3099–3104.

15. K. Q. Huang, R. S. Tichy, and J. B. Goodenough, *J. Am. Ceram. Soc.*, 1998, **81**, 2565–2575.

16. C. Haavik, E. M. Ottesen, K. Nomura, J. A. Kilner, and T. Norby, *Solid State Ionics*, 2004, **174**, 233–243.

17. F. Blanc, D. S. Middlemiss, Z. H. Gan, and C. P. Grey, *J. Am. Chem. Soc.*, 2011, **133**, 17662–17672.

18. P. Lacorre, F. Goutenoire, O. Bohnke, R. Retoux, and Y. Laligant, *Nature*, 2000, **404**, 856–858.

19. S. Georges, F. Goutenoire, F. Altorfer, D. Sheptyakov, F. Fauth, E. Suard, and P. Lacorre, *Solid State Ionics*, 2003, **161**, 231–241.

20. I. R. Evans, J. A. K. Howard, and J. S. O. Evans, *Chem. Mater.*, 2005, **17**, 4074–4077.

21. P. W. Betteridge, J. R., Carruthers, R. I., Cooper, K., Prout, and D. J., Watkin, *J. Appl. Crystallogr.*, 2003, **36**, 1487.

22. L. Malavasi, H. Kim, S. J. L. Billinge, T. Proffen, C. Tealdi, and G. Flor, *J. Am. Chem. Soc.*, 2007, **129**, 6903–6907.

23. S. Nakayama, H. Aono, and Y. Sadaoka, *Chem. Lett.*, 1995, 431–432.

24. S. Nakayama, T. Kageyama, H. Aono, and Y. Sadaoka, *J. Mater. Chem.*, 1995, **5**, 1801–1805.

25. S. Nakayama and M. Highchi, *J. Mater. Sci. Lett.*, 2001, **20**, 913–915.

26. S. S. Pramana, W. T. Klooster, and T. J. White, *Acta Crystallogr. B*, 2007, **63**, 597–602.

27. L. Malavasi, A. Orera, P. R. Slater, P. M. Panchmatia, M. S. Islam, and J. Siewenie, *Chem. Commun.*, 2011, **47**, 250–252.

28. P. M. Panchmatia, A. Orera, G. J. Rees, M. E. Smith, J. V. Hanna, P. R. Slater, and M. S. Islam, *Angew. Chem. Int. Ed.*, 2011, **50**, 9328–9333.

29. A. Orera and P. R. Slater, *Chem. Mater.*, 2010, **22**, 675–690.

30. M. Rozumek, P. Majewski, L. Sauter, and F. Aldinger, *J. Am. Ceram. Soc.*, 2004, **87**, 662–669.

31. M. Rozumek, P. Majewski, H. Schluckwerder, F. Aldinger, K. Kunstler, and G. Tomandl, *J. Am. Ceram. Soc.*, 2004, **87**, 1795–1798.

32. X. Kuang, M. A. Green, H. Niu, P. Zajdel, C. Dickinson, J. B. Claridge, L. Jantsky, and M. J. Rosseinsky, *Nat. Mater.*, 2008, **7**, 498–504.

33. L. Bindi, P. Bonazzi, M. Dusek, V. Petricek, and G. Chapuis, *Crystallogr. B*, 2001, **57**, 739–746.

34. F. X. Wei, T. Baikie, T. An, M. Schreyer, C. Kloc, and T. J. White, *J. Am. Chem. Soc.*, 2011, **133**, 15200–15211.

Chapter 4

The Local Structure of SOFC Materials Investigated by X-Ray Absorption Spectroscopy

Antonino Martorana,[a] **Francesco Giannici,**[a] **and Alessandro Longo**[b]

[a]*Dipartimento di Fisica e Chimica, Università di Palermo, viale delle Scienze, 90128 Palermo, Italy*
[b]*ISMN-CNR, via Ugo La Malfa, 153, 90146 Palermo, Italy*

antonino.martorana@unipa.it

This chapter is devoted to the analysis of the local atomic structure of solid oxide fuel cell (SOFC) electrolyte and electrode materials. Among the experimental techniques able to provide information about the local structure of materials, the X-ray absorption spectroscopy has the peculiarity of element selectivity, allowing to investigate the chemical environment of specific atoms embedded in a matrix. Solid oxide electrolytes allow the conduction of ionic charge carriers between the electrodes of a SOFC device; the mechanism of ion conduction depends on the type of carrier, and it is finely tuned—or even only possible—if the solid matrix is suitably tailored by insertion of doping species that modify the local structure and the dynamics of the lattice. The oxygen

Structural Characterization Techniques: Advances and Applications in Clean Energy
Edited by Lorenzo Malavasi
Copyright © 2016 Pan Stanford Publishing Pte. Ltd.
ISBN 978-981-4669-34-4 (Hardcover), 978-981-4669-35-1 (eBook)
www.panstanford.com

reduction and fuel oxidation processes are catalyzed at the respective electrodes; moreover, the cathode and anode layers must: (1) allow an efficient exchange of reactants with the environment, (2) convey the ionic species to/from the electrolyte and (3) ensure the conduction of the electrons involved in the reduction and oxidation processes. The chemical and physical stability of the interface with the electrolyte layer is another essential issue of electrode materials. The chapter begins with a section describing the basic theory underlying the X-ray absorption spectroscopy and the experimental set-ups used in fuel cell applications. The second section reports on case studies and perspectives of future development of fuel cell materials under the keynote of local structure.

4.1 X-Ray Absorption Spectroscopy

X-Ray Absorption Spectroscopy (XAS) is an atomic absorption spectroscopy. In the following paragraph, we will see how it is used to gain insights on the local atomic structure of a single element in a solid oxide. Different acronyms are used in the literature to refer to XAS techniques. These are EXAFS—extended X-ray absorption fine structure, the oscillations of the XAS spectrum far from the absorption edge; XANES—X-ray absorption near-edge structure, the features of the XAS spectrum superimposed on the absorption edge; XAFS—X-ray absorption fine structure, comprising both XANES and EXAFS. Let us consider a monochromatic beam of hard X-rays (with energy 5–50 keV) interacting with a ceramic oxide (e.g., CeO_2, or $Y:BaZrO_3$).[1] The X-ray interaction with matter in this case is dominated by photoelectric absorption: when the energy of the impinging photons is larger than the binding energy of a core electron, this is ejected to the continuum (photoelectron). The intensity of the

---

[1]We restrict here to the case that is most relevant for SOFCs, while XAS can be employed on glassy, liquid or gaseous samples, and is not restricted to hard X-rays. However, the data analysis scheme presented here is valid for hard X-rays only. Soft X-rays, used for the analysis of lighter atoms, involve completely different experimental setup and data analysis models: moreover, the information contained in the XAS spectra of lighter elements (for which the term NEXAFS, Near Edge XAFS, is often used) mainly concerns the electronic structure rather than the atomic structure.

incoming and transmitted beams is labeled I_0 and I_1, respectively. The X-ray absorption coefficient of a sample of thickness x, defined as

$$\mu = \frac{1}{x} \ln \frac{I_0}{I_1},$$ (4.1)

decreases smoothly with increasing energy (the X-rays being more penetrating as their energy grows), until the energy matches the binding energy of a core electron: At this point, the absorption coefficient rises accordingly. The sudden increase of μ as a function of E is called the absorption edge.

This is not different from other absorption spectroscopies: In particular, since the X-ray energy is high, the photons are able to excite electrons from core states, which are atomic rather than molecular. Therefore, the transition energy is defined only by the atomic species rather than by bonding or oxidation state. In conclusion, XAS is an atomic spectroscopy like AAS or XPS: A single element can be probed selectively by tuning the radiation energy in order to match the energy of the atomic transition, regardless of the oxidation state, coordination environment, or spatial distribution within different phases. This is the first main feature of XAS: Using the right X-ray energy it is possible to focus on one atomic species at a time (e.g., X-rays of 19 keV only excite the 1s electrons of niobium, see Fig. 4.1).

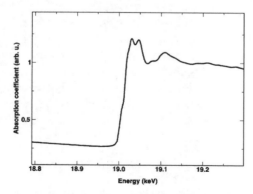

Figure 4.1   An X-ray absorption spectrum around the K-edge of niobium (19 keV).

The transition of a core electron to the continuum is labeled using letters, so that the ejection of a 1s electron is called K edge,

2s is called L_1 edge, and 2p electrons give rise to the L_2 and L_3 edges.[2] The hard X-ray range covers approximately the K edges of elements heavier than Sc, and also the L edges of heavier elements, from about Sn onwards. For the heaviest elements (lanthanides and beyond), the K edges lie at very high energies (40–80 keV), which present experimental difficulties: For this reason, the L edges of such elements are often used.

4.1.1 EXAFS Theory

The following is a simplified picture of the absorption process, and of the derivation of the relevant EXAFS equation that is used for quantitative data analysis. While this is only valid under certain assumptions, it is nonetheless useful to grasp the physical basis of XAS.[3]

The photoelectron coming off the absorber atom propagates as an outgoing spherical wave: for an isolated atom, the photoelectron does not interact with anything, and the XAS spectrum is smooth (this absorber-only atomic contribution, μ_0, is of pivotal importance in data analysis). The fine-structure modulation of the absorption is the result of the quantum interference of the photoelectron wave with itself, after interacting with the atoms around the absorber.

It is possible to derive the EXAFS oscillations quantitatively from first principles, under certain assumptions that are only met outside of the near-edge region.[4] As the outgoing wave impinges with a neighboring atom, it is scattered back as an incoming wave that interferes with the outgoing wave (like the ripples on water hitting the border of a pond).

Since the interatomic distance is fixed, the interference of the waves is alternately constructive and destructive as a function of the photoelectron wavevector **k**, as defined by the following relation:

---

[2]Due to spin-orbit splitting into $2p_{1/2}$ and $2p_{3/2}$. The sequence of edge energies is $L_3 < L_2 < L_1 < K$.

[3]Thorough treatments of EXAFS theory are presented in the classical works by Teo [1] and Stern [2] and were reviewed by Rehr and Albers [3]. A recent primer to the topic is [4].

[4]These are: (1) only one electron is ejected; (2) the X-ray wavelength is much larger than the core orbital; (3) the photoelectron energy is high enough that all the other electrons are frozen in place during the process.

$$k = \sqrt{(2m_e/\hbar^2)(E - E_0)} = \sqrt{0.263(E - E_0)}, \qquad (4.2)$$

where E_0 is the edge position (i.e., the electron binding energy), and E the incoming beam energy. Therefore the $E - E_0$ term is the energy carried by the outgoing photoelectron. The second form of the equation is valid for the energy in eV and wavevector in Å, as it is customary. The relation between the interatomic distance and the constructive interference condition is shown in Fig. 4.2a, while destructive interference is represented in Fig. 4.2b. It can be demonstrated that the EXAFS fine structure equals the amplitude of this interference, and that it appears as an additional oscillatory contribution to the absorption coefficient plot.

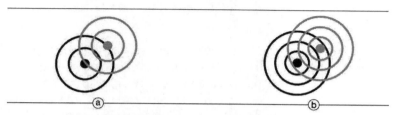

Figure 4.2   (a) The outgoing wave (black) interferes constructively with the incoming wave (gray); (b) Changing the wavelength, the interference is now destructive.

The fine structure term features: (1) an oscillatory term that takes into account the constructive and destructive interference as a function of k; (2) a $1/kR^2$ term that comes from the spherical wave amplitude; (3) the overall amplitude and phase shift functions $F(\mathbf{k})$ and $\delta(\mathbf{k})$, that represent the quantum-mechanical process of ejection and backscattering. These functions arise from the interactions between photoelectrons and atoms, so they are determined by the nature of the absorber-backscatterer pair, and they carry the chemical information contained in the EXAFS spectrum. Amplitudes and phase shifts used to be measured from model compounds, but nowadays they are calculated with programs like FEFF or GNXAS for any given atomic configuration.

The contribution from each of the atoms in a coordination shell is additive, so N_i atoms in the i-th coordination shell, placed at distance R_i from the absorber, give rise to the EXAFS signal:

$$\chi(k) \propto \sum_i \frac{N_i F_i(k)}{kR_i^2} \sin(2kR_i + \delta_i(k))$$ (4.3)

Further refinements of the model involve (1) the photoelectron mean free path, $\lambda(\mathbf{k})$; (2) the variance of the interatomic distance, σ^2, accounting for the static and vibrational disorder blurring the pair distribution function (often referred to as the Debye–Waller factor, although this should not be confused with the disorder factor of diffraction with the same name); (3) an overall amplitude parameter S_0^2 (slightly lower than unity) accounting for inelastic effects. In conclusion,

$$\chi(k) = S_0^2 \sum_i \frac{N_i F_i(k)}{kR_i^2} \sin(2kR_i + \delta_i(k)) e^{-2\sigma_i^2 k^2} e^{-2R_i/\lambda(k)}$$ (4.4)

that is the complete EXAFS equation in harmonic approximation. The main points to note are: (1) the kR^2 term at denominator, and the limited mean free path of the photoelectron, restrict the range of the outgoing wave to about 6 Å in most cases; (2) the disorder severely dampens the signal at high k values, so that an ordered structure frozen at 20 K can have a good signal up to $k = 25$ Å^{-1}, but the spectrum of a glass or a crystal at high temperatures may fall off at about 10 Å^{-1}. This is the second main feature of XAS: it only probes the local environment of the absorbing atom, comprising a few coordination shells, and it is extremely sensitive to local disorder.

All of the above, derived for a single scattering event, can be generalized for every multiple scattering (MS) path between the absorber and any other group of neighboring atoms. MS paths are in general less important than single scattering, since they have lower $F(\mathbf{k})$ and higher σ^2, but they have to be taken into account especially in the following cases: (1) collinear arrangements of atoms, e.g., in symmetric structures like perovskite; (2) low k-values, where the disorder damping is less important.[5]

---

[5]MS can also arise between two atoms, if the photoelectron bounces back and forth more than once. The probability of this event is lower than single scattering but it can be significant nonetheless when modeling a spectrum quantitatively.

4.1.2 EXAFS Data Analysis

The experimental fine structure term is conveniently normalized so that it is independent on the total absorption of the sample:

$$\chi = \frac{\mu - \mu_0}{\mu_0} \qquad (4.5)$$

The first conundrum of EXAFS analysis is that μ_0 (the isolated absorber contribution) cannot be measured, so it must be defined recursively as the total spectrum minus the fine-structure contribution from the neighboring atoms (while EXAFS is defined using μ_0 itself). The subtraction of the background (extraction) is arbitrary to a degree, and it is one of the pitfalls of the EXAFS analysis. In practice, μ_0 is approximated as a smooth function of E, while the oscillatory features are attributed to the interatomic correlations.[6] This may be better visualized and understood using the Fourier transform (FT). An EXAFS spectrum and the corresponding FT are shown in Fig. 4.3.

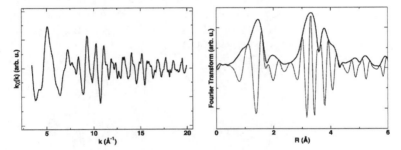

Figure 4.3   An EXAFS spectrum in k-space (left) and its Fourier Transform in R-space (right). The real part and the magnitude of the FT are plotted as thin and thick black lines, respectively.

The interatomic correlations contribute to the EXAFS signal with superimposing sinusoidal waves, and the frequency of each wave increases with the interatomic distance R. The Fourier transform can be employed on the $\chi(\mathbf{k})$ spectrum (vs. Å^{-1}) to

---

[6]A number of mathematical models have been proposed in the literature, most of them based on smoothing splines. More sophisticated approaches employ additional functions to reproduce multi-electron transitions appearing as smaller secondary absorption edges.

obtain a $\chi(R)$ spectrum (vs. Å), where each peak corresponds to a coordination shell, as a function of the distance from the absorber. In this way, the μ_0 background represents a low-frequency contribution placed at distances that cannot correspond to any neighboring atoms (i.e., $R < 1$ Å). By minimizing this low-R signal, one obtains the real EXAFS signal free from atomic contributions due to the absorber only. The different structural parameters all have direct effects on the height and shape of peaks in the FT plot: coordination number affects peak height, $F(\mathbf{k})$ affects the peak shape, disorder affects peak width, and distance controls the peak position.

Since the single components are weighted by $F(\mathbf{k})$, a simple qualitative analysis of the FT is not feasible, especially when MS is relevant. For this reason, a multiparametric least-square fitting is commonly used to extract the structural parameters from the spectra. Sophisticated data analysis methods have been described in the literature, but they are far outside the scope of this introduction.[7]

Choosing a reasonable model, and finding the global minimum in the parameter space is a difficult task. Model fitting is carried out with minimization algorithms, usually providing also a graphical insight into the model suitability (Fig. 4.4).

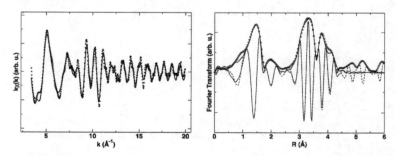

Figure 4.4 A multi-shell fitting in k-space (left) and in R-space (right). The experimental spectra and models are plotted as dots and lines, respectively.

The information extracted from the spectrum is model-dependent, so it is possible to find many models that fit the data, but that do not make any physical sense. For this reason, the data

---

[7]The interested reader is referred to the documentation of the VIPER free software: http://www.cells.es/Beamlines/CLAESS/software/viper.html.

extraction and modeling are to be conducted in the most economical way, i.e., refining the least number of independent parameters. An oft-quoted figure is the number of independent points from the Nyquist theorem:

$$N_{ind} \approx \frac{2\Delta k \Delta R}{\pi} \qquad (4.6)$$

A cautious strategy is to have at least twice independent points than fitting parameters. During the refinement, some parameters are usually correlated (e.g., N and σ^2 both affect amplitude, MS path length and disorder correlate with those of simple scattering, etc.), so a quantitative assessment of the uncertainties of each parameter of the fitting is difficult. Reasonable estimates of uncertainty are about 0.5 for coordination numbers, 0.01 Å for distances, and 10% for disorder. An example of EXAFS data analysis, reporting explicit uncertainties, is shown in Table 4.1.

Table 4.1 Results derived from the EXAFS analysis of a single coordination shell (the Ge-Ge first shell coordination in amorphous germanium at 77 K)

		a-Ge		
N	—	4.0	±	0.2
R	(Å)	2.468	±	0.005
σ^2	$(10^{-3}$ Å$^2)$	2.2	±	0.2

Source: Adapted with permission from [5]. Copyrighted by The American Physical Society.

4.1.3 XANES Analysis

Quantitative modeling of XANES data is very difficult for the increasing complexity of the MS model near the absorption edge, and relatively few cases exist in the literature. However, very important qualitative information is extracted easily from near-edge features.

The oxidation state of a metal ion determines the depth of the energy of the core electrons, so that higher oxidation states (higher charge) correspond to higher binding energies, and therefore to the absorption edges being shifted to the right. In many cases, the presence and shape of pre-edge peaks, which are due to transitions between core states and valence states, also help in identifying the oxidation state (see Fig. 4.5). With the aid of model compounds, comparison between the measured and reference spectra can resolve precisely even slight changes in electronic states [6]. The shape of the absorption edge is also determined by the shape of the first coordination shell, and can be used as a sort of fingerprint: In some cases, pre-edge transitions between bound states may be forbidden in octahedral symmetry and can be used for instance to discriminate between octahedral and tetrahedral coordination.

The broadening of near-edge features increases with E, so that lower-energy edges (typically K-edges of first row transition metals, and L-edges of heavier elements) are more often used in the XANES analysis.

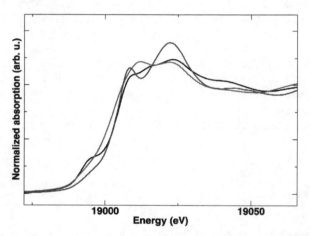

Figure 4.5   Normalized XANES spectra on the Nb K-edge of: NbO_2 (red), Nb_2O_5 (black) and $BaCe_{0.84}Y_{0.1}Nb_{0.06}O_3$ (blue). Both oxidation state and coordination environment have an effect on the near-edge features, and give information on the state of Nb in the perovskite.

4.1.4   XAS Experiments

XAS experiments are performed in dedicated beamlines at synchrotron radiation facilities, which provide a monochromatic, tunable, intense X-ray source. Synchrotrons are large-scale electron storage rings (about 100 m in radius) where electrons are accelerated at a few GeV: The constant acceleration needed to keep the electron beam on a circular orbit leads to the emission of intense radiation along the horizontal tangent to the orbit. Synchrotron radiation is continuous in the IR-X-ray range, easily collimated in microscopic spots, and it is exceedingly intense if compared to laboratory sources. Even higher brilliance and collimation is achieved with so-called insertion devices, in which the electron orbit is subjected to alternating magnetic fields. A complete introduction to the accelerator physics and to the experimental techniques available with synchrotron radiation can be found in [7].

The most common configurations in XAS experiments are (1) transmission geometry (Fig. 4.6a), in which the absorption coefficient is measured from the intensity of the incoming and transmitted beam through the Beer–Lambert law described in Eq. 4.1; (2) fluorescence geometry (Fig. 4.6b), in which the absorption coefficient is derived indirectly from the intensity of the fluorescence radiation that comes from the sample as a result of the absorption process, I_f. In this case, the absorption coefficient is proportional to I_f/I_0.[8]

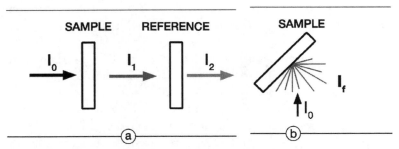

Figure 4.6   (a) Transmission geometry with sample and reference standard; (b) Fluorescence geometry (aerial view), with the sample surface 45° from both the incoming beam and detector.

Transmission geometry, where possible, assures the best signal-to-noise ratio (s/n), fast acquisition and less sources of errors. A usable spectrum can be measured if the absorber is concentrated enough: ideally, the best s/n is achieved with an absorption jump around 1, but reasonably good data can still

---

[8]Other configurations, less frequently exploited, are possible (e.g., total electron yield, reflection geometry, time-resolved fast measurements).

be collected with a jump of around 0.1. At the same time, the total absorption of the sample, which is due to all the elements present, must not be too high. The optimal total absorption is around 1–2. Higher total absorption can cause systematic errors in the transmitted beam intensity. The total absorption and the absorption edge jump are calculated from the sample composition and weight using tabulated X-ray absorption coefficients.[9] In practice, samples for transmission are prepared as self-supporting pellets by pressing the sample with a suitable dilutant (cellulose or boron nitride are transparent to X-rays), like one does with infrared spectroscopy. To improve homogeneity, the sample can also be suspended in an inert solvent and deposited on a Millipore filter.

Ionization chambers are used as fast and accurate detectors that also let the X-ray beam pass through, so the incident I_0 and transmitted I_1 beam intensity can be measured in a straightforward way. The common setup also involves a reference sample being measured at the same time: the transmitted beam, I_1, acts as an incoming beam, and a third ionization chamber I_2 is used to measure the beam transmitted by the reference. The absorption edge of the reference is then used as an absolute energy reference for all measurements.

If transmission cannot be used, e.g., when the absorber atom is very dilute, and increasing the amount of sample would just make it totally opaque, the sample is tilted 45° from the incoming beam, and the fluorescence radiation is collected by a detector covering a large solid angle about 90° from the incoming beam. Energy-resolving semiconductors are used as detectors, with several elements in parallel to improve the lower detection limit, which can reach about 10^{14} atoms/cm². Good samples for fluorescence are either thin and concentrated (e.g., a thin film) or thick and dilute. This minimizes the systematic errors connected with self-absorption of the fluorescence radiation by the sample itself. Fluorescence is typically most suited for higher-energy edges, since the yield of the radiative de-excitation mechanism increases with energy, and the fluorescence peaks are easier to resolve.

---

[9] *XAFSmass* and *Hephaestus* are freely available via the Internet.

4.2 Solid Oxide Fuel Cells: Materials for Electrolytes and Electrodes

Modern fuel cell technology is based on the assembly of different solid components [8]; a central role is played by the electrolytic membrane, which determines the operative temperature of the device and the overall balance of plant. To date, a good deal of research activity is focused on the improvement of solid-oxide electrolyte materials, which allow to build robust, modular and low-operative-cost plants for energy production. Among solid oxide electrolytes, anionic conductors, performing the transport of O^{2-} anions from cathode to anode, are currently exploited in actual facilities. A scheme of an anion-conduction SOFC is drawn in Fig. 4.7. A mature technology for stationary fuel cell plants is based on yttria-stabilized zirconia (YSZ) electrolytes. The insertion of Y^{3+} in the zirconia matrix has the effect of formation of oxygen vacancies, according to the defect equation:

$$2Zr_{Zr}^{X} + O_{O}^{X} + Y_2O_3 \leftrightarrow 2Y_{Zr}' + V_{o}^{\cdot\cdot} + 2ZrO_2 \tag{4.7}$$

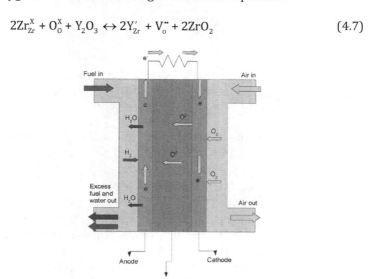

Figure 4.7 Scheme of anion-conduction SOFC.

So, the trivalent dopant insertion improves anion conductivity, by providing empty lattice sites for O^{2-} diffusion paths. Most of the solid oxides with a high anion conductivity crystallize in the fluorite structure (Fig. 4.8) that is ideally composed of edge-sharing MO_8 cubic boxes. On average, YSZ is cubic (space group *Fm-3m*), while undoped zirconia exhibits a tetragonal distortion of the parent fluorite structure. Energy production plants exploiting YSZ have a high operative temperature (about 1000°C), allowing to work in cogenerative mode and improving the overall process efficiency. On the other hand, such high temperatures require the use of expensive materials and reduce the lifetime of the cell components.

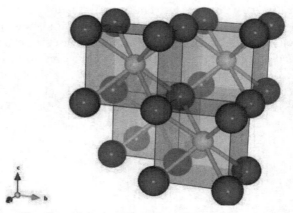

Figure 4.8   The fluorite structure. The cubic oxide cages around the cations are shown (Drawing produced by VESTA [9]).

For anion-conducting electrolytes, the search of alternatives to YSZ has been mainly directed to other fluorites like SDC (samaria-doped ceria) and GDC (gadolinia-doped ceria) [10, 11], and to LSGM ($La_{1-x}Sr_xGa_{1-y}Mg_yO_3$), which has a perovskite structure [12]. The issues concerning the ceria-based electrolytes are focused on the suppression of electronic conduction, that can depend on Ce^{4+} reducibility and, for LSGM, on phase segregation that lowers the grain boundary conductivity.

The electrolyte materials with the highest anionic conductivity, related to δ-Bi_2O_3, are the subject of an intense research activity that aims to stabilize the fluorite structure [13], so far with only partially positive results.

A drawback of anionic conductors, stemming from the simultaneous presence of fuel and reaction products (e.g., water) at the anode compartment, is the necessity of implementing fuel recirculation to improve the device efficiency. A way to simplify the fuel management is that of using protonic conductors (Fig. 4.9).

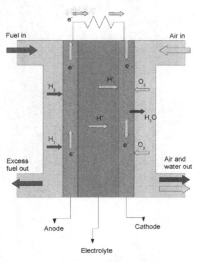

Figure 4.9 Scheme of a proton-conduction SOFC.

To date, the proton-conduction fuel cells that have reached the phase of mature technology are the PEMFC, in which the electrolyte is a polymer membrane, Nafion, or similar materials. The drawback of the PEMFC is the low working temperature (less than 100°C in actual devices), producing easy poisoning of the noble-metal anode catalyst by pollutants such as the carbon monoxide present in the fuel [14].

The consequent request of high-purity (under a few ppm) feeding streams can be overcome by the development of new polymeric materials working at a higher temperature, or to seek for proton conducting ceramics working at definitely higher temperatures [15].

The state-of-the-art proton-conducting ceramics in the temperature range 350–750°C are currently based on strontium and barium cerates and on calcium and barium zirconates [15, 16]. These oxides have a perovskite-type ABO_3 structure, in which the B^{4+} cation lies in an octahedral cage of oxygens; the octahedra share the vertices and the A^{2+} cations are located in cuboctahedral cavities formed by the network of the octahedral cages (Fig. 4.10).

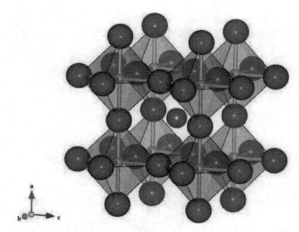

Figure 4.10 ABO$_3$ perovskite structure. The octahedral oxide cages around the B^{4+} cations are shown. The A cations lie in the cavities formed by the BO$_6$ octahedra (Drawing produced by VESTA [9]).

In order to introduce protons in the perovskite, the B site is doped with an M trivalent species. Charge neutrality is accomplished by formation of one oxygen vacancy every two M^{3+} cations introduced in the host structure, giving rise to an oxygen-defective solid with formula AB$_{1-x}$M$_x$O$_{3-\delta}$. In hydration conditions, an OH$^-$ group is introduced in an anionic vacancy, while a proton H$^+$ binds to a lattice oxygen. Equations 4.8–4.9 account for the defect equilibrium in barium cerate.

$$2Ce_{Ce}^X + O_O^X + Y_2O_3 \leftrightarrow 2Y_{Ce}' + V_O^{\cdot\cdot} + 2CeO_2 \tag{4.8}$$

$$O_O^X + V_O^{\cdot\cdot} + H_2O \leftrightarrow 2OH_O^{\cdot} \tag{4.9}$$

Overall, in the assumption that all the oxygen vacancies are filled, the number of protons introduced in the structure is equal to the number of dopant M^{3+} cations; the mechanism of proton conduction is based on the hopping of proton between neighboring oxygens, assisted by lattice vibrations [17].

The chemical stability of the above-cited cerates with respect to the reaction with acid compounds in the atmosphere, such as CO$_2$ or SO$_2$, is quite limited and leads to the decomposition of the proton conductor. For instance, $BaCeO_3$ reacts with CO_2, producing barium carbonate and cerium oxide. On the other hand, the zirconates have a definitely higher chemical stability, but also a high grain boundary resistivity, likely due to oxide demixing at the needed sintering temperatures and/or reduction of symmetry that affects the probability of proton diffusion paths [18].

These drawbacks of proton-conducting ceramics prevented, so far, the exploitation of these materials in practical devices different from hydrogen sensors. One of the challenges of the chemistry of materials is therefore represented by the development of new ceramics that join high proton conductivity with chemical stability, thus allowing implementation in actual energy production plants.

In the assembly of an FC device, the electrolyte is complemented by the electrode compartments. Electrode SOFC materials accomplish various tasks: (1) provide catalytic fuel oxidation sites at the anode and oxygen reduction at the cathode; (2) transport ionic species to/from the interface with the electrolyte; (3) convey electrons coming from fuel oxidation to the external circuit (anode) and allow their transport to the species to be reduced at the cathode. Moreover, electrode materials should be stable in reaction environment and a good compatibility with the electrolyte, in terms of similar thermal expansion coefficients and absence of diffusion processes leading to the formation of unwanted interface phases, is also needed. The fulfillment of the cell electrochemical reaction needs the contact between the ion conduction, the electron conduction and the gas phases, constituting the so-called triple phase boundary (TPB) [19].

The TPB spatial extent is crucial for the device performance and can be effectively improved by exploiting materials that have mixed ionic-electronic conduction (MIEC). Among the anode materials meeting this requisite, the cermets are composite ceramic-metallic materials whose oxide phase is in charge of ionic transport and electrolyte interface compatibility, while the metal phase provides the catalytic sites and the electronic conduction. However, these materials have the drawback of poor resistance to poisoning, especially when the FC devices are fed with hydrocarbon-containing fuels, and of metal particles sintering [20]. To overcome these problems, in the last years the possibility was investigated of using mixed oxides encompassing in a single phase all the properties required for anode materials [20, 21]. The issue of mixed ionic-electronic conductivity, beside oxygen reduction activity, was addressed also for cathodes [22]; starting from the perovskite $La_{1-x}Sr_xMnO_3$ (LSM), so far a wide variety of cathode oxides have been formulated and tested in SOFC applications [21].

4.2.1 Case Study 1: Tailoring the Grain Boundary in Nanocrystalline Ceria

The grain boundary is the interfacial, ill-ordered, contact region between differently oriented crystallites of a polycrystalline material. Grain boundary structures are typically present in SOFC electrolyte membranes, whose full-density sintering is necessary in order to prevent leakage of unreacted fuel to the cathode. A TEM micrograph of a full-density YSZ electrolyte is shown in Fig. 4.11.

Taking into account the issue of electrical conduction in ceria and zirconia doped with trivalent species, the grain boundary is characterized by an accumulation of positive charge carriers inducing, by charge compensation, a depletion of carriers of the same sign in the space charge layers adjacent to the grain boundary core [24, 25]. In a typical ceramic anion conductor, e.g., Y- or Yb-doped ceria, the trivalent dopants constitute effective negative defects, while the doubly positively charged oxygen vacancies (Eq. 4.7) are the actual mobile charge carriers. In the sintering process, the negative dopants are mobilized towards the grain boundary core, partially neutralizing the positive potential originated by the excess of oxygen vacancy concentration at the grain boundary core. The still present depletion of positive oxygen vacancies in the adjacent space charge layers is at the origin of the low grain boundary conductivity affecting these solid oxide electrolytes and, similarly, also YSZ. So, a possible way to overcome the lack of grain boundary conductivity in ceria and zirconia-based electrolytes could be that of a suitable modification of the grain boundary composition.

Figure 4.11   High-resolution transmission electron microscopy of grain boundaries in a sample of YSZ with an average grain size of 120 nm. Reprinted from *Prog. Mater. Sci.*, 51, Guo and Waser, Electrical properties of the grain boundaries of oxygen ion conductors: Acceptor-doped zirconia and ceria, pp. 151–210, Copyright 2006, with permission from Elsevier [23].

This hypothesis was examined in a study involving the comparison between homogeneous Y-, Yb-, and Bi-doped ceria electrolytes and the oxides modified by the same heteroatoms but prepared by grain boundary decoration [26]. While the homogeneously doped samples were prepared by coprecipitation, the decoration was achieved by dissolution of the dopant nitrate in water, addition of undoped ceria, drying and final calcination at 450°C. X-ray powder diffraction allowed to demonstrate that both routes produced a single crystalline fluorite phase; some relevant results of the local structure analysis carried out by EXAFS analysis are reported below. Figure 4.12 shows the Fourier-transformed EXAFS spectra of the Y-doped samples, both homogeneous and decorated. The reference Y_2O_3 spectrum confirms the XRD evidence that secondary phases, even if poorly crystallized, are absent. It is also evident by inspection the difference between homogeneously doped and decorated samples, pointing to a different distribution of dopants in the host oxide.

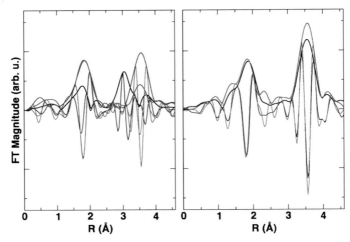

Figure 4.12 FT EXAFS data on the Y K-edge. Left panel: Y_2O_3 (black); Y-decorated powder (red); Y-decorated sintered (blue). Right panel: Y-doped powder (black); Y-doped sintered (red). Thick lines are moduli, thin lines are imaginary parts. Reproduced with permission from *J. Electrochem. Soc.*, 159, B417 (2012). Copyright 2012, The Electrochemical Society [26].

Table 4.2 reports the details of the EXAFS analysis carried out on the sintered homogeneous and decorated YDC samples on both the Ce and Y edges. It seems particularly significative the comparison between the disorder factors: The lower value of σ_{Ce-O} in the decorated sample can be attributed to the grain boundary segregation of dopants and, consequently, to the lesser number of perturbed bulk Ce atoms; on the contrary, the higher σ values on the Y side are assigned to the large variety of different local structures that can accommodate the Y atoms in the perturbed grain boundary region.

Table 4.2 EXAFS analysis of the sintered homogeneously doped and decorated YDC samples

	R_{Ce-O} (Å)	σ_{Ce-O} (10^{-3} Å^2)	$R_{Y-O,1}$ (Å)	$R_{Y-O,2}$ (Å)	σ_{Y-O} (10^{-3} Å^2)	R_{Y-Ce} (Å)	σ_{Y-Ce} (10^{-3} Å^2)
Homogeneous	2.32	10	2.31	2.46	2.5	3.80	7.1
Decorated	2.33	8.3	2.28	2.40	3.0	3.79	9.3

Source: Adapted with permission from [26]. Copyrighted by The Electrochemical Society.
Note: Uncertainty is on the last digit.

The local structure analysis is coherent with the conductivity data obtained by complex impedance spectroscopy: While homogeneously doped samples shows two clearly distinguishable conductivity contributions, respectively attributed to bulk and grain boundary anion diffusion paths, the decorated samples show a single contribution that, on the basis of the EXAFS analysis, was attributed to the preferential anion diffusion into the heavily doped grain boundary region.

As a final remark, the complementary knowledge achieved about long/short range structure and conductivity in the investigated materials allowed to demonstrate that it is viable to tailor the grain boundary structure and composition of solid oxide electrolytes in order to improve FC performances.

4.2.2 Case Study 2: The Local Structure of δ-Bi$_2$O$_3$

Bismuth oxide presents a complex pattern of phase transitions in the range from room temperature up to the melting temperature. The monoclinic α form is stable until 729°C, while the δ form exists between 729 and the melting point at 824°C. On cooling, transitions to the metastable β and γ forms are encountered. The δ-Bi$_2$O$_3$ has a oxide-defective fluorite-like structure, with 25% of missing oxide ions; it is the best oxide ion conductor, with a conductivity reaching 1 S/cm at 750°C, but many factors hinder the FC applications, including stability in a wider thermal range, chemical reactivity in reductive environment and low mechanical strength [27]. However, the scientific literature on bismuth oxide-based conductors is considerable, owing to possible applications for oxygen separators and to studies aiming at a deeper insight in the oxide conduction mechanism, eventually leading to the design of new FC materials.

The structure of δ-Bi$_2$O$_3$ has been investigated mainly by X-ray and neutron powder diffraction [28]. The long-range analysis showed that the oxide atoms can occupy, beside the regular tetrahedral 8c sites of the fluorite structure, also the interstitial 32f sites of the *Fm-3m* space group. For undoped Bi$_2$O$_3$, the proposed mechanism of oxide diffusion from a tetrahedral occupied site to neighboring empty involves low-energy diffusion paths through the interstitial 32f and the octahedral cavity, as shown in Fig. 4.13.

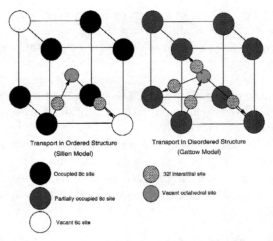

Transport in Ordered Structure
(Sillen Model)

Transport in Disordered Structure
(Gattow Model)

● Occupied 8c site

▨ 32f interstitial site

⬤ Partially occupied 8c site

◯ Vacant octahedral site

◯ Vacant 6c site

Figure 4.13   Diffusion paths in ordered and disordered δ-Bi$_2$O$_3$ through insterstitial 32f sites. Reprinted from *Solid State Ionics*, 140, Boyapati et al., Effect of oxygen sublattice ordering on interstitial transport mechanism and conductivity activation energies in phase-stabilized cubic bismuth oxides, pp. 149–160, Copyright 2001, with permission from Elsevier [28].

The slow transition from the disordered to the ordered pattern of oxygen vacancies takes place on cooling below 600°C and involves a remarkable drop of oxide conductivity, due to the reduced probability of finding a suitably oriented diffusion path.

The effect of doping Bi$_2$O$_3$ with isovalent or aliovalent cations results in the stabilization to low temperature of the δ phase, at the expense of a loss of oxide conductivity depending on the type and concentration of dopants introduced in the host matrix. To this concern, the best performing stabilized δ-Bi$_2$O$_3$ compounds were obtained with a composition Bi$_{12.5}$RE$_{1.5}$ReO$_{24.5}$ (RE = La, Nd), with the cations randomly distributed in the 4a (0,0,0) and the oxygens partitioned between the 8c (0.25,0.25,0.25) and the 32f (x,x,x), $x \approx 0.37$, sites of the *Fm-3m* space group. Interestingly, the smaller dopants Y and Er have similar x value but a conductivity value similar to the Re-free compounds [13]. The cited authors recognized that a detailed analysis of the local environment of cations was necessary, but only partial results, concerning the Er doped compounds, were published. The k^3-weighted FT of the respective cation L_3 edges (the FT of the Er L_3 edge is shown in Fig. 4.14) did not gave structural information beyond the first shell, leading to the conclusion that the oxide shell around Er and Bi are highly disordered, even if the reported Debye–Waller coefficients ($\sigma^2 = 0.007$ Å^2 and $\sigma^2 = 0.006$ Å^2, respectively) are not exceedingly high. Further investigation about the local structure of stabilized delta-bismuth oxides seems suitable, also to shed light in the mechanism of oxide diffusion in fluorites that could improve the design of new anion conductors. With this respect, a synergetic complement with simulation approaches, like the ab initio MD study recently reported for $Bi_{1-x}V_xO_{1.5+x}$ [30], can be very useful.

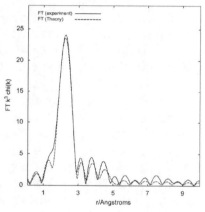

Figure 4.14 Fourier-transformed EXAFS data of the Er L_3-edge of $Bi_{12.5}Er_{1.5}ReO_{24.5}$. Reprinted from *J. Phys. Chem. Solids*, 69, Punn et al., The local environment of cations in $Bi_{12.5}Er_{1.5}ReO_{24.5}$, pp. 2687–2690, Copyright 2008, with permission from Elsevier [29].

4.2.3 Case Study 3: The Role of the Dopant in Proton-Conducting Perovskites

Proton-conducting perovskites (PCP) have a general formula M^{3+}: $A^{2+}B^{4+}O_3$, in which the trivalent M cation substitutes the B cation, and protons are incorporated as described by Eqs. 4.8–4.9. The research activity on PCP, starting in the 1980s, was based on the combination of a wide range of different ABO_3 compounds (mostly $ACeO_3$ cerates and $AZrO_3$ zirconates), and various dopants.

Eventually, all of the proposed compounds presented some chemical, structural, or phase instability that hindered a real-life fuel cell application. A growing interest was then directed at studying the structural mechanisms underlying the shortcomings in chemical stability, and proton mobility. Several techniques (pulsed-field gradient NMR, quasielastic neutron scattering, neutron diffraction and MD simulations) have been used to probe the dynamics of the proton and the structure of the proton binding sites.

In an attempt to give a systematic approach to proton conduction in oxides, Kreuer proposed that "not only a good size matching but also acid/base matching is required in the choice of the acceptor dopant with respect to an optimization of proton mobility" [31]. This proposition was put forward even more openly, on the basis of combined molecular dynamics simulations, hydration thermochemistry, and conductivity experiments, when Y^{3+} was identified as the best possible dopant for $BaZrO_3$, since "the enthalpy of formation of protonic defects is virtually unchanged by the presence of the dopant" [32].

The reported values of proton mobility and activation energy in groups of differently doped perovskites suffer from a lack of consistency, since there is a strong correlation between transport properties and the preparation history of the pellets–especially in zirconates, which are notoriously difficult to sinter. In general, a very large number of impedance spectroscopy studies are available for almost every PCP, while the information gained on their fundamental solid-state chemistry has been relatively low.

An element-selective, local probe like X-ray absorption spectroscopy is ideally suited to investigate the dopant sites in the solid state, while also providing good statistical average (some 10^{18} perovskite unit cells are probed in a XAS experiment). The main results on $BaCeO_3$ and $BaZrO_3$ doped with various trivalent cations are reported below.

Peculiar coordination environments are revealed by EXAFS analysis in various PCP. These arise from the specific interaction of the trivalent dopants with the host oxide. Two cases are especially notable: the YO_6 octahedra in $Ba(Ce,Y)O_3$ are more axially elongated than CeO_6 [33]; the Gd-Ba second coordination shell is distorted and contracted in $Ba(Ce,Gd)O_3$, despite the GdO_6 octahedra are larger than the corresponding CeO_6 [34].

The concept of a fixed ionic radius, widely used to design new compounds, and to derive structure-property relations, was found to be not totally adequate to describe the local coordination environments of host and dopant cations alike. For instance, In^{3+} has a variable size—with In-O bonds stretching from 2.11 to 2.16 Å as a function of the oxide overall composition, adapting its size to the host oxide in both $BaCeO_3$ and $BaZrO_3$ [36, 37].

The case of $BaZrO_3$ doped with Y^{3+} can be described instead as a rigid cation in a rigid host matrix. The dopant retains its ionic radius, thereby expanding the YO_6 octahedra with respect to ZrO_6. The overall cation framework of the parent pure $BaZrO_3$, however, is retained on doping, so that only the anion sublattice (first and third coordination shells) expands around Y^{3+} (as shown in Fig. 4.15), and the cation sublattice (second and fourth shells) is the same around both Y^{3+} and Zr^{4+} [37].

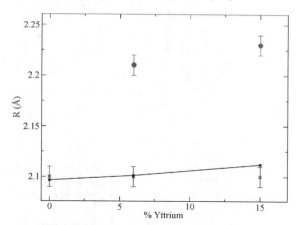

Figure 4.15 First-shell distances around B-site cations in $BaZr_{1-x}Y_xO_3$ as a function of Y content, as determined by X-ray diffraction (average) and X-ray absorption (site-selective). Y-O plotted as red circles, Zr-O as blue crosses, average M-O as black squares. Reprinted with permission from Giannici et al., *Chem. Mater.*, **23**, pp. 2994–3002. Copyright 2011 American Chemical Society [37].

Besides static structural evidence, EXAFS also provided information on the interaction between proton defects and dopant sites: This was achieved by comparing the spectra of the host and dopant sites in both protonated and deprotonated samples (Fig. 4.16). A neat example is $BaCe_{0.98}Y_{0.02}O_3$, the proton insertion causes only the Y-O, Y-Ba, and Y-Ce bonds to be significantly more disordered, while the corresponding bonds around Ce^{4+} are unaffected. The preferential interaction between defects depends on the particular dopant-host pair: In fact, it is not observed in $BaZr_{0.94}Y_{0.06}O_3$–corroborating the theoretical prediction that there is no difference in basicity between the oxygen sites around Y and Zr, so that the protons bond equally well to either one [32].

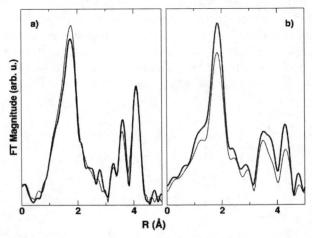

Figure 4.16 The Fourier-transformed EXAFS data of $BaCe_{0.98}Y_{0.02}O_3$ on the Ce K-edge (panel a), and on the Y K-edge (panel b). The thick lines refer to the protonated samples, the thin lines to the deprotonated samples. Data originally presented in Giannici et al., Local environment of barium, cerium and yttrium in yttrium-doped barium cerate, *Solid State Ionics*, 178, pp. 587–591, Copyright 2007 Elsevier [38].

If a trivalent M^{3+} dopant is not completely incorporated in the perovskite oxide, excess M_2O_3 may form at grain boundaries. This is usually poorly crystallized, so that it is often invisible to diffraction techniques, but the distinctive M-M bonds that are typical of M_2O_3 are easily recognized in the EXAFS spectra. For instance, the solubility limit of Y^{3+} in $BaCeO_3$ is around 17%, while nominal compositions around $BaCe_{0.7}Y_{0.3}O_3$ might appear as single-phase with XRD [38]. There is little correlation between solubility and ionic size: Y^{3+} shows a similar ionic size with Ce^{4+}, while In^{3+} can be inserted in $BaCeO_3$ and $BaZrO_3$ despite a noticeable size mismatch with both Ce^{4+} and Zr^{4+} [35, 36]. In fact, it is worth noting that $BaCeO_3$ and $BaZrO_3$ themselves are miscible despite showing very different symmetry and size: It is clear that the successful insertion of the trivalent dopant depends on chemical parameters that cannot be restricted merely to ionic size.

In conclusion, X-ray absorption spectroscopy provides information on different aspects of the fundamental crystal chemistry behind the doping process in PCP, and on the interaction between lattice defects.

4.2.4 Case Study 4: Electronic Conductivity and Catalytic Activity of LSCM

LSCM ($La_{1-x}Sr_xCr_{1-y}Mn_yO_{3-\delta}$) is a perovskite ABO_3 oxide that combines the high oxidation activity of $LaMnO_3$ and the good stability in reducing environment of $LaCrO_3$. The electronic conduction, obtained by Sr-doping of the A site, is likely related to a small-polaron hopping mechanism. The electronic conduction and the catalytic behavior were investigated by the complementary use of different techniques involving in particular X-ray absorption spectroscopy [39, 40]. In typical LSCM compositions, such as $x = 0.1$–0.3 and $y = 0.5$, doping the La site with a bivalent cation involves the introduction of a negative defect, so that charge neutrality is maintained by the formation of positive point defects, e.g., by formation of oxygen vacancies or modification of the oxidation state of the B species. Possible mechanisms are

$$[Sr'_{La}] = 2[V_O^{\bullet\bullet}] + [B_B^{\bullet}] \tag{4.10}$$

or

$$[Sr'_{La}] + [B'_B] = 2[V_O^{\bullet\bullet}] \tag{4.11}$$

In the former case, a p-type conduction takes place, while the latter involves *n*-type.

X-ray absorption spectroscopy is the most suited technique to achieve selective information about the B-site oxidation state, and hence on the electronic conductivity of LSCM. An analysis of the XANES at the Cr and Mn K-edges of $(La_{1-x}Sr_xCr_{1-y}Mn_yO_{3-\delta})$ (see Fig. 4.17) allowed to show that the valence of Cr does not vary in response to a change in reducing/oxidizing environment. On the contrary, the shift towards higher energies of the Mn K-edge in oxidizing ambient is evidence that Mn changes its oxidation state, likely from 3+ to 4+.

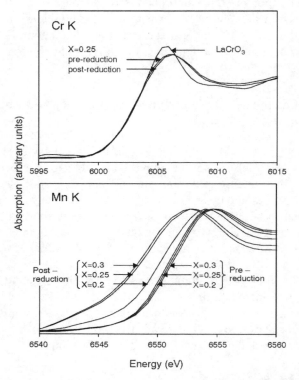

Figure 4.17 The K-edges of Cr and Mn in reducing/oxidizing environment. Reprinted from *Solid State Ionics*, 177, Plint et al., Electronic transport in the novel SOFC anode material $La_{1-x}Sr_xCr_{0.5}Mn_{0.5}O_{3\pm\delta}$, pp. 2005–2008, Copyright 2006, with permission from Elsevier [40].

Then, the defect equilibrium reaction for the Mn oxidation can be expressed as

$$\frac{1}{2}O_2 + V_O^{\cdot\cdot} + 2Mn_{Mn}^X \leftrightarrow O_O^X + Mn_{Mn}^{\cdot} \qquad (4.12)$$

and the electronic conductivity is p-type. Actually, the corresponding equilibrium constant would imply that $[Mn_{Mn}^{\bullet}]$, and hence the electronic conductivity, be dependent on $P_{O2}^{1/4}$, whereas the experimental evidence showed a $P_{O2}^{1/8}$ dependence. This was attributed to a disproportionation of Mn^{3+} in Mn^{2+} and Mn^{4+}, so that the effective electroneutrality condition could be defined, by the complementary X-ray absorption and conductivity experiments, as

$$[Sr_{La}'] + [Mn_{Mn}'] = 2[V_O^{\bullet\bullet}] + [Mn_{Mn}^{\bullet}] \qquad (4.13)$$

The EXAFS analysis of LSCM allowed to demonstrate that also the local structure around Cr is not modified on reduction/oxidation, whereas the EXAFS spectra showed a decrease of the oxygen coordination number around Mn. A model of LSCM in reducing environment was then put forth, according to the bidimensional scheme reported in Fig. 4.18.

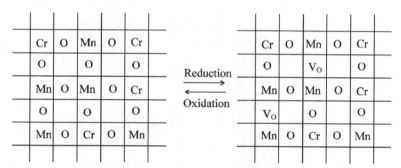

Figure 4.18 Bidimensional scheme of the preferential distribution of $V_O^{\bullet\bullet}$ around Mn. Reprinted with permission from Tao et al., *J. Phys. Chem. B*, **110**, pp. 21771–21776. Copyright 2006 American Chemical Society [39].

The reported case studies show the importance of a local structure analysis in different topics concerning fuel cell solid oxide materials. In summary, the examples, concerning (1) anion-conducting electrolytes, (2) proton-conducting electrolytes, (3) electrolyte grain boundaries and (4) an electrode material, have been chosen as representative of the different compartments of a SOFC device and of the related research issues. Of course, several further examples could be proposed, but we would also outline the fundamental use, in all the reported examples, of complementary experimental techniques allowing, by cross-analyzing the various pieces of information, to get an overall picture of the investigated materials.

Acknowledgments

We thank Dario Caia for drawing Figs. 4.2 and 4.6 and for help with the page layout.

References

1. Teo, B.-K. (1986). *EXAFS: Basic Principles and Data Analysis* (Springer, Berlin).

2. Stern, E. A. (1987). Theory of EXAFS (Koningsberger, D. C., Prins, R., eds.), in: *X-ray Absorption: Principles, Applications, Techniques of EXAFS, SEXAFS, and XANES*, Chapter 1, Wiley-VCH, Weinheim, pp. 3–53.

3. Rehr, J. J., Albers, R. C. (2000). Theoretical approaches to X-ray absorption fine structure, *Rev. Mod. Phys.*, **72**, 621–892.

4. Bunker, G. (2010). *Introduction to XAFS: A Practical Guide to X-Ray Absorption Fine Structure Spectroscopy* (Cambridge University Press, UK).

5. Dalba, G., Fornasini, P., Grazioli, R., Rocca, F. (1995). Local disorder in crystalline and amorphous germanium, *Phys. Rev. B*, **52**, 11034.

6. Wilke, M., Farges, F., Petit, P.-E., Brown, G. E., Martin, F. (2001). Oxidation state and coordination of Fe in minerals: An Fe K-XANES spectroscopic study, *Am. Mineral.*, **86**, 714–730.

7. Margaritondo, G. (2002). *Elements of Synchrotron Light: For Biology, Chemistry and Medical Research* (Oxford University Press, UK).

8. Larminie, J., Dicks, A. (2002). *Fuel Cell Systems Explained* (John Wiley, Chichester).

9. Momma, K., Izumi, F. (2011). VESTA 3 for three-dimensional visualization of crystal, volumetric and morphology data, *J. Appl. Cryst.*, **44**, 1272–1276.

10. Benamira, M., Ringuedé, A., Albina, V., Vannier, R.-N., Hildebrandt, L., Lagergren, C., Cassir, M. (2011). Gadolinia-doped ceria mixed with alkali carbonates for solid oxide fuel cell applications: I. A thermal, structural and morphological insight, *J. Power Sources*, **196**, 5546–5554.

11. Timurkutluk, B., Timurkutluk, C., Mat, M. D., Kaplan, Y. (2011). Novel structured gadolinium doped ceria based electrolytes for intermediate temperature solid oxide fuel cells, *J. Power Sources*, **196**, 9361–9364.

12. Marrero-López, D., Ruiz-Morales, J. C., Peña-Martínez, J., Martín-Sedeño, M. C., Ramos-Barrado, J. R. (2011). Influence of phase segregation on the bulk and grain boundary conductivity of LSGM electrolytes, *Solid State Ionics*, **186**, 44–52.

13. Punn, R., Feteira, A. M., Sinclair, D. C., Greaves, C. (2006). Enhanced oxide ion conductivity in stabilized δ-Bi_2O_3, *J. Am. Chem. Soc.*, **128**, 15386–15387.

14. Kreuer, K.-D. (2001). On the development of proton conducting polymer membranes for hydrogen and methanol fuel cells, *J. Membr. Sci.*, **185**, 29–39.

15. Iwahara, H., Asakura, Y., Katahira, K., Tanaka, M. (2004). Prospect of hydrogen technology using proton-conducting ceramics, *Solid State Ionics*, **168**, 299–310.

16. Kreuer, K.-D. (2003). Proton-conducting oxides, *Annu. Rev. Mater. Res.*, **33**, 333–359.

17. Kreuer, K.-D., Paddison, S. J., Spohr, E., Schuster, M. (2004). Transport in proton conductors for fuel-cell applications: Simulations, elementary reactions, and phenomenology, *Chem. Rev.*, **104**, 4637–4678.

18. Iguchi, F., Sata, N., Tsurui, T., Yugami, H. (2007). Microstructures and grain boundary conductivity of $BaZr_{1-x}Y_xO_3$ (x = 0.05, 0.10, 0.15) ceramics, *Solid State Ionics*, **178**, 691–695.

19. O'Hayre, R., Barnett, D. M., Prinz, F. B. (2005). The triple phase boundary. A mathematical model and experimental investigations for fuel cells, *J. Electrochem. Soc.*, **152**, A439–A444.

20. McIntosh, S., Gorte, R. J. (2004). Direct hydrocarbon solid oxide fuel cells, *Chem. Rev.*, **104**, 4845–4865.

21. Tsipis, E. V., Kharton, V. V. (2011). Electrode materials and reaction mechanisms in solid oxide fuel cells: A brief review. III. Recent trends and selected methodological aspects, *J. Solid State Electrochem.*, **15**, 1007–1040.

22. McEvoy, A. J. (2001). Materials for high-temperature oxygen reduction in solid oxide fuel cells, *J. Mater. Sci.*, **36**, 1087–1091.

23. Guo, X., Waser, R. (2006). Electrical properties of the grain boundaries of oxygen ion conductors: Acceptor-doped zirconia and ceria, *Prog. Mater. Sci.*, **51**, 151–210.

24. Maier, J. (1986). On the conductivity of polycrystalline materials, *Ber. Bunsenges. Phys. Chem.*, **90**, 26–33.

25. Litzelman, S. J., De Souza, R. A., Butz, B., Tuller, H. L., Martin, M., Gerthsen, D. (2009). Heterogeneously doped nanocrystalline ceria films by grain boundary diffusion: Impact on transport properties, *J. Electroceram.*, **22**, 405–415.

26. Lupetin, P., Giannici, F., Gregori, G., Martorana, A., Maier, J. (2012). Effects of grain boundary decoration on the electrical conduction of nanocrystalline CeO_2, *J. Electrochem. Soc.*, **159**, B417–B425.

27. Kharton, V. V., Marques, F. M. B., Atkinson, A. (2004). Transport properties of solid oxide electrolyte ceramics: A brief review, *Solid State Ionics*, **174**, 135– 149.

28. Boyapati, S., Wachsman, E. D., Jiang, N. (2001). Effect of oxygen sublattice ordering on interstitial transport mechanism and conductivity activation energies in phase-stabilized cubic bismuth oxides, *Solid State Ionics*, **140**, 149–160.

29. Punn, R., Gameson, I., Berry, F., Greaves, C. (2008). The local environment of cations in $Bi_{12.5}Er_{1.5}ReO_{24.5}$, *J. Phys Chem. Solids*, **69**, 2687–2690.

30. Kuang, X., Payne, J. L., Johnson, M. R., Radosavljevic Evans, I. (2012). Remarkably high oxide ion conductivity at low temperature in an ordered fluorite-type superstructure, *Angew. Chem. Int. Ed.*, **51**, 690–694.

31. Kreuer, K.-D. (1999). Aspects of the formation and mobility of protonic charge carriers and the stability of perovskite-type oxides, *Solid State Ionics*, **125**, 285–302.

32. Kreuer, K.-D., Adams, S., Münch, W., Fuchs, A., Klock, U., Maier, J. (2001). Proton conducting alkaline earth zirconates and titanates for high drain electrochemical applications, *Solid State Ionics*, **145**, 295–306.

33. Longo, A., Giannici, F., Balerna, A., Ingrao, C., Deganello, F., Martorana, A. (2006). Local environment of yttrium in yttrium-doped barium cerate, *Chem. Mater.*, **18**, 5782–5788.

34. Giannici, F., Longo, A., Balerna, A., Martorana, A. (2009). Dopant-host oxide interaction and proton mobility in $Gd:BaCeO_3$, *Chem. Mater.*, **21**, 597–603.

35. Giannici, F., Longo, A., Balerna, A., Kreuer, K.-D., Martorana, A. (2007). Indium doping in barium cerate, *Chem. Mater.*, **19**, 5714–5720.

36. Giannici, F., Longo, A., Balerna, A., Kreuer, K.-D., Martorana, A. (2009). Proton dynamics in in:$BaZrO_3$: Insights on the atomic and electronic structure from X-ray absorption spectroscopy, *Chem. Mater.*, **21**, 2641–2649.

37. Giannici, F., Shirpour, M., Longo, A., Martorana, A., Merkle, R., Maier, J. (2011). Long-range and short-range structure of proton-conducting Y:$BaZrO_3$, *Chem. Mater.*, **23**, 2994–3002.

38. Giannici, F., Longo, A., Deganello, F., Balerna, A., Arico', A. S., Martorana, A. (2007). Local environment of barium, cerium and yttrium in yttrium-doped barium cerate, *Solid State Ionics*, **178**, 587–591.

39. Tao, S., Irvine, J. T. S., Plint, S. M. (2006). Methane oxidation at redox stable fuel cell electrode $La_{0.75}Sr_{0.25}Cr_{0.5}Mn_{0.5}O_{3-\delta}$, *J. Phys. Chem. B*, **110**, 21771–21776.

40. Plint, S. M., Connor, P. A., Tao, S., Irvine, J. T. S. (2006). Electronic transport in the novel SOFC anode material $La_{1-x}Sr_xCr_{0.5}Mn_{0.5}O_{3\pm\delta}$, *Solid State Ionics*, **177**, 2005–2008.

Chapter 5

Proton Dynamics in Oxides: An Insight into the Mechanics of Proton Conduction from Quasielastic Neutron Scattering

Maths Karlsson

Department of Applied Physics, Chalmers University of Technology, SE-412 96 Göteborg, Sweden

maths.karlsson@chalmers.se

5.1 Introduction

Neutron scattering is now a well-established technique in the field of solid-state ionics, i.e., the study of solid electrolytes and their uses, and has played a crucial role in contributing to the current understanding of ion conducting solids. This encompasses studies of both crystal structures, via neutron diffraction (ND), surface and near-surface phenomena via neutron reflectivity (NR), as well as of the dynamical nature of materials via inelastic and quasielastic neutron scattering (INS and QENS). Whereas the majority of previous neutron work has focused on structural investigations

Structural Characterization Techniques: Advances and Applications in Clean Energy
Edited by Lorenzo Malavasi
Copyright © 2016 Pan Stanford Publishing Pte. Ltd.
ISBN 978-981-4669-34-4 (Hardcover), 978-981-4669-35-1 (eBook)
www.panstanford.com

using ND techniques, less work has been directed towards dynamical studies using INS and QENS.

This chapter is specifically concerned with the application of QENS for dynamical studies of proton conducting oxides. The primary interest in these materials, which may be classified according to their structure type, comes from their potential to contribute to a sustainable future, in particular through their use as electrolytes in next-generation, intermediate-temperature ($\approx$200–500°C) solid oxide fuel-cell (SOFC) technology, (Kreuer, 2003; Malavasi et al., 2010; Steele and Heinzel, 2001) as well as through their use as electrolytes in hydrogen sensors and through their relatively unexplored potential as catalytic materials (Gelling and Bouwmeester, 1992).

A particularly promising class of proton conducting oxides are ABO_3-type perovskites, where A is a relatively large cation, with oxidation state commonly +2, and B is a cation with oxidation state commonly +4 (Kreuer, 2003). The incorporation of protons into these structures relies on acceptor doping to the B site, such as Y^{3+} substituted for Ce^{4+} in $BaCeO_3$, followed by hydration. The acceptor doping creates oxygen vacancies, which can be subsequently filled with oxygens during the hydration procedure (Kreuer, 2003). The hydration is usually performed by heat treatment of the sample in a humid atmosphere, a process during which the water molecules in the gaseous phase dissociate into hydroxyl groups (–OH^-) and protons (H^+) on the surface of the sample. The –OH^- groups then stick to oxygen vacancies, whereas the (other) protons bind to lattice oxygens of the oxide host lattice. In the Kröger–Vink notation (Kröger and Vink, 1956), this reaction may be written as

$$H_2O + V_O^{\cdot\cdot} + O_O^x \Leftrightarrow 2\,(OH_O^{\cdot}), \tag{5.1}$$

where $V_O^{\cdot\cdot}$ denotes an oxygen vacancy, O_O^x denotes a lattice oxygen, and $OH_O^{\cdot}$ denotes a proton bound to a lattice oxygen (the superscripts $\cdot$ and $\times$ denote positive and neutral charges, respectively).

The protons are not stuck to any particular oxygens but are rather free to move from one oxygen to another one and with time they will therefore diffuse into the bulk of the material.

At the same time as protons diffuse into the bulk, the counter diffusion of oxygen vacancies from the bulk to the surface allows the dissociation of other water molecules on the surface of the sample. This leads to an increase of the proton concentration in the material, and so it is believed that the process continues until most, if not all, of the (bulk) oxygen vacancies are filled.

The incorporation of protons during hydration in itself means that the protons have to be mobile. The mobility of protons is routinely characterized by impedance spectroscopy techniques, with which the conductivity of protons can be determined on a macroscopic length-scale. In the case of polycrystalline samples, the impedance spectra may allow the separation of bulk conductivity from contributions from the grain boundaries (GBs). The conductivity in GBs is lower than in the bulk. This is thought to be due to either a structural misalignment in the GB region, leading to lower proton conductivity, or the appearance of a space-charge layer around the GB core, which leads to Schottky barriers and the depletion of mobile protons. At present the latter explanation is the predominating one (Chen et al., 2011; Shirpour et al., 2012), but the details of the GB core are not fully understood.

The connection between macroscopic proton conductivity, σ, and proton diffusion coefficient, D_σ, is given by the Nernst–Einstein equation:

$$D_\sigma = \sigma(T)\frac{k_B T}{e^2 N},\tag{5.2}$$

where k_B is the Boltzmann constant, T the temperature, e the proton charge, and N the number density of the mobile protons. The proton diffusion coefficient, D_σ, is proportional to the proton self-diffusion coefficient, D_σ, via the Haven ratio $H_R = D_s/D_\sigma$. The Haven ratio, which may have values both smaller or larger than 1, reflects correlation effects, such as deviations from directional and/or temporal randomness of consecutive proton jumps, whereas D_σ is the quantity that is normally measured in QENS experiments. QENS can give information about both the time-scale and spatial geometry of dynamical processes, which is unique compared to other spectroscopic techniques. This deeper understanding of the dynamical aspects of the proton diffusion is achieved through the analysis of the momentum and energy transferred in the scattering event.

The aim of this chapter is to introduce the non-specialist reader to the basic concepts of QENS, its advantages and disadvantages, and to review the QENS studies that have been done on proton conducting oxides so far, as well as to discuss the state of the art and prospectives and importance for future work in this field. The chapter has also been published recently as a Perspective Article in *Phys. Chem. Chem. Phys.* (Karlsson, 2015). Articles concerned with the use of neutron scattering techniques for studies of solid-state ionics in a wider context and not specialized on QENS, are reported elsewhere (Karlsson, 2013; Sosnowska, 1999).

5.2 Neutron Scattering Experiments

5.2.1 Neutron Sources and the Production of Free Neutrons

Neutron scattering experiments are performed at large-scale neutron scattering facilities, where neutrons are produced either by nuclear fission or by spallation. In nuclear fission, certain isotopes of very heavy elements, such as uranium or plutonium, are bombarded with neutrons during which other neutrons, as well as a great deal of energy, are released from the nuclei of the isotopes. If the free neutrons are let to react with other atoms, then even more neutrons are released and as a consequence a self-sustaining chain reaction is created. In spallation sources, on the other hand, neutrons are released (spallated) by the bombardment of protons on a heavy metal target. In both types of neutron sources, the produced neutrons are of very high energy (MeV), much higher than what is useful for neutron scattering experiments. The neutrons are therefore slowed down in a, so-called, moderator, before they are guided to large instrument halls containing instruments designed for certain types of experiments. The type and temperature of the moderator determine the energy of the neutrons. Generally, neutron energies in the range 0.1–10 meV refer to cold neutrons, neutron energies in the range 10–100 meV refer to thermal neutrons, and neutron energies in the range 100–1000 meV refer to hot neutrons. Cold and thermal neutrons are particularly useful in QENS experiments, since their energies and wavelengths match the energies of relevant dynamical processes and interatomic distances in condensed matter. The implication of this is two-fold: First, it implies that the scattered neutrons may take up or lose a large part of their incoming energy, which means that dynamics can be measured with high accuracy; secondly, it implies that interference effects of the scattered neutrons occur, which gives structural information. Furthermore, the interaction of neutrons with matter is for most materials weak, which ensures that the bulk sample is being probed and not just surface or near-surface states that may behave differently from the bulk.

Examples of state-of-the-art neutron research reactors are the Institut Laue-Langevin (ILL) in France, the NIST Centre for Neutron Research (NCNR) in the US, the Laboratoire Léon Brillouin (LLB) in France, the FRM-II facility in Germany, and the OPAL neutron source of the Australian Nuclear Science and Technology Organisation (ANSTO), which are all continuous neutron sources, whereas the IBR-2M reactor of the Frank Laboratory of Nuclear Research in Russia is a pulsed source. Examples of spallation sources are the ISIS neutron facility in the UK, the Spallation Neutron Source (SNS) in the US, and the Japan Proton Accelerator Research Complex (J-PARC) in Japan, which are pulsed sources, and the Swiss Spallation Neutron Source (SINQ) in Switzerland which is a continuous source. The next-generation neutron source is the European Spallation Source (ESS), a pulsed source which is being constructed in Sweden and that will come into operation around 2020.

5.2.2 Scattering Theory and Scattering Cross Sections

As in all scattering experiments, the energy and momentum are conserved during a neutron scattering event. The energy of a neutron is given by $E = \hbar^2 k^2 / 2m$, where m is the neutron's mass and k is the magnitude of the associated wave vector, $|\boldsymbol{k}| = k = 2\pi/\lambda$, and λ is the wavelength of the neutron. Expressions for the momentum and energy transferred from the sample to the neutron during the scattering event may then be written as

$$\hbar \boldsymbol{Q} = \hbar(\boldsymbol{k}_0 - \boldsymbol{k}_1), \tag{5.3}$$

$$|Q|^2 = |k_0|^2 + |k_1|^2 - 2|k_0|\,|k_1|\cos 2\theta, \tag{5.4}$$

and

$$\hbar\omega = E_0 - E_1 = \frac{\hbar^2}{2m}(|k_0|^2 - |k_1|^2), \tag{5.5}$$

where k_0 and E_0 are the wave vector and energy of the incident neutron and k_1 and E_1 that of the scattered, and 2θ is the scattering angle. As the vast majority of QENS studies of proton conducting oxides are done on powder samples, which do not have any preferred orientation, all that generally matters is the magnitude of Q. Therefore, the vector character of Q is ignored in the following.

The measured quantity in most experiments is the double differential scattering cross section, $d^2\sigma/d\Omega dE$, which represents the number of neutrons scattered into the solid angle $d\Omega$ with energy in the range dE. The amplitude of the scattered wave depends on the type of nuclei on which the neutrons are scattered and is also isotope and spin dependent, thus averages have to be taken for each element. The total cross section per scatterer, σ, reflects the effective areas of nuclei as seen by the incident neutrons and is obtained by integrating over all energies and solid angles,

$$\sigma = \int dE \int d\Omega \, \frac{d^2\sigma}{d\Omega dE} = 4\pi \langle b^2 \rangle. \tag{5.6}$$

Here b is the scattering length, which can be either real or complex. The real part is usually positive (with the notable exception of H, which has a negative scattering length) and means a repulsive potential between the neutron and nucleus, whereas a negative scattering length means that the neutron is subjected to an attractive potential. The imaginary part relates to the probability that the neutron is absorbed rather than scattered. The total scattering cross section can be split into coherent and incoherent parts. The coherent part, σ_{coh}, corresponds to an average over all isotopes and nuclear spin states and may be written as

$$\sigma_{coh} = 4\pi \langle b \rangle^2 = 4\pi b_{coh}^2. \tag{5.7}$$

The incoherent part, σ_{inc}, corresponds to the difference between the total and coherent scattering cross sections and is given by

$$\sigma_{inc} = 4\pi(\langle b^2 \rangle - \langle b \rangle^2). \tag{5.8}$$

It represents therefore the mean square deviation from the mean potential, which is due to isotopic and/or spin dependent effects of the scattering length.

As in the case for the scattering cross sections, the measured quantity in neutron scattering experiments, i.e., the double differential scattering cross section, can be separated into one coherent and one incoherent part according to

$$\frac{d^2\sigma}{d\Omega\,dE} = \frac{k_1}{k_0}\frac{1}{4\pi\hbar}[\sigma_{coh}S_{coh}(Q,\omega) + \sigma_{inc}S_{inc}(Q,\omega)].$$

(5.9)

Here $S_{coh}(Q, \omega)$ and $S_{inc}(Q, \omega)$ are known as the coherent and incoherent dynamical structure factors, respectively, which are the functions obtained in most QENS experiments. The coherent part gives information about interference effects in materials, thus it provides information about the behavior of atoms in relation to each other, whereas the incoherent part relates to scattering from individual atoms. The Fourier transforms of $S_{coh}(Q, \omega)$ and $S_{inc}(Q, \omega)$ give the so-called intermediate scattering functions, $I_{coh}(Q, t)$ and $I_{inc}(Q, t)$, which in turn are the Fourier transforms of the total and self real-space time correlation functions, $G(r, t)$ and $G_{self}(r, t)$. $G_{self}(r, t)$ gives the probability that the same particle will be found at the position r at a later time t. Finally, one should note that since r and t are the Fourier-transformed variables of Q and ω, long distances in real space correspond to small Q, and vice versa. Analogously, slow diffusivities, implying long times in $G(r, t)$, correspond to small ω.

5.2.3 Quasielastic Neutron Scattering

QENS refers to those inelastic processes that are almost elastic. The term is usually considered to mean a broadening of the elastic line in the neutron energy spectrum, $S(Q, \omega)$, rather than the appearance of discrete peaks associated with inelastic scattering.[1] This is illustrated schematically in Fig. 5.1. The elastic component is due to scattering from atoms which are localized in space, or in other words move too slowly to be resolved within

---

[1]However, in case the intermediate scattering function, $I(Q, t)$, is measured, as is the case in neutron spin-echo experiments, the quasielastic scattering is manifested as a relaxational decay with time.

the resolution of the instrument. The inelastic peaks arise from scattering from atoms which vibrate in a periodic manner and with a fixed frequency. Analogously to inelastic light scattering (by Raman spectroscopy), the inelastically scattered neutrons can either loose energy (Stokes scattering) or gain energy (anti-Stokes scattering), respectively; however, in comparison to its optical counterpart, INS does not rely on any selection rules.[2] The QENS broadening is due to scattering from atoms that are moving in a stochastic manner.

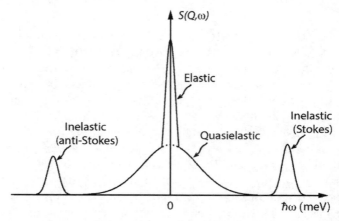

Figure 5.1   Schematic illustration of a neutron scattering spectrum, containing elastic, inelastic, and quasielastic components. The inelastic scattering has contributions from Stokes (neutron energy loss) and anti-Stokes (neutron energy gain) scattering, respectively. Although purely elastic scattering is defined as $\hbar\omega = 0$, every instrument has a finite resolution and therefore the elastic component has here been broadened to reflect this.

Just as for other kinds of neutron scattering, QENS contains both coherent and incoherent scattering contributions. As mentioned above, the coherent scattering yields information about interference phenomena between atoms, which in QENS measurements means that information about collective dynamics, e.g., transport properties, may be obtained. The incoherent scattering, on the contrary, relates to scattering from individual

---

[2] The activation of Raman scattering relies on changes in polarizability of the vibrating moieties. In INS, all modes are *active* and in principle measurable.

atoms, thus providing information about single-particle motions, also known as self-dynamics.

5.2.4   QENS Techniques

QENS techniques can be largely grouped into time-of-flight, backscattering, and neutron spin-echo (NSE) spectroscopy. The majority of previous QENS studies on proton conducting oxides have been performed by the use of time-of-flight and backscattering techniques, which give access to the time-scale of picoseconds, extended up to ≈1 ns in some cases, whereas even slower time-scales can be accessed with the NSE technique. Figure 5.2 shows, as an example, approximate (Q, $\hbar\omega$) domains as covered by the various spectrometers at the ILL. Included in the figure are the (Q, $\hbar\omega$) ranges of relevance for diffusional dynamics in proton conducting oxides, as will be discussed further below.

A brief description of the various QENS techniques, emphasizing the essentials of each method, is presented in the following. A comprehensive description of the techniques can be found elsewhere (Springer, 1972; Bée, 1988; Liang et al., 2009).

5.2.4.1   Time-of-flight spectroscopy

The typical energy resolution of time-of-flight spectrometers ranges between approximately 1 μeV and 1000 μeV, which implies that dynamics with characteristic time-scales faster than some hundreds of picoseconds usually can be investigated, cf. Fig. 5.2. These spectrometers can be designed to operate in either (i) the direct-geometry or (ii) the indirect-geometry mode. Direct-geometry spectrometers work with a pulsed monochromatic neutron beam impinging on the sample. The monochromator usually consists of a system of rotating disc choppers, which selects neutrons with a specific velocity out of an incoming broad distribution of neutron velocities as defined by the neutron moderator. The chopper system also serves to pulse the neutron beam in time. The final energy is determined by the time-of-flight between the sample and detector. In this way, the distribution of scattered neutron velocities (energies) can be determined. In indirect-geometry spectrometers, on the contrary, a specific energy of the scattered neutrons is detected. In practice, this means using a *quasi-white* beam which is illuminating the sample

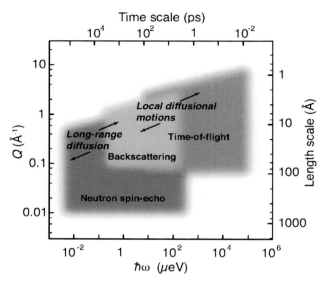

Figure 5.2 Neutron spectroscopy methods at the ILL encompass a large range of time- and length-scales. The $(Q, \hbar\omega)$ ranges of relevance for dynamical processes in proton conducting oxides are indicated. The figure has been modified after Jobic et al. (Jobic and Theodorou, 2007).

and analyzing the wavelength of the scattered neutrons by Bragg diffraction from a monocrystal. By differentiating Bragg's law, it can be shown that the energy resolution for these inverted-geometry spectrometers is given by

$$\Delta E/E = 2\Delta\lambda/\lambda = 2\sqrt{(\cot\theta \cdot \Delta\theta)^2 + (\Delta d/d)^2}, \qquad (5.10)$$

where θ is the Bragg angle and d the lattice parameter of the monocrystal analyzer. As the lattice parameter can be determined with very high precision (typically, $\Delta d/d \approx 10^{-4}$), the latter term can be ignored and instead the dominant term is $\cot\theta \cdot \Delta\theta$. It follows that the highest energy resolution is achieved when the Bragg angle approaches 90° since then $\cot\theta$ tends to zero, and therefore these spectrometers are also called backscattering spectrometers. Figure 5.3 shows schematic illustrations of the major components of the two types of instruments. An overview of the beam trajectories by means of distance–time diagrams is also shown.

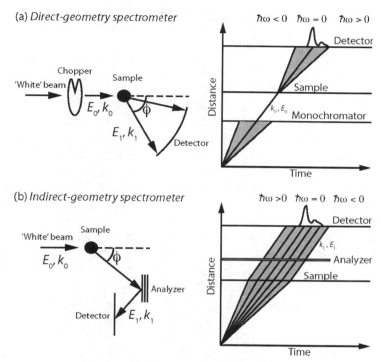

Figure 5.3 Schematic illustrations of direct-geometry (a) and indirect-geometry (b) spectrometers, together with their corresponding distance–time diagrams for single pulses of neutrons.

When planning an experiment on a time-of-flight spectrometer, the interplay of instrumental energy resolution and signal intensity is an important concern. Generally, the resolution increases with the use of longer neutron wavelengths; however, the intensity is then usually decreased; for instruments on guide tubes the intensity λ^{-3} varies as at long wavelengths. A further disadvantage of increasing the neutron wavelength is that the accessible region in (Q, $\hbar\omega$) space gets reduced. This is determined by the laws of conservation of energy and momentum in the scattering process (Eqs. (5.4–5.5)) and depends on the particular values of neutron energy and scattering angle. For a direct-geometry spectrometer, it follows that the accessible region is limited by

$$\hbar^2 Q^2 / 2m = 2E_0 - \hbar\omega - 2\sqrt{E_0(E_0 - \hbar\omega)} \cos 2\theta, \tag{5.11}$$

whereas for an indirect-geometry spectrometer, the accessible region is limited by

$$\hbar^2 Q^2/2m = 2E_1 + \hbar\omega - 2\sqrt{E_1(E_1 + \hbar\omega)}\, \cos 2\theta. \qquad (5.12)$$

Figure 5.4 shows the accessible regions for the two types of spectrometers and two choices of neutron energy. Note that for fixed incident energy (as in direct-geometry spectrometers) and for fixed analyzed energy (as in indirect-geometry spectrometers), the curves that define the measurable $(Q, \hbar\omega)$ region are identical in shape but are each other's mirror image. Furthermore, one should note that direct-geometry spectrometers cannot measure neutron energy losses that are larger than the value of the incident neutron energy, since the final neutron energy can never be less than zero. Similarly, inverted-geometry spectrometers cannot measure neutron energy gains larger than the value of the neutron energy measured by the analyzer. Examples of currently operational time-of-flight spectrometers include IN4 (ILL), IN5 (ILL), IN6 (ILL), TOFTOF (FRM-II), FOCUS (PSI), MAPS (ISIS), MARI (ISIS), MERLIN (ISIS), LET (ISIS), DCS (NCNR), ARCS (SNS), CNCS (SNS), SEQUOIA (SNS), PELICAN (OPAL), and HRC and AMATERAS (J-PARC).

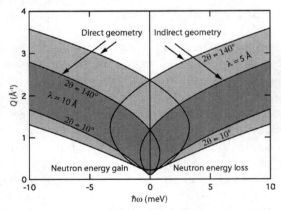

Figure 5.4 Plots of the accessible region in $(Q, \hbar\omega)$ space for direct-geometry and indirect-geometry spectrometers, with neutrons of wavelength 5 and 10 Å (energy 3.272 and 0.818 meV, respectively). The minimum and maximum scattering angles are 10° and 140°, respectively.

5.2.4.2 Backscattering Spectroscopy

Whereas time-of-flight spectrometers utilize either direct- or indirect-scattering geometry, the technique known as backscattering is the limiting case of the latter. Specifically, it has the energy analyzer positioned in perfect or near backscattering geometry ($\theta_A \approx 90°$), in addition it utilizes a monochromator, also that in perfect or near backscattering geometry ($\theta_M \approx 90°$), before the sample, cf. Fig. 5.5. Using the same argument as for the "conventional" indirect-geometry time-of-flight spectrometers, the backscattering geometry increases the energy resolution according to Eq. (5.10). Furthermore, as both the monochromator and analyzer are set in backscattering geometry, the energy transfer is fixed. This means that if one wants to achieve a dynamical range of say 10 times the resolution, the energy of the incoming neutrons has to change by the same amount. The manner in which this is done is by giving the monochromator a translational motion (Doppler broadening) (Birr et al., 1971) or by thermal expansion of the lattice parameters of the monochromator crystal (Cook et al., 1992). The former approach requires much shorter measuring times and is usually adopted. However, the latter one yields a much larger dynamical range not limited by the speed of the Doppler driven monochromator.

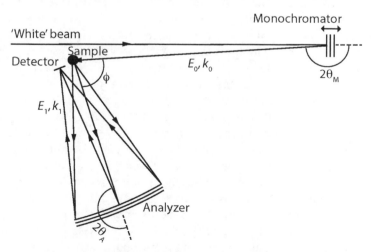

Figure 5.5   Schematic illustration of a backscattering spectrometer based on Doppler broadening.

Backscattering spectrometers are characterized by a higher energy resolution than time-of-flight spectrometers. Typical energy resolutions are between 0.3 and 1 µeV. This translates into the time-scale of nanoseconds, that is much slower than the time-scales probed by most time-of-flight spectrometers. Although most backscattering spectrometers have been built on neutron research reactors and make use of monocrystal monochromator, backscattering spectrometers built on spallation sources do not use such monochromators, but instead the incident neutron energy is determined from the overall time-of-flight between the neutron source and the detectors. A dynamical range of several hundred µeV is achievable. Currently operational backscattering spectrometers include IN10 (ILL), IN13 (ILL), IN16B (ILL), SPHERES (FRM-II), IRIS (ISIS), OSIRIS (ISIS), HFBS (NCNR), and BASIS (SNS).

5.2.4.3 Spin-echo spectroscopy

As described above, time-of-flight and backscattering spectrometers rely on the determination of the exchange in neutron energy via the measurements of time-of-flight before and after the scattering event, respectively, or by monochromization by monocrystals. The smaller the energy exchange is, the more precise the neutron speed has to be defined. This can be achieved only at the expense of infinitely low count rate and sets a practical resolution limit of 0.1–1 µeV for these types of instruments. In NSE spectroscopy, on the other hand, the energy resolution is decoupled from the neutron intensity and as a consequence it is possible to measure the energy exchange of each individual neutron in the scattering event irrespective of their energy (Mezei, 1972, 1980; Mezei et al., 2003). Currently available NSE instruments achieve energy resolutions of the order of 0.1 to 1 neV, which means that time-scales as long as hundreds of nanoseconds can be reached, thus allowing studies of relatively slow diffusional processes but, importantly, still on an atomic length-scale. In addition, NSE covers a very wide time-range, of several decades, often with the same instrumental setting (Mezei, 1980, 1972; Mezei et al., 2003). It follows that NSE spectroscopy offers unique opportunities to obtain information about dynamical processes occurring on significantly different time-scales in the same measurement.

The basic principle of NSE is as follows. First, neutrons from a cold moderator are monochromized with the use of a neutron velocity selector, which gives a relatively wide range of neutron wavelengths ($\Delta\lambda/\lambda \approx 15\%$ FWHM). These neutrons are then polarized along their velocity direction (x), before their spins are rotated to a direction perpendicular to the velocity direction (z) by the use of a $\pi/2$ spin flipper (see Fig. 5.6a). Then, the neutrons travel in the first precession coil through a magnetic field aligned along the x direction. Here, the neutrons undergo a specific number of Larmor precessions in the yz plane, determined by the neutron velocity (v), length of the coil (L), and magnetic field strength (B). Accordingly, the total precession angle (in radians) over the length of the first solenoid can be expressed as

$$\varphi_1 = \frac{\gamma B L}{v}, \tag{5.13}$$

where γ is the neutron gyromagnetic ratio. For a typical flux density line integral BL (or more strictly $\int^{L} \boldsymbol{B}d\boldsymbol{l}$) of 0.3 Tm, the polarization of 10 Å neutrons will undergo more than 20,000 precessions. It is clear that the relatively wide range of neutron wavelengths is rapidly dephased and the final net polarization at the end of the first solenoid will be zero. Before the neutrons are scattered by the sample, the neutron spins are rotated by 180° around the z axis by a π spin flipper. After the scattering event, the neutrons travel through the second solenoid, which is identical to the first one, with the consequence being that the neutrons now precess in the opposite direction.

If the scattering is purely elastic, the neutron spin direction at the end of the second coil will equal that at the beginning of the first coil and the total precession angle is then zero, $\varphi = \varphi_1 - \varphi_2 = 0$, irrespective of the spread of neutron velocities (see Fig. 5.6b). The final neutron polarization is measured by flipping the neutron spins back into the longitudinal x-direction using a $\pi/2$-flipper and finally analyzing it with an array of supermirrors in front of the detector that transmits only neutrons of one polarization direction. Since the angle between the neutron polarization and the analyzer direction is φ, then the probability that a neutron is transmitted is $\cos(\varphi)$. What is measured experimentally is the expectation value (average) over all the scattered neutrons, i.e., $\langle\cos(\varphi)\rangle$.

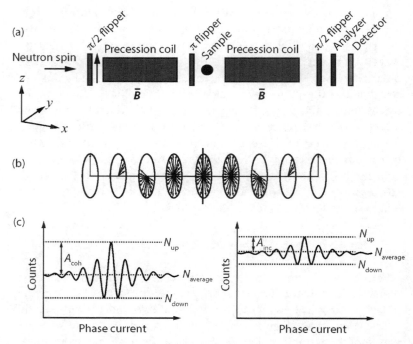

Figure 5.6 (a) The layout of a generic spin-echo spectrometer showing its principal components. (b) Schematic representation of the dephasing of the precessing neutron spins along the first arm of the spectrometer, followed by a π spin flip and subsequent rephasing along the second arm. (c) NSE signal, for a fixed Q-value, as a function of the phase difference between the incident and scattered beams, in the case of purely coherent and incoherent scattering, respectively. A_{coh} and A_{inc} are the echo amplitudes for coherent and incoherent scattering, $N_{average}$ is the average count rate outside the echo, and N_{up} and N_{down} are the count rates of non-spin-flip (π flipper off) and spin-flip (π flipper on) measurements made with the $\pi/2$ flippers off.

If the scattering is quasielastic, the situation is different since the energy and hence the velocities of the neutrons will change at the scattering event, and the neutrons' spins will therefore not return to their initial state. Accordingly, the accumulated precession angle will be

$$\varphi = \gamma BL\left(\frac{1}{v_1} - \frac{1}{v_2}\right),$$ (5.14)

where v_1 and v_2 are the velocities of the incident and scattered neutrons, respectively. Expressing the energy transfer in terms of $\hbar\omega = m/2(v_2^2 - v_1^2)$, it can be shown that the accumulated precession angle with respect to the echo condition is

$$\varphi = \frac{\hbar\gamma BL}{mv_1^3}\,\omega = t\omega.$$ (5.15)

The proportionality constant $t = \hbar\gamma BL/mv_1^3$ has the units of time and is called the *spin-echo* or *Fourier time*. Noting that at a given Q, the probability for scattering with an energy exchange $\hbar\omega$ is by definition $S(Q, \hbar\omega)$, thus the final beam polarization measured at the echo position (where the field integrals in the first and second arm are exactly matched) is[3]

$$P_x = \langle\cos(t\omega)\rangle \propto \int \cos(t\omega)S(Q, \omega)d\omega$$ (5.16)

This is nothing else than the Fourier transform of $S(Q, \omega)$ with respect to ω. Thus, the measurement of the final beam polarization for a given Fourier time, t, is simply a measurement of the intermediate scattering function, $I(Q, t)$

$$P_x = \langle\cos(t\omega)\rangle \propto I(Q, t).$$ (5.17)

In other words, data is recorded as a function of real time, and not as a function of energy transfer as in the case of time-of-flight and backscattering spectroscopy. Different *Fourier times* are measured by varying the field integral (by the precession field of the first coil) around the symmetry point between the two coils. This will give an echo group as a function of phase current (Fig. 5.6c), where the periodicity of the damped oscillation is determined by the average wavelength and its envelope is the Fourier transform of the wavelength distribution.

As in all types of neutron scattering experiments, the $I(Q, t)$ can be divided into coherent and incoherent parts, $I(Q, t) = I_{\text{coh}}(Q, t)$

---

[3] The proportionality constant originates from instrumental factors which can be accounted for.

+ $I_{inc}(Q, t)$. Incoherent scattering is featured by a 2/3 probability of flipping the spins of the neutrons, effectively reducing the incoherent NSE signal by 2/3, and, in addition, contributing to a background (Fig. 5.6c; Farago, 2002). Hence, the intermediate scattering function measured by NSE can be expressed as

$$I_{NSE}(Q, t) = I_{coh}(Q, t) - \frac{1}{3} I_{inc}(Q, t). \tag{5.18}$$

Generally, NSE provides the normalized intermediate scattering function obtained as

$$\frac{I_{NSE}(Q, t)}{I_{NSE}(Q, t = 0)} = \frac{2A}{N_{up} - N_{down}}, \tag{5.19}$$

where A is the echo amplitude and N_{up} and N_{down} are the maximal and minimal count rates, respectively. These are usually determined by performing measurements with the π flipper on and off, respectively, while having the $\pi/2$ flippers off. It implies that the instrument is setup in such a way that the neutrons' spins and the magnetic fields are aligned parallel effectively zeroing the precession. The amplitudes of coherent and incoherent scattering, $I_{coh}(Q, t = 0) = S_{coh}(Q)$ and $I_{inc}(Q, t = 0) = S_{inc}(Q)$, respectively, can also be determined by measuring the intensities of spin-flip and non-spin flip scattering.

As it has been highlighted before, a wealth of information is obtained by analyzing the Q-dependence of the QENS component. Whereas time-of-flight and backscattering instruments allow the collection of data in the whole accessible range of Q-values in ones, NSE spectrometers, generally, collect data from a limited range of Q-values for each configuration. This is a big hindrance for all NSE experiments in which the signal of interest is not concentrated in a limited Q-range. The availability of a detector covering 30° of scattering angle on IN11-C at the ILL partially overcomes this disadvantage, although at the expense of a limitation in the maximum Fourier time achieved. The WASP instrument, which is currently being built at the ILL and which will allow to collect data over even larger scattering angle ranges should allow in the future for a much more efficient data collection in many chemical physics experiments, including investigations of proton conduction. Currently operational NSE spectrometers include IN11 and IN11-C (ILL), IN15 (ILL), J-NSE and RESEDA (FRMII), NSE (NCNR), NSE (SNS) and MUSES (LLB).

5.3 QENS on Proton Conducting Oxides

QENS has played a central role in the field of proton conducting oxides and provided important information about the dynamics of protons in this class of technologically important materials. The usefulness of QENS for studies of proton conducting oxides comes from the fact that it gives access to the relevant time- and length-scales on which the atomic-scale dynamics of protons occur. In addition, the very large incoherent neutron scattering cross section of protons of 80.26 barns (1 barn = 10^{-24} cm^2), far larger than all other nuclei (<10 barns), and relatively small coherent scattering cross section (1.76 barns), enables one to observe protons essentially free from constructive interference, i.e., information about proton self-diffusion can be obtained, whereas the correlation between the dynamical behavior of an ensemble of protons can be neglected.[4] Furthermore, the strong scattering signal from protons provides a good contrast in experiments and enables studies of proton self-diffusion in systems containing only relatively small amounts of protons. It follows that the total dynamical structure factor, $S(Q, \omega)$, can, in most cases, be approximated with the incoherent dynamical structure factor, i.e., $S(Q, \omega) \approx S_{inc}(Q, \omega)$. The measured structure factor is a convolution of $S_{inc}(Q, \omega)$ and the resolution function of the instrument, $R(Q, \omega)$, that is

$$S_{meas}(Q, \omega) = S_{inc}(Q, \omega) \otimes R(Q, \omega). \qquad (5.20)$$

The resolution function is usually determined by a measurement of the sample at very low temperature (<10 K), where the diffusional dynamics is *frozen-in*, or on a "perfectly" elastic, incoherent, scatterer, such as vanadium, of the same geometry as the sample.

When the QENS is accompanied by an elastic component, which is the case for localized motions, the dynamical structure factor may be expressed as

---

[4] For a complete list of the thermal neutron scattering cross sections of all elements and their isotopes, the reader is referred to Sears (1992).

$$S_{inc}(Q, \omega) = e^{-\langle u^2 \rangle Q^2} \{S_{inc}^{el}(Q)\delta(\omega) + S_{inc}^{inel}(Q, \omega)\}. \tag{5.21}$$

Here, the exponential factor is known as the Debye–Waller factor, which accounts for the decrease in elastic and quasielastic intensity due to vibrational motions of atoms (i.e., inelastic scattering). $\langle u^2 \rangle$ is the total mean square displacement of all atoms due to vibrational motions in the material. $S_{inc}^{el}(Q)\delta(\omega)$ and $S_{inc}^{inel}(Q, \omega)$ represent the elastic and quasielastic contributions, respectively. Studying their dependence on Q and temperature will bring a wealth of information, such as the time-scale and geometry of the diffusive process(es) in the system under investigation.

5.3.1 Diffusion Models

Theoretical models are based on the van Hove correlation function formalism and they predict the profile of $S(Q, \omega)$ and $I(Q, t)$, according to the kind of dynamics in the system. Generally, the quasielastic part of $S(Q, \omega)$ can be described by one or more Lorentzian functions, related to one or more dynamical processes, i.e.,

$$S_{inc}^{inel}(Q, \omega) = \sum_{l=1} A_l(Q) L_l(Q, \omega), \tag{5.22}$$

where the Lorentzian function is

$$L_l(Q, \omega) = \frac{1}{\pi} \frac{\Gamma(Q, \omega)_l}{(\hbar\omega)^2 + \Gamma(Q)_l^2} \tag{5.23}$$

and $\Gamma(Q)_l$ is its half-width at half-maximum (HWHM). Here, the Q-dependence of the latter provides information about the geometry of the dynamics and hence adds a useful means to distinguish between different models. For random (Brownian) translational diffusion, $\Gamma(Q)$ follows a parabolic increase with increasing Q, i.e.,

$$\Gamma(Q) = \hbar D_s Q^2, \tag{5.24}$$

where D_s is the self-diffusion coefficient. D_s relates to the relaxation time τ, according to

$$\tau = \frac{1}{D_s Q^2}. \tag{5.25}$$

Random translational diffusion, also known as continuous diffusion, is, however, only observed at small Q-values, which correspond to large distances in real space. At larger Q-values, the motion is no more continuous and underlying microscopic mechanisms are at play. To describe such mechanistic detail, several types of jump-diffusion models have been developed. These all describe long-range diffusion as a series of successive jumps and contain as parameters the characteristic jump length and time between successive jumps (the latter is referred to as residence or relaxation time). One of the most used models is that developed by Chudley and Elliott (1961), which assumes a constant jump length, r, a residence (relaxation) time, τ, and a negligible jump time. At sufficiently small Q-values, the $\Gamma(Q)$ still follows a Q^2-behavior, as in the case for continuous diffusion, but at larger Q-values $\Gamma(Q)$ follows an oscillatory behavior according to

$$\Gamma(Q)_{C-E} = \frac{\hbar}{\tau}\left(1 - \frac{\sin(Qr)}{Qr}\right). \tag{5.26}$$

Related jump-diffusion models are the Hall–Ross model (Hall and Ross, 1981), which is characterized by a Gaussian distribution of jump lengths, and the Singwi–Sjölander model (Singwi and Sjölander, 1960), which is characterized by an exponential distribution of jump lengths. However, one should note that diffusion processes are often more complicated and cannot always be categorized into these relatively simple cases, hence more sophisticated models must be developed. A detailed description and survey of different models can be found in several textbooks and review articles, see, e.g., refs (Bée, 1988; Hempelmann, 2000).

5.4 Overview of QENS Studies

This section reviews the literature on QENS studies on proton conducting oxides. The aim is not to give an exhaustive account for all the work that has been done in this field, but to illustrate different uses of QENS and to summarize some of the key results obtained so far. This is followed by my critical remarks as well as a discussion about the prospectives for future studies in this area of research.

5.4.1 Perovskite Structured Oxides

The majority of previous QENS studies on proton conducting oxides have been performed using time-of-flight and backscattering methods and on perovskite structured materials, such as doped variants of $BaZrO_3$ and $BaCeO_3$ based compounds; these studies are here summarized briefly. The initial studies were performed by Hempelmann et al. (1995) and Matzke et al. (1996) in the mid-1990s on a hydrated sample of $SrCe_{0.95}Yb_{0.05}O_{2.975}$. Figure 5.7 shows the QENS spectra measured at different temperatures. From the low-Q data, it was possible to extract the proton self-diffusion constant as a function of temperature and this was found to be comparable to the bulk proton conductivity measured with impedance spectroscopy (Hempelmann et al., 1995). The high-Q data was also analyzed and this contains information about the mechanistic detail of the proton conduction. Analysis showed that the QENS spectra could be reproduced by two quasielastic

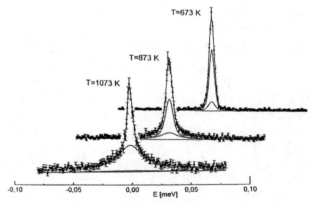

Figure 5.7 Neutron scattering spectra, $S(Q, \omega)$, of $SrCe_{0.95}Yb_{0.05}H_{0.02}O_{2.985}$ for different temperatures at momentum transfer $Q = 0.29$ Å^{-1}. The solid lines show the total scattering function as well as the two components of the two-state model. Reprinted with permission from Hempelmann et al. (1995), copyright Elsevier, 1995.

components, corresponding to two different localized proton motions with different activation energies, suggesting the existence of two different structural sites occupied by the protons. More detailed analysis showed that the QENS data was in agreement with a two-state model superimposed on the Chudley–Elliott model. The Chudley–Elliott model suggests in this case that the proton conduction occurs as a series of proton jumps (transfers) between neighboring oxygens, O(1) and O(2), and rotational diffusion of the –OH group between such transfers (see Fig. 5.8a), whereas the two-state model indicates that the proton diffusion consists of some sort of trapping and release events.

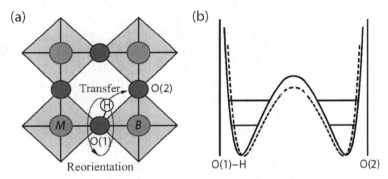

Figure 5.8 (a) Schematic of the elementary local dynamical processes in the proton conduction mechanism in a $AB_{1-x}M_xO_3H_x$ type perovskite with a cubic structure, where M is the acceptor dopant. (b) The proton occupies a double Morse type potential with barrier height dependent on the separation distance between neighboring oxygens, O(1)–O(2). The horizontal lines depict vibrational energy levels for the O–H stretch mode. The dashed curve indicates the change in potential energy due to phonons of the perovskite host lattice.

The O(1)–H···O(2) transfer direction may be modeled by a double Morse type potential, with a barrier height dependent on the separation distance between O(1) and O(2) and on the vibrational level of the O–H stretch mode, which is illustrated in Fig. 5.8b. Thus, the rate of proton diffusion is believed to be strongly coupled to the vibrational dynamics of the system. In particular, the proton performs localized O–H stretch and wag modes, which may be seen as precursors to the transfer and reorientational step, respectively, and moreover the dynamics of the oxygen sub-lattice induce large fluctuations in the distances between O(1) and O(2) with time (Karlsson et al., 2005, 2008b).

Such a proton conduction mechanism in perovskites has later found support from several computer simulations and experiments on different proton conducting oxide systems ever since. In particular, muon spin-relaxation experiments (Hempelmann et al., 1998) and several simulations (Kreuer et al., 1998; Münch et al., 1996; Münch et al., 1997; Shimojo et al., 1997) have indicated that the dopant atoms are responsible for the trapping effect in these materials, thus decreasing the overall proton conductivity. Simulations have for example reproduced the experimental trend in proton conductivity in the $BaZr_{0.9}M_{0.1}O_{2.95}$ (M = Y, In, Sc and Ga) series for which the conductivity differs several orders of magnitude depending on the type of dopant atom (Kreuer et al., 2001). More recently, the trapping view was further supported by combined thermogravimetric and a.c. impedance spectroscopy data on $BaZr_{0.8}Y_{0.2}O_3H_{0.2}$ (Yamazaki et al., 2013). However, converse to the view that dopant atoms act as localized trapping centers for the proton diffusion, it has also been proposed that the dopant atoms may affect the proton transport in a more nonlocal manner (Kreuer et al., 1997; Kreuer, 1999).

Following the pioneering work by Hempelmann et al. (1995) and Matzke et al. (1996), Karmonik et al. (1996) investigated the proton dynamics in the double perovskite structured material $Ba[Ca_{0.39}Nb_{0.61}]O_{2.91}$ which, similarly to the previous studies on $SrCe_{0.95}Yb_{0.05}O_{2.975}$, gave support for a proton conduction mechanism divided into proton jumps and reorientational motions. Subsequently, Pionke et al. (1997) reported on the proton self-diffusion constant for protons in the same material. Later, Groß et al. (2001) and Beck et al. (2001) investigated the influence of particle size on the atomic-scale proton diffusion in $BaZr_{0.85}M_{0.15}O_{2.925}$ (M = Y, In, and Ga). A key result is that only the microcrystalline samples showed a clear quasielastic signal related to proton motions. It was imagined that in the nanocrystalline samples, the protons are concerted mainly to the GB regions or to the surface of the crystallites. More recently, Wilmer et al. (2007) investigated the proton dynamics in $BaZr_{0.90}Y_{0.10}O_{2.95}$. Attempts to interpret the data in the framework of the two-state model yielded unconvincing results. A simpler approach using the isotropic Chudley–Elliott model yielded reasonable values for the proton self-diffusivities but also unusually large values for the jump distance which was found to be close to the mean distance between dopants of approximately 9 Å. Furthermore, Malikova et al. (2007) performed a simultaneous structural and dynamic study on $BaCe_{0.90}Y_{0.10}O_{2.95}$, by combining neutron diffraction with QENS. A key result was that the dehydration occurs over a large temperature range (from 500 to 800°C), providing evidence for the presence of proton sites with a variable degree of hydrogen bonding strengths to the perovskite lattice. Slodczyk et al. (2008) investigated proton dynamics in Yb-doped $BaZrO_3$, and they observed the onset of proton diffusion at a temperature of approximately 600°C, whilst Karlsson et al. (2010a) reported on a QENS study of $BaZr_{0.90}M_{0.10}O_{2.95}$ (M = Y and Sc). In the latter study, the authors revealed a localized proton motion on the ps time-scale and with a small activation energy of 10–30 meV, for both materials. Comparison of the QENS results to density functional theory calculations suggests that for both materials this motion may be ascribed to intra-octahedral proton transfers occurring close to a dopant atom. Braun et al. (2009) reported on the Y-doped material, $BaZr_{0.90}Y_{0.10}O_{2.95}$, and found two different activation energies for proton diffusion at different ranges of temperature. Colomban et al. (2010) reported on a change in local proton dynamics across a structural phase transition in $(Ba/Sr)Zr_{1-x}Ln_xO_{3-\delta}$, whilst Slodczyk et al. (2013) investigated proton dynamics in $SrZr_{0.90}Yb_{0.10}O_{2.95}$ and $BaZr_{0.90}Yb_{0.10}O_{2.95}$. Measurements taken in the temperature range from 400 to 700 °C showed on a peak in the mean square displacement of the protons at around 500°C, suggesting a maximum in proton diffusivity around this temperature. Most recently, Chen et al. (2013) measured simultaneously macroscopic proton conductivity and atomic-scale proton diffusivity in $BaCe_{0.8}Y_{0.2}O_{2.9}$, by means of an *in-situ* impedance spectroscopy cell in combination with the QENS measurements. A key result was that the QENS data could be interpreted in terms of inter-octahedral proton transfer.

Whereas all the above-mentioned work was done with the use of time-of-flight and backscattering methods, there are only three reports (Jalarvo et al., 2013b; Karlsson et al., 2010b,c) on the use of NSE spectroscopy for studies on proton conducting oxides, despite its unique benefits. The initial work was done by Karlsson et al. (2010b) on a hydrated sample of $BaZr_{0.90}Y_{0.10}O_{2.95}$.

A key result was that the protonic self-diffusion constant, measured over a length scale of 5–8 unit cell lengths, is comparable with that as extracted from conductivity experiments. This suggests that already on a length-scale as short as ≈ 20 Å, the effect of potential local traps or other "imperfections" in the structure that can be expected to affect the proton dynamics, has averaged out. That is, there are no features revealed on a larger length-scale that have not been experienced by the proton on the shorter length-scale probed by NSE.

More recently, Karlsson et al. (2010c) investigated the dopant concentration dependence of the local proton dynamics in $BaZr_{1-x}$ $In_xO_{3-x/2}$ (x = 0.10 and 0.50). Figure 5.9 shows the normalized intermediate scattering function, $I(Q, t)/I(Q, 0)$, for the two materials at 500 K and Q = 1.05 Å^{-1}. The relaxational decay with increasing Fourier time relates to dynamics of the protons. A key result is that the shape of the $I(Q, t)/I(Q, 0)$s differ significantly for the two materials. For x = 0.10, the $I(Q, t)/I(Q, 0)$ is reflected by a single exponential decay and a constant, $I(Q, t)/I(Q, 0) = [1 - c(Q)]e^{-t/\tau}(Q) + c(Q)$, where τ = 60 ps is interpreted as the characteristic relaxation time for a localized proton motion, whereas the plateau at long time-scales (c = 0.32) relates to the scattering from protons that are essentially immobile within the experimental NSE time-window. For x = 0.50, on the other hand, the $I(Q, t)/I(Q, 0)$ is stretched in time and fits much better to a Kohlrausch–Williams–Watts (KWW) stretched exponential function (Kolhrausch, 1854; Williams and Watts, 1990) $I(Q, t)/I(Q, 0) = e^{-[t/\tau_{KWW}(Q)]^{\beta(Q)}}$, where $\tau_{KWW}(Q) \approx 4$ ns is a characteristic time of a relaxational process and $\beta(Q) \approx 0.42$ is the, so-called, stretching parameter. The authors interpreted the stretched relaxational decay in terms of a large distribution of diffusional rates for the protons as due to many different local structural environments around the protons in the material. This is physically reasonable since the high concentration of In is known to induce strong short-range structural perturbations of the longer-range, average, cubic perovskite structure. The structural distortions become more and more pronounced with increasing dopant level and it has been suggested that they are related to tilting of the $(In/Zr)O_6$ octahedra due to the size difference between the In^{3+} and Zr^{4+} ions (Karlsson et al., 2008a). Further, it has been suggested that there is a compositional "threshold" between $x = 0.10$ and $x = 0.25$ above which the dopant induced structural distortions distribute throughout the entire perovskite structure, although with no long-range coherence in terms of the length-scales typically probed by diffraction (Karlsson et al., 2008a). Thus, the more well-defined time-scale of the proton motion observed for $x = 0.10$ is likely to result from the more ordered local structure of this material. Interestingly, the idea of a compositional "threshold" between $x = 0.10$ and $x = 0.25$ compares to a rise in conductivity from 2.9×10^{-5} S/cm for $x = 0.10$ to 2.6×10^{-4} S/cm for $x = 0.25$, which may indicate that some structural disorder is favorable for high proton conduction in perovskite type oxides (Karlsson et al., 2008a).

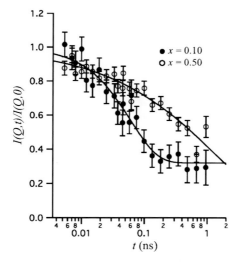

Figure 5.9 $I(Q, t)/I(Q, 0)$ of $BaZr_{1-x}In_xO_{3-x/2}$ ($x = 0.10$ and 0.50) at 500 K and $Q = 1.05$ Å^{-1}. The lines represent fits with a single exponential plus a constant ($x = 0.10$) and a KWW stretched exponential function ($x = 0.50$), respectively. Reprinted with permission from Karlsson et al. (2010c), copyright American Chemical Society, 2010.

5.4.2   Novel Structure Types

Clearly, ABO_3-type perovskites continue to be the materials that are accumulating the largest interest within the solid-state ionics community. However, there is a growing interest in alternative, more complicated, structure types and particularly in structure

(a)

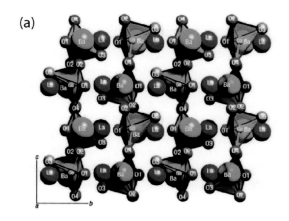

(b)

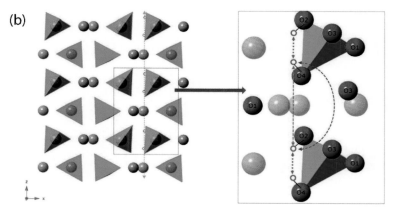

Figure 5.10 (a) Crystal structure of LaBaGaO$_4$, which is comprised of GaO$_4$ distorted tetrahedra and ordered alternating layers of lanthanum and barium ions. The GaO$_4$ tetrahedra are isolated from one another (with an elongated Ga–O3 bond). (b) Protons are represented as small grey-colored circles bound to particular corners of the GaO$_4$ tetrahedra. The proton migration takes place along the c axis, shown as a gray dashed arrow. The insert shows a slice parallel to the ac plane with the elementary steps: the intratetrahedron path is represented with gray arrows and two possibilities for intertetrahedra paths are represented with (i) blue and (ii) purple arrows. Reprinted with permission from Jalarvo et al. (2013b), copyright American Chemical Society, 2013, and from Kendrick et al. (2007), copyright Nature Publishing Group, 2007.

types containing tetrahedral moieties, such as lanthanum barium gallates, i.e., $LaBaGaO_4$-based compounds (Kendrick et al., 2007). The structure of $LaBaGaO_4$ consists of discrete GaO_4 tetrahedra, which are charge balanced by the Ba/La ions (Fig. 5.10a). Increasing the Ba:La ratio results in the formation of oxygen vacancies, $La_{1-x}Ba_{1+x}GaO_{4-x/2}$, and similarly to perovskite type oxides such oxygen vacancies can be filled with hydroxyl groups during a hydration reaction. The presence of oxygen vacancies leads to considerable relaxation of neighboring GaO_4 tetrahedra, resulting in the formation of Ga_2O_7 units so that the Ga retains tetrahedral coordination; however, the hydration can lead to the breaking up of such units.

Recently, Jalarvo et al. (2013a,b) investigated atomic-scale dynamics of protons in a hydrated sample of $La_{0.8}Ba_{1.2}GaO_{3.9}$, using neutron backscattering and NSE spectroscopy. The backscattering spectra were fitted to two Lorentzian components: one narrow and one broader one, representing proton dynamics on different time-scales. The analysis of the narrow component showed that it can be related to continuous proton diffusion with an activation energy of 0.44 eV. This activation energy is somewhat smaller than that extracted from conductivity experiments (0.56 eV), but in perfect agreement with the activation energy for intratetrahedron proton jumps as determined by calculations that suggests this process to be rate-limiting for the longer-range proton diffusion (Jalarvo et al., 2013a). The analysis of the broader component shows that this is related to localized proton motions with an activation energy of 0.068 eV, which is similar to the calculated intertetrahedra proton transfer value. On the basis of these results, it was suggested that the proton conduction occurs as a series of intratetrahedron proton jumps between the O2 and O4 sites, and intertetrahedron proton jumps from O4 to O2 (cf. Fig. 5.10b). The intertetrahedron proton jumps are suggested to take place either directly along the *c* axis, or via the O3 site of a neighboring GaO4 tetrahedron, whereas the overall long-range proton transport takes place along the *c* axis. The proton conduction mechanism is thus so-called *Grotthuss*-like, which means that the protons diffuse stepwise throughout the structure of the material. Between each proton jump, the proton is covalently bound to an oxygen and performs O–H stretch and wag vibrational motions, superimposed of the vibrational dynamics of the oxygen lattice. These motions induce fluctuations in the distance between the proton and a neighboring oxygen to which the proton may jump, thus creating transient hydrogen bonds that affect strongly the probability for proton transfer.

5.5 Critical Remarks and Outlook

It has been shown that the majority of QENS studies have been performed on classic proton conducting perovskites, in particular on materials based on $BaZrO_3$ and $BaCeO_3$, whereas only a few studies have been performed on other structure types. Although, clearly, these studies have provided important information about the dynamical behavior of protons in oxides, several of them have suffered from either a weak scattering signal or from the limited (Q, ω) range as accessed with the variety of instruments that have been used. As a consequence, it has often been difficult or impossible to find models that reliably describe the data and therefore to draw any firm conclusions on what type of motions that were observed. Furthermore, there are, in some cases, disagreements between the results obtained in different studies, even when the same material was investigated. However, in view of the different types of instruments and instrumental settings that have been used, some reproducibility problems may be expected. In addition, the structural and physiochemical details of the investigated samples, as partly related to the details of the sample preparation, are of important concern.[5] In this context, the studies by Groß et al. (2001) and Beck et al. (2001) already highlighted the importance of particle size, hence synthesis route, on the atomic-scale proton diffusion in $BaZr_{0.85}M_{0.15}O_{2.925}$ ($M = Y$, In, and Ga) proton conductors, but many more factors may be at play. Therefore, there is a need to perform systematic investigations, using the same experimental conditions and on well-characterized samples, in order to be able to make good comparisons between different measurements. Such studies should include systematic investigations of the effect of type and concentration of dopant atoms, crystal structure, and level of hydration, on the atomic-scale proton dynamics, for example.

---

[5]This also accounts for the spread in proton conductivities for the same type of systems, as reported in the literature, Kreuer (2003).

Although this chapter has highlighted the advantages of neutron scattering for research on proton conducting oxides, as with all techniques, QENS has its disadvantages. The primary drawback of QENS is that neutron scattering is an intensity-limited technique. In studies of proton conducting oxides, typically at least 10 grams of the sample is needed to obtain data of sufficient quality. These are very large samples for most other analytical techniques and obtaining a sufficient quantity can be problematic, particularly for new, complex, materials that may only be available in much smaller quantities. On the positive side, the large sample size does mean that concerns about representative sampling are much less severe than for techniques that operate on the milligram or smaller scale. Moreover, measuring times are at least a few hours per instrumental setting, thus kinetic measurements by QENS are generally not feasible. Any instrumental improvements with respect to advances in neutron flux and detector coverage, allowing faster acquisition times and smaller samples, in the form of single crystals or even thin films, to be investigated, are therefore highly welcome. For the future application of proton conducting oxides as fuel-cell electrolytes, one would indeed use a (thin) film of the proton conductor sandwiched between the anode and cathode materials. Other than in powder samples, such films can be highly textured and strained, which may affect significantly the proton conducting properties. Addressing diffusive processes in oxide films is however a lot more challenging than in bulk powder samples due to the heavily reduced sample volume. However, with the vision of the ESS, which, in comparison to present-day neutron sources, will offer considerably higher neutron flux, such experiments might become possible on a routine basis. Increasing the neutron flux may further open up for studies using polarization analysis, for the separation of coherent and incoherent scattering. Such analysis would not only distinguish between collective and self-dynamics but may also give information about proton-proton interactions, for example. Similar information may be obtained by the use of nuclear polarization methods, which offer exciting opportunity to tune continuously the spin-dependent scattering cross section of hydrogen nuclei and thereby the contrast between coherent and incoherent scattering (Piegsa et al., 2013). Furthermore, there is a clear trend towards the developments of *in-situ* sample environments, which allow for at least one additional materials property to be measured simultaneously with the collection of the QENS spectra. In this way the inherent uncertainty that comes from correlating separate measurements can be avoided, or allow for measurements which today are not even feasible separately. We have already noted the recent study by Chen et al. (2013), who combined QENS with impedance spectroscopy, thus allowing for the direct correlation between proton dynamics on significantly different time- and length-scales. Future work in this direction is likely to expand and will include the development and subsequent use of *in-situ* electrochemical cells, which allow for measurements under conditions that mimic fuel cell operating conditions.

5.6   Conclusions

To conclude, QENS is an important technique in the field of proton conducting oxides and has already contributed greatly to the understanding of proton dynamics in these materials, nevertheless the technique shows great potential for advancing further this understanding. Future work in this area is likely to comprise systematic investigations of well-characterized samples of both classic proton conducting perovskites as well as of new compounds and will take great advantage of the upgrade of existing neutron spectrometers and from the development of new instrumentation along with the construction of next-generation neutron sources. A better understanding of the mechanism of proton conduction in a wider family of oxide proton conductors is seen as crucial for the development of strategies for developing new materials with higher proton conductivity. This is in turn critical to future breakthroughs in the development of next-generation devices based on proton conducting oxides, such as intermediate-temperature fuel cells, hydrogen sensors, or other electrochemical devices. Even small or gradual advancements of the current understanding of proton conduction mechanisms in oxides may therefore be of considerable environmental and economic impact.

Acknowledgments

Financial support from the Swedish Research Council (grant No. 2010-3519 and 2011-4887) is gratefully acknowledged. Finally, many thanks to Antonio Faraone at the NIST Centre for Neutron Research for time and discussions and for valuable comments on the writing of this chapter.

References

Beck, C., Janssen, S., Gross, B., and Hempelmann, R. (2001). *Scripta Mater.*, **44**, 2309–2313.

Bée, M. (1988). *Quasielastic Neutron Scattering* (IOP Publishing, Bristol, D.J. Millen ed.).

Birr, M., Heidemann, A., and Alefeld, B. (1971). *Nucl. Instr. Meth.*, **95**, 435.

Braun, A., Duval, S., Ried, P., Embs, J., Juranyi, F., Strässle, T., Stimming, U., Hempelmann, R., Holtappels, P., and Graule, T. (2009). *J. Appl. Electrochem.*, **39**, 262103.

Chen, C. T., Danel, C. E., and Kim, S. (2011). *J. Mater. Chem.*, **21**, 5435.

Chen, Q., Banyte, J., Zhang, X., Embs, J. P., and Braun, A. (2013). *Solid State Ion.*, **252**, 2–6.

Chudley, C. T., and Elliott, R. J. (1961). *Proc. Phys. Soc. (London).*, **77**, 353.

Colomban, P., Slodczyk, A., Lamago, D., Andre, G., Zaafrani, O., Lacroix, O., Willemin, S., and Sala, B. (2010). *J. Phys. Soc. Jpn.*, **79**, 1.

Cook, J. C., Petry, W., Heidemann, A., and Barthelemy, J.-F. (1992). *Nucl. Instrum. Methods Phys. Res., A*, **312**, 553.

Farago, B. (2002). The basics of neutron spin-echo, in: *Neutron Data Booklet*, Chapter 2.8 (Institut Laue-Langevin, Grenoble, France).

Gelling, P. J., and Bouwmeester, H. J. M. (1992). *Catal. Today.*, **12**, 1–105.

Groß, B., Beck, C., Meyer, F., Krajewski, T., Hempelmann, R., and Altgeld, H. (2001). *Solid State Ion.*, **145**, 325–331.

Hall, P., and Ross, D. K. (1981). *Mol. Phys.*, **42**, 673.

Hempelmann, R. (2000). *Quasielastic Neutron Scattering and Solid State Diffusion (Clarendon Press, Oxford).*

Hempelmann, R., Karmonik, C., Matzke, T., Cappadonia, M., Stimming, U., Springer, T., and Adams, M. A. (1995). *Solid State Ion.*, **77**, 152–156.

Hempelmann, R., Soetratmo, M., Hartmann, O., and Wäppling, R. (1998). *Solid State Ion.*, **107**, 269–280.

Jalarvo, N., Gourdon, O., Bi, Z., Gout, D., Ohl, M., and Paranthaman, M. P. (2013a). *Chem. Mater.*, **25**, 2741.

Jalarvo, N., Stingaciu, L., Gout, D., Bi, Z., Paranthaman, M. P., and Ohl, M. (2013b). *Solid State Ion.*, **252**, 12.

Jobic, H., and Theodorou, D. N. (2007). *Micropor. Mesopor. Mater.*, **102**, 21.

Karlsson, M. (2013). *Dalton Trans.*, **42**(2), 317–329.

Karlsson, M. (2015). *Phys. Chem. Chem. Phys.*, **17**, 26–38.

Karlsson, M., Ahmed, I., Matic, A., and Eriksson, S. (2010a). *Solid State Ion.*, **181**, 126.

Karlsson, M., Björketun, M. E., Sundell, P. G., Matic, A., Wahnström, G., Engberg, D., Börjesson, L., Ahmed, I., Eriksson, S. G., and Berastegui, P. (2005). *Phys. Rev. B.*, **72**, 094303-1–7.

Karlsson, M., Engberg, D., Björketun, M. E., Matic, A., Wahnström, G., Sundell, P. G., Berastegui, P., Ahmed, I., Falus, P., Farago, B., Börjesson, L., and Eriksson, S. (2010b). *Chem. Mater.*, **22**, 740–742.

Karlsson, M., Fouquet, P., Ahmed, I., and Maccarini, M. (2010c). *J. Phys. Chem. C.*, **114**, 3293.

Karlsson, M., Matic, A., Knee, C. S., Ahmed, I., Börjesson, L., and Eriksson, S. G. (2008a). *Chem. Mater.*, **20**, 3480–3486.

Karlsson, M., Matic, A., Parker, S. F., Ahmed, I., Börjesson, L., and Eriksson, S. G. (2008b). *Phys. Rev. B.*, **77**, 104302.

Karmonik, C., Hempelmann, R., Cook, J., and Güthoff, F. (1996). *Ionics*, **2**, 69.

Kendrick, E., Kendrick, J., Knight, K. S., Islam, M. S., and Slater, P. R. (2007). *Nat. Mater.*, **6**, 871–875.

Kolhrausch, R. (1854). *Annu. Phys.*, (Weinheim, Ger.) **1**, 179.

Kreuer, K. D. (1999). *Solid State Ion.*, **125**, 285–302.

Kreuer, K. D. (2003). *Annu. Rev. Mater. Res.*, **33**, 333–359.

Kreuer, K. D., Adams, S., Münch, W., Fuchs, A., Klock, U., and Maier, J. (2001). *Solid State Ion.*, **145**, 295–306.

Kreuer, K. D., Münch, W., Ise, M., He, T., Fuchs, A., Traub, U., and Maier, J. (1997). *Ber. Bunsenges. Phys. Chem.*, **101**, 1344.

Kreuer, K. D., Münch, W., Traub, U., and Maier, J. (1998). *Ber. Bunsenges. Phys. Chem.*, **102**, 552–559.

Kröger, F. A., and Vink, H. J. (1956). *Solid State Physics: Advances in Research and Applications* (Academic Press).

Liang, L., Rinaldi, R., and Schober, H. (2009). Neutron scattering instrumentation, in: *Neutron Applications in Earth, Energy and Environmental Sciences*, Chapter 3 (Springer Science + Business Media, Heidelberg, New York).

Malavasi, L., Fisher, C. A. J., and Islam, M. S. (2010). *Chem. Soc. Rev.*, **39**, 4370.

Malikova, N., Loong, C. K., Zanotti, J. M., and Fernandez-Alonso, F. (2007). *J. Phys. Chem. C.*, **111**, 6574–6580.

Matzke, T., Stimming, U., Karmonik, C., Soetramo, M., Hempelmann, R. and Güthoff, F. (1996). *Solid State Ion.*, **86–88**, 621–628.

Mezei, F. (1972). *Z. Phys.*, **255**, 146–160.

Mezei, F. (1980). *Neutron Spin Echo: Lecture Notes in Physics*, vol. 28 (Springer, Heidelberg).

Mezei, F., Pappas, C., and Gutberlet, T. (2003). *Neutron Spin Echo Spectroscopy: Basics, Trends and Applications, Lecture Notes in Physics*, vol. 601 (Springer Verlag, Berlin, Heidelberg, New York).

Münch, W., Seifert, G., Kreuer, K. D., and Maier, J. (1996). *Solid State Ion.*, **86–88**, 647–652.

Münch, W., Seifert, G., Kreuer, K. D., and Maier, J. (1997). *Solid State Ion.*, **97**, 39–44.

Piegsa, F. M., Karlsson, M., van den Brandt, B., Carlile, C. J., Forgan, E. M., Hautle, P., Konter, J. A., McIntyre, G. J., and Zimmer, O. (2013). *J. Appl. Cryst.*, **46**, 30–34.

Pionke, M., Mono, T., Schweika, W., Springer, T., and Schober, H. (1997). *Solid State Ion.*, **97**, 497–504.

Sears, V. F. (1992). *Neutron News,* **3**(3), 26–37.

Shimojo, F., Hoshino, K., and Okazaki, H. (1997). *J. Phys. Soc. Jpn.*, **66**, 8–10.

Shirpour, M., Merkle, R., Lin, C. T., and Maier, J. (2012). *Phys. Chem. Chem. Phys.*, **14**, 730.

Singwi, K., and Sjölander, A. (1960). *Phys. Rev.*, **120**, 1093.

Slodczyk, A., Colomban, P., Lamago, D., Limage, M.-H., Raomain, F., Willemin, S., and Sala, B. (2008). *Ionics*, **14**, 215–222.

Slodczyk, A., Colomban, P., Malikova, N., Zaafrani, O., Longeville, S., Zanotti, J.-M., Lacroix, O., and Sala, B. (2013). *Solid State Ion.*, **252**, 7–11.

Sosnowska, I. M. (1999). *Solid State Ion.*, **119**, 261–268.

Springer, T. (1972). *Quasielastic Neutron Scattering for the Investigation of Diffusive Motions in Solids and Liquids*, Springer Tracts in Modern Physics, v. 64 (Springer Verlag, Berlin, Heidelberg, New York).

Steele, B. C. H., and Heinzel, A. (2001). *Nature*, **414**, 345–352.

Williams, G., and Watts, D. C. (1970). *Trans. Faraday Soc.*, **66**, 80.

Wilmer, D., Seydel, T., and Kreuer, K. D. (2007). *Mater. Res. Soc. Proc.*, **972**, 15.

Yamazaki, Y., Blanc, F., Okuyama, Y., Buannic, L., Lucio-Vega, J. C., Grey, C. P., and Haile, S. M. (2013). *Nat. Mater.*, **12**, 647.

Chapter 6

In situ Powder Diffraction for the Study of Hydrogen Storage Materials: A General Introduction

Francesco Dolci and Emilio Napolitano

European Commission-DG Joint Research Centre,
Institute for Energy and Transport, Westerduinweg 3,
Petten, 1755 ZG, The Netherlands

francesco.dolci@ec.europa.eu

6.1 Introduction

It can be easily stated that the complexity of objects studied by materials science grew more and more as the discipline developed. As soon as a field moves from the comprehension of model systems and the underlying fundamental mechanisms, to systems closer to real life applications, complexity increases exponentially. When "objects"[1] operate under realistic conditions, different

---

[1]With the term "object," one can try to identify any association of materials used for a specific application, especially for commercial use. A battery, for instance, in its simplest constituents, is composed by anode, cathode and electrolyte, plus a casing and not simply by the materials involved in the redox reaction. "System or material" defines instead the chemical compounds used within the energy storage "object".

Structural Characterization Techniques: Advances and Applications in Clean Energy
Edited by Lorenzo Malavasi
Copyright © 2016 Pan Stanford Publishing Pte. Ltd.
ISBN 978-981-4669-34-4 (Hardcover), 978-981-4669-35-1 (eBook)
www.panstanford.com

challenges have to be faced by the experimental investigator who wants to have a picture as close as possible to reality. Finding non-destructive techniques able to probe the full system under working conditions, can be seen as one of the ultimate goals of modern materials science. Not always the complexity of the system allows for a complete characterization, and often each object has to be broken down in its constituents, each characterized under operative conditions. Diffraction is a non-destructive technique which can rely on a significant historic experience. Its use is widespread and virtually every laboratory working within the large boundaries of solid-state chemistry makes routinely use of diffraction [1–3]. In particular the use of powder diffraction techniques is commonly employed because obtaining single crystals of necessary size and quality is often difficult, especially when time constraints are strict. Also, powder diffraction is well suited to perform Bragg scattering analysis in non-ambient conditions (temperature, pressure, different gaseous atmospheres, electromagnetic fields, etc.) monitoring the structural/micro-structural variation of the technological materials under real operating conditions [49, 50].

In the past 50 years, diffraction and powder diffraction methods witnessed an ever-growing development. A major breakthrough in the use of powder diffraction techniques as a quantitative tool in materials sciences occurred in 1969 with the introduction of the so-called whole pattern fitting profile-structure refinement approach, or the Rietveld method. This method paved the way for quantitative structural and microstructural characterization also on multiphase polycrystalline samples. From this point onwards, the continuous increase of the experimental possibilities offered by neutron and synchrotron facilities and the simultaneous availability of more powerful computers and more efficient algorithms, allowed more and more complex experiments to be planned and carried out [4, 5]. The approach to an in situ diffraction experiment is basically the same of a standard diffraction experiment. Its two main requirements are the availability of an experimental set-up able to match the conditions needed, without compromising the quality of the recorded data, and the use of a detection system able to capture the modification of the sample as they occur. Energy storage systems, by their very nature, undergo significant changes as the energy storage reaction occurs. An energy storage material is releasing or storing energy when specific physical parameters are changed within the system. For instance, these parameters can be voltage, as in the case of batteries, or hydrogen-pressure and temperature, as in the case of hydrogen storage materials. During an in situ experiment, the control over these key parameters is of crucial importance. Monitoring an evolving energy storage system, and clearly defining the reaction pathway of a specific process, is the typical scope of an in situ diffraction experiment. Identifying the sequence of phases formed and consumed during the energy storage reaction, offers the opportunity to clearly recognize the key passages in the storage mechanism; it defines their relevance and possibly helps in finding solutions to specific problems. It is obvious that the dimensions of the field touched by the broad definition "energy storage materials" are vast. In the following, we will discuss only the class of materials used for solid-state hydrogen storage, and even among these, we will try to restrict our survey primarily to the group of materials labelled as "complex hydrides" [6, 7]. Nevertheless, many general considerations made for this material class are relevant for other energy storage materials as well. Phase transformations and redox reaction processes, for instance, are common, and they can be found in both battery and solid-state hydrogen storage materials [8]. The main difference between the two classes lies in the physical parameter used to control the reaction process and the occurrence of a redox reaction split between two different electrodes for batteries, whereas a single reaction environment is used for solid-state hydrogen storage materials. Sometimes, even the borders between hydrogen storage and battery materials are not strict, and metal hydrides can be used as electrodes in lithium and hydride batteries [9–12].

6.2   Hydrogen Storage Materials

Hydrogen can be considered as a promising energy carrier, due to its high gravimetric energy content. Its main drawback is a relatively low volumetric energy density. Solid-state hydrogen storage materials offer the opportunity to improve the volumetric density of the energy storage system at the expense of its gravimetric energy density. Historically, the development of hydrogen storage materials stems from the metallurgy field, being pure metals such as palladium, or alloys such as $LaNi_5$, or FeTi among the first and best studied examples of solid-state hydrogen storage materials [13–16]. Many of the materials of scientific and technological interest are synthesized in polycrystalline form. Powder diffraction is then the main candidate for reliable and non-destructive bulk analysis. The end of 1990s saw a general rise of interest for the hydrogen storage possibilities of the complex hydrides material class [7, 17]. Despite having a high hydrogen gravimetric content, the members of this materials class have thermodynamic properties which are often far away from those needed for practical applications. Among different proposals for improving the performance of the hydrogen storage system, the idea of mixing together a complex metal hydride and a standard metal hydride has been extensively explored. The mixture produced with this approach, can be called "reactive hydride composite" (RHC). The first RHCs had a hydrogenated state composed by only two phases [18–20]; however, with time, more phases have been added, improving the overall performance of the system but significantly increasing its complexity [21–23]. Often, not only the multi-phase mixture has to be characterized, but also the single components inside the hydrogen storage material have been poorly studied. A significant example in this respect can be taken from the borohydride family [24, 25]. Another important fact which has to be kept well in mind is that many hydrogen storage materials often contain a promoter phase (usually called "catalyst"). When the promoter is mixed with the system [17, 26, 27], it can significantly improve the performance of the material, in terms of both kinetics and reversibility. Almost always, the additive reacts with the other components of the system and it is modified during hydrogen cycling. The final state of the "catalyst" and the modifications it induces in the main component phases can be easily investigated with the help of diffraction.

For the interested reader, many reviews and books are available and can be consulted for obtaining more detailed information on the behaviour of a specific hydrogen storage material [7, 28–35]. An exhaustive overview of all the results obtained by analysing solid-state hydrogen storage materials, through the use powder diffraction or in situ powder diffraction, is outside the scope and the possibilities of this chapter. In the following, some general considerations, with a special focus on some practical aspects, will be made for in situ powder diffraction experiments. Only the class of solid-state hydrogen storage materials will be considered, and the RHC family, in particular, used as a reference. This should not be considered as an indication of the limited possibilities of in situ powder diffraction for the study of hydrogen storage materials.

For instance, in situ diffraction experiments have also been used for studying other hydrogen storage options such as MOFs or clathrates [36, 37].

6.3 The in situ Powder Diffraction Experiment

Choosing the right set of experiments is of fundamental importance for achieving a profitable and effective material characterization. Before aiming immediately at the description of the system under operative conditions, it is convenient to approach the experimental study in gradual steps. An activity such as bibliographic research should not be overlooked. Despite the relative novelty of many materials used for hydrogen storage, it is often possible to retrieve important historical traces about compounds which have not been considered for a long time. Two interesting examples are the class of borohydrides and amide materials. Before their "re-discovery" as hydrogen storage materials in the last decade [18, 38], a considerable amount of information on their properties was already present in past scientific literature [39–41]. Even if information obtained in this way should be critically assessed, bibliographic research can be a method for avoiding time-consuming characterizations. It is important to stress once again the complexity of many solid-state hydrogen storage materials. They can easily contain more than four main elements and are often mixed with additives ("catalysts"). When possible, before analysing directly the multi-phase system, the single component phases, if their behaviour is unknown, should be investigated. It could very well be possible that the decomposition products of one of the phases inside the fully hydrogenated mixture are not known. Therefore, designing a starting set of experiments aimed at elucidating the decomposition mechanism of only one of the components of the multiphase system becomes a necessity. Diffraction is easily the preferred choice for such a task. Such fundamental information makes any further analysis of the real, complex system, easier. Using a reliable set of data as a starting point can significantly speed up the analysis of an intricate reaction mechanism for a multi-component mixture. A reference is therefore given by the reaction mechanisms of the single components. By using diffraction, it is possible to build up a library of reactions, which can be compared with more complex systems. As a result, differences between the reaction pathways of single phases and multi-phase mixtures can be highlighted [42–46]. It is clear, for instance, that it will be really difficult to understand what is specific of a multi-component system [22], if we do not know how a subset of components behaves [47, 48]. Having an accurate thermodynamic assessment of a multi-element system might be impossible for a large temperature/pressure window. Nevertheless, probing specific areas is an acceptable challenge. In situ diffraction can follow the evolution of the system during its development from a mixture of reagents to a mixture of products. Through diffraction techniques, the experimentalist takes a "group snapshot" of all the different phases present inside the system in a given moment. For instance, known phases can be present, but in a different form from those adopted at room temperature and pressure [45], and new phases can be clearly indentified, often for the first time [48, 51–53]. This approach offers also the advantage of complementing and supplying data, which can be used for building up thermodynamic libraries by means of ab-initio modelling. In fact, density functional theory (DFT) modelling requires reliable crystal structure data for obtaining accurate results out of the calculations performed [54, 55]. X-ray powder diffraction and neutron powder diffraction are the two available options for every in situ diffraction experiment. These two techniques have specific advantages and inconveniences, as it will be discussed in the following sections.

6.3.1 Approach to a New Experiment

Before planning a new in situ diffraction experiment, it is important to have clear in mind what kind of information has to be obtained from the experiment itself. A single analysis can answer different questions, but the experimentalists need to have a clear idea of the information which will be extracted from the diffraction data. It might sound trivial and obvious, but a clear experimental project helps in every subsequent step. For instance, materials' synthesis can be approached in different ways according to the kind of experiment planned: X-rays or neutrons diffraction (for neutrons, the isotopic identity of the different elements is relevant), new phase identification (in this situation, the material should be crystalline and pure), elucidation of reaction pathways (pre-treatment conditions and the number of components should be carefully chosen), clarification of the role of a promoter (the amount of promoting phase present inside the mixture has to abundant enough in order to be visible), etc. Before starting with a detailed experimental plan, all the possible information available should be gathered, and the behaviour of the sample should be at least partially known. All information is important and helps in defining the experimental conditions and the necessary environment. Once the scope of the in situ investigation is defined, and its objectives are clear, it is possible to think about the best way to achieve them. For example, a phase identification problem necessitates the use of high-resolution diffraction, and the contamination of the diffraction pattern by scattering from the sample cell should be kept to a minimum. Ideally the diffraction experiment should take place using a cell which allows ample margins for temperature and pressure, and virtually gives no contribution to the diffraction pattern. In the end, the experimental constrains will eventually dictate the best possible compromise between the desired conditions and what is available. Having well clear in mind what the final objectives are, helps in defining what can easily be discarded and what is crucial for the success of the experiment. An excellent reference for having a detailed overview about cell design, is given by Gray and Webb [56]. Due to their very nature, in situ experiments can produce a considerable amount of data. These data have to be analysed and interpreted. It is therefore important to choose beforehand the level of detail and the amount of information which will have to be extracted from the recorded data. Quick visualization methods and automatic data logging can be employed for having a general and quick reference during execution of the experiment.

In the following, the three available options for powder diffraction experiments will be briefly described and their peculiarities with respect to solid-state hydrogen storage materials analysis outlined.

Laboratory X-rays offer the advantage of a relatively easier operability. In principle, any experienced user can buy an in situ system or build a new one. The possibility to avoid the typical time constraints linked to the use of large-scale facilities is a significant advantage, because it allows more time to tailor the system to the specific needs of the users, or to repeat a failed experiment. The main disadvantage of using a laboratory-scale machine for in situ powder diffraction experiments on hydrogen storage materials (and any other lightweight based system) is the relatively weak scattering power of elements with low atomic numbers. Hydrogen in particular, is basically invisible and its presence can only be inferred by lattice distortions; for instance, modified lattice parameters. Despite the intrinsic limitations of this option, laboratory X-rays can offer the chance to gather important information on the main reaction steps a hydrogen storage system undergoes during thermal treatment. Two possible examples can be found in the paper on sodium alanate decomposition by Gross et al. [57, 58] and the paper on mixed Li-Mg-N-H systems by Xiong et al. [59]. In both cases, the general reaction processes are outlined, and some important transformations are clearly evidenced.

Synchrotron powder diffraction Synchrotron facilities are the most powerful source of X-ray radiation available nowadays. The generated X-ray beam is extremely intense, the high brilliance achievable in a third synchrotron generation source is about 12 orders of magnitude higher than a laboratory one. This corresponds to better counting statistic (more intense peaks), leading to an improved signal to noise ratio. Moreover, the excellent vertical collimation (with a divergence of few mrad) gives the possibility to improve instrument resolution, obtaining a high-angular-resolution data collection. In this manner, problems due to peak overlap can be reduced. The high photon flux reaching the sample enables the use of small specimens and a drastic reduction in the data acquisition time. A caveat about the use of synchrotron radiation for the study of hydrogen storage materials is, however, necessary. As for the case of laboratory X-rays, the scattering power of the different atoms is directly proportional to their atomic number. A good example of the care with which X-ray powder diffraction data obtained from hydrogen storage materials should be treated is given by the high temperature polymorph of yttrium borohydride. Recently, two crystallographic models were published by Ravnsbæk et al. [60] and Frommen et al. [61]. While the first paper is based on an X-ray powder diffraction experiment, the second one is based on neutron diffraction data. Despite the similarity in the arrangement of yttrium and boron atoms, the structure model obtained with X-rays does not report the correct hydrogen atom arrangement, which is instead detected with the use of neutrons (see Fig. 6.1).

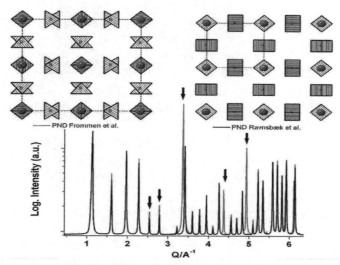

Figure 6.1   Simulated neutron powder diffraction patterns (PND) for the high temperature polymorph of Yttrium borohydride according to the structural models of Frommen et al. and Ravnsbæk et al. The structure on the left has a unit cell which is twice as big as the one for the structure on the right. $[BH_4]^{4-}$ tetrahedra and their orientations are clearly resolved with help of neutron diffraction. The model based on x-rays of Ravnsbæk et al. does not distinguish $[BH_4]^{4-}$ orientations and averages the positions of the tetrahedra over the vertices of a cube. PND is able to distinguish between the two models and give rise to the peaks highlighted by arrows. X-ray diffraction is not able to distinguish between the two models.

Neutron powder diffraction can be used profitably for the study of hydrogen storage materials. A fundamental specificity is linked to the neutron scattering phenomenon. Neutrons are scattered by their interaction with atomic nuclei, rather than with the electron density. This phenomenon gives the possibility to detect with more accuracy the presence of light atoms (e.g. H) also in presence of heavier ones [62]. Neutrons can easily discriminate between different isotopes. Due to this peculiarity, special attention should be paid to the isotopical composition of the sample. Certain isotopes such as ^{10}B should be avoided, if possible, due to their very high neutron absorption cross section, while others such as ^{1}H can give rise to a significant background, due to loss of coherent scattering. As mentioned above, scattering for neutrons is a nuclear process and happens with a lower probability than the scattering of an X-ray photon by an electron cloud. The lower neutron scattering probability has three main practical consequences:

- the use of a significantly larger amount of sample than the low quantity used for X-rays (synchrotron radiation in particular)
- much larger penetration power of the neutron beam than that of an X-ray beam
- relatively long collection times, which are usually larger than for X-rays

The deeper penetration depth of neutrons allows the use of denser materials such as steel for building up reaction cells, or the use of larger and more complex sample environment facilities around the sample cell, such as furnaces. On the other hand, sample handling operations can be made more complex and potentially dangerous by the formation of radioactive isotopes. Due to their special sensitivity to hydrogen atoms, neutrons can be considered the preferential choice when the material studied is a hydrogen storage material. The use of deuterated samples is the most common solution to the problems caused by the incoherent scattering cross section of hydrogen. This approach is not free from consequences. As evidenced by Weller et al. [63, 64], it is necessary to take into account that the picture obtained by using powder neutron diffraction is influenced by the isotopic enrichment of the sample. If a high neutron flux combined with a suitable instrumental resolution is available, even non-isotopically enriched samples can be successfully studied [63, 65]. The biggest challenge that in situ neutron diffraction experiments have to face is time resolution, since the relatively low penetration power of neutrons requires lager collection times. This is not an issue when diffraction is used for probing specific points along a pressure composition isotherm (PCI) [69]. It is, however, possible to obtain relevant kinetic information if the neutron flux is intense enough [37, 70–72].

6.3.2   Cell Design

The design and realization of a suitable cell, or reaction chamber for the in situ experiment is possibly the most difficult challenge which has to be overcome before the in situ experiment can take place. As stated before, every in situ sample cell is a compromise between what can be achieved within a series of specific constrains (e.g. time available, instrument used, safety, cost, ...), and what the experiment requires. A good cell design should be as much versatile as possible. Despite the necessity to tailor a certain design to a specific scope and instrument, it is always convenient, whenever possible, to build up the cell following a modular approach which can then be adapted to different situations with as little effort as possible. On the other hand, tailoring a cell to a specific instrument offers the best guarantee of obtaining more easily good results, but it limits the choice of available instruments. The mechanical strength of the cell should be calculated before its production begins [56, 66]. Water pressure testing it is usually employed for post-construction testing. It is also necessary to leak-test the rig attached to the sample cell. A helium (which has a density relatively close to hydrogen) pressure test can be profitably used for this purpose. The possibility of having automatic and remotely controlled valves can improve significantly the smooth execution of the experiment. If thermocouples are used to monitor the temperature of the cell these should be positioned as close as possible to the sample, without being illuminated by the beam. If they are inserted within the cell, their positioning should not compromise the overall mechanical stability. If the thermal expansion coefficient for the crystal lattice of the material used for the walls of the cell (or alternatively of an inert compound present inside the irradiated volume of the cell) is known, the shift of its diffraction peaks can be used as a reference for the sample temperature [51]. The peaks of the sample cell present in the collected diffraction pattern can be used as an internal intensity standard for monitoring phase evolution within the sample [46]. Another important aspect which should be considered is the practicality of cell and sample handling within a given experimental set-up. If a cell has been thoroughly developed for a single instrument, there should not be any major problem, since all the parameters are optimized for a specific configuration. On the contrary, if the cell can be used on many different instruments, all the different steps, from sample loading inside the cell, to cell placement within the beam and the final sample disposal, should be considered and planned. A careful design should be based on technical drawings; multiple options considered and possibly tried before the experiment takes place. Placing and centring the sample in the neutron beam usually requires a design for the in situ cell, which has to be as close as possible to the original configuration. Thermocouples and tubing should be carefully placed and machined keeping well in mind any possible obstacle (flanges, heat shields, etc.). Connections have to be hydrogen and temperature resistant. Permanent sealing of parts needed for accessing the sample must be avoided. Copper, for instance, should not be used for high temperatures.

Sample handling for air-sensitive compounds, such as solid-state hydrogen storage materials, is critical. Sample cells should allow sample loading and transport under a protective atmosphere (usually provided by a glove box). Keeping a potentially combustible or explosive material safe from any contaminant such as moisture and water is always necessary, even more so if the sample is radioactive. Vacuum pumps should be attached to the rig and provide a good level of vacuum for the whole rig. Excess hydrogen pressure must be vented safely and filters avoiding sample loss inside the rig are usually needed. Extra volumes for reducing high pressures are always necessary if pressures above 3 bar are used. A sufficient hydrogen (or deuterium) reservoir has to be available during the whole experiment, and safety requirements should be carefully checked. The volume of the cell has to be chosen in relation to the kind of test planned. Pressure should not vary significantly during a single experiment. When volumetric measurements are coupled with in situ diffraction experiments, adequate combinations of reservoir volumes and pressure transducers have to be chosen [56]. An appropriate reservoir volume of gas is therefore required.

Many different options for cell design are available in the literature. Following the distinctions used in the previous section, some general remarks on cell designs will be given for laboratory X-rays, synchrotron and neutron diffraction experiments. The interested reader is referred to specific literature [56]. Special emphasis will be put on original designs, rather than commercial ones.

Laboratory X-rays Two examples for cell designs used in conventional laboratory X-ray machines for the study of hydrogen storage materials are given by Gross et al. [57] and Mauron et al. [67]. Due to the widespread use of laboratory X-ray diffractometer manufactures, commercial solutions for performing in situ experiments are often available. The usual configuration adopted is the Bragg–Brentano geometry. This arrangement offers the advantage of being robust and avoids cumbersome alignment operations. An X-ray transparent window is necessary for keeping the experiment atmosphere confined. The usual choice is a beryllium window. Beryllium should be cooled and kept separated from any reactive atmosphere (such as hydrogen or gaseous products desorbed by the sample, e.g. boranes), in order to preserve its integrity. The possible reaction of the sample with the beryllium window, in case of direct contact of the two, must be avoided too.

Synchrotron radiation has been extensively used for the study of hydrogen storage materials [66]. The typical sample-holder cell used for in situ diffraction studies on hydrogen storage materials is a capillary made of quartz or sapphire, connected to a gas handling system, but other materials can be used as well [66, 68]. Coupling a monocrystalline sapphire tube with an area detector offers the significant advantage of having single diffraction spots on the 2D diffracted image. These spots can be masked during the experiment or at a later stage, during data analysis: The remaining pattern is composed only by diffraction from the sample. Particular care must be taken in tinkering with the system, due to the fragility of many capillary cells, and any possible cause of cracks should be carefully avoided. The particularly small volume of the cell should be taken into account if volumetric measurement are performed [56]. The routine use of resistance heaters or hot air blowers can also be problematic for an accurate temperature control.

Neutron Diffraction Due to the high penetrating power of neutrons, the possibilities offered by different materials can be used for cell construction: The materials used can range from low scattering alloys such as $Ti_{2.08}Zr$ or metals such as V, to strong scattering high strength alloys, such as Inconel. Scattering contribution from the cell, if null scattering materials are not used, can be minimized by using collimators [56]. It is also possible to use cells made of amorphous quartz or even single-crystal sapphire [73]. As in the case of X-rays, the cell has to be inert, and all possible reactions between the sample and the cell, or the cell and the atmosphere should be avoided. In the case of neutrons, activation of the cell materials has to be considered too. In the event of mechanical failure, the amount of sample lost is potentially much larger than for X-ray samples. In this case, it could be dispersed inside hot furnaces or other machinery controlling the sample environment. Samples containing group I or II elements can compromise the mechanical stability of quartz, and vanadium. $Ti_{2.08}Zr$ reacts easily with hydrogen, causing embrittlement. If these materials are used, a protective and inert layer has to be applied to the cell [74]. If a diffraction pattern from the cell is present, it has to be recorded, and special attention to possible overlapping areas between the pattern from the sample and the pattern from the cell carefully checked. A specific advantage of using cells with a bigger volume, is an enhancement in the precision of the gas absorption results obtained through the Sievert method [56]. The high penetration power of neutrons has also been exploited for coupling together in situ diffraction and gravimetric hydrogen measurements [75].

6.4 Examples of in situ Diffraction Experiments for Hydrogen Storage Materials Investigation

The amount of experimental work done on hydrogen storage materials by using in situ powder diffraction experiments is substantial, and a complete survey is beyond the scope of this chapter. We will present some examples where in situ diffraction provided important information on solid-state hydrogen storage materials. These examples can be used as a reference for other possible experiments, and they should be considered as specific cases of more general problems. An important advantage offered by in situ diffraction measurements is to complement data obtained from widespread techniques such as temperature programmed desorption and differential scanning calorimetry, or from volumetric (or gravimetric) techniques. The last case is more relevant for hydrogen storage materials, since pressure composition isotherms or kinetics curves are routinely used for sample analysis. Important details on the hydrogen absorption/desorption processes can be obtained for the above-mentioned techniques, but they lack any kind of sensitivity to the chemical composition of the sample. Ex situ measurements are often employed to characterize the materials after investigation, but it is not always possible to stop a reaction in a specific transient moment. The obtained materials can be formed by a reversible interaction with the gaseous atmosphere produced by sample decomposition, or decompose further from the point of interest. This is especially true when the point of interest lies between two reaction processes, and a considerable amount of precision is required. An example in this respect is given by the PCI traces of many reactive hydride mixtures. RHCs usually show complex reaction pathways, and they react with hydrogen following a two- or three-step mechanism. This has been clearly evidenced in different systems, with the help of in situ neutron diffraction [51, 76, 77]. For both Li-N-H and Li-Mg-N-H mixtures, intermediate steps have been identified. For the Li-N-H system, the appearance of a non-stoichiometric quasi-imide phase, together with a previously unreported Li_4NH phase, was detected under low equilibrium hydrogen pressures. By using in situ diffraction, the stability of these phases was obtained as a function of the applied hydrogen activity (pressure). Another example of intermediate reaction steps, clearly evidenced by the use of in situ diffraction, can be found for Li-Mg-N-H systems [69]. The PCI of the system, shown in Fig. 6.2, evidenced an intermediate step in the hydrogenation pathway. In situ neutron diffraction measurements could be used to associate the low hydrogen content region of the PCI curve to an incomplete hydrogenation step. Both for the Li-N-H system [78] and for the Li-Mg-N-H system [79], ex situ measurements revealed the occurrence of intermediate reaction steps. The advantage of in situ diffraction measurements is that they not only confirmed the previously proposed mechanisms but also allowed a more detailed characterization of the hydrogen absorption process. Moreover, the use of in situ neutron diffraction unambiguously showed the presence of high hydrogen content intermediate phases, such as Li_4NH and $Li_2Mg_2(NH)_3$, and allowed to obtain a structural model for previously unknown phases. Literature offers also other examples for similar in situ neutron diffraction probing of PCIs for conventional metal hydrides [80–84].

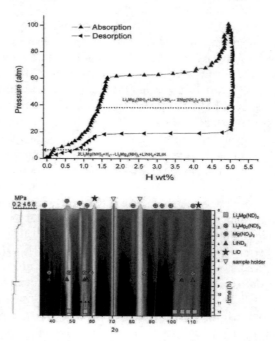

Figure 6.2   Upper part: PCI for the $Mg(NH_2)_2/2LiH$ hydrogen storage system obtained at 200°C. Lower part: in situ neutron powder diffraction data (wavelength 2.42 Å) for the same system kept at 200°C. The sample holder used was made of ASI-316L steel.

The possibility to resolve hydrogen (deuterium) positions within the phases present inside the storage mixture [82] makes this technique a useful tool for completely assessing the structure of a single-phase hydrogen storage material within a well-defined pressure and temperature range. Reversibility is often a major issue for many different solid-state hydrogen storage mixtures. The reaction pathway followed by the system during its first hydrogenation or dehydrogenation cycle can be incomplete and never be fully recovered during subsequent cycling. Knowing the evolution of the sample helps in clarifying the nature of the hydrogen-material interactions, and it detects the parameters responsible for a specific behaviour. For instance, the effect of stoichiometry and pressure on the performance of RHC based on borohydride/hydride mixtures has been extensively studied by different authors [53, 85–88]. The formation of unwanted products or intermediates can be held responsible for the unachieved total reversibility of the system. Representative is the case of the closo-dodecaborate phases, which have been identified as "dead-end intermediates" in all known borohydride based systems, such as $NaBH_4$ [89], $LiBH_4$ [90], $Mg(BH_4)_2$ [91] and $Ca(BH_4)_2$ [92]. The appearance of mixed hydrides phases such as $Ca_3Mg_4H_{14}$, observed during the desorption of $Ca(BH_4)_2/MgH_2$ [93], or the ternary hydride $NaMgH_3$, observed during hydrogenation of a desorbed $NaBH_4/MgH_2$ mixture [53], is also a typical example of unwanted reaction steps. Their occurrence is strongly related to the driving force (hydrogen pressure, stoichiometry and temperature) the systems are subjected to. These intermediate phases always occur in specific conditions under which the reaction is driven towards a different outcome from the one expected. For these systems, in situ diffraction gives the possibility to resolve the sequence of phases appearing during hydrogen absorption/desorption reactions. Unknown intermediates are clearly determined, and the appearance of amorphous or liquid components is evidenced by large and broad peaks [53]. By varying one of the main controlling parameters—pressure, stoichiometry and temperature—it is possible to have a direct image of the reaction pathway taken by the material [85, 88]. A good example is given by Price et al. [88]. By carrying out a thorough investigation on $LiBH_4/MgH_2$ mixtures, it has been possible to show how the effect of pressure impacts the products formed after dehydrogenation. In situ neutron and X-ray diffraction experiments evidenced the formation of Li-Mg alloys in the desorption products obtained at high temperature. Monitoring through diffraction the cooling process clearly evidenced a change in the phase composition of the sample, highlighting the effect of stoichiometry and the quality of the vacuum used. The pumping efficiency of the used vacuum pumps affected the final reaction products, favouring or preventing the formation of a passivating layer of LiH on magnesium particles. The real nature of the hydrogen desorption process within the system was revealed only by using in situ diffraction techniques. The ambiguities resulting from ex situ analysis of the system were thus explained and resolved. This example is especially interesting because it shows the impact that an analysis on a system under non-operative conditions might have on the interpretation of results.

Another important possibility offered by in situ diffraction is the capability to highlight structural differences between a component in an operative environment, and the same component under non-reacting conditions (the typical reference for hydrogen storage materials is given by the material kept at room temperature). For example, it is possible to consider the heat treatment of magnesium amide ($Mg(NH_2)_2$) [45], and the system MgH_2/Nb_2O_5, studied during hydrogenation [94].

Broadly speaking, magnesium amide can be considered as part of the class of complex metal hydrides [7], and it is a major component in different reversible hydrogen storage mixtures [95]. By following with in situ neutron diffraction the decomposition process of magnesium amide, it was possible to indentify significant, but reversible structural changes caused by the thermal treatment.

From the diffraction patterns shown in Fig. 6.3, it is immediately evident how the peaks of $Mg(NH_2)_2$ change in position and intensity. These changes can be modelled through the use of Rietveld method and are explained with a significant deformation in the magnesium and nitrogen arrangement, which move away from the positions they occupy at room temperature. When $Mg(NH_2)_2$ is mixed with LiH, forming a RHC hydrogen storage material, no significant hydrogen release is detected before 150°C, despite having an estimated thermodynamic equilibrium hydrogen pressure of around 1 bar at 90°C [96]. Transforming the desorbed single-phase compound ($Li_2Mg(NH)_2$) to the fully hydrogenated two-phase mixture ($Mg(NH_2)_2/2LiH$) likely involves cations diffusion and phase segregation. The presence of a kinetic barrier is to be expected. In situ diffraction evidenced how one of the two materials forming the hydrogenated RHC mixture modifies its structure before the hydrogen release reaction can occur. The use of in situ diffraction can also help in detecting the subtle changes a hydrogen storage material goes through. A system based on MgH_2 doped with Nb was studied by in situ neutron diffraction [94]. The occurrence of a non-stoichiometric magnesium hydride phase was evidenced by Rietveld refinement of the diffracted pattern. The use of deuterium allowed the neutron diffraction pattern to be sensitive to changes in the occupancy of the hydrogen sites inside different crystal structures. The occurrence of previously unreported mixed Mg-Nb-O phases was also detected and a structural model was produced. In this example, in situ powder diffraction showed with a high level of detail, how the real hydrogen storage system evolved during operative conditions. The role of a minor component ("catalyst"), such as Nb, was directly investigated, and the modifications it causes clearly linked to changes in the diffraction pattern. The importance of hydrogen diffusion within the system was suggested on the basis of the obtained results, and the role of the additive explained within this context.

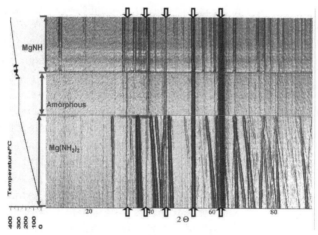

Figure 6.3 In situ neutron powder diffraction (wavelength 1.868 Å) for thermal treatment of $Mg(NH_2)_2$. The arrows highlight the positions of the peaks from an ASI-316L steel sample holder. Their presence can be easily identified in the section where only the amorphous component is present.

As a last example we refer to the most basic, but extremely useful, application of in situ diffraction: the possibility to screen the decomposition pathways of different combinations of reagents

[97, 98], or single compounds [45, 99, 100]. With this approach, the occurrence of delicate (such as easily decomposing intermediates), or transitory products (such as high temperature polymorphs), can be identified and characterized. The big advantage of in situ diffraction is the possibility to control sample atmosphere and monitor the effect different changes have on the reaction pathway: both the gaseous atmosphere inside the sample cell and the temperature of the sample can be directly modified by the experimentalist, until the appearance of a specific product phase occurs (see, for instance, the example shown in Fig. 6.3).

6.5 Conclusions

The complexity of solid-state hydrogen storage materials and their chemistry requires a significant experimental effort for characterizing their reactivity and behaviour. In situ powder diffraction is an extremely versatile technique, which can vary in purpose and approach: From basic and qualitative investigations to more refined analysis and high-resolution experiments. Planning is an essential part of the in situ investigation. Different goals require different approaches, and both cell design and the choice of the instrument used have to be considered according to the experimentalist's necessities. In particular, the different elemental-contrast possibilities offered by neutrons and X-rays should always be kept in mind. As a final word, it is necessary to point out the limits of in situ powder diffraction for the analysis of solid-state hydrogen storage materials. Despite being a powerful and versatile technique, it requires sufficient crystallinity for directly identifying reaction intermediates. This is even more true if structure determination is the main scope of the experiment. Amorphous or poorly resolved peaks can cause significant difficulties in interpreting unambiguously the outcome of a powder diffraction experiment, in particular when a complex multi-element system is under study. For this reason, in situ diffraction experiments on multi-element/multi-phase solid-state hydrogen storage materials should ideally always be complemented with other types of analysis, such as nuclear magnetic resonance, volumetric or gravimetric techniques, Raman and infrared spectroscopies, thermal desorption spectrometry, and differential scanning calorimetry. The changes which are not identified by use of powder diffraction methods can then be explained with the results obtained with techniques which are responsive to different transformations within the sample. Facing an in situ experiment with the help of ancillary information (from the amount and the identity of the desorbed gases, to the entity of the reaction heats) helps in unambiguously defying the reaction mechanism under study, and it reduces the risks associated with the approximations and the assumptions often made in this context.

References

1. Giacovazzo, C., Monaco, H. L., Artioli, G., Viterbo, D., Milanesio, M., Gilli, G., Gilli, P., Zanotti, G., Ferraris, G. (2011). *Fundamentals of Crystallography* (Oxford University Press).

2. Dinnebier, R. E., Billinge, S. J. L. editors (2008). *Powder Diffraction: Theory and Practice* (RCS publishing).

3. Kisi, E. H., and Howard, C. J. (2008). *Applications of Neutron Powder Diffraction*, Oxford Series on Neutron Scattering in Condensed Matter (Oxford University Press).

4. Young, R. A. editor (1995). *The Rietveld Method*, International Union of Crystallography Monographs on Crystallography (Oxford University Press).

5. David, W. I. F., Shankland, K., McCusker, L. B., Bärlocher, C. editors (2006). *Structure Determination from Powder Diffraction Data*, International Union of Crystallography Monographs on Crystallography (Oxford University Press).

6. Yvon, K., and Renaudin, G. (2006). Hydrides: Solid State Transition Metal Complexes, *Encyclopedia of Inorganic Chemistry*.

7. Orimo, S.-i., Nakamori, Y., Eliseo, J. R., Züttel, A., and Jensen, C. M. (2007). Complex hydrides for hydrogen storage, *Chem. Rev.*, **107**, 4111–4132.

8. Fichtner, M. (2011). Conversion materials for hydrogen storage and electrochemical applications—Concepts and similarities, *J. Alloys Compounds*, **509**, Supplement 2, S529–S534.

9. Kleperis, J., Wójcik, G., Czerwinski, A., Skowronski, J., Kopczyk, M., and Beltowska-Brzezinska, M. (2001). Electrochemical behavior of metal hydrides, *J. Solid State Electrochem.*, **5**, 229–249.

10. Latroche, M., Chabre, Y., Decamps, B., Percheron-Guégan, A., and Noreus, D. (2002). In situ neutron diffraction study of the kinetics of metallic hydride electrodes, *J. Alloys Compounds*, **334**, 267–276.

11. Ying, T. K., Gao, X. P., Hu, W. K., Wu, F., and Noréus, D. (2006). Studies on rechargeable NiMH batteries, *Int. J. Hydrogen Energy*, **31**, 525–530.

12. Oumellal, Y., Rougier, A., Nazri, G. A., Tarascon, J. M., and Aymard, L. (2008). Metal hydrides for lithium-ion batteries, *Nat. Mater.*, **7**, 916–921.

13. Alefeld, G., Völkl, J. editors (1978). *Hydrogen in Metals I: Basic Properties*, Topics in Applied Physics (Springer).

14. Alefeld, G., Völkl, J. editors (1978). *Hydrogen in Metals II: Application-Oriented Properties*, Topics in Applied Physics (Springer).

15. Schlapbach, L. editor (1988). *Hydrogen in Intermetallic Compounds I: Electronic, Thermodynamic, and Crystallographic Properties, Preparation*, Topics in Applied Physics (Springer).

16. Schlapbach, L. editor (1992). *Hydrogen in Intermetallic Compounds II-Surface and Dynamic Properties, Applications*, Topics in Applied Physics (Springer).

17. Bogdanović, B., and Schwickardi, M. (1997). Ti-doped alkali metal aluminium hydrides as potential novel reversible hydrogen storage materials, *J. Alloys Compounds*, **253–254**, 1–9.

18. Chen, P., Xiong, Z., Luo, J., Lin, J., and Tan, K. L. (2002). Interaction of hydrogen with metal nitrides and imides, *Nature*, **420**, 302–304.

19. Vajo, J. J., Skeith, S. L., and Mertens, F. (2005). Reversible storage of hydrogen in destabilized LiBH$_4$, *J. Phys. Chem. B*, **109**, 3719–3722.

20. Barkhordarian, G., Klassen, T., Dornheim, M., and Bormann, R. (2007). Unexpected kinetic effect of MgB$_2$ in reactive hydride composites containing complex borohydrides, *J. Alloys Compounds*, **440**, L18–L21.

21. Hu, J., Liu, Y., Wu, G., Xiong, Z., Chua, Y. S., and Chen, P. (2008). Improvement of hydrogen storage properties of the Li–Mg–N–H system by addition of LiBH$_4$, *Chem. Mater.*, **20**, 4398–4402.

22. Yang, J., Sudik, A., Siegel, D. J., Halliday, D., Drews, A., Carter, R. O., Wolverton, C., Lewis, G. J., Sachtler, J. W. A., Low, J. J., Faheem, S. A., Lesch, D. A., and Ozoliņš, V. (2008). A self-catalyzing hydrogen-storage material, *Angew. Chem. Int. Ed.*, **47**, 882–887.

23. Wang, J., Liu, T., Wu, G., Li, W., Liu, Y., Araújo, C. M., Scheicher, R. H., Blomqvist, A., Ahuja, R., Xiong, Z., Yang, P., Gao, M., Pan, H., and Chen,

P. (2009). Potassium-modified $Mg(NH_2)_2/2LiH$ system for hydrogen storage, *Angew. Chem. Int. Ed.,* **48**, 5828–5832.

24. Filinchuk, Y., Chernyshov, D., and Dmitriev, V. (2008). Light metal borohydrides: Crystal structures and beyond, *Zeitschrift für Kristallographie Crystal. Mater.,* **223**, 649–659.

25. Dmitriev, V., Filinchuk, Y., Chernyshov, D., Talyzin, A. V., Dzwilewski, A., Andersson, O., Sundqvist, B., and Kurnosov, A. (2008). Pressure-temperature phase diagram of $LiBH_{\{4\}}$: Synchrotron x-ray diffraction experiments and theoretical analysis, *Phys. Rev. B,* **77**, 174112.

26. Barkhordarian, G., Klassen, T., and Bormann, R. (2003). Fast hydrogen sorption kinetics of nanocrystalline Mg using Nb_2O_5 as catalyst, *Scripta Mater.,* **49**, 213–217.

27. Castro, J. F. R. de, Yavari, A. R., LeMoulec, A., Ishikawa, T. T., and Botta F, W. J. (2005). Improving H-sorption in MgH_2 powders by addition of nanoparticles of transition metal fluoride catalysts and mechanical alloying, *J. Alloys Compounds,* **389**, 270–274.

28. Grochala, W., and Edwards, P. P. (2004). Thermal decomposition of the non-interstitial hydrides for the storage and production of hydrogen, *Chem. Rev.,* **104**, 1283–1316.

29. Walker, G. editor (2008). *Solid-State Hydrogen Storage: Materials and Chemistry*, Woodhead Publishing Series in Electronic and Optical Materials No. 14 (Woodhead Publishing Limited).

30. Léon, A. editor (2008). *Hydrogen Technology-Mobile and Portable Applications*, Green Energy and Technology (Springer).

31. Hirscher, M. editor (2010). Front Matter, *Handbook of Hydrogen Storage,* pp. I-XX.

32. Eberle, U., Felderhoff, M., and Schüth, F. (2009). Chemical and physical solutions for hydrogen storage, *Angew. Chem. Int. Ed.,* **48**, 6608–6630.

33. Yang, J., Sudik, A., Wolverton, C., and Siegel, D. J. (2010). High capacity hydrogen storage materials: Attributes for automotive applications and techniques for materials discovery, *Chem. Soc. Rev.,* **39**, 656–675.

34. Broom, D. P. (2011). *Hydrogen Storage Materials: The Characterisation of Their Storage Properties*, Green Energy and Technology (Springer).

35. Reardon, H., Hanlon, J. M., Hughes, R. W., Godula-Jopek, A., Mandal, T. K., and Gregory, D. H. (2012). Emerging concepts in solid-state hydrogen storage: The role of nanomaterials design, *Energy Environ. Sci.,* **5**, 5951–5979.

36. Yan, Y., Telepeni, I., Yang, S., Lin, X., Kockelmann, W., Dailly, A., Blake, A. J., Lewis, W., Walker, G. S., Allan, D. R., Barnett, S. A., Champness,

N. R., and Schröder, M. (2010). Metal–organic polyhedral frameworks: High H_2 adsorption capacities and neutron powder diffraction studies, *J. Am. Chem. Soc.,* **132**, 4092–4094.

37. Zhao, Y., Xu, H., Daemen, L. L., Lokshin, K., Tait, K. T., Mao, W. L., Luo, J., Currier, R. P., and Hickmott, D. D. (2007). High-pressure/low-temperature neutron scattering of gas inclusion compounds: Progress and prospects, *Proc. Natl. Acad. Sci.,* **104**, 5727–5731.

38. Chlopek, K., Frommen, C., Leon, A., Zabara, O., and Fichtner, M. (2007). Synthesis and properties of magnesium tetrahydroborate, $Mg(BH_4)_2$, *J. Mater. Chem.,* **17**, 3496–3503.

39. Dafert, F. W., and Miklauz, R. (1910). Uber einige neue verbindungen von stickstoff und wasserstoff mit lithium, *Monatsch. Chem.,* **31**, 981–996.

40. Juza, R. (1964). Amides of the alkali and the alkaline earth metals, *Angew. Chem. Int. Ed. English,* **3**, 471–481.

41. Soloveichik, G. L., Gao, Y., Rijssenbeek, J., Andrus, M., Kniajanski, S., Bowman Jr, R. C., Hwang, S.-J., and Zhao, J.-C. (2009). Magnesium borohydride as a hydrogen storage material: Properties and dehydrogenation pathway of unsolvated $Mg(BH_4)_2$, *Int. J. Hydrogen Energy,* **34**, 916–928.

42. Balogh, M. P., Jones, C. Y., Herbst, J. F., Hector Jr, L. G., and Kundrat, M. (2006). Crystal structures and phase transformation of deuterated lithium imide, Li_2ND, *J. Alloys Compounds,* **420**, 326–336.

43. Riktor, M. D., Sorby, M. H., Chlopek, K., Fichtner, M., Buchter, F., Zuttel, A., and Hauback, B. C. (2007). In situ synchrotron diffraction studies of phase transitions and thermal decomposition of $Mg(BH_4)_2$ and $Ca(BH_4)_2$, *J. Mater. Chem.,* **17**, 4939–4942.

44. Maehlen, J. P., Yartys, V. A., Denys, R. V., Fichtner, M., Frommen, C., Bulychev, B. M., Pattison, P., Emerich, H., Filinchuk, Y. E., and Chernyshov, D. (2007). Thermal decomposition of AlH_3 studied by in situ synchrotron X-ray diffraction and thermal desorption spectroscopy, *J. Alloys Compounds,* **446–447**, 280–289.

45. Dolci, F., Napolitano, E., Weidner, E., Enzo, S., Moretto, P., Brunelli, M., Hansen, T., Fichtner, M., and Lohstroh, W. (2010). Magnesium imide: Synthesis and structure determination of an unconventional alkaline earth imide from decomposition of magnesium amide, *Inorg. Chem.,* **50**, 1116–1122.

46. Paskevicius, M., Pitt, M. P., Webb, C. J., Sheppard, D. A., Filsø, U., Gray, E. M., and Buckley, C. E. (2012). In-situ X-ray diffraction study of γ-$Mg(BH_4)_2$ decomposition, *J. Phys. Chem. C,* **116**, 15231–15240.

47. Meisner, G. P., Scullin, M. L., Balogh, M. P., Pinkerton, F. E., and Meyer, M. S. (2006). Hydrogen release from mixtures of lithium borohydride and lithium amide: A phase diagram study, *J. Phys. Chem. B*, **110**, 4186–4192.

48. Rijssenbeek, J., Gao, Y., Hanson, J., Huang, Q., Jones, C., and Toby, B. (2008). Crystal structure determination and reaction pathway of amide–hydride mixtures, *J. Alloys Compounds*, **454**, 233–244.

49. Schlögl, R. (2009). Chapter 5 x-ray diffraction: A basic tool for characterization of solid catalysts in the working state, *Adv. Catal.*, **52**, 273–338.

50. Kandemir, T., Wallacher, D., Hansen, T., Liss, K.-D., Naumann d'Alnoncourt, R., Schlögl, R., and Behrens, M. (2012). In situ neutron diffraction under high pressure—Providing an insight into working catalysts, *Nucl. Instrum. Methods Phys. Res. Section A*, **673**, 51–55.

51. Weidner, E., Dolci, F., Hu, J., Lohstroh, W., Hansen, T., Bull, D. J., and Fichtner, M. (2009). Hydrogenation reaction pathway in $Li_2Mg(NH)_2$, *J. Phys. Chem. C*, **113**, 15772–15777.

52. Riktor, M. D., Sorby, M. H., Chlopek, K., Fichtner, M., and Hauback, B. C. (2009). The identification of a hitherto unknown intermediate phase CaB_2H_x from decomposition of $Ca(BH_4)_2$, *J. Mater. Chem.*, **19**, 2754–2759.

53. Pistidda, C., Garroni, S., Minella, C. B., Dolci, F., Jensen, T. R., Nolis, P., Bösenberg, U., Cerenius, Y., Lohstroh, W., Fichtner, M., Baró, M. D., Bormann, R. de, and Dornheim, M. (2010). Pressure effect on the $2NaH + MgB_2$ hydrogen absorption reaction, *J. Phys. Chem. C*, **114**, 21816–21823.

54. Kim, K. C., Kulkarni, A. D., Johnson, J. K., and Sholl, D. S. (2011). Examining the robustness of first-principles calculations for metal hydride reaction thermodynamics by detection of metastable reaction pathways, *Phys. Chem. Chem. Phys.*, **13**, 21520–21529.

55. Kim, K. C., Allendorf, M. D., Stavila, V., and Sholl, D. S. (2010). Predicting impurity gases and phases during hydrogen evolution from complex metal hydrides using free energy minimization enabled by first-principles calculations, *Phys. Chem. Chem. Phys.*, **12**, 9918–9926.

56. Gray, E. M., and Webb, C. J. (2012). In-situ diffraction techniques for studying hydrogen storage materials under high hydrogen pressure, *Int. J. Hydrogen Energy*, **37**, 10182–10195.

57. Gross, K. J., Guthrie, S., Takara, S., and Thomas, G. (2000). In-situ X-ray diffraction study of the decomposition of $NaAlH_4$, *J. Alloys Compounds*, **297**, 270–281.

58. Gross, K. J., Sandrock, G., and Thomas, G. J. (2002). Dynamic in situ X-ray diffraction of catalyzed alanates, *J. Alloys Compounds*, **330–332**, 691–695.

59. Xiong, Z. T., Wu, G. T., Hu, J. J., and Chen, P. (2006).Investigations on hydrogen storage over Li–Mg–N–H complex—the effect of compositional changes, *J. Alloys Compounds*, **417**, 190–194.

60. Ravnsbæk, D. B., Filinchuk, Y., Černý, R., Ley, M. B., Haase, D. R., Jakobsen, H. J., Skibsted, J. R., and Jensen, T. R. (2010). Thermal polymorphism and decomposition of Y(BH₄)₃, *Inorg. Chem.*, **49**, 3801–3809.

61. Frommen, C., Aliouane, N., Deledda, S., Fonneløp, J. E., Grove, H., Lieutenant, K., Llamas-Jansa, I., Sartori, S., Sørby, M. H., and Hauback, B. C. (2010). Crystal structure, polymorphism, and thermal properties of yttrium borohydride Y(BH₄)₃, *J. Alloys Compounds*, **496**, 710–716.

62. https://www.ncnr.nist.gov/resources/n-lengths/ (**2012**), pp.

63. Ting, V. P., Henry, P. F., Kohlmann, H., Wilson, C. C., and Weller, M. T. (2010). Structural isotope effects in metal hydrides and deuterides, *Phys. Chem. Chem. Phys.*, **12**, 2083–2088.

64. Weller, M. T., Henry, P. F., Ting, V. P., and Wilson, C. C. (2009). Crystallography of hydrogen-containing compounds: Realizing the potential of neutron powder diffraction, *Chem. Commun.*, **7**, 2973–2989.

65. Chater, P. A., David, W. I. F., Johnson, S. R., Edwards, P. P., and Anderson, P. A. (2006). Synthesis and crystal structure of Li₄BH₄(NH₂)₃, *Chem. Commun.*, **0**, 2439–2441.

66. Jensen, T. R., Nielsen, T. K., Filinchuk, Y., Jorgensen, J.-E., Cerenius, Y., Gray, E. M., and Webb, C. J. (2010). Versatile in situ powder X-ray diffraction cells for solid-gas investigations, *J. Appl. Crystallogr.*, **43**, 1456–1463.

67. Mauron, P., Bielmann, M., Remhof, A., and Zuttel, A. (2011). High-pressure and high-temperature x-ray diffraction cell for combined pressure, composition, and temperature measurements of hydrides, *Rev. Sci. Instrum.*, **82**, 065108–065107.

68. Moorhouse, S. J., Vranjes, N., Jupe, A., Drakopoulos, M., and O'Hare, D. (2012). The Oxford-Diamond in situ cell for studying chemical reactions using time-resolved X-ray diffraction, *Rev. Sci. Instrum.*, **83**, 084101.

69. Dolci, F., Weidner, E., Hoelzel, M., Hansen, T., Moretto, P., Pistidda, C., Brunelli, M., Fichtner, M., and Lohstroh, W. (2010). In-situ

neutron diffraction study of magnesium amide/lithium hydride stoichiometric mixtures with lithium hydride excess, *Int. J. Hydrogen Energy,* **35**, 5448–5453.

70. Day, P., Enderby, J. E., Williams, W. G., Chapon, L. C., Hannon, A. C., Radaelli, P. G. and Soper, A. K. (2004). GEM: The general materials diffractometer at ISIS—multibank capabilities for studying crystalline and disordered materials, *Neutron News,* **15**, 19.

71. Isnard, O. (2007). A review of in situ and/or time resolved neutron scattering, *Comptes Rendus Phys.,* **8**, 789–805.

72. Hansen, T. C., Henry, P. F., Fischer, H. E., Torregrossa, J., and Convert, P. (2008). The D20 instrument at the ILL: A versatile high-intensity two-axis neutron diffractometer, *Meas. Sci. Technol.,* **19**, 034001.

73. Widenmeyer, M., Niewa, R., Hansen, T. C., and Kohlmann, H. (2013). In situ neutron diffraction as a probe on formation and decomposition of nitrides and hydrides: A case study, *Zeitschrift für anorganische und allgemeine Chemie,* **639**, 285–295.

74. Iwase, K., Mori, K., Hishinuma, Y., Hasegawa, Y., Iimura, S., Ishikawa, H., Kamoshida, T., and Ishigaki, T. (2011). Development of sample holder for in situ neutron measurement of hydrogen absorbing alloy, *Int. J. Hydrogen Energy,* **36**, 3062–3066.

75. David, W. I. F., Sommariva, M., Jones, M. O., Johnson, S., and Edwards, P. (2007). In-situ neutron diffraction and gravimetric studies of H_2 cycling in hydrides, *Acta Crystallogr.,* A63. s76.

76. Weidner, E., Bull, D. J., Shabalin, I. L., Keens, S. G., Telling, M. T. F., and Ross, D. K. (2007). Observation of novel phases during deuteration of lithium nitride from in situ neutron diffraction, *Chem. Phys. Lett.,* **444**, 76–79.

77. Bull, D. J., Weidner, E., Shabalin, I. L., Telling, M. T. F., Jewell, C. M., Gregory, D. H., and Ross, D. K. (2010). Pressure-dependent deuterium reaction pathways in the Li-N-D system, *Phys. Chem. Chem. Phys.,* **12**, 2089–2097.

78. David, W. I. F., Jones, M. O., Gregory, D. H., Jewell, C. M., Johnson, S. R., Walton, A. P., and Edwards, P. (2007). *J. Am. Chem. Soc.,* **129**, 1594.

79. Hu, J., Liu, Y., Wu, G., Xiong, Z., and Chen, P. (2007). Structural and compositional changes during hydrogenation/dehydrogenation of the Li–Mg–N–H system, *J. Phys. Chem. C,* **111**, 18439–18443.

80. Kisi, E. H., Mac A. Gray, E., and Kennedy, S. J. (1994). A neutron diffraction investigation of the $LaNi_5D$ phase diagram, *J. Alloys Compounds,* **216**, 123–129.

81. Gray, E. M., Cookson, D. J., and Blach, T. P. (2006). X-ray diffraction cell for studying solid-gas reactions under gas pressures to 100 bar, *J. Appl. Crystallogr.*, **39**, 850–855.

82. Nakamura, Y., Nakamura, J., Iwase, K., and Akiba, E. (2009). Distribution of hydrogen in metal hydrides studied by in situ powder neutron diffraction, *Nucl. Instrum. Methods Phys. Res. Section A*, **600**, 297–300.

83. Yartys, V. A., Denys, R. V., Webb, C. J., Mæhlen, J. P., Gray, E. M., Blach, T., Isnard, O., and Barnsley, L. C. (2011). High pressure in situ diffraction studies of metal–hydrogen systems, *J. Alloys Compounds*, **509**, Supplement 2, S817–S822.

84. Sakaki, K., Terashita, N., Tsunokake, S., Nakamura, Y., and Akiba, E. (2011). In Situ X-ray Diffraction Study of Phase Transformation of $Mg_{2-x}Pr_xNi_4$ during hydrogenation and dehydrogenation (x = 0.6 and 1.0), *J. Phys. Chem. C*, **116**, 1401–1407.

85. Walker, G. S., Grant, D. M., Price, T. C., Yu, X., and Legrand, V. (2009). High capacity multicomponent hydrogen storage materials: Investigation of the effect of stoichiometry and decomposition conditions on the cycling behaviour of $LiBH_4$–MgH_2, *J. Power Sources*, **194**, 1128–1134.

86. Bösenberg, U., Ravnsbæk, D. B., Hagemann, H., D'Anna, V., Minella, C. B., Pistidda, C., van Beek, W., Jensen, T. R., Bormann, R., and Dornheim, M. (2010). Pressure and temperature influence on the desorption pathway of the $LiBH_4$–MgH_2 composite system, *J. Phys. Chem. C*, **114**, 15212–15217.

87. Price, T. E. C., Grant, D. M., Legrand, V., and Walker, G. S. (2010). Enhanced kinetics for the $LiBH_4$:MgH_2 multi-component hydrogen storage system–The effects of stoichiometry and decomposition environment on cycling behaviour, *Int. J. Hydrogen Energy*, **35**, 4154–4161.

88. Price, T. E. C., Grant, D. M., Weston, D., Hansen, T., Arnbjerg, L. M., Ravnsbæk, D. B., Jensen, T. R., and Walker, G. S. (2011). The effect of H_2 partial pressure on the reaction progression and reversibility of lithium-containing multicomponent destabilized hydrogen storage systems, *J. Am. Chem. Soc.*, **133**, 13534–13538.

89. Garroni, S., Milanese, C., Pottmaier, D., Mulas, G., Nolis, P., Girella, A., Caputo, R., Olid, D., Teixdor, F., Baricco, M., Marini, A., Suriñach, S., and Baró, M. D. (2011). Experimental evidence of $Na_2[B_{12}H_{12}]$ and Na formation in the desorption pathway of the $2NaBH_4$ + MgH_2 system, *J. Phys. Chem. C*, **115**, 16664–16671.

90. Yan, Y., Li, H.-W., Maekawa, H., Miwa, K., Towata, S.-I., and Orimo, S.-I. (2011). Formation of intermediate compound $Li_2B_{12}H_{12}$ during the dehydrogenation process of the $LiBH_4$-MgH_2 system, *J. Phys. Chem. C*, **115**, 19419–19423.

91. Li, H.-W., Miwa, K., Ohba, N., Fujita, T., Sato, T., Yan, Y., Towata, S., Chen, M. W., and Orimo, S. (2009). Formation of an intermediate compound with a $B_{12}H_{12}$ cluster: Experimental and theoretical studies on magnesium borohydride $Mg(BH_4)_2$, *Nanotechnology*, **20**, 204013.

92. Bonatto Minella, C., Garroni, S., Olid, D., Teixidor, F., Pistidda, C., Lindemann, I., Gutfleisch, O., Baró, M. D., Bormann, R. D., Klassen, T., and Dornheim, M. (2011). Experimental evidence of $Ca[B_{12}H_{12}]$ formation during decomposition of a $Ca(BH_4)_2$ + MgH_2 based reactive hydride composite, *J. Phys. Chem. C*, **115**, 18010–18014.

93. Barkhordarian, G., Jensen, T. R., Doppiu, S., Bosenberg, U., Borgschulte, A., Gremaud, R., Cerenius, Y., Dornheim, M., Klassen, T., and Bormann, R. (2008). Formation of $Ca(BH_4)_2$ from hydrogenation of CaH_2 + MgB_2 composite, *J. Phys. Chem. C*, **112**, 2743–2749.

94. Schimmel, H. G., Huot, J., Chapon, L. C., Tichelaar, F. D., and Mulder, F. M. (2005). Hydrogen cycling of niobium and vanadium catalyzed nanostructured magnesium, *J. Am. Chem. Soc.*, **127**, 14348–14354.

95. Gregory, D. H. (2008). Lithium nitrides, imides and amides as lightweight, reversible hydrogen stores, *J. Mater. Chem.*, **18**, 2321–2330.

96. Luo, W. F., and Ronnebro, E. (2005). Towards a viable hydrogen storage system for transportation application, *J. Alloys Compd.*, **404**, 392–395.

97. Rude, L. H., Filinchuk, Y., Sørby, M. H., Hauback, B. C., Besenbacher, F., and Jensen, T. R. (2011). Anion substitution in $Ca(BH_4)_2$-CaI_2: Synthesis, structure and stability of three new compounds, *J. Phys. Chem. C*, **115**, 7768–7777.

98. Ravnsbæk, D. B., Sørensen, L. H., Filinchuk, Y., Besenbacher, F., and Jensen, T. R. (2012). Screening of metal borohydrides by mechano-chemistry and diffraction, *Angew. Chem. Int. Ed.*, **51**, 3582–3586.

99. Buchter, F., Łodziana, Z., Remhof, A., Friedrichs, O., Borgschulte, A., Mauron, P., Züttel, A., Sheptyakov, D., Palatinus, L., Chłopek, K., Fichtner, M., Barkhordarian, G., Bormann, R., and Hauback, B. C. (2009). Structure of the orthorhombic γ-phase and phase transitions of $Ca(BD_4)_2$, *J. Phys. Chem. C*, **113**, 17223–17230.

100. David, W. I. F., Callear, S. K., Jones, M. O., Aeberhard, P. C., Culligan, S. D., Pohl, A. H., Johnson, S. R., Ryan, K. R., Parker, J. E., Edwards,

P. P., Nuttall, C. J., and Amieiro-Fonseca, A. (2012). The structure, thermal properties and phase transformations of the cubic polymorph of magnesium tetrahydroborate, *Phys. Chem. Chem. Phys.,* **14**, 11800–11807.

Chapter 7

Structure of Crystallographically Challenged Hydrogen Storage Materials from Total Scattering

Hyunjeong Kim

Research Institute of Energy Frontier,
National Institute of Advanced Industrial Science and Technology,
Tsukuba West, 16-1 Onogawa, Tsukuba, Ibaraki 305-8569, Japan

hj.kim@aist.go.jp

This chapter presents a brief introduction of the atomic pair distribution function (PDF) analysis of total scattering data and shows the use of the PDF to elucidate the key structural features that are closely linked to the hydrogen storage properties of various types of materials. We present some examples from our PDF work on materials whose structures are difficult to characterize by using conventional crystallographic techniques alone. Examples include NH_3BH_3 confined in mesoporous silica, mechanically alloyed amorphous-like Mg_xCo_{100-x} and heavily disordered $V_{1-x}Ti_xH_2$. We also briefly discuss how extracted structural information is linked to their hydrogen storage properties. The PDF technique can be applied to any materials and the goal of this chapter is to

Structural Characterization Techniques: Advances and Applications in Clean Energy
Edited by Lorenzo Malavasi
Copyright © 2016 Pan Stanford Publishing Pte. Ltd.
ISBN 978-981-4669-34-4 (Hardcover), 978-981-4669-35-1 (eBook)
www.panstanford.com

make readers familiar with the PDF technique and its potential in solving structural characterization problems.

7.1   Introduction

As global warming emerges as one of issues that cannot be ignored any longer and the energy problems start to take a heavy toll on our daily lives, the use of hydrogen as an alternative fuel for transportation is attracting attention more than ever. At first glance, powering vehicles with hydrogen may not sound difficult; we simply feed a fuel cell with hydrogen to generate necessary energy. However, supplying hydrogen in a mobile unit turns out to be quite a challenging task. An average modern compact car has a ~42 L gasoline tank. With a full tank of gasoline, one can drive ~500 km. To cover the same range using a fuel cell car, 5 kg of hydrogen is needed. At room temperature under atmospheric pressure, hydrogen is in a gas form and 5 kg of hydrogen occupies a volume of 60,000 L (=60 m^3). This means your fuel cell car should have a huge hydrogen gas tank with dimensions of 3.9 m × 3.9 m × 3.9 m. Obviously, this is not a picture of our future transportation.

How to pack such a large volume of hydrogen in a safe and compact way for fuel cell vehicles is one of great challenges that we are facing now. Simply one could think of storing gaseous hydrogen in a high-pressure gas tank or liquid or solid hydrogen in a cryogenic storage system but these methods are rather risky and inefficient [1]. At present, many believe that the most promising way of storing hydrogen for fuel cell vehicles is the use of materials that can reversibly absorb and desorb hydrogen (hydrogen storage materials). For practical onboard applications, a material that can absorb more than 5~6 wt% and 40 kg m^{-3} of hydrogen is required [2]. In addition, the material should work at ~373 K under the operating pressure of 0.1~10 MPa and a refueling time of less than 3.3 min and a minimum lifetime of 1500 hydrogenation and dehydrogenation cycles are expected. There are many types of hydrogen storage materials such as interstitial hydrides, which are reactive metals, metal alloys, or intermetallic compounds that reversibly absorb atomic hydrogen into their interstitial sites, complex hydrides where atomic hydrogen is bound either covalently or ionically and released through decomposition, and microporous adsorbents, which adsorb molecular hydrogen at low temperature. An overview of hydrogen storage properties of these types of materials can be found in Ref. [1–4] and references therein. Although a wide range of hydrogen storage materials are available at present, none of them meet the targets.

A great effort has been made in the material science field either to enhance the hydrogen storage properties of currently available materials or to develop novel highly efficient materials. Some of examples are synthesizing new Mg-based materials by the mechanical milling method [5] and destabilizing stable hydrides like MgH_2 and complex hydrides via nano-sizing or nano-confinement [6]. All of these approaches yield favorable improvements in the hydrogen storage properties of materials.

For any materials, the first step to understanding their characteristic properties is to obtain structural information closely linked to the properties. It is not an overstatement to say that the ability to determine the structure has been the basis for the remarkable advances in physical, chemical and material science fields and crystallography has been making a great contribution to solving structures for almost a century. However, modern technologically important materials often show structural disorders or distortions and reduction in size to nano length scales and crystallography alone is not able to give sufficient information for full understanding of the properties of these types of materials. Many of novel hydrogen storage materials prepared by mechanical milling and nano-sizing or nano-confinement methods fall in this category. They are often lack of long-range structural order. Figure 7.1 shows the X-ray diffraction patterns of mechanically milled $Mg_{50}Co_{50}$ alloy using the laboratory X-ray source of a Cu tube [7]. Only one broad peak appears in the diffraction data. What kind of structural information can be extracted from this data? Obviously, it is quite challenging to solve the structure problems of this type of materials using crystallography alone. Because of this reason, we call them crystallographically challenged hydrogen storage materials. Many emerging complex functional materials possess similar characteristics and the development of robust structural characterization methods for crystallographically challenged materials is a big issue in materials science, physics, and chemistry communities [8].

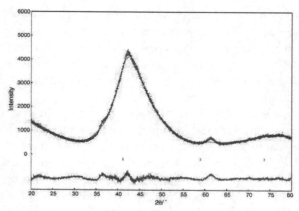

Figure 7.1 The X-ray diffraction patterns and a Rietveld fit of $Mg_{50}Co_{50}$ alloy mechanically milled for 100 h [7].

7.2 Atomic Pair Distribution Function

Our approach to tackling the structural characterization problems of crystallographically challenged hydrogen storage materials is the use of the atomic pair distribution function (PDF) analysis of total scattering data [9]. Among various definitions [9, 10], the atomic PDF, $G(r)$, that we are going to use in this chapter is defined as:

$$G(r) = 4\pi r[\rho(r) - \rho_0], \tag{7.1}$$

where ρ_0 is the average atomic number density, $\rho(r)$ is the microscopic pair-density and r is a radial distance [9]. The PDF gives information about the number of atoms in a spherical shell of unit thickness at a distance r from a reference atom.

For a simple example, let us think of a square lattice sheet in which one type of atom sit on each lattice point (Fig. 7.2a). If we select the atom indicated by an "X" mark as our reference, the PDF shows peaks at the distances between the reference and other atoms (Fig. 7.2b). For instance, the first PDF peak arises from the pairs of the reference and its first nearest neighbor atoms. There are four of them. The second peak is due to the reference and its second nearest neighbor atoms. Note the fourth peak at around 4.47 Å is twice as high as the first peak because there are eight atoms 4.47 Å apart from the reference atom. Therefore, the area of a peak is closely related to the coordination number. If the sheet is large enough to make the fraction of atoms on the four sides negligible, whichever atom you pick, except the atoms on or near the sides, the same distribution profile would be obtained. Therefore, the PDF gives in some sense a probability of finding an atom pair separated by distance r. If structural defects or distortions are introduced to the sheet without breaking the average symmetry, they bring some changes to PDF peaks, especially to a first few peaks, like the broadening or splitting of peaks or the development of new intensities. The deviation of PDF intensities from the average structure gives us an idea how structural modifications occur locally.

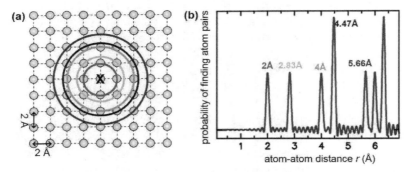

Figure 7.2   (a) A square lattice sheet and (b) the corresponding PDF.

The experimental PDF is obtained from X-ray or neutron diffraction data of an isotropic sample like a powder. Therefore, from an experimental point of view, a PDF experiment is not much different from a regular powder diffraction experiment. What makes the PDF technique distinct from the conventional crystallographic technique is that it makes use of both Bragg and diffuse intensities (the total scattering). For an average structural study, Bragg intensities are solely used and diffuse intensities underneath the Bragg peaks are neglected. However, diffuse intensities include valuable information about local atomic distortions and the PDF takes full advantage of them [9].

Because the PDF does not presume long-range order or translational periodicity, its application is not limited to crystalline materials. In fact, the PDF has been used for studying noncrystalline materials like liquids and glasses [10, 11] for a long time and only recently applied to studying crystalline and nanocrystalline materials [12–16].

The process of acquiring the PDF starts by obtaining the total scattering structure function, $S(Q)$, from the experimental powder diffraction data. The measured diffracted intensity is expressed as

$$I(Q) = I^{coh} + I^{inc} + I^{mul} + I^{back}, \tag{7.2}$$

where I^{coh} is the coherent scattering intensity, I^{inc} is the incoherent scattering intensity, and I^{mul} is the multiple scattering intensity. I^{back} is the background scattering intensity from air, a sample container and an experimental setup. Q is the magnitude of the diffraction vector for elastic scattering which is related to the scattering angle, 2θ, and the wavelength of the radiation, λ as follows:

$$Q = \frac{4\pi \sin\theta}{\lambda}. \tag{7.3}$$

After making proper background subtraction, correction (like absorption and polarization) and normalization (by the incident flux and the number of atoms in the sample) [9], the corrected coherent scattering intensity, $I^{corr.coh}$, is used to obtain $S(Q)$ using a following equation:

$$S(Q) = \frac{I^{corr.coh}(Q) - \sum_i c_i |f_i(Q)|^2}{\left|\sum_i c_i f_i(Q)\right|^2} + 1, \tag{7.4}$$

where c_i and f_i are the atomic concentration and X-ray atomic form factor (a Q-dependent function), respectively, for the atomic species of type i. In the case of neutron data, the neutron scattering lengths (Q-independent), b_i, is used instead of f_i. Finally, the PDF, $G(r)$, is obtained by a sine Fourier transform

$$G(r) = \frac{2}{\pi} \int_0^{Q_{max}} Q[S(Q) - 1]\sin(Qr)dQ. \tag{7.5}$$

Q_{max} is the maximum Q value used for Fourier transforming the experimental data. Real-space resolution is roughly determined by $\delta r \sim \pi/Q_{max}$ [9]. The higher the Q_{max} value, the better the real-space resolution of the PDF. In principle, the PDF can be obtained using powder diffraction data from laboratory X-ray sources. If sin $\theta = 1$ in Eq. 7.3, Cu K_α gives $Q_{max} \sim 8$ Å^{-1} and Mo K_α gives $Q_{max} \sim 16$ Å^{-1} and these result in relatively low real-space resolution of $\delta r \sim 0.4$ Å and ~ 0.2 Å, respectively. In addition, the finite Q range of experimental data causes artificial oscillation called termination ripples. Therefore, for high accuracy and good real-space resolution of the PDF data, $Q_{max} > 30$ Å^{-1} is desirable [9]. The importance of Q_{max} is clearly demonstrated in Ref. [17, 18]. Because detailed features in the PDF are determined by the high-Q portion of the data, excellent statistics at the high-Q region is also required.

Because the PDF provides structural information over a wide length scale, it is also useful for investigating features extending to several nano-meters like nano-domains [19–24] or nanoparticles [16, 25–31]. Some of these studies require the PDF profile out to high r, like more than 100 Å. The experimental PDF peaks normally decay with increasing r due to the finite resolution in Q-space. Therefore, obtaining high resolution diffraction data is important to study the medium range structural correlation.

Considering all the requirements of diffraction data for the PDF study discussed above, it is best to carry out the PDF experiments at synchrotron X-ray or spallation neutron sources where high-energy (short-wavelength), high-flux X-rays and neutrons are available. Basically, any facility providing data satisfying above specifications can be used, but there are several beamlines or instruments optimized for PDF measurements. Some of them are NPDF [32] at the Lujan Neutron Scattering Center (http://www.lansce.lanl.gov), NOVA at J-PARC (http://is.j-parc.jp/index-e.html), and NOMAD at the Spallation Neutron Source (http://neutron.ornl.gov) for neutron experiments and 11-ID-B at the Advanced Photon Source (http://www.aps.anl.gov) for X-ray experiments.

There are several software programs available for processing diffraction data to the PDF. One of widely used data processing programs for neutron and X-ray PDFs are PDFgetN [33] and

PDFgetX2 [34], respectively. The PDFgetN program can be downloaded from http://pdfgetn.sourceforge.net and the PDFgetX2 program from http://www.pa.msu.edu/cmp/billinge-group/programs/PDFgetX2.

The PDF can be calculated from a structural model using

$$G(r) = \frac{1}{r} \sum_i \sum_j \left[\frac{f_i(0)f_j(0)}{\langle f(0) \rangle^2} \delta(r - r_{ij}) \right] - 4\pi r \rho_0, \tag{7.6}$$

where $f_i(0)$ is the atomic form factor of atom i evaluated at $Q = 0$, $\langle f(0) \rangle$ is the average atomic form factor of the sample at $Q = 0$, r_{ij} is the distance between atoms i and j, and ρ_0 is the average atomic number density [12]. The value of the atomic form factor at $Q = 0$ approximates to the number of electrons in the atom, Z. In the case of neutron PDF, the atomic form factors should be replaced by neutron scattering lengths, b_i. The sums go over all the atoms in the structural model. It is worth noting that the intensity of a PDF peak locating at r is proportional to the number of atom pairs separated by distance r and $f_i(0)f_j(0)/\langle f(0) \rangle^2$ (or $b_i b_j/\langle b \rangle^2$ for neutron) value of the atom pair.

A lot of information can be extracted from the PDF by modeling. Full profile fitting of the experimental PDF data analogous to the Rietveld refinement [35] can be carried out using the program PDFgui [36]. This program uses least-squares and allows us to refine the structural parameters of the model used, like lattice parameters, isotropic or anisotropic atomic displacement parameters, atomic positions and site occupancies. This analysis program is useful for study requiring a model consisting of a relatively small number of atoms. The PDFgui program can be downloaded from http://www.diffpy.org. For study requiring a model made up of a large number of atoms, the reverse Monte Carlo (RMC) technique [37, 38] is an alternative choice. In this case, a residual function is minimized by changing the occupancy or displacing randomly selected atoms in the model by a random amount. One of popularly used programs for the RMC analysis is RMCProfile program [39], which can be downloaded from http://www.rmcprofile.org. In this chapter, some of example studies using the least-squares approach, i.e. the PDFgui program, will be presented.

7.3 Practical Examples

7.3.1 Nano-Confined NH₃BH₃

Ammonia borane (AB), NH_3BH_3, has attained considerable attention as a potential material for hydrogen storage. At low temperature, this molecular crystal has an orthorhombic structure, and upon warming it undergoes an orthorhombic-to-tetragonal phase transition at 225 K [40–45]. Some of hydrogen is released at ~373 K and approximately 15 wt% of hydrogen is released from AB at ~423 K. Despite the high hydrogen yields, several material challenges must be overcome for fuel cell applications such as high hydrogen releasing temperatures, long induction time prior to hydrogen release and the formation of by-products like borazine, which is harmful to fuel cells.

One compelling approach to overcome these obstacles is nanocomposition of AB by loading AB in mesoporous silica materials [46]. This approach successfully reduces the induction time and the hydrogen releasing temperature of AB. Furthermore, the formation of borazine was significantly suppressed. It was also shown that the alterations in hydrogen releasing properties of AB strongly depend on the level of AB loading in mesoporous silica. Bulk AB-like nature was recovered in high AB loading nanocomposite samples. Although the improvement in hydrogen releasing properties was striking, the mechanism responsible for the enhanced properties is not known. This is partly because of the absence of structural information of AB inside mesoporous silica; structural determination using the crystallographic method and transmission electron microscope (TEM) was not successful because of its lack of long-range structural order and weak scattering signals compared to the host materials.

A hyperpolarized (HP) ^{129}Xe nuclear magnetic resonance (NMR) study provided a general picture of where supported AB resides in the mesoporous silica host, MCM-41, with increasing the AB loading level [47]. It was revealed that at the weight ratio of AB:MCM-41 = 1:2 all the AB resides inside the mesopores but as the loading increases, AB fills the pores completely and excess AB begins to accumulate outside the pores forming AB aggregates. Schematic illustrations of AB loaded MCM-41 with different loading levels are shown in Fig. 7.3. The HP ^{129}Xe NMR results provide important preliminary knowledge of this material necessary to the PDF study: the sample with the weight ratio of AB:MCM-41 = 1:2 should be used in order to obtain the structural information of nano-confined AB in MCM-41. Otherwise, we need to put extra effort into separating the nano-confined AB signals from those of AB aggregates and this is obviously not an easy task.

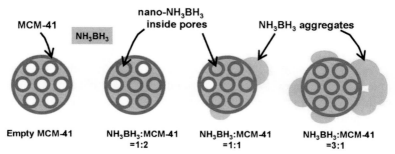

Figure 7.3   Schematic illustrations of nano-confined NH_3BH_3 in mesoporous silica MCM-41 with different NH_3BH_3 loading.

The goal of this study is to find out how AB molecules are arranged inside MCM-41 and how their structural response to temperature differs from bulk AB. This is only possible with high-quality data in which the noise level is sufficiently low to distinguish weak signals from nano-confined AB. Because the third-generation synchrotron X-ray sources provide intense beams and require only a small amount of samples for PDF studies, we carried out the X-ray total scattering experiments on bulk AB, empty MCM-41 and nano-confined AB inside MCM-41 samples at the 11-ID-B beamline at the Advanced Photon Source at Argonne National Laboratory. The rapid acquisition pair distribution function (RA-PDF) setup was used [48]. Each sample was measured at various temperatures from 80 to 300 K during warming. Experimental details can be found in Ref. [49].

Figure 7.4 shows the raw diffraction data of an empty MCM-41 and nanocomposite samples with weight ratios of AB: MCM-41 = 1:2 and 1:1. It can be clearly seen that the 1:2 sample does not show any sharp diffraction peaks and its diffraction patterns are similar to those of the empty MCM-41. Meanwhile, the 1:1 sample shows small sharp peaks sitting on the MCM-41 signals. Taking into account the [129]Xe NMR results, we can speculate that those sharp peaks of the 1:1 sample are from AB aggregates.

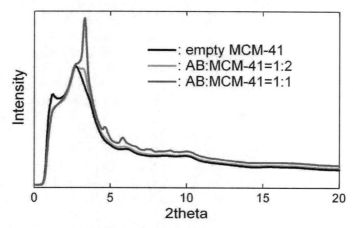

Figure 7.4   Synchrotron X-ray diffraction patterns of nano-confined NH_3BH_3 in mesoporous silica MCM-41 and empty MCM-41 obtained at 240 K.

Instead of directly analyzing the PDF, we investigated the difference between PDFs obtained at two adjacent temperature points. The difference curves obtained by subtracting the PDF at higher temperature from the PDF at lower temperature are shown in Fig. 7.5. Large structural changes are observed from the PDF of bulk AB for the 80 K through 200 K temperature range (Fig. 7.5a) probably due to continuous change in the tilting angle of AB molecules along the *c*-axis [50]. The orthorhombic-to-tetragonal phase transition at 225 K is clearly evident from the characteristic curve related to the 220 and 225 K data sets. Note that the similar looking difference curve was also obtained from the AB: MCM-41 = 3:1 sample at the transition temperature indicating the 3:1 sample undergoes the same phase transition as bulk AB at 225 K (Fig. 7.5b). In addition, the orthorhombic and tetragonal structural models explain the experimental PDFs of the 3:1 sample below and above 225 K, respectively, well. This suggests that AB aggregates are nothing but bulk AB. On the other hand, a flat difference curve was obtained from the 1:2 sample at 225 K indicating the absence of the phase transition at 225 K (Fig. 7.5c). This is consistent with results using differential scanning calorimetry (DSC) and anelastic spectroscopy [51]. Huge change occurs in the PDF of the 1:2 sample between the 240 and 270 K: well-defined features were observed in the difference curve up to 40 Å, which is the size of pores in MCM-41, and no signal was found above 40 Å. These features are indeed characteristic of the bulk AB structure in the tetragonal phase. Figure 7.6 shows how well the tetragonal structure model explains these features. This indicates that below 240 K AB molecules inside mesopores are arranged in the same way as bulk AB in the tetragonal phase. This tetragonal-like structural order extends to many neighbors in the length scale of 40 Å. However, above 270 K, AB loses medium range order and as a result, the difference curve contains the structural correlations that have been lost at the higher temperatures. While the structure of AB inside mesopores turns out to be similar to the structure of bulk AB in the tetragonal phase, its structural response to temperature is substantially different from that of bulk AB. This is a strong indication that the nano-confinement of AB using a mesoporous silica scaffold greatly alters the intermolecular interaction of AB, thus stabilizing the high temperature tetragonal phase at lower temperature altering the dehydrogenation properties of AB.

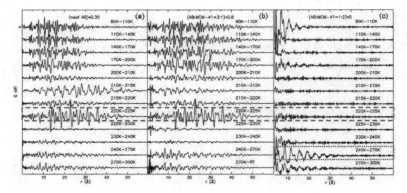

Figure 7.5 Difference between PDFs obtained at two adjacent temperature points. Each difference curve was obtained by subtracting the higher temperature PDF from the lower temperature PDF of (a) bulk AB, (b) AB:MCM-41 = 3:1, and (c) AB:MCM-41=1:2 samples [49].

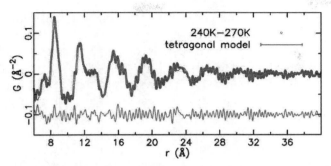

Figure 7.6 PDF refinement results on the difference curve of 240 and 270 K PDFs of AB:MCM-41=1:2 using the tetragonal model [49].

7.3.2   Mechanically Alloyed Mg_xCo_{100-x}

Mg is one of currently available materials that can absorb hydrogen more than the requirement for hydrogen fuel cell vehicles [1]. However, its high hydrogen absorption and desorption temperature and poor kinetics are major drawbacks that hinder on-board application. To overcome these challenges, many efforts have been made to develop new Mg-based materials. Mg_xCo_{100-x} is one of them.

Mg_xCo_{100-x} alloy can be synthesized by the mechanical milling method. Although $MgCo_2$ (=$Mg_{33}Co_{66}$) is the only known stable phase in the Mg–Co binary phase diagram, metastable Mg_xCo_{100-x} alloy is formed in the composition range of $20 \leq x \leq 63$ [7]. Furthermore, $MgCo_2$ is known not to absorb hydrogen but mechanically alloyed Mg_xCo_{100-x} with $x > 33$ absorbs hydrogen at ambient conditions (e.g., $Mg_{50}Co_{50}$ absorbs ~2.1 wt% of hydrogen). Mg-rich compositions tend to absorb more hydrogen than Mg-poor compositions. Even though hydrogenation occurs at more favorable temperature than pure Mg, Mg_xCo_{100-x} does not desorb hydrogen at 373 K even under vacuum. This is an indication of the formation of a stable hydride.

The X-ray diffraction patterns using Cu K_α radiation show one broad peak indicating the amorphous-like nature of Mg_xCo_{100-x} (Fig. 7.1) [7, 52]. Obviously, it is difficult to apply conventional crystallography methods to extract structural information of this type of materials. One of structure probing tools routinely used for mechanically alloyed materials is high-resolution TEM. Using TEM, nanocrystals embedded in amorphous matrix of $Mg_{50}Co_{50}$

was revealed [53]. Moreover, selected area electron diffraction patterns (SAEDP) suggested that both nanocrystals and amorphous matrix have a body-centered cubic (bcc) structure with the uniform distribution of Mg and Co atoms.

Although the X-ray diffraction patterns of $Mg_{50}Co_{50}$ was virtually unaltered after hydrogenation [7], TEM images and SAEDP studies showed bcc crystals grown more than 100 Å in size [53]. In addition, the face-centered cubic (fcc) Co phase and a phase with a composition close to Mg_2Co were also found in hydrogenated samples. It was reported that when $Mg_{50}Co_{50}$ was heated above 413 K under 4 MPa of hydrogen pressure Mg_2CoH_5 and Co peaks started to appear on top of broad amorphous intensities in X-ray diffraction patterns [7]. A further increase in temperature above 481 K led to the formation of an additional phase, $MgCo_2$ [52]. It is probable that intense electron beams promoted crystal growth observed in TEM images. The TEM study provided some of structural information of $Mg_{50}Co_{50}$ and its hydride but the information is not enough to understand the hydrogen storage properties of Mg_xCo_{100-x} alloys. In this example, we will show how to extract the structural information of this amorphous-like alloy using PDF analysis.

As it is mentioned earlier, if one studies hydrogen-containing materials, he/she would think of carrying out neutron experiments because the structural information including hydrogen positions can be easily obtained by substituting hydrogen with deuterium. However, for this particular example of $Mg_{50}Co_{50}$, we would largely benefit from obtaining both neutron and X-ray PDFs. Note that the contribution of each pair of atoms to the PDF is $b_i b_j / <b>^2$ (Eq. 7.6). Table 7.1 shows these values for all possible atom pairs in $Mg_{50}Co_{50}$. Because Co interacts more strongly with X-ray but weakly with neutron than Mg, signals from Co-related pairs appear predominantly in the X-ray PDF but insignificantly in the neutron PDF and signals from Mg-related pairs appear the other way around. Table 7.2 shows the $b_i b_j / <b>^2$ values for all possible pairs in $Mg_{50}Co_{50}D_{75}$.

Synchrotron X-ray and neutron total scattering data of $Mg_{50}Co_{50}$ and $Mg_{50}Co_{50}D_{75}$ were collected at the 11-ID-B beamline at the Advanced Photon Source at Argonne National Laboratory and at the NPDF instrument at the Lujan Neutron Scattering Center at Los Alamos National Laboratory, respectively. In addition, Mg_xCo_{100-x} (x = 35, 40, 45 and 55) samples were also measured at the 11-ID-B. Experimental details can be found in Refs. [54–56].

Table 7.1 $b_ib_j/<b>^2$ values for all possible pairs in $Mg_{50}Co_{50}$

	Mg-Mg	Mg-Co	Co-Co
X-ray	0.379	0.853	1.918
neutron	1.869	0.866	0.401

Note: For X-ray, b_{Mg} = 12 and b_{Co} = 27 were used and for neutron, b_{Mg} = 5.375 and b_{Co} = 2.49 were used [5].

Table 7.2 $b_ib_j/<b>^2$ values for all possible pairs in $Mg_{50}Co_{50}D_{75}$

	Mg-Mg	Mg-Co	Co-Co	D-Mg	D-Co	D-D
X-ray	1.075	2.420	5.444	0.090	0.202	0.007
neutron	1.108	0.513	0.238	1.375	0.637	1.707

Note: For X-ray, b_{Mg} = 12, b_{Co} = 27, and b_D = 1 were used and for neutron, b_{Mg} = 5.375, b_{Co} = 2.49, and b_D = 6.671 were used [5].

By simply plotting experimental PDFs together, we can learn various things. Figure 7.7 shows neutron and X-ray PDFs of $Mg_{50}Co_{50}$ and $Mg_{50}Co_{50}D_{75}$. Huge changes were observed in neutron PDFs, especially low-r regions after deuteration (Fig. 7.7a). On the contrary, besides the scale, the X-ray PDF stays almost unchanged (Fig. 7.7b). Change in the PDF scale is due to change in the average scattering power $<b>$ by introducing deuterium. This figure suggests that $Mg_{50}Co_{50}$ bears large spaces which can accommodate D atoms without influencing the metal substructure significantly. Newly appearing intensities in neutron data is probably due to pairs associated with D and Mg atoms.

If Mg and Co atoms were randomly distributed over the bcc lattice in $Mg_{50}Co_{50}$ as suggested by TEM, no difference between X-ray and neutron PDFs would be expected as shown in our calculated PDFs using the bcc structural model in Fig. 7.8a. However, this is not what we see from the experimental data. As shown in Fig. 7.8b, X-ray and neutron experimental PDFs look quite different. This strongly indicates that the local structure of $Mg_{50}Co_{50}$ is more complicated than a simple bcc structure. Such differences, like peak shapes and the positions of the intensity maxima of the first peaks, are due to a large contrast in X-ray and neutron scattering powers of Mg and Co mentioned earlier. Taking this into account, our PDF data suggested that ~2.47 Å Co–Co (the first X-ray peak position), ~2.96 Å Mg–Mg (the first neutron peak position) and ~2.7 Å Mg–Co (overlapped intensity) pairs exist.

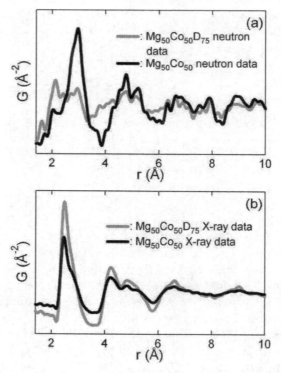

Figure 7.7   Experimental (a) neutron and (b) X-ray PDFs of $Mg_{50}Co_{50}$ and $Mg_{50}Co_{50}D_{75}$ [55].

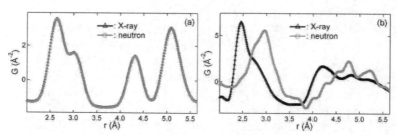

Figure 7.8   Comparison between (a) calculated and (b) experimental X-ray and neutron PDFs of $Mg_{50}Co_{50}$. The bcc structural model was used for calculation [55].

Interestingly, three shortest interatomic distances found in $MgCo_2$ (Fig. 7.9a) are 2.4 Å Co–Co, 2.84 Å Mg–Co, and 2.98 Å Mg–Mg distances, which are close to what we found from the experimental data [57]. In fact, the $MgCo_2$ model successfully reproduced the main features of X-ray and neutron PDFs, especially their first peak shapes [55]. It is likely that the local atomic arrangements of $Mg_{50}Co_{50}$ are closely related to the $MgCo_2$ structure.

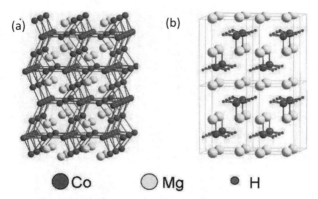

(a)   (b)

● Co   ○ Mg   • H

Figure 7.9   The crystal structure of (a) $MgCo_2$ and (b) Mg_2CoH_5 [55].

Although the $MgCo_2$ model explains the characteristic features of X-ray and neutron PDFs reasonably well, it lacks Mg of being $Mg_{50}Co_{50}$. Furthermore, it does not account for the hydrogenation properties of $Mg_{50}Co_{50}$ since $MgCo_2$ is known not to absorb hydrogen. Therefore, to make a physically reasonable model, it is necessary to introduce a hydrogen (deuterium in this case) absorbing phase consisting of Mg or Mg and Co. From the literature, we found three possible hydride phases for our model. They are MgH_2 [58], Mg_2CoH_5 [59], and $Mg_6Co_2H_{11}$ [60]. $Mg_{50}Co_{50}$ models composed of $MgCo_2$ and one of these hydride phases are $MgCo_2$ + MgH_2, $MgCo_2$ + Mg_2CoH_5, and $MgCo_2$ + $0.25Mg_6Co_2H_{11}$. These models can contain a maximum 1.2, 2.0, and 1.3 mass% of hydrogen, respectively. Since $Mg_{50}Co_{50}$ is known to absorb more than 2.1 mass% of hydrogen, we consider the $MgCo_2$ + Mg_2CoH_5 model for the local structure of $Mg_{50}Co_{50}$. The crystal structure of Mg_2CoH_5 is shown in Fig. 7.9b.

We constructed a supercell model containing the structural features of both $MgCo_2$ and Mg_2CoH_5 phases and calculated neutron and X-ray PDFs. They are shown in Fig. 7.10 together with experimental PDFs. The model qualitatively explains the experimental data. It reproduces the almost identical X-ray PDFs of alloy and deuteride samples and huge changes in neutron PDF peaks after deuteration. This suggests that the structure of $Mg_{50}Co_{50}$ is mainly comprised of $MgCo_2$- and Mg_2Co-like atomic arrangements whose correlations die out quickly with increasing interatomic distances. Hydrogen is absorbed by Mg_2Co-like parts.

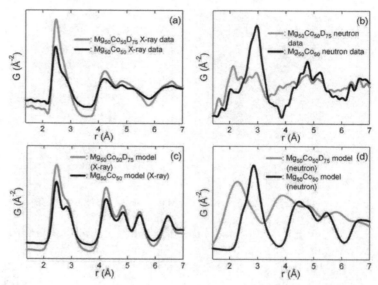

Figure 7.10 (a) Experimental X-ray and (b) neutron PDFs of $Mg_{50}Co_{50}$ and $Mg_{50}Co_{50}D_{75}$. Calculated (c) X-ray and (d) neutron PDFs using the two-phase model consisting of $MgCo_2$- and Mg_2CoD_5-like structural features [55].

Because the two-phase model consisting of $MgCo_2$ and Mg_2Co explains the experimental PDFs of $Mg_{50}Co_{50}$ and $Mg_{50}Co_{50}D_{75}$, we further examine the model to see whether it allows us to understand the various characteristics of Mg_xCo_{100-x} [56]. For this purpose, we obtained the X-ray PDFs of Mg_xCo_{100-x}. Although the PDFs of Mg_xCo_{100-x} look similar in appearance, systematic changes with increasing Mg content, x, were clearly observed (Fig. 7.11). The change can be more readily seen from the difference curves between two PDFs of different compositions. In Fig. 7.12, two difference curves obtained by subtracting the experimental PDF of Mg-poor composition from that of Mg-rich composition are shown. These curves represent changes in the local structure of Mg_xCo_{100-x} with increasing x. We also plotted difference between calculated PDFs using Mg_2Co and $MgCo_2$ structural models. Three curves overlap amazingly well. This strongly indicates that the Mg_2Co-like phase continuously increases while the $MgCo_2$-like phase decreases with increasing Mg content x in MgxCo$_{100-x}$.

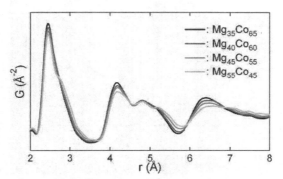

Figure 7.11   Low-r regions of X-ray PDFs of Mg_xCo_{100-x}. Composition-dependent changes are clearly seen [56].

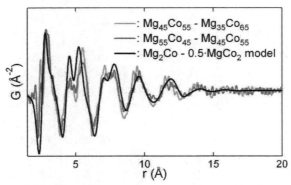

Figure 7.12   Difference curves obtained by subtracting the PDF of Mg-poor composition from that of Mg-rich composition are plotted with difference between calculated PDFs using Mg_2Co and $MgCo_2$ structural models [56].

An increase of the Mg_2Co-like phase in Mg_xCo_{100-x} means the hydrogen capacity should increase with x since the Mg_2Co-like phase absorbs hydrogen in our two-phase model. Can the two-phase model explain the hydrogen capacity of Mg_xCo_{100-x}? We constructed the two-phase models describing several compositions of Mg_xCo_{100-x} and estimated their maximum hydrogen content. The calculated values from the models are plotted in Fig. 7.13 with measured values from Ref. [7] and they are in good agreement.

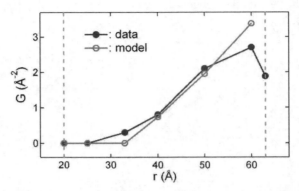

Figure 7.13 The hydrogen capacity of Mg_xCo_{100-x}. Experimental values are plotted with calculated values using the two-phase model. The alloy formation range is specified with vertical dashed lines [4].

7.3.3 $V_{1-x}Ti_x$ bcc Alloys

Vanadium is considered one of promising hydrogen storage materials since it can absorb and desorb a large amount of hydrogen in ambient conditions. Because of its high cost, alloying with other cheap elements is favorable. However, it is well known that alloying V with other elements often leads to poor cyclic stability, that is to say, the reversible hydrogen capacity gradually decreases as the hydrogen absorption and desorption process is repeated. Then, what causes degradation in the reversible hydrogen capacity? Numerous studies reported that V-based bcc alloys with poor cyclic stability show significant diffraction peak broadening [61, 62]. Therefore, identifying the origin of diffraction peak broadening will provide us an important insight into the cyclic stability of V-based bcc alloys. To tackle this problem, we employ the PDF technique.

Synchrotron X-ray total scattering data of $V_{1-x}Ti_xH_2$ ($x = 0, 0.2$ and 0.5) underwent several hydrogen absorption and desorption cycles were collected at Japan Atomic Energy Agency (JAEA) beamline of BL22XU at SPring-8 [63]. Details of sample preparation, experimental setup and conditions can be found in Ref. [64].

X-ray PDFs of $V_{1-x}Ti_xH_2$ (x = 0, 0.2 and 0.5) which underwent one (labeled with 1st) and five (labeled with 5th) or ten (labeled with 10th) hydrogen absorption and desorption cycles are compared over a wide-r range in Fig. 7.14. One striking feature observed is rapid damping of PDF peaks with increasing interatomic distance r in alloy hydride samples. There is almost no cycle-induced change in the PDF of VH_2 (Fig. 7.14a) but 20% substitution of V with Ti dramatically attenuates the PDF profile: initially, decaying was comparable to that of VH_2 but after ten cycles the PDF falls off markedly faster (Fig. 7.14b). Further increase of Ti (or decrease of V) accelerates the decaying (Fig. 7.14c). Even the PDF of $V_{0.5}Ti_{0.5}H_2$ of the first cycle falls off faster than that of $V_{0.8}Ti_{0.2}H_2$ of the 10th cycle.

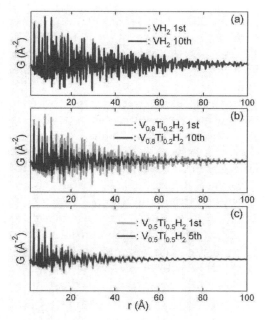

Figure 7.14 X-ray PDFs of (a) VH_2, (b) $V_{0.8}Ti_{0.2}H_2$ and (c) $V_{0.5}Ti_{0.5}H_2$. The PDF of the first and higher cycle (the 10th cycle for VH_2 and $V_{0.8}Ti_{0.2}H_2$ and the 5th cycle for $V_{0.5}Ti_{0.5}H_2$) are plotted top on each other in light and dark color, respectively [64].

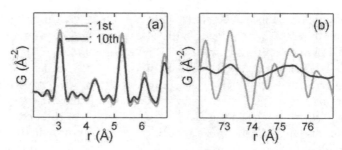

Figure 7.15 Peaks at (a) low- and (b) high-r regions of X-ray PDFs of $V_{0.8}Ti_{0.2}H_2$ samples of the 1st and the 10th cycle [64].

A close examination of the X-ray PDFs of $V_{0.8}Ti_{0.2}H_2$, where cycle-induced change was readily seen, reveals that the rapid PDF profile damping is due to a progressive increase in the width of PDF peaks as r increases (r-dependent peak broadening). As it is seen in Fig. 7.15 the broadening of the low-r peaks of $V_{0.8}Ti_{0.2}H_2$ after 10 cycles is insignificant but that of the high-r peaks is significant. The broadening of PDF peaks reflects the weakening of the structural correlation. Hence, it is most probable that the hydrogen absorption and desorption reaction creates lattice defects or distortions which largely disturb the mid-to-long range structural order.

Various structural defects were reported to form in V-based ternary alloys during the hydrogenation and dehydrogenation process. For instance, stacking faults, twin boundaries and dislocations were observed in the high-resolution transmission electron microscopy (TEM) images of V-Ti-Mn alloys [65] and the formation of vacancy defects and dislocations was identified in $V_{0.4}Ti_{0.24}Cr_{0.36}$ by positron annihilation lifetime measurements [66]. Thus, we need to examine how these defects appear in the PDF and identify which defect is responsible for the rapid PDF profile decaying in cycled samples.

Several fcc VH_2 structural models including one of defects mentioned above, i.e., vacancies, stacking faults, and twin boundaries, were prepared. Because the formation process and resultant characteristics of dislocations in fcc VH_2 are not well understood, we simulated dislocations in the bcc V structure instead. Randomly distributed vacancy defects do not induce the rapid decaying of the PDF. This is consistent with earlier study [67]. Stacking faults increase the attenuation of PDF via *r*-dependent peak broadening but broadening is not as significant as our data and some of peaks remain sharp. These sharp peaks are from atom pairs in the (111) planes of the fcc structure since the in-plane structural correlation of the (111) planes is not disturbed by introducing stacking faults [27]. Twin boundaries give similar effects on the PDFs. These defects, i.e., stacking faults and twin boundaries, are probably present in our samples but no peak remains sharp in our experimental PDFs. This suggests that there exists another type of defects that can induce much stronger *r*-dependent peak broadening than these two planar defects.

Indeed, dislocations provide an interesting result. In Fig. 7.16a, calculated X-ray PDFs using the dislocation and dislocation-free bcc models are plotted on top of each other. Clearly, dislocations cause the rapid fall-off of the PDF. This is because of the significant broadening of the PDF peak width with increasing *r* (Fig. 7.16b,c). As the dislocation density increases, the broadening becomes stronger. The degree of broadening is comparable to our experimental data. In addition, unlike the planar defect case, no peaks remain sharp. Therefore, it is highly probable that a large number of dislocations are present in our $V_{0.8}Ti_{0.2}H_2$ samples inducing unusually rapid PDF profile damping.

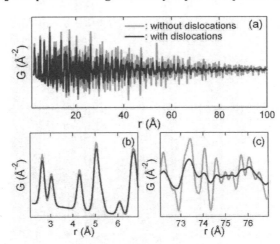

Figure 7.16 (a) Calculated X-ray PDFs using the bcc V structural model with and without dislocations. The dislocation density was 4.6×10^{11} cm^{-2}. Effect of dislocations, i.e., broadening of PDF peaks, is small in (b) low-*r* regions but large in (c) high-*r* regions [64].

We estimated the degree of broadening by fitting the fcc di-hydride phase model to the $V_{0.8}Ti_{0.2}H_2$ experimental PDFs. In the PDFgui program, a parameter called Q_{broad} gives rise to r-dependent peak broadening [68]. The Q_{broad} values obtained from the PDF refinements are plotted against cycle number in Fig. 7.17a. Figure 7.17b shows the amount of absorbed hydrogen by $V_{0.8}Ti_{0.2}$ as a function of cycle number. Interestingly, there is a close correlation between Q_{broad} and the reversible hydrogen storage capacity. During the first five cycles when the Q_{broad} value increases quickly, the amount of absorbed hydrogen is reduced rapidly. In subsequent cycles, changes in both Q_{broad} and the reversible hydrogen storage capacity become small. The strong correlation between the Q_{broad} value and the hydrogen storage capacity leads us to an idea that dislocation defects are generated over cycles and they probably play an important role in degradation in the reversible hydrogen storage capacity of $V_{0.8}Ti_{0.2}$.

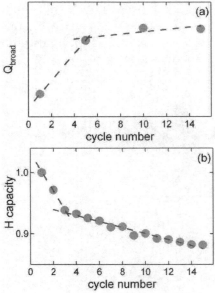

Figure 7.17 (a) The Q_{broad} values obtained from the PDF refinements of $V_{0.8}Ti_{0.2}H_2$ data and (b) the reversible hydrogen capacity of $V_{0.8}Ti_{0.2}$ at 413 K are plotted as a function of cycle number. The reversible hydrogen storage capacity was normalized by the value of the first cycle. Dashed lines are for guidance [64].

7.4 Summary

In this chapter, we have presented examples of how the PDF analysis of X-ray and neutron total scattering data can be used to reveal key structural features of crystallographically challenged hydrogen storage materials and how those features are responsible for their hydrogen storage properties. Numerous advanced energy materials share similar structural characterization problems as our examples and we believe readers can benefit largely from this powerful emerging technique for studying their materials.

Acknowledgments

This work was partly supported by the New Energy and Industrial Technology Development Organization (NEDO) under Advanced Fundamental Research Project on Hydrogen Storage Materials (HYDRO-STAR). This work has benefited from the use of NPDF at the Lujan Neutron Scattering Center at Los Alamos National Laboratory, funded by the DOE office of Basic Energy Sciences. Los Alamos National Laboratory is operated by Los Alamos National Security LLC under Contract DE-AC52-06NA25396. Use of the Advanced Photon Source, an Office of Science User Facility operated for the U.S. Department of Energy (DOE) Office of Science by Argonne National Laboratory, was supported by the U.S. DOE under Contract No. DE-AC02-06CH11357. Work at SPring-8 was performed under the Shared Use Program of JAEA Facilities under Proposal No. 2011A3703 and No. 2011B3784.

References

1. Schlapbach, L., and Züttel, A. (2001). Hydrogen-storage materials for mobile applications, *Nature*, **414**, 353–358.

2. Broom, D. P. (2011). *Hydrogen Storage Materials: The Characterisation and Their Hydrogen Storage Properties* (Springer-Verlag, London).

3. Seayad, A. M., and Antonelli, D. M. (2004). Recent advances in hydrogen storage in metal-containing inorganic nanostructures and related materials, *Adv. Mater.*, **16**, 765–777.

4. van den Berg, A. W. C., and Areán, C. O. (2008). Materials for hydrogen storage: current research trends and perspectives, *Chem. Commun.*, **2008**, 668–681.

5. Huot, J., Ravnsbæk, D. B., Zhang, J., Cuevas, F., Latroche, M., and Jensen, T. R. (2013). Mechanochemical synthesis of hydrogen storage materials, *Prog. Mater. Sci.*, **58**, 30–75.

6. de Jongh, P. E., and Adelhelm P. (2010). Nanosizing and nanoconfinement: New strategies towards meeting hydrogen storage goals, *ChemSusChem*, **3**, 1332–1348.

7. Zhang, Y., Tsushio, Y., Enoki, H., and Akiba, E. (2005). The study on binary Mg-Co hydrogen storage alloys with BCC phase, *J. Alloys Compounds*, **393**, 147–153.

8. Billinge, S. J. L., and Levin, I. (2007). The problem with determining atomic structure at the nanoscale, *Science*, **316**, 561–565.

9. Egami, T. and Billinge, S. J. L. (2003). *Underneath the Bragg Peaks: Structural Analysis of Complex Materials* (Pergamon Press Elsevier, Oxford, England).

10. Warren, B. E. (1990). *X-Ray Diffraction* (Dover, New York).

11. Benmore, C. J. (2012). A review of high-energy X-ray diffraction from glasses and liquids, *ISRN Mater. Sci.*, 2012, 852905.

12. Billinge, S. J. L., and Kanatzidis, M. G. (2004). Beyond crystallography: The study of disorder, nanocrystallinity and crystallographically challenged materials with pair distribution functions, *Chem. Commun.*, **2004**, 749–760.

13. Proffen, T., Billinge, S. J. L., Egami, T., and Louca, D. (2003). Structural analysis of complex materials using the atomic pair distribution function: A practical guide, *Z. Kristallogr.*, **218**, 132–143.

14. Proffen, T., and Kim, H. (2009). Advances in total scattering analysis, *J. Mater. Chem.*, **19**, 5078–5088.

15. Malavasi, L. (2011). Total scattering investigation of materials for clean energy applications: The importance of the local structure, *Dalton Trans.*, **40**, 3777–3788.

16. Hurd, A., and Sinha, S. (2012) *Neutrons and Nanoscience* (Springer, New York).

17. Petkov, V., Jeong, I. K., Chung, J. S., Thorpe, M. F., Kycia, S., and Billinge, S. J. L. (1999). High real-space resolution measurement of the local structure of $Ga_{1-x}In_xAs$ using X-ray diffraction, *Phys. Rev. Lett.*, **83**, 4089–4092.

18. Peterson, P. F., Proffen, T., Jeong, I. K., Billinge, S. J. L., Choi, K. S., Kanatzidis, M. G., and Radaelli, P. G. (2001). Local atomic strain in $ZnSe_{1-x}Te_x$ from high real-space resolution neutron pair distribution function measurements, *Phys. Rev. B.*, **63**, 165211.

19. Qiu, X. Y., Proffen, T., Mitchell, J. F., and Billinge, S. J. L. (2005). Orbital correlations in the pseudocubic O and rhombohedral R phases of $LaMnO_3$, *Phys. Rev. Lett.*, **94**, 177203.

20. Sartbaeva, A., Wells, S. A., Thorpe, M. F., Bozin, E. S., and Billinge, S. J. L. (2006) Geometric simulation of perovskite frameworks with Jahn-Teller distortions: applications to the cubic manganites, *Phys. Rev. Lett.*, **97**, 065501.

21. Kim, H. J., Bozin, E. S., Haile, S. M., Snyder, G. J., and Billinge, S. J. L. (2007). Nanoscale α-structural domains in the phonon-glass thermoelectric material β-Zn_4Sb_3, *Phys. Rev. B*, **75**, 134103.

22. Lin, H., Bozin, E. S., Billinge, S. J. L., Quarez, E., and Kanatzidis, M. G. (2005). Nanoscale clusters in the high performance thermoelectric $AgPb_mSbTe_{m+2}$, *Phys. Rev. B*, **72**, 174113.

23. Paglia, G., Bozin, E. S., and Billinge, S. J. L. (2006). Fine-scale nanostructure in γ-Al_2O_3, *Chem. Mater.*, **18**, 3242–3248.

24. Bozin, E. S., Malliakas, C. D., Souvatzis, P., Proffen, T., Spaldin, N. A., Kanatzidis, M. G., and Billinge, S. J. L. (2010). Entropically stabilized local dipole formation in lead chalcogenides, *Science*, **330**, 1660–1663.

25. Gilbert, B., Huang, F., Zhang, H. Z., Waychunas, G. A., and Banfield, J. F. (2004). Nanoparticles: Strained and stiff, *Science*, **305**, 651–654.

26. Page, K., Proffen, T., Terrones, H., Terrones, M., Lee, L., Yang, Y., Stemmer, S., Seshadri, R., and Cheetham, A. K. (2004). Direct observation of the structure of gold nanoparticles by total scattering powder neutron diffraction, *Chem. Phys. Lett.*, **393**, 385–388.

27. Neder, R. B., and Korsunskiy, V. I. (2005). Structure of nanoparticles from powder diffraction data using the pair distribution function, *J. Phys. Condens. Matter*, **17**, S125–S134.

28. Juhas, P., Cherba, D. M., Duxbury, P. M., Punch, W. F., and Billinge, S. J. L. (2006). Ab initio determination of solid-state nanostructure, *Nature*, **440**, 655–658.

29. Masadeh, A. S., Bozin, E. S., Farrow, C. L., Paglia, G., Juhas, P., Billinge, S. J. L., Karkamkar, A., and Kanatzidis, M. G. (2007). Quantitative size-dependent structure and strain determination of CdSe nanoparticles using atomic pair distribution function analysis, *Phys. Rev. B*, **76**, 115413.

30. Page, K., Proffen, T., Niederberger, M., and Seshadri, R. (2010). Probing local dipoles and ligand structure in $BaTiO_3$ nanoparticles, *Chem. Mater.*, **22**, 4386–4391.

31. Newton, M. A., Chapman, K. W., Thompsett, D., and Chupas, P. J. (2012). Chasing changing nanoparticles with time-resolved pair distribution function methods, *J. Am. Chem. Soc.*, **134**, 5036–5039.

32. Proffen, T., Egami, T., Billinge, S. J. L., Cheetham, A. K., Louca, D., and Parise, J. B. (2002), Building a high resolution total scattering powder diffractometer upgrade of NPD at MLNSC, *Appl. Phys. A Mater. Sci. Process.*, **74**, S163–S165.

33. Peterson, P. F., Gutmann, M., Proffen, T., and Billinge, S. J. L. (2000). PDFgetN: A user-friendly program to extract the total scattering structure factor and the pair distribution function from neutron powder diffraction data, *J. Appl. Crystallogr.*, **33**, 1192.

34. Qiu, X. Y., Thompson, J. W., and Billinge, S. J. L. (2004). PDFgetX2: A GUI driven program to obtain the pair distribution function from X-ray powder diffraction data, *J. Appl. Crystallogr.*, **37**, 678.

35. Rietveld, H. (1969). A profile refinement method for nuclear and magnetic structures, *J. Appl. Crystallogr.*, **2**, 65–71.

36. Farrow, C. L., Juhás, P., Liu, J. W., Bryndin, D., Božin, E. S., Bloch, J., Proffen, T. and Billinge, S. J. L. (2007). PDFfit2 and PDFgui: Computer programs for studying nanostructure in crystals, *J. Phys Condens. Matter*, **19**, 335219.

37. McGreevy, R. L. (2001). Reverse Monte Carlo modeling, *J. Phys. Condens. Matter.*, **13**, R877–R913.

38. Tucker, M. G., Dove, M. T., and Keen, D. A. (2001). Application of the reverse Monte Carlo method to crystalline materials, *J. Appl. Cryst.*, **34**, 630–638.

39. Tucker, M. G., Keen, D. A., Dove, M. T., Goodwin, A. L., and Hui, Q. (2007). RMCProfile: Reverse Monte Carlo for polycrystalline materials, *J. Phys. Condens. Matter.*, **19**, 335218.

40. Hoon, C. F., and Reynhardt, E. C. (1983). Molecular dynamics and structures of amine boranes of the type $R_3N.BH_3$. 1. X-ray investigation of $H_3N.BH_3$ at 295 and 110 K, *J. Phys. C Solid State Phys.*, **16**, 6129–6236.

41. Hess, N. J., Bowden, M. E., Parvanov, V. M., Mundy, C., Kathmann, S. M., Schenter, G. K., and Autrey, T. (2008). Spectroscopic studies of the phase transition in ammonia borane: Raman spectroscopy of single crystal NH_3BH_3 as a function of temperature from 88 to 330 K, *J. Phys. Chem.*, **128**, 034508.

42. Hess, N. J., Schenter, G. K., Hartman, M. R., Daemen, L. L. Proffen, T., Kathmann, S. M., Mundy, C. J., Hartl, M., Heldebrant, D. J., Stowe, A. C.,

and Autrey, T. (2009). Neutron Powder diffraction and molecular simulation study of the structural evolution of ammonia borane from 15 to 340 K, *J. Phys. Chem. A*, **113**, 5723–5735.

43. Paolone, A., Palumbo, O., Rispoli, P., Cantelli, R., and Autrey, T. (2009). Hydrogen dynamics and characterization of the tetragonal-to-orthorhombic phase transformation in ammonia borane, *J. Phys. Chem. C*, **113**, 5872–5878.

44. Penner, G. H., Chang, Y. C. P., and Hutzal, J. (1999). A deuterium NMR spectroscopic study of solid BH_3NH_3, *Inorg. Chem.*, **38**, 2868–2873.

45. Gunaydin-Sen, O., Achey, R., Dalal, N. S., Stowe, A., and Autrey, T. (2007). High resolution ^{15}N NMR of the 225 K phase transition of ammonia borane (NH_3BH_3): Mixed order-disorder and displacive behavior, *J. Phys. Chem. B*, **111**, 677–681.

46. Gutowska, A., Li, L., Shin, Y., Wang, C. M., Li, X. S., Linehan, J. C., Smith, R. S., Kay, B. D., Schmid, B., Shaw, W., Gutowski, M., and Autrey, T. (2005). Nanoscaffold mediates hydrogen release and the reactivity of ammonia borane, *Angew. Chem. Int. Ed.*, **44**, 3578–3582.

47. Wang, L.-Q., Karkamkar, A., Autrey, T., and Exarhos, G. J. (2009). Hyperpolarized Xe-129 NMR investigation of ammonia borane in mesoporous silica, *J. Phys. Chem. C*, **113**, 6485–6490.

48. Chupas, P. J., Qiu, X., Hanson, J. C., Lee, P. L., Grey, C. P., and Billinge, S. J. L. (2003). Rapid-acquisition pair distribution function (RA-PDF) analysis, *J. Appl. Crystallogr.*, **36**, 1342–1347.

49. Kim, H., Karkamkar, A., Autrey, T., Chupas, P. J., and Proffen, T. (2009). Determination of structure and phase transition of light element nanocomposites in mesoporous silica: case study of NH_3BH_3 in MCM-41, *J. Am. Chem. Soc.*, **131**, 13749–13755.

50. Yang, J. B., Lamsal, J., Cai, Q., James, W. J., and Yelon, W. B. (2008). Structural evolution of ammonia borane for hydrogen storage, *Appl. Phys. Lett.*, **92**, 091916.

51. Paolone, A., Palumbo, O., Rispoli, P., Cantelli, R., Autrey, T., and Karkamkar, A. (2009) Absence of the structural phase transition in ammonia borane dispersed in mesoporous silica: evidence of novel thermodynamic properties, *J. Phys. Chem. C*, **113**, 10319–10321.

52. Shao, H., Asano, K., Enoki, H., and Akiba, E. (2009). Fabrication, hydrogen storage properties and mechanistic study of nanostructured $Mg_{50}Co_{50}$ body-centered cubic alloy, *Scr. Mater.*, **60**, 818–821.

53. Matsuda, J., Shao, H., Nakamura, Y., and Akiba, E. (2009). The nanostructure and hydrogenation reaction of $Mg_{50}Co_{50}$ BCC alloy prepared by ball-milling, *Nanotechnology*, **20**, 204015.

54. Kim, H., Nakamura, J., Shao, H., Nakamura, Y., Akiba, E., Chapman, K. W., Chupas, P. J., and Proffen, T. (2011). Local structural evolution of mechanically alloyed $Mg_{50}Co_{50}$ using atomic pair distribution function analysis, *J. Phys. Chem. C*, **115**, 7723–7728.

55. Kim, H., Nakamura, J., Shao, H., Nakamura, Y., Akiba, E., Chapman, K. W., Chupas, P. J., and Proffen, T. (2011). Insight into the hydrogenation properties of mechanically alloyed $Mg_{50}Co_{50}$ from the local structure, *J. Phys. Chem. C*, **115**, 20335–20341.

56. Kim, H., Nakamura, J., Shao, H., Nakamura, Y., Akiba, E., Chapman, K. W., Chupas, P. J., and Proffen, T. (2012). Variation in the ratio of Mg_2Co and $MgCo_2$ in amorphous-like mechanically alloyed Mg_xCo_{100-x} using atomic pair distribution function analysis, *Z. Kristallogr.*, **227**, 299–303.

57. Buschow, K. H. J. (1975). Magnetic properties of $MgCo_2$, $MgNi_2$ and Mg_2Ni, *Solid State Commun.*, **17**, 891–893.

58. Zachariasen, W. H., Holley, C. E., and Stamper, J. F. (1963). Neutron diffraction study of magnesium deuteride, *Acta Crystallogr.*, **16**, 352–353.

59. Zolliker, P., Yvon, K., Fischer, P., and Schefer, J. (1985). Dimagnesium cobalt(I) pentahydride, Mg_2CoH_5, containing square-pyramidal CoH_5^{4-} anions, *Inorg. Chem.*, **24**, 4177–4180.

60. Černý, R., Bonhomme, F., Yvon, K., Fischer, P., Zolliker, P., Cox, D. E., and Hewat, A. (1992). Hexamagnesium dicobalt undecadeuteride $Mg_6Co_2D_{11}$: containing $[CoD_4]^{5-}$ and $[CoD_5]^{4-}$ complex anions conforming to the 18-electron rule, *J. Alloys Compounds*, **187**, 233–241.

61. Itoh, H., Arashima, H., Kubo, K., Kabutomori, T., and Ohnishi, K. (2005). Improvement of cyclic durability of BCC structured Ti-Cr-V alloys, *J. Alloys Compounds*, **404–406**, 417–420.

62. Aoki, M., Noritake, T., Ito, A., Ishikiriyama, M., and Towata, S. (2011). Improvement of cyclic durability of Ti-Cr-V alloy by Fe substitution, *Int. J. Hydrogen Energy*, **36**, 12329–12332.

63. Watanuki, T., Machida, A., Ikeda, T., Ohmura, A., Kaneko, H., Aoki, K., Sato, T. J., and Tsai, A. P. (2007). Development of a single-crystal X-ray diffraction system for hydrostatic-pressure and low-temperature structural measurement and its application to the phase study of quasicrystals, *Philos. Mag.*, **87**, 2905–2911.

64. Kim, H., Sakaki, K., Ogawa, H., Nakamura, Y., Nakamura, J., Akiba, E., Machida, A., Watanuki, T., Proffen, T. (2013). Origin of Degradation in the Reversible Hydrogen Storage Capacity of $V_{1-x}Ti_x$ Alloys from

the Atomic Pair Distribution Function Analysis, *J. Phys. Chem. C*, **117**, 26543–26550.

65. Matsuda, J., Nakamura, Y., and Akiba, E. (2011). Microstructure of Ti-V-Mn BCC alloys before and after hydrogen absorption-desorption, *J. Alloys Compounds*, **509**, 4352–4356.

66. Kawasuso, A., Arashima, H., Maekawa, M., Itoh, H., and Kabutomori, T. (2009). TiCrV hydrogen storage alloy studied by positron annihilation spectroscopy, *J. Alloys Compounds*, **486**, 278–283.

67. Murray Gibson, J. (2007). Understanding the limits of pair-distribution functions for nanoscale correlation function measurement, *J. Phys. Condens. Matter*, **19**, 455217.

68. Farrow, C. L., Juhás, P., Liu, J. W., Bryndin, D., Božin, E. S., Bloch, J., Proffen, T., and Billinge, S. J. L. (2009). PDFgui User Guild.

Chapter 8

Precise Structure Analysis of Inorganic Materials for Clean Energy by Maximum-Entropy Method: Neutron and Synchrotron X-Ray Powder Diffraction Studies

Masatomo Yashima

Department of Chemistry and Materials Science, Tokyo Institute of Technology, 2-12-1-W4-17, O-okayama, Meguro-ku, Tokyo, 152-8551, Japan

yashima@cms.titech.ac.jp

This chapter presents a review on the field of clean energy, including materials, crystal structure, electron/nuclear-density distribution, and diffusional pathway of mobile ions. The electron/nuclear-density analysis based on the maximum-entropy method (MEM) and MEM-based pattern fitting using neutron and synchrotron powder diffraction data is powerful to investigate the diffusional pathway of mobile ions and the chemical bonding of materials for clean energy. Structural disorder and/or diffusional pathways of mobile oxide ions and copper cations have been visualized in various fluorite-type materials (ceria solid solution,

Structural Characterization Techniques: Advances and Applications in Clean Energy
Edited by Lorenzo Malavasi
Copyright © 2016 Pan Stanford Publishing Pte. Ltd.
ISBN 978-981-4669-34-4 (Hardcover), 978-981-4669-35-1 (eBook)
www.panstanford.com

$Ce_{0.93}Y_{0.07}O_{1.96}$; bismuth oxide solid solution, $Bi_{1.4}Yb_{0.6}O_3$; yttrium tantalum oxide, $Y_{0.785}Ta_{0.215}O_{1.715}$; copper iodide, CuI; ceria-zirconia, $Ce_xZr_{1-x}O_2$ ($x = 0.12$, 0.5 and 1.0)) and perovskite-type and perovskite–related materials (($La_{0.80}Sr_{0.20}$)($Ga_{0.80}Mg_{0.15}Co_{0.05}$)$O_{2.8}$, $LaGaO_3$, $La_{0.6}Sr_{0.4}CoO_{3-\delta}$, $La_{0.4}Ba_{0.6}CoO_{3-\delta}$, $La_{0.6}Sr_{0.4}Co_{0.8}Fe_{0.2}O_{3-\delta}$, $La_{0.64}(Ti_{0.92}Nb_{0.08})O_{2.99}$). The diffusional pathway of mobile ions through the interstitialcy or interstitial mechanism has also been investigated in $Pr_2(Ni_{0.75}Cu_{0.25})_{0.95}Ga_{0.05}O_{4+\delta}$, $Pr_2Ni_{0.75}Cu_{0.25}O_{4+\delta}$, $(Pr_{0.9}La_{0.1})_2(Ni_{0.74}Cu_{0.21}\text{-}Ga_{0.05})O_{4+\delta}$, and $La_{9.69}(Si_{5.70}Mg_{0.30})O_{26+\delta}$. Electron-density analysis of visible-light photocatalysts enables the visualization of covalent and ionic bonds. The covalent bonding makes the bandwidth wider and the band gap narrower, which leads to the visible-light response of these materials. We also describe the electron-density analysis of a visible-light photocatalyst $(Ga_{0.885}Zn_{0.115})(N_{0.885}O_{0.115})$.

8.1   Introduction

Ionic conducting ceramic materials are keys for the clean energy, because the electrolyte and cathode materials for solid oxide fuel cells require the high ionic conductivity and the ionic-electronic mixed conductors are used for oxygen separation membrane [1–7]. The nuclear/electron-density distribution obtained by the maximum-entropy method (MEM) analysis of neutron, X-ray and synchrotron X-ray diffraction data enables the visualization of diffusional pathways of mobile ions and anisotropic/anharmonic atomic thermal motions in ionic conducting ceramic materials [5, 6, 8, 9]. In this review, I describe the results of MEM analyses for various ionic conducting ceramic materials.

Overall water splitting using a photocatalyst is an attractive solution for the supply of clean and recyclable hydrogen energy. A large number of photocatalysts have been proposed to date; however, most photocatalysts work only in the ultraviolet ($\lambda <$ 400 nm, energy fraction of about 4% in the sunlight) region (e.g., titania (TiO_2) [10]) due to the large band gap of metal oxides. Recently various metal oxynitrides and metal oxysulfides have been proposed to be visible-light (more than 40% energy of sunlight) responsive photocatalysts [11]. Crystal structure and chemical bonding influence on the band gap and visible-light response of the photocatalysts. In the present review, I also describe the crystal structure and electron-density distribution of visible-light responsive photocatalyst.

8.2 Method of the Precise Structure Analysis of Ionic Conducting Ceramic Materials and Photocatalysts

The ionic conductivity of an ionic conducting material increases with an increase of temperature. The electrochemical devices such as solid oxide fuel cells and oxygen sensors efficiently work at high temperatures. However, there exists a lack of crystallographic and geometric information of mobile ions in particular at high temperatures. The ionic conduction occurs through the diffusion of mobile ions; therefore, it is required to investigate the diffusional pathways of the mobile ions in the crystal lattice of ionic conducting materials at high temperatures. The visualization of diffusional pathways of mobile ions is essential to establish the mechanism of the diffusion and ionic conduction.

Neutron powder diffraction is powerful to investigate the position and spatial distribution of light elements such as oxygen, hydrogen and lithium atoms in the crystal lattice of a mixed compound consisting of heavy metal and light atoms. We devised and fabricated new furnaces which enable in situ measurements of quality neutron powder diffraction data up to 1860 K in air [12] and high-angular-resolution synchrotron powder diffraction data up to 1770 K in air [13, 14].

Figure 8.1 shows a photograph of the neutron diffractometer HERMES [15] and the furnace for high-temperature measurements [12]. The combination of the furnace and HERMES diffractometer enables the collection of high-quality neutron powder diffraction data, which leads to precise nuclear-density distribution of ceramic materials in air up to 1860 K.

The diffusional pathway of mobile ions in the ionic conducting materials has been studied by expressing the spatial distribution of mobile ions using the split-atom model, anharmonic thermal vibration and Fourier transform of the structure factor. However, the split-atom model is not appropriate to describe the continuous and complicated spatial distribution of mobile ions. It is difficult to refine the higher terms of anharmonic atomic displacement parameters. The Fourier synthesis makes the ghost due to the termination effect. On the contrary, the nuclear/electron density analysis through the maximum-entropy method (MEM) using the limited number of structure factors is able to describe precisely the continuous and complicated spatial distribution of mobile ions. We have used a computer program PRIMA [9] for the MEM calculations. A successor of PRIMA, Dysnomia is developed by Izumi's group.

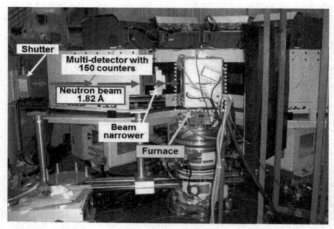

Figure 8.1 A photograph of the neutron diffractometer HERMES [15] equipped with the furnace for high-temperature measurements [12].

In the MEM analysis, observed structure factors and their errors are required. First we perform the Rietveld analysis of neutron/synchrotron X-ray powder diffraction data using a computer program (e.g., RIETAN-FP [8]). We obtain the observed structure factors F_O(Rietveld) and their errors δF_O(Rietveld) as an output of the Rietveld analysis. Although the MEM is a model-free method, the MEM nuclear- and electron-density distributions are biased by the Rietveld analysis result. By the MEM-based pattern fitting (MPF) (see Fig. 8.2), we can obtain more reliable nuclear- and electron-density distributions. The MPF is the total pattern fitting of the neutron/synchrotron powder diffraction data by fixing the structure factors to the calculated ones F_C(MEM). The MPF yields the observed structure factors F_O(MPF) and their errors, which are used in the next MEM analysis. This analysis process is iterated (REMEDY cycle), which can improve the MEM results. The crystal structure and nuclear/electron-density distributions are drawn with computer programs VEATA or VENUS [9, 16]. In this review, I describe examples of Rietveld, MEM and MPF analyses of ionic conducting materials and photocatalysts.

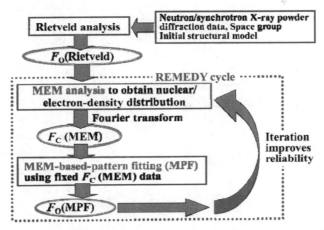

Figure 8.2 Flow chart of the MEM-based pattern fitting (MPF), including the Rietveld and MEM analyses, MPF and REMEDY cycle.

8.3 Examples of MEM and MPF Analysis of Oxide-Ion Conducting Ceramic Materials (Oxygen Vacancy Mechanism)

The diffusion of mobile ions occurs by (i) vacancy mechanism, (ii) interstitial mechanism, or (iii) interfacial mechanism. In this section, I describe the MEM and MPF analysis of ionic conducting materials where the ions move via the vacancy mechanism.

8.3.1 Fluorite-Type and Related Ionic Conducting Materials

Figure 8.3 shows the Rietveld pattern of neutron powder diffraction data of an yttria-doped ceria material ($Ce_{0.93}Y_{0.07}O_{1.96}$, space group: $Fm\bar{3}m$) taken at 1434°C in air [17]. The Rietveld analysis was carried out assuming the fluorite-type structure with the $Fm\bar{3}m$

symmetry where the cation (Ce^{4+} and Y^{3+}) and anions (O^{2-} and its vacancy) were put at $4a$ 0,0,0 and at $8c$ 1/4,1/4,1/4, respectively. The reliability factors were R_{wp} = 6.58%, R_B = 2.19%, and R_F = 1.36%. $Ce_{0.93}Y_{0.07}O_{1.96}$ has the defect fluorite-type structure. The occupancy factor of the oxygen atom is fixed to 0.98175, which indicates the existence of anion vacancy (fraction at the anion site = 0.01825). The oxide ion moves via the vacancy mechanism. Figure 8.4 shows the MEM nuclear-density distribution of $Ce_{0.93}Y_{0.07}O_{1.96}$ at (a) 23 and (b) 1434°C. At 23°C the oxygen atoms are localized near the $8c$ 1/4,1/4,1/4 position, while the oxide ions are spread over widely at 1434°C. The spatial distribution of nuclear densities of an oxygen atom is connected with that of the nearest neighbor oxygen atom at 1434°C. The connected nuclear density is the diffusional pathway of oxide ions, which is not straight but curved. The curved diffusional pathway exists along the <100> directions, which forms a three-dimensional network (Figs. 8.4b and 8.5a).

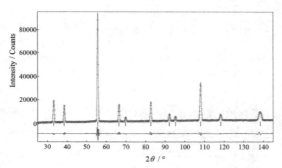

Figure 8.3 Rietveld pattern of neutron powder diffraction data of $Ce_{0.93}Y_{0.07}O_{1.96}$ taken at 1434°C [17].

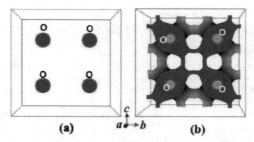

Figure 8.4 MEM nuclear-density distribution of $Ce_{0.93}Y_{0.07}O_{1.96}$ at (a) 23 and (b) 1434°C ($0.15 \leq x \leq 0.3$) [17].

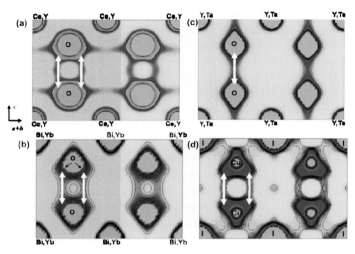

Figure 8.5   Nuclear-density distributions on the (110) planes of the fluorite-type structured (a) $Ce_{0.93}Y_{0.07}O_{1.96}$ (1434°C) [17], (b) $Bi_{1.4}Yb_{0.6}O_3$ (738°C) [18] and (c) $Y_{0.785}Ta_{0.215}O_{1.715}$ (535°C) [20]. (d) Electron-density distribution on the (110) planes of the fluorite-type structured copper iodide CuI (487°C) [21].

The neutron powder diffraction data of $Bi_{1.4}Yb_{0.6}O_3$ were collected in air at 384°C and at 738°C [18]. The MEM calculations were carried out with 64 × 64 × 64 pixels. After the REMEDY cycle, the R-factors based on the Bragg intensities, R_B, were improved from 7.73% to 1.00% and from 6.94% to 0.84% for the neutron data taken at 384°C and 738°C, respectively. The R-factors based on the structure factors, R_F, were also improved by the REMEDY cycle from 5.08% to 0.61% and from 4.33% to 0.58% for the data measured at 384°C and 738°C, respectively. Figure 8.5b shows the MEM nuclear-density distribution on the (110) plane in δ-$Bi_{1.4}Yb_{0.6}O_3$ at 738°C. The oxide ions have a complicated disorder spreading over a wide area, as compared to the cations. The disorder is more significant at higher temperatures, which is consistent with the higher oxide-ion conductivity and the higher atomic displacement parameters at higher temperatures [18]. The oxide ions shift to the opposite direction from the cations of Bi and Yb, probably due to the repulsive force between the cations and anions (black arrows in Fig. 8.5b). Similar positional disorder was observed in MEM nuclear-density distribution in the cubic defect fluorite-type δ-Bi_2O_3 [19] and yttrium tantalum oxide $Y_{0.785}Ta_{0.215}O_{1.715}$ (Fig. 8.5c) [20]. It is interesting to point out that the diffusional pathway along the <100> directions is observed not only in the oxide-ion conducting fluorite-type oxides (Figs. 8.5a–8.5c) but also the Cu^+-cation conductor CuI (Fig. 8.5d) [21]. Here I have demonstrated that the combination of MEM with Rietveld and MPF analysis is powerful to investigate the positional disorder and diffusional pathway of fluorite-type ionic conductors [22].

Ceria-zirconia ($Ce_xZr_{1-x}O_2$) materials are widely used as exhaust gas catalysts [22–26]. The oxide ions in $Ce_{0.5}Zr_{0.5}O_2$ are spread over a significantly wider area compared with other $Ce_xZr_{1-x}O_2$ (x = 0.12 and 1.0) (Fig. 8.6), which suggests the high bulk diffusivity of the oxide ions and high catalytic activity of $Ce_{0.5}Zr_{0.5}O_2$ [25]. The ceria-zirconia materials exhibit lower oxide-ion diffusivity compared with typical superionic conductors, thus, it is difficult to visualize the connected diffusional pathway in MEM nuclear-density map. Using the bond valence mapping [27], we can obtain the possible diffusional pathway of oxide ions in nanocrystalline $Ce_{0.5}Zr_{0.5}O_2$ [26]. Figure 8.7 shows the bond valence map on the (100) plane of nanocrystalline $Ce_{0.5}Zr_{0.5}O_2$ [26], which indicates the possible diffusional pathway of oxide ions along the <100> (arrows in Fig. 8.7) and <110> directions.

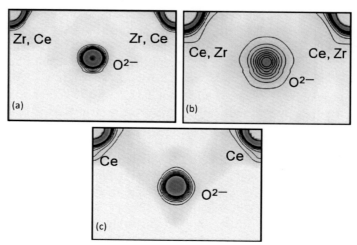

Figure 8.6 Electron-density distribution of bulk ceria-zirconia materials $Ce_xZr_{1-x}O_2$ [25]. (a) x = 0.12, (b) x = 0.5 and (c) x = 1.0.

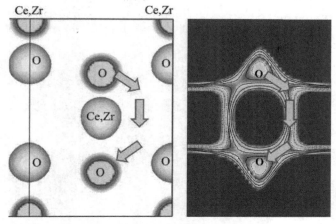

Figure 8.7   (a) MEM nuclear-density distribution and (b) bond valence map on the (100) plane of nanocrystalline $Ce_{0.5}Zr_{0.5}O_2$ [26], which indicates the possible diffusional pathway of oxide ions along the <100> and <001> directions. (a) 299 K and (b) 1176 K.

8.3.2   Perovskite-Type and Double Perovskite-Type Ionic Conducting Materials

Perovskite-type oxide-ion conducting materials have been utilized as electrolytes and cathodes of solid-oxide fuel cells (SOFCs) for clean energy [28, 29]. Lanthanum gallate-based material $(La_{0.80}Sr_{0.20})$-$(Ga_{0.80}Mg_{0.15}Co_{0.05})O_{2.8}$ (LSGMC) is used as the electrolyte of SOFCs, because this composition exhibits high oxide-ion conductivity. Refined crystal structure of LSGMC at 1392°C indicates highly anisotropic thermal motions (Fig. 8.8a). The MEM nuclear-density distribution clearly shows the connected probability density of oxide ions (Fig. 8.8b). The diffusional pathway (e.g., Oa-Ob in Fig. 8.8b) is not straight (black dotted line in Fig. 8.8b) but curved keeping the (Ga,Mg,Co)-oxygen distance to some degree (white line with arrows in Fig. 8.8b). Figures 8.9a–8.9c indicate that the spatial distribution of oxide ions becomes larger with an increase of temperature, which is consistent with the fact that the ionic conductivity also increases with temperature. The mother material $LaGaO_3$ does not exhibit connected nuclear densities between nearest-neighbor oxygen sites even at 1390°C (Fig. 8.9d), but the LSGMC clearly shows the connected diffusional pathway of oxide ions at 1392°C (Figs. 8.8b and 8.9a). This is consistent with the higher ionic conductivity of LSGMC than that of the mother material $LaGaO_3$.

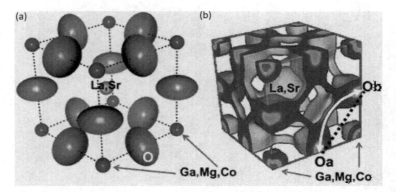

Figure 8.8   (a) Refined crystal structure and (b) isosurface of nuclear density of $(La_{0.80}Sr_{0.20})(Ga_{0.80}Mg_{0.15}Co_{0.05})O_{2.8}$ (1392°C) [28].

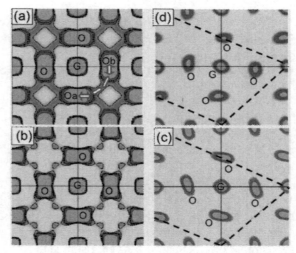

Figure 8.9   Nuclear-density distributions of $(La_{0.80}Sr_{0.20})(Ga_{0.80}Mg_{0.15}Co_{0.05})O_{2.8}$ ((a) 1392°C, (b) 1198°C, (c) 796°C) [28, 29] and $LaGaO_3$ (1390°C) [29, 30].

Lanthanum cobaltite ($LaCoO_3$)-based materials are oxide-ion and electronic mixed conductors, which are utilized as cathode materials for SOFCs and oxygen separation membranes. Next, I describe the MEM nuclear-density distributions of $LaCoO_3$-based materials ($La_{0.4}Ba_{0.6}CoO_{3-\delta}$, $La_{0.6}Sr_{0.4}CoO_{3-\delta}$, and $La_{0.6}Sr_{0.4}Co_{0.8}$ $Fe_{0.2}O_{3-\delta}$) [31–33]. In all three compositions the oxide ions exhibit highly anisotropic thermal motions where the thermal vibration perpendicular to the Co-O or (Co,Fe)-O bonds is larger. The MEM nuclear densities of $La_{0.6}Sr_{0.4}CoO_{3-\delta}$ and $La_{0.6}Sr_{0.4}Co_{0.8}Fe_{0.2}O_{3-\delta}$ did not exhibit connected diffusional pathway of oxide ions, thus, we proposed a possible curved diffusional pathway considering the highly anisotropic thermal motion around the stable position [31, 32]. Recently, we successfully visualized the connected oxide-ion diffusional pathway in $La_{0.4}Ba_{0.6}CoO_{3-\delta}$ at 1277°C (P1-P2-P3 path in Fig. 8.10d) [33], which strongly suggests its higher oxide-ion diffusivity. The higher oxide-ion diffusivity in $La_{0.4}Ba_{0.6}CoO_{3-\delta}$ was validated by (i) higher bottleneck size for oxide-ion diffusion and (ii) higher concentration of carrier (oxygen vacancy) concentration [33].

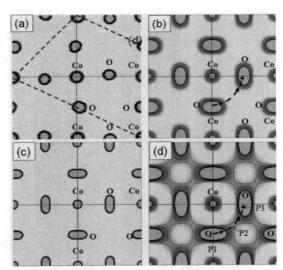

Figure 8.10 Nuclear-density distribution of $La_{0.6}Sr_{0.4}CoO_{3-\delta}$ at (a) 27.5°C and (b) 1258°C in air. Nuclear-density distribution of $La_{0.4}Ba_{0.6}CoO_{3-\delta}$ at (c) 27°C and (d) 1277°C in air.

The diffusion pathway of mixed conductor $La_{0.4}Ba_{0.6}CoO_{3-\delta}$ (Fig. 8.10d) is similar to that of ionic conductor ($La_{0.80}Sr_{0.20}$) ($Ga_{0.80}Mg_{0.15}Co_{0.05}$)-$O_{2.8}$ (Fig. 8.9a). The path of cubic perovskite-type ABO_3-based ionic conducting materials is curved keeping the distance from the B site cation to some degree. The path is along the <100> direction near the stable oxygen position (P1, P3 in Fig. 8.10d), while along <110> around the center of the path (P2 in Fig. 8.10d). The perovskite-type ionic and mixed conductors form three-dimensional network of oxide-ion diffusional pathways.

We visualized the diffusional pathway of oxide ions in the nuclear-density distribution of double perovskite-type compound $La_{0.64}(Ti_{0.92}Nb_{0.08})O_{2.99}$ (Fig. 8.11) [34]. The crystal structure of $La_{0.64}(Ti_{0.92}Nb_{0.08})O_{2.99}$ consists of alternative La-occupied La1-O1 and La-defective La2-O2 one (Fig. 8.11a). The oxide ions diffuse along the edge of $(Ti_{0.92}Nb_{0.08})O_6$ octahedron ($O3_a$–$O3_b$ in Fig. 8.11). The path is not straight (dotted line L in Fig. 8.11) but curved (white line with arrows C in Fig. 8.11). These features of the diffusion path of double perovskite are similar to those of cubic perovskite. It should be noted that the $O3_a$–$O3_b$ path is connected by the nuclear densities and that the O1-O3 and O2-O3 paths are not connected. The $O3_a$–$O3_b$ path forms two-dimensional network, which leads to anisotropic diffusion. The MEM nuclear- and electron-density analysis enables the direct visualization of anisotropic diffusion. The minimum nuclear density value on the $O3_a$–$O3_b$ path increases with an increase of temperature, which indicates higher oxide-ion diffusivity at higher temperatures.

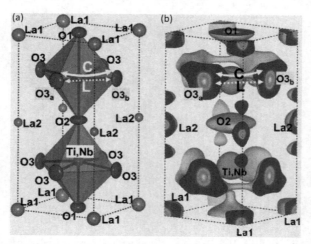

Figure 8.11 (a) Refined crystal structure and (b) isosurface of nuclear density of double perovskite-type $La_{0.64}(Ti_{0.92}Nb_{0.08})O_{2.99}$ [34].

8.4 MEM and MPF Analysis of Oxide-Ion Conducting Ceramic Materials Where the Diffusion Occurs via the Interstitialcy or the Interstitial Mechanism

The MEM and MPF are able to be applied to the nuclear/electron density analysis of materials where the diffusion occurs via the interstitialcy or interstitial mechanism [35–40]. In the interstitialcy mechanism, an ion moves from a lattice site to an interstitial one, then to another lattice site.

MEM nuclear density distributions clearly show the interstitial oxygen O3 in hyperstoichiometric $Pr_2(Ni_{0.75}Cu_{0.25})_{0.95}Ga_{0.05}O_{4.31}$ and $Pr_2Ni_{0.75}Cu_{0.25}O_{4.19}$ (Figs. 8.12d and 8.12e). On the contrary, there exists no interstitial oxygen in the defective $Sr_2Ti_{0.9}Co_{0.1}O_{3.98}$ (Fig. 8.12f). MEM nuclear/electron-density distribution can detect atoms which are not included in the Rietveld refinement. In a Rietveld fit, it is often difficult to refine accurately the occupancy factor and atomic displacement parameters. The Rietveld refinement and MEM density map should be consistent with each other. MEM density maps also show the highly anisotropic distribution of the apical O2 atom (Figs. 8.12d and 8.12e), which is consistent with the highly anisotropic thermal ellipsoids in the refined structures (Figs. 8.12a and 8.12b). The high anisotropic O2 atomic displacements are mainly static components and are ascribed to the repulsion between the O2 and interstitial O3 atoms. This origin is supported also by the ab initio structural optimization [37].

Figure 8.13 shows the Refined structure and MEM nuclear density distribution of $(Pr_{0.9}La_{0.1})_2(Ni_{0.74}Cu_{0.21}Ga_{0.05})O_{4+\delta}$ at 1016°C [35]. To express the large spatial distribution of oxygen atom around the interstitial O3 site, a split-atom model is used (Fig. 8.13a), but not appropriate for the description of the continuous, complicated distribution as shown in Fig. 8.13b. The connected nuclear densities between the apical O2 and interstitial O3 sites indicate the diffusional pathway of mobile oxide ions.

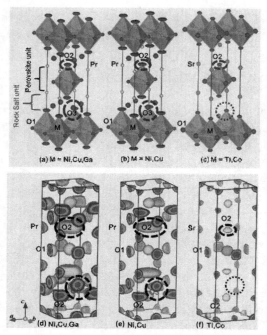

Figure 8.12 Refined crystal structures of hyperstoichiometric (a) $Pr_2(Ni_{0.75}Cu_{0.25})_{0.95}$-$Ga_{0.05}O_{4.31}$, (b) $Pr_2Ni_{0.75}Cu_{0.25}O_{4.19}$, and (c) defective $Sr_2Ti_{0.9}Co_{0.1}O_{3.98}$ at room temperature (RT). Isosurfaces of the nuclear density at ±0.05 fm Å^{-3} of (d) $Pr_2(Ni_{0.75}Cu_{0.25})_{0.95}Ga_{0.05}O_{4.31}$, (e) $Pr_2Ni_{0.75}Cu_{0.25}O_{4.19}$, and (f) $Sr_2Ti_{0.9}Co_{0.1}O_{3.98}$ at RT [37].

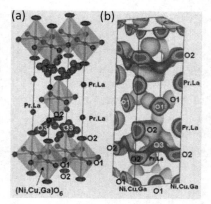

Figure 8.13 (a) Refined structure and (b) MEM nuclear density distribution of $(Pr_{0.9}La_{0.1})_2(Ni_{0.74}Cu_{0.21}Ga_{0.05})O_{4+\delta}$ at 1016°C.

Temperature dependence of nuclear density includes useful information on the diffusion mechanism of ionic conducting materials. Figure 8.14a shows that the probability density of O3 interstitial decreases with an increase of temperature, which is consistent with the decrease of hyperstoichiometric excess oxygen amount obtained by thermogravimetry [37]. On the contrary, the minimum nuclear density at the cross (×) point on the O2-O3 path increases with temperature, which is consistent with the increase of oxygen permeation rate [37]. It should be noted that the oxygen permeation rate increases with an increase of the minimum nuclear density on the O2-O3 path (Fig. 8.14b). The minimum nuclear density on the diffusion path is a useful microscopic parameter, which can be a measure of oxide-ion diffusivity [37].

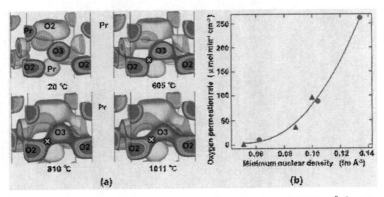

Figure 8.14 (a) Isosurfaces of the nuclear density at 0.05 fm $Å^{-3}$ of Pr_2 $(Ni_{0.75}Cu_{0.25})_{0.95}Ga_{0.05}O_{4+\delta}$ at different temperatures [37]. (b) Relationship between the oxygen permeation rate and minimum nuclear density at the cross (×) point on the O2-O3 diffusional pathway in Panel (a) [37]. Red circles and blue triangles denote the data of $Pr_2(Ni_{0.75}Cu_{0.25})_{0.95}Ga_{0.05}O_{4+\delta}$ and $Pr_2(Ni_{0.75}Cu_{0.25})O_{4+\delta}$, respectively.

It is interesting to compare the nuclear- and electron-density distributions of $(Pr_{0.9}La_{0.1})_2(Ni_{0.74}Cu_{0.21}Ga_{0.05})O_{4+\delta}$ at 1016°C [35]. The interstitial oxygen is clearly observed in the nuclear-density map, while the (Ni,Cu,Ga)-O2 covalent bond is visualized in the MEM electron- and theoretical valence electron-density distributions in Figs. 8.15b and 8.15c, respectively. The interstitial oxygen is also supported in the theoretical optimized structure (Fig. 8.15c).

The (Ni,Cu,Ga)-O2 covalent bond is weaker than the (Ni,Cu,Ga)-O1 (Figs. 8.15b and 8.15c), which strongly suggests that the apical O2 is more mobile compared with the equatorial O1 atom [37]. Therefore the apical O2 can be a part of the O2-O3 oxide-ion diffusional pathway [37].

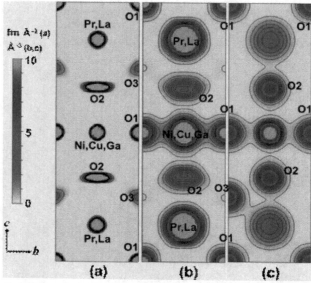

Figure 8.15 (a) MEM nuclear-density distribution and (b) MEM electron-density distribution of $(Pr_{0.9}La_{0.1})_2(Ni_{0.74}Cu_{0.21}Ga_{0.05})O_{4+\delta}$ at room temperature [36]. (c) A part of the theoretical valence electron-density distribution of an approximated supercell, $Pr_{36}La_4Ni_{15}Cu_4GaO_{84}$ [36].

We have also visualized the diffusional pathway of oxide ions in apatite-type ionic conductor $La_{9.69}(Si_{5.70}Mg_{0.30})O_{26.24}$ at 1558°C (Fig. 8.16) [38]. Oxide ions O4 in apatite-type $La_{9.69}(Si_{5.70}Mg_{0.30})O_{26.24}$ diffuse through a one-dimensional tunnel extending along the c axis of the hexagonal framework (orange arrows in Fig. 8.16), while the oxygen atoms O3, which are member of $(Si_{0.95}Mg_{0.05})O_4$ tetrahedron, show a short-range movement among the O3-O5-O4-O5-O3 atoms following a curved path (black and white arrows in Fig. 8.16) [38]. The MEM and MPF are applicable to the nuclear/electron density analysis of lithium-cation conductors [39, 40] and of proton conducting materials [41].

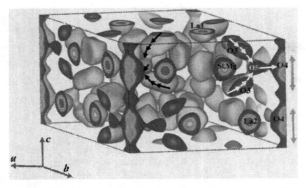

Figure 8.16 Nuclear-density distribution of apatite-type La$_{9.69}$(Si$_{5.70}$Mg$_{0.30}$) O$_{26.24}$ (1558°C) [38]. Arrows denote the oxide-ion diffusional pathways.

8.5 MEM and MPF Analysis of Visible-Light Responsive Photocatalysts

Chemical bonding is an important factor in the visible-light response of the photocatalysts, because the covalent bonds make the valence bandwidth wider, which leads to narrower band gap. We have visualized the covalent and ionic bonds in the MEM electron-density distributions of various visible-light responsive photocatalysts [42–45].

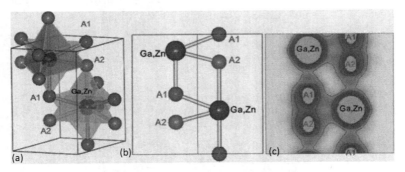

Figure 8.17 (a, b) Refined crystal structure and MEM electron-density distribution of (Ga$_{0.885}$Zn$_{0.115}$)(N$_{0.885}$O$_{0.115}$) [44].

Figure 8.17 shows a first example of the experimental visualization of covalent bonding, positional disorders and split anion sites (A1, A2: (N,O)) the visible-light responsive gallium zinc oxynitride photocatalyst $(Ga_{0.885}Zn_{0.115})(N_{0.885}O_{0.115})$ [44]. By the covalent bonding, the ZnO substitution into GaN reduces the band gap, which leads to the visible-light response. Density functional theory–based calculations supported the experimental results.

Acknowledgments

The author would like to thank many coauthors in the References for the coworking and Prof. K. Ohoyama, Prof. T. Ida, Dr. J. Kim, Mr. M. Ohkawara and facility staffs for their arrangements and support on the neutron and synchrotron diffraction experiments. A part of this work was financially supported by the Ministry of Education, Culture, Sports, Science and Technology of Japan, through a Grant-in-Aid for Scientific Research (A) No. 24246107 and Challenging Exploratory Research No. 23655190. The neutron diffraction measurements were carried out as projects approved by the Neutron Science Laboratory, Institute for Solid State Physics, University of Tokyo (Proposal Nos. 10766, 10768, 9723 and 8767) and by the Japan Proton Accelerator Research Complex (J-PARC) and Institute of Materials Structure Science of KEK (proposal Nos. 2010A0030 and 2010A0037). The synchrotron experiments were performed as projects approved by the Photon Factory of KEK (Proposal Nos. 2011G185, 2011G640, 2010G144, 2005G157 and 2009G072) and by the Japan Synchrotron Radiation Research Institute (JASRI) (Proposal Nos. 2010B1788, 2011B1995, 2012A1415 and 2011A1442).

References

1. Ten Elshof, J. E., Bouwmeester, H. J. M., and Verweij, H. (1995). Oxidative coupling of methane in a mixed-conducting perovskite membrane reactor., *Appl. Catal. A,* **130**, 195–212.

2. Steele, B. C. H., and Heinzel, A. (2001). Materials for fuel-cell technologies, *Nature,* **414**, 345–352.

3. Drioli, E., and Romano, M. (2001). Progress and new perspectives on integrated membrane operations for sustainable industrial growth, *Ind. Eng. Chem. Res.,* **40**, 1277–1300.

4. Adler, S. B. (2004). Factors governing oxygen reduction in solid oxide fuel cell cathodes, *Chem. Rev.,* **104**, 4791–4843.

5. Yashima, M. (2008). Crystal structures, structural disorders and diffusion paths of ionic conductors from diffraction experiments, *Solid State Ionics*, **179**, 797–803.

6. Yashima, M. (2009). Diffusion pathway of mobile ions and crystal structure of ionic and mixed conductors-A brief review, *J. Ceram. Soc. Jpn.*, **117**, 1055–1059.

7. Malavasi, L., Fisher, C. A. J., and Islam, M. S. (2010). Oxide-ion and proton conducting electrolyte materials for clean energy applications: Structural and mechanistic features, *Chem. Soc. Rev.* **39**, 4370–4387.

8. Izumi, F., and Momma, K. (2007). Three-dimensional visualization in powder diffraction, *Solid State Phenom.*, **130**, 15–20.

9. Izumi, F., and Dilanian, R. A. (2002). Structure refinement based on the maximum-entropy method from powder diffraction data, *Recent Res. Dev. Phys.*, **3**, 699–726.

10. Fujishima, A., and Honda, K. (1972). Electrochemical photolysis of water at a semiconductor electrode, *Nature*, **238**, 37–38.

11. Maeda, K., and Domen, K. (2007). New non-oxide photocatalysts designed for overall water splitting under visible light, *J. Phys. Chem. C*, **111**, 7851–7861.

12. Yashima, M. (2002). In situ observations of phase transition using high-temperature neutron and synchrotron x-ray powder diffractometry, *J. Am. Ceram. Soc.*, **85**, 2925–2930.

13. Yashima, M., Tanaka, M., Oh-uchi, K., and Ida, T. (2005). A compact furnace for synchrotron powder diffraction measurements up to 1807 K, *J. Appl. Crystallogr.*, **38**, 854–855.

14. Yashima, M., Oh-uchi, K., Tanaka, M., and Ida, T. (2006). A compact furnace for synchrotron powder diffraction experiments up to 1800 K, *J. Am. Ceram. Soc.*, **89**, 1395–1399.

15. Ohoyama, K., Kanouchi, T., Nemoto, K., Ohashi, M., Kajitani, T., and Yamaguchi, Y. (1998). The new neutron powder diffractometer with a multi-detector system for high-efficiency and high-resolution measurements, *Jpn. J. Appl. Phys., Part 1*, **37**, 3319–3326.

16. Momma, K., and Izumi, F. (2008). VESTA: A three-dimensional visualization system for electronic and structural analysis, *J. Appl. Crystallogr.*, **41**, 653–658.

17. Yashima, M., Kobayashi, S., and Yasui, T. (2007). Positional disorder and diffusion path of oxide ions in the yttria-doped ceria $Ce_{0.93}Y_{0.07}O_{1.96}$, *Faraday Discuss.*, **134**, 369–376.

18. Yashima, M., and Ishimura, D. (2005). Visualization of the diffusion path in the fast oxide-ion conductor $Bi_{1.4}Yb_{0.6}O_3$, *Appl. Phys. Lett.*, **87**, 221909.

19. Yashima, M., and Ishimura, D. (2003). Crystal structure and disorder of the fast oxide-ion conductor cubic Bi_2O_3, *Chem. Phys. Lett.*, **378**, 395–399.

20. Yashima, M., and Tsuji, T. (2007). Crystal structure, disorder and diffusion path of oxygen ion conductors $Y_{1-x}Ta_xO_{1.5+x}$ (x = 0.215 and 0.30), *Chem. Mater.*, **19**, 3539–3544.

21. Yashima, M., Xu, Q., Yoshiasa, A., and Wada, S. (2006). Crystal structure, electron density and diffusion path of the fast-ion conductor copper iodide CuI, *J. Mater. Chem.*, **16**, 4393–4396.

22. Yashima, M. Crystal structure, structural disorder and oxide-ion diffusional pathway of the fluorite-type oxides and fluorite-related phases (Nakamura, A., and Mizusaki, J., eds.), *Fluorite Oxides*, Chapter X, Nova Science Publisher, New York, in press.

23. Yashima, M. Crystal and electronic structures, structural disorder, phase transformation and phase diagram of ceria-zirconia and ceria-based materials (Trovarell, A., and Fornasiero, P., eds.), *Catalysis by Ceria and Related Materials 2*nd *Edition*, Chapter 1, Imperial College Press, London, in press.

24. Wakita, T., and Yashima, M. (2008). Structural disorder in the cubic $Ce_{0.5}Zr_{0.5}O_2$ catalyst, A possible factor of the high catalytic activity, *Appl. Phys. Lett.*, **92**, 101921.

25. Yashima, M., and Wakita, T. (2009). Atomic displacement parameters and structural disorder of oxygen ions in the $Ce_xZr_{1-x}O_2$ solid solutions ($0.12 \leq x \leq 1.0$): Possible factors of high catalytic activity of ceria-zirconia catalysts, *Appl. Phys. Lett.*, **94**, 171902.

26. Yashima, M., Sekikawa, T., Sato, D., Nakano, H., and Omoto, K. Crystal structure and oxide-ion diffusion of nano-crystalline, compositionally homogeneous ceria-zirconia $Ce_{0.5}Zr_{0.5}O_2$ up to 1176 K, *Cryst. Growth and Design*, in review.

27. Sale, M., and Avdeev, M. (2012). 3DBVSMAPPER: A program for automatically generating bond-valence sum landscapes, *J. Appl. Crystallogr.*, **45**, 1054–1056.

28. Yashima, M., Nomura, K., Kageyama, H., Miyazaki, Y., Chitose, H., and Adachi, K. (2003). Conduction path and disorder in the fast oxide-ion conductor $(La_{0.8}Sr_{0.2})(Ga_{0.8}Mg_{0.15}Co_{0.05})O_{2.8}$, *Chem. Phys. Lett.*, **380**, 391–396.

29. Yashima, M. (2009). Structural Disorder, Diffusion Pathway of Mobile Oxide Ions, and Crystal Structure in Perovskite-Type Oxides and Related Materials (Ishihara, T., ed.), in: *Perovskite Oxide in Solid Oxide Fuel Cells, Series: Fuel Cells and Hydrogen Energy,* Chapter 6, Springer-Verlag Press, Dordrecht, pp. 117–145.

30. Nomura , K., and Yashima, M. (2006). A study on the ion diffusion path of perovskite-type ionic conductors by high-temperature neutron diffractometry (Ida, T., and Kamiyama, T., eds.), in: *Proc. Symposium on Powder Diffraction III, KEK Proceedings* 2005-19, pp. 45–48 (in Japanese).

31. Yashima, M., and Tsuji, T. (2007). Structural investigation of the cubic perovskite-type doped lanthanum cobaltite $La_{0.6}Sr_{0.4}CoO_{3-\delta}$ at 1531 K: Possible diffusion path of oxygen ions in an electrode material, *J. Appl. Crystallogr.,* **40**, 1166–1168.

32. Yashima, M., and Kamioka, T. (2008). Neutron diffraction study of the perovskite-type lanthanum cobaltite $La_{0.6}Sr_{0.4}Co_{0.8}Fe_{0.2}O_{3-\delta}$ at 1260°C and 394°C, *Solid State Ionics,* **179**, 1939–1943.

33. Chen, Y.-C., Yashima, M., Ohta, T., Ohoyama, K., and Yamamoto, S. (2012). Crystal structure, oxygen deficiency and oxygen diffusion path of perovskite-type lanthanum cobaltites $La_{0.4}Ba_{0.6}CoO_{3-\delta}$ and $La_{0.6}Sr_{0.4}CoO_{3-\delta}$, *J. Phys. Chem. C,* **116**, 5246–5254.

34. Ali, R., Yashima, M., and Izumi, F. (2007). Diffusion path of oxide ions in an oxide-ion conductor $La_{0.64}(Ti_{0.92}Nb_{0.08})O_{2.99}$ with a double perovskite-type structure, *Chem. Mater.,* **19**, 3260–3264.

35. Yashima, M., Enoki, M., Wakita, T., Ali, R., Matsushita, Y., Izumi, F., and Ishihara, T. (2008). Structural disorder and diffusional pathway of oxide ions in a doped Pr_2NiO_4-based mixed conductor, *J. Am. Chem. Soc.,* **130**, 2762–2763.

36. Yashima, M., Sirikanda, N., and Ishihara, T. (2010). Crystal structure, diffusion path and oxygen permeability of a Pr_2NiO_4-based mixed conductor $(Pr_{0.9}La_{0.1})_2(Ni_{0.74}Cu_{0.21}Ga_{0.05})O_{4+\delta}$, *J. Am. Chem. Soc.,* **132**, 2385–2392.

37. Yashima, M., Yamada, H., Nuansaeng, S., and Ishihara, T. (2012). Role of Ga^{3+} and Cu^{2+} in the high interstitial oxide-ion diffusivity of Pr_2NiO_4-based oxides: Design concept of interstitial ion conductors through the higher-valence d^{10} dopant and Jahn-Teller effect, *Chem. Mater.,* **24**, 4100–4113.

38. Ali, R., Yashima, M., Matsushita, Y., Yoshioka, H., Ohoyama, K., and Izumi, F. (2008). Diffusion path of oxide ions in an apatite-type ionic conductor $La_{9.69}(Si_{5.70}Mg_{0.30})O_{26.24}$, *Chem. Mater.,* **20**, 5203–5208.

39. Yashima, M., Itoh, M., Inaguma, Y., and Morii, Y. (2005). Crystal structure and diffusion path in the fast lithium-ion conductor $La_{0.62}Li_{0.16}TiO_3$, *J. Am. Chem. Soc.*, **127**, 3491–3495.

40. Nishimura, S., Kobayashi, G., Ohoyama, K., Kanno, R., Yashima, M., and Yamada, A. (2008). Lithium diffusion in Li_xFePO_4: An experimental visualization, *Nat. Mater.*, **7**, 707–711.

41. Yashima, M., Yonehara, Y., and Fujimori, H. (2011). Experimental visualization of chemical bonding and structural disorder in hydroxyapatite through charge and nuclear-density analysis, *J. Phys. Chem. C*, **115**, 25077–25087.

42. Yashima, M., Lee, Y., and Domen, K. (2007). Crystal Structure and electron density of tantalum oxynitride, a visible light responsive photocatalyst, *Chem. Mater.*, **19**, 588–593.

43. Yashima, M., Ogisu, K., and Domen, K. (2008). Structure and electron density of oxysulfide $Sm_2Ti_2S_2O_{4.9}$ as a visible light responsive photocatalyst, *Acta Crystallogr. B*, **64**, 291–298.

44. Yashima, M., Yamada, H., Maeda K., and Domen, K. (2010). Experimental visualization of covalent bonds and structural disorder in a gallium zinc oxynitride photocatalyst $(Ga_{1-x}Zn_x)(N_{1-x}O_x)$, Origin of visible light absorption, *Chem. Comm.*, **46**, 2379–2381.

45. Yashima, M., Saito, M., Nakano, H., Takata, T., Ogisu, K., Domen, K. (2010). *Imma* perovskite-type oxynitride $LaTiO_2N$, Structure and electron density, *Chem. Commun.*, **46**, 4704–4706.

Index

Conflict Management and Dialogue in Higher Education

A Global Perspective

A Volume in
International Higher Education

Series Editors
Fredrick M. Nafukho and Beverly Irby
Texas A&M University

International Higher Education

Fredrick. M. Nafukho and Beverly Irby, Series Editors

Conflict Management and Dialogue in Higher Education:
A Global Perspective (2016)
by Nancy T. Watson, Karan L, Watson, and Christine A. Stanley

Governance and Transformations of Universities in Africa:
A Global Perspective (2014)
edited by Fredrick M. Nafukho, Helen M. A. Muyia, and Beverly Irby

Conflict Management and Dialogue in Higher Education

A Global Perspective

by

Nancy T. Watson

Karan L. Watson

Christine A. Stanley
Texas A&M University

INFORMATION AGE PUBLISHING, INC.
Charlotte, NC • www.infoagepub.com

Library of Congress Cataloging-in-Publication Data

CIP record for this book is available from the Library of Congress
http://www.loc.gov

ISBNs: 978-1-68123-520-2 (Paperback)

978-1-68123-521-9 (Hardcover)

978-1-68123-522-6 (ebook)

Printed in the United States of America

CONTENTS

SECTION III: SCHOLARSHIP ON MANAGING CONFLICT

SECTION IV: PERSONNEL AND PROGRAMS IN
MANAGING CONFLICT

FOREWORD

Nancy and Karan Watson and Christine Stanley have written a very important book.

During a Foreign Service career in the Middle East, I learned something about conflict, both political and physical such as the fights being waged today in that area. I also learned something about negotiations. There are negotiations to end conflicts, to strengthen relations, to find compromises and sometimes to clarify that in fact no agreement is possible and that conflict must continue.

When I arrived as a dean at Texas A&M, it did not take me long to figure out that conflict also permeates institutions of higher education. It may not be as spectacularly violent as the Middle Eastern variants, but understanding and managing it are just as important. The authors start with a crucial point. Whether we watch it on TV or experience it in the workplace, a common reaction is to see conflict as something negative, something to be avoided. Not so, we are told. Conflict is itself neither positive or negative. Indeed, conflict is often the necessary driver for organizational change. No conflict, no change. This also holds true for personal growth.

The first chapter lays out the fundamentals. Conflict is part of life—we all experience it, and we all have our own style of dealing with conflict, even if we are not aware of it. Similarly, all organizations have conflict and an organizational culture that defines how conflict is managed. Strong organizations have to evolve, and change means conflict. The key for healthy organizations and individuals is how conflict is managed, and the book

Conflict Management and Dialogue in Higher Education: A Global Perspective, pp. ix–xi
Copyright © 2016 by Information Age Publishing

makes an important point: not all conflicts can be resolved, but they can all be managed.

National issues of diversity and inclusion have been much in the news lately, and they have been highly contentious. No surprise for our authors who make the observation that diversity creates conflict. Indeed, diversity requires conflict. Again, the critical factor is how that conflict is managed.

There are many common threads in conflict and conflict management that are relevant in almost any circumstances. At the same time, organizations have unique cultures that affect how conflict is perceived and managed. Higher education is no exception, and the book devotes a very useful chapter to a description of who we are, what we seek and how we work, and how all of that has an impact on conflict and its management.

Moving from the institutional to the individual, the book lays out first the personal skills required for effective conflict management. It makes clear that good conflict managers are made, not born. We all can learn to do this. As so much does in life, it starts with self awareness, an understanding of who we are and how we operate, including traits of which we may not be conscious, such as implicit bias. Speaking of bias, the book plays to one of mine by underscoring the importance of listening. I discovered long ago that the most important attribute of effective diplomacy and negotiation is the ability to listen well.

Having set the stage by defining conflict and identifying institutional and individual characteristics that relate to it, the book then moves to a practical discussion of how to deal with conflict situations. The key is communication. The authors lay out the elements that go into effective difficult dialogues with some very helpful examples before turning to the importance of mediation as a key form of conflict intervention, again with concrete examples.

Of course, no scholarly work on the subject would be complete without a discussion of the body of scholarship on conflict management, and the book has this. However, it is a work solidly grounded in the world of experience by three uniquely qualified authors. Nancy Watson is a professional counselor and mediator who has spoken and written extensively on conflict management. Karan Watson manages conflict every single day as Provost of Texas A&M University. Christine Stanley is A&M's Vice President and Associate Provost for Diversity. They know what they are talking about.

Anyone with management responsibilities in higher education should read this book. Its relevance also goes well beyond the academy. Conflict is universal, as are many of the techniques for dealing with it. I found its analyses and prescriptions as applicable to the world of conflict and diplomacy that I left as it is to the one I am in now. It is a major contribution to the literature on this important subject, but it is also a field manual for the effective management of conflict in daily life.

Ryan Crocker, Dean, Bush School of Government and Public Service-Texas A&M University

Former ambassador to Afghanistan, Iraq, Pakistan, Syria, Kuwait and Lebanon

ACKNOWLEDGMENTS

Our individual and collective work and experiences with organizations and groups in the public, government, and education sectors across the United States and in other countries, and particularly in higher education settings, have taught us that conflict is not only an inevitable part of life, but recognizing and learning how to manage it, are equally important. Strategic conflict engagement and conflict management can lead to deeper dialogue and increased understanding for effective communication.

We would like to express our sincere appreciation to the people who have taught us about strategic conflict engagement and dialogue. Your reflections, the challenging dialogues, and your courage have shaped our thinking about conflict management over the years. We remain indebted to you, for without your insights and urging, the development of this book would not have been possible.

Nanc, Karan, and Christine

Conflict Management and Dialogue in Higher Education: A Global Perspective, pp. xiii–xiii
Copyright © 2016 by Information Age Publishing

PRELUDE AND BOOK ORGANIZATION

This book addresses the important topics of conflict, mediation, and dialogue in higher education. Conflicts are a part of life. Although many people assume conflicts are negative and, therefore, should be avoided, conflict is truly neutral; however, how one engages in the conflict is what can be perceived as constructive or destructive. There are many positive outcomes for a conflict that is managed well, hence the necessity for this book. One of the most important reasons for management rather than avoidance of conflict is some level of conflict drives most change that occurs in organizations. In order to manage change, we must learn, grow, and develop effective conflict management skills. The conflicts we engage in our personal lives and in the workplace are essential to personal, professional, and organizational development. However, when managed poorly, conflicts can escalate to the point where they can harm the health and vitality of individuals and organizations. As illustrated in this book, *the key to managing conflict is to expect, understand, and embrace conflict* in a manner that allows it to be beneficial to individuals and the organization. The alternative to well managed conflict is not the absence of conflict, but typically the costly loss of talented personnel, an unhealthy organizational climate, or even lead to lawsuits. The book provides approaches for one of the most recognized and useful alternative methods of managing conflicts —mediation. Further, this book shares important communication tools for

Conflict Management and Dialogue in Higher Education: A Global Perspective, pp. xv–xvii
Copyright © 2016 by Information Age Publishing

addressing conflict and the value of using dialogue to address social and cultural differences.

The contents of this book reflect areas of importance addressed in work of The Center for Change and Conflict Resolution (CCCR) Mediation: alternative dispute resolution practices, conflict management intervention options, models of thinking about conflict, the mediation format, and the skill set needed for a person to be a strong conflict manager and mediator. We challenge readers to reflect upon personal biases and beliefs that may negatively impact conflict and the mediation process.

Chapter 1 provides definitions and explanations for our framing of conflict, which is essential if it is to be managed. This includes when we should expect conflict, whether conflict is positive or negative, and the need for appropriate engagement in conflict for individuals and an organization. Finally, we will discuss the point of framing the challenge with conflict to ensure management of conflict which is not always the resolution of a conflict.

Section I, of this book, Defining Conflict, introduces the framing, realities, and attributes about conflict and conflict management that we have with conflict in Higher Education. This section includes Chapter 2, 3, and 4. Chapter 2, "Realities About Conflict," shares information related to the multi-facet consequences of conflict especially when is conflict negative and when is conflict positive. The idea of management of conflict to promote the positive consequences, and finally how an organization can affect its organizational culture through its approach to conflict management.

Chapter 3, "Unique Attributes Around Conflict in Higher Education," discusses the core missions of higher education, the community of higher education, and how leadership and conflict are often viewed differently than in other work settings.

Section II will focus on more details to attend to when creating a conflict management approach for units in higher education. This section includes Chapters 4, 5, and 6. Chapter 4, "Personal Skills Required to be a Good Conflict Manager," provides an approach to personal conflicts, and how to translate such personal competencies into organization approaches. Finally, we will explicitly discuss the molding of a unit's organizational culture and climate through its approach to conflict.

Chapter 5, "Dialogue as a Conflict Managing Strategy," discusses a communication strategy, *Dialogue*, as a tool that is useful to support an organization particularly when there is a difficult process, issue, or conflict to decide upon or discuss

Chapter 6, "Mediation Skills in Managing Conflict," focuses on a specific method of conflict intervention, mediation. As discussed in this chapter, mediation is a structured conflict management process where the parties in conflict work to generate solutions to their issues. Mediation is a useful con-

flict management intervention strategy in higher education because it gives the power of the solution/outcome to the parties in conflict. The mediators are responsible for establishing an environment where the parties in conflict can have a productive dialogue and the mediators are responsible for the structure and process the conflicting parties will go through to work to address their conflicts.

Section III: Scholarship on Managing Conflict includes Chapter 7, "Conflict Management in Higher Education: A Review of Selected Literature Managing Conflict in Higher," presents not only some of the literature concerning conflict in higher education, but our own scholarly work on conflict management at some of the institutions we have worked with

Finally, Section IV: Personnel and Programs in Managing Conflict, includes Chapters 8, 9, and 10. Chapter 8, "Conflict Management from a Practitioners Perspective," focuses on a specific method of conflict intervention, mediation. As discussed in this chapter, mediation is a structured conflict management process where the parties in conflict work to generate solutions to their issues. Mediation is a useful conflict management intervention strategy in higher education because it gives the power of the solution/outcome to the parties in conflict. The mediators are responsible for establishing an environment where the parties in conflict can have a productive dialogue and the mediators are responsible for the structure and process the conflicting parties will go through to work to address their conflicts

Chapter 9, "Unit Leaders' Responsibilities With Conflict," discusses the unique issues of managing conflict at an institution of higher education. There are some conflict issues unique to higher education, particularly ones where there is no one person 'in charge' of faculty. Higher education structures often differ from business and industry, or even other nonprofit entities, and therefore effective conflict engagement and strategies for engagement differ.

Chapter 10 is the book's "Conclusion and the Way Forward" It concludes with a brief summary and discusses the "way forward" looking particularly at the areas of conflict management and dialogue in higher education and its implications for the future.

SECTION I

DEFINING CONFLICT

CHAPTER 1

WHY FOCUS ON
MANAGING CONFLICT?

It is possible to conceive conflict as not necessarily a wasteful outbreak of incompatibilities, but a normal process by which socially valuable differences register themselves for the enrichment of all concerned.

—Mary Parker Follett

In this book, we address the important topics of conflict, conflict management, and dialogue in higher education. Conflicts are a part of everyday life. Conflict for many people is defined as a *fight*, and therefore, it is something we learn to avoid until it is the last resort. However, as individuals who live and work in an increasingly diverse and global society, we should learn to manage conflict. When one person perceives his/her needs or interests are being denied by another, conflict rises, even if no one else recognizes that a conflict exists. Considering this definition, many people assume that all conflicts are negative and, therefore, should be avoided; however, conflict itself is truly neutral. Specifically, how one chooses to engage in the conflict can produce either constructive or destructive outcomes. Managing and engaging in conflict constructively yields many positive outcomes; thus, we hope that you find the contents of this book to be useful in your personal and professional lives.

Useful Definitions

It is important to have a common vocabulary when discussing conflict, engaging in meaningful conflict, and strategically addressing conflict. Following are terms that we will discuss in this book.

- *Conflict* is a struggle or contest between people with opposing values, needs, ideas, beliefs, or goals (Watson & Watson, 2011) or a social interaction of two or more interdependent parties who perceive incompatible goals (Kolb & Putnam, 1992).
- *Dialogue* is two or more sides working toward understanding, suspending judgment, and listening for new information.
- *Difficult Dialogue* is any conversation between two or more people where at least one person experiences "dis-ease" in engaging in the topic or issue with others.
- *Facilitation* is a structured conversation between two or more parties involved in a conflict.
- *Facilitator* is a third party who makes it easier for people to understand one another.

Foundation of Individual Conflict Responses

Individuals develop a mental model of how to deal with a conflict early in childhood; it happens at an unconscious level. Most continue to use strategies that were modeled by primary caregivers or significant role models while growing up. Some had excellent adult role models who taught them how to effectively manage conflict. Others had adult role models who taught us that conflict is bad and should be avoided at all cost. Some were even taught to "get others before they get us"—attack before someone attacks. Individuals carry these mental models of what is the appropriate behavior when faced with a conflict, and often are unconscious of the reasons for making a particular choice of behavior.

Unless individuals make a conscious choice to look at their unconscious mental model for conflict engagement, they generally just react to conflict with their old unconscious, coping behavior. They continue to engage or ignore conflict consistently with how they were taught as children. Those who were taught to fight continue to do so almost anytime there is a conflict. Those who were taught to avoid and "pretend there is no conflict" continue to ignore and avoid the conflict. Individuals practice what they unconsciously learned and then often are unsatisfied with the outcome of our conflict engagement. There is nothing inherently wrong with the mental model for conflict management developed in childhood. However,

it is often ineffective for specific conflicts. If we have a framework for understanding our unconscious, behavior choices when facing a conflict as well as other modes of behavior, then we can make our choices more consciously, while recognizing other possible choices as well.

What Are Mental Models?

According to Peter Senge (1990), "mental models are deeply held internal images of how the world works, images that limit us to familiar ways of thinking and acting. Very often, we are not consciously aware of our mental models or the effects they have on our behavior" (pp. 232, 262). Figure 1.1 demonstrates how much of what occurs prior to our making a decision on an action is internal, aware to only to us.

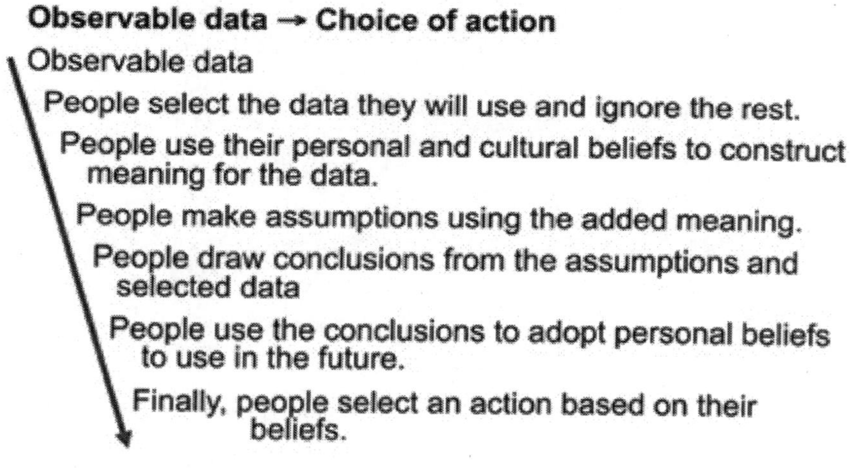

Observable data → Choice of action
Observable data
People select the data they will use and ignore the rest.
People use their personal and cultural beliefs to construct meaning for the data.
People make assumptions using the added meaning.
People draw conclusions from the assumptions and selected data
People use the conclusions to adopt personal beliefs to use in the future.
Finally, people select an action based on their beliefs.

Source: Model adapted from Senge (1990) by K. Watson. Reprinted with permission.

Figure 1.1.—Ladder of inference.

Because these thoughts and feelings are internal to the individual, other people cannot *know* the individual's thoughts and feelings. They can only see the actions. Individuals' mental models determine how they navigate the world. This is one of the fundamental reasons conflict occurs. When a person focuses on something different from another person, assumptions are usually made about who is right. And who is right is typically related to *my mental model is the true mental model; and, if you deviate from it you might be trying to undermine me.*

A Framework for Understanding the Modes of Behavior in Conflict

Blake and Mouton (1975) created a framework, which illustrates five different conflict modes or types. The modes lie on a grid that compares the response to conflict by noting the levels of cooperation and assertiveness. The Thomas-Kilmann Conflict Mode Instrument (TKI) is based upon the Blake and Mouton's conflict framework. This self-report instrument reflects the propensity of individuals to respond to conflict in one of five modes as shown in Figure 1.2.

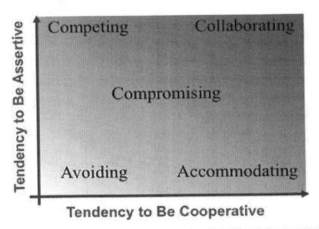

Thomas-Kilmann Conflict Mode Instrument

Source: Consulting Psychologist Press (1999). Reprinted with permission.

Figure 1.2. Conflict modes grid.

This framework illustrates that individuals respond to conflict by consciously or unconsciously using one of the following five modes (Thomas & Kilmann, 1974): (a) Avoiding, (b) Competing, (c) Compromising, (d) Accommodating, and (e) Collaborating. Each of these modes can be depicted along two scales: assertiveness and cooperation. None of these modes are wrong to use when responding to conflict, however there are times when the use of a particular mode is constructive or destructive (see Figure 1.3).

The TKI is designed to show which style(s) an individual has the greatest tendency to use in a conflict. However, different conflicts and their associ-

ated factors warrant different styles. The more that individuals understand the strengths and weaknesses of each style, the more they are able to choose a style most conducive for managing the conflict.

The avoiding conflict mode is characterized by low assertiveness and low cooperation. The avoiding mode is appropriate to use when there are issues of low importance. It is also used when we want to reduce tensions, buy some time, or when we are in a position that has little to no power. Avoiding skills include the:

- Ability to withdraw
- Ability to sidestep issues
- Ability to leave things unresolved
- Ability to discern a sense of timing

The competing conflict mode is characterized by high assertiveness and low cooperation. The competing mode is appropriate to use when quick action needs to be taken, unpopular decisions need to be made, vital issues must be handled, or one is protecting self-interests. Competing skills include:

- Arguing or debating
- Using rank or influence
- Standing your ground
- Asserting your opinions, thoughts and feelings
- Stating your position clearly

The compromising conflict mode is characterized by moderate assertiveness and moderate cooperation. Some people define compromise as "giving up more than you want," while others see compromise as winning for both parties. The compromising mode is appropriate to use when there are issues of moderate importance, equal power status, or parties have a strong commitment for resolution. The compromising mode can also be used as a temporary solution when there are time constraints. Compromising skills include:

- Negotiating
- Finding a middle ground
- Assessing value
- Making concessions

The accommodating conflict mode is characterized by low assertiveness and high cooperation. The accommodating mode is appropriate to use, to show reasonableness, develop performance, create good will, or keep peace. Some people use the accommodating mode when the issue or outcome is of low importance to them. Accommodating skills include:

- Forgetting your desires
- Selflessness
- Ability to yield
- Obeying orders

The collaborating conflict mode is characterized by high assertiveness and high cooperation. The collaborative mode has been described as "putting an idea on top of an idea on top of an idea, in order to achieve the best solution to a conflict." (S. Luera, personal communication, 1998). Collaborating can take a great deal of time and energy. Therefore, the collaborating mode should be used when the conflict warrants the time and energy. The collaborative mode is appropriate to use when the conflict is important to people who are working to construct an integrative solution. Collaboration skills include:

- Active listening
- Identifying needs and concerns
- Nonthreatening confrontation
- Analyzing input

Figure 1.3.   Utilization of TKI conflict behavioral modes.

Individuals will choose a conflict style depending upon personal and organizational norms, as well as the current escalation level of the conflict. In order to skillfully manage a conflict, individuals must choose a style that will lead to de-escalation of the conflict and, ultimately, a level of resolution that minimizes the resources and energy surrounding the issues in the conflict (Algert & Froyd, 2002). Once a person determines what conflict mode he/she will use for a given conflict situation the next step involves reflecting on what conflict modes are being used by the other parties in conflict. This process is known as framing a conflict and will be discussed in Chapter 4.

Conflict Responses in Organizations

Windle and Warren (2009) shared three common responses from people within organizations when conflicts arise. Conflicts are typically addressed in the following ways:

- Pave over the conflict with superficial gestures
- Blaming, talking, or complaining about situation with friends or third parties (while failing to talk directly to the other party we are in disagreement with)
- Trying to get hired guns to deal with the problem (they should be able to intimidate the other party)

Paving over the conflict involves the parties discussing everything except the conflict. The individuals may discuss the weather, the search for a new college dean, or even the school's athletic programs; however, the parties never discuss the conflict. When the conflict is not discussed, there is a *grain of sand* of divisiveness between the two parties. The one-grain may not create a large problem. However, the cumulative effect of multiple *unresolved* conflicts, or multiple grains of sand, leads to distrust between the parties. On the other hand, if the organization's style of managing conflict is to blame others, it may quickly become a very unwelcoming environment. And finally, if an organization's primary response is to passively wait for someone else to fix the conflicts, it may get stuck, with no internal skills to progress.

In addition, the researchers have shown that an organization will normally develop a dominant behavioral mode for dealing with conflict (Algert & Watson, 2002). Furthermore, responses to conflict are learned and people who stay in the organization usually adapt their personal styles to the environment over time. Researchers have demonstrated that conflict behavior modes are often driven by the majority, especially over time when people in titled leadership and managerial positions, as well as the people

who choose to stay with the organization and thus with the greatest longevity are setting the culture of the organization (Algert & Watson, 2002).

Change Creates Conflicts

Change will often cause conflicts to occur in an organization, whether it is a college or university, department, or a particular program. Figure 1.4 illustrates a change process model, which explains how an individual transitions through various stages of change in an organization. When an organization is experiencing change, it is common for an individual to believe others are simultaneously in the same stage related to the change process; this is typically not accurate. People in the organization will move through the change steps at different rates of speed. Even though the individuals are all moving through the process, some will be leading the change initiative and expending a lot of energy, while others will spend a lot of energy resisting the change. Individuals in a group or team will experience different levels of resistance to change, so we are all at different stages of the internal change process.

Colleges and universities are prime examples of organizations where change is a constant. When leaders plan for change, they often engage their leadership team about the process and outcomes over a considerable time period. As a group, they have progressed through the change process and are therefore committed to the decision to change. However, when the change is announced, levels of resistance that accompany change often shock leaders. Leaders should always anticipate resistance and understand that other people in the organization might not yet have the opportunity to work through the change process. Individuals need sufficient time to think about the change, grow interest in the change, and commit to the change, or even to work against the change. Satir and Banmen's (1991) change model, Figure 1.5, depicts the normal shift over time that occurs as individuals (as well as groups and organizations) are confronted with a change. The time scales for individuals and for a particular change may vary tremendously within an organization. Part of managing change involves handling the complexity of people being in different stages of resisting or accepting the change.

Diversity Creates Conflict

Colleges and universities are becoming increasingly socially and culturally diverse. In many ways, college campuses are microcosms of society, the workforce, and the world. The diversity that enriches an organization

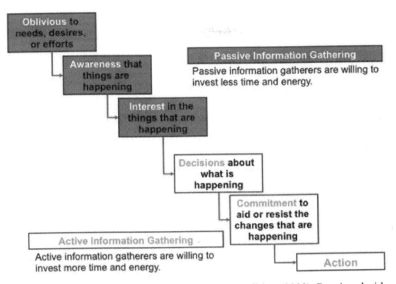

Source: Synthesized by K. L. Watson from Foundation Coalition (2000). Reprinted with permission.

Figure 1.4.   Staged change model.

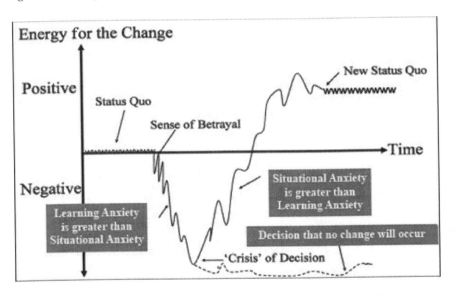

Source: Adapted from Satir, Banmen, Gerber, and Gomori (1991) by Algert and Watson (2005). Reprinted with permission.

Figure 1.4.   Satir's model for individuals and organizations.

or a campus environment will often lead to conflict. As we noted before, how individuals choose to engage in the conflict, can either be constructive or destructive. We firmly believe that diversity creates an opportunity for productive dialogue that raises awareness, enhances communication, leads to perspective taking, and increases knowledge and understanding about self and others. Consequently, when there is a diversity of mental models operating, there is increased likelihood that they are going to open the door for conflicts to arise. In addition, when we consider the diversity of an individual's preferred conflict behavioral modes and where individuals are in the change process, conflicts will likely occur.

Individuals who have been historically marginalized or underrepresented in society represent an intersection of social and cultural identity factors, such as age, cultural identity, gender identity or expression, nationality, physical or mental ability, political and ideological perspectives, racial and ethnic identity, religious and spiritual identity, sexual orientation, and social and economic status. One cannot expect to espouse diversity and not value what all members of an organization or a campus community bring to the educational enterprise. Similarly, one should fully expect that diversity of identity, thought, opinion, and life experiences will challenge ways of knowing and doing in an organization. These attributes are likely to create differences in how conflict is perceived and managed, and also the behaviors associated with the conflict.

- *Gender:* Individuals are often socialized to use particular conflict modes because of their gender. For example, in some cultures, males are taught to "always stand up to someone, and, if you have to fight, then fight." A person socialized this way would be more likely to use assertive conflict modes versus cooperative modes. Similarly, some females are socialized to accommodate when a conflict arises, especially if the conflict is with a male.
- *Privilege:* In their work on racism and white privilege curriculum design, Adams, Bell, and Griffin (2007) shared the following comments:

> Participants bring to a course on racism a wide range of feelings and experiences, and often misinformation, confusion, and bias. White participants may sincerely want to learn about racism and figure out how to play a role in making their communities, schools, and workplaces welcoming places for all, but fail to see the role white skin privilege and accumulated white advantage play in perpetuating racial inequality. Participants of color may want to figure out how to break through the silence about racism as a historic and contemporary force that differentially shapes their lives, but fear having their concerns dismissed, being viewed as too sensitive or as troublemakers, or be-

ing misunderstood by white peers and teachers. Participants from all racial groups may be reluctant to explore racism, especially in mixed groups, given the complex and often painful web of emotions that discussions about racism inevitably raise. (p. 123)

- *Self-concept:* How people think and feel about themselves affects how they approach conflict. For example, do they think their thoughts, feelings, and opinions are valuable in the current situation.
- *Position (Power):* What is an individual's power status (i.e., equal to, more than, or less than) in relation to the person with whom we are in conflict?

Vibrant Organizations Change and Have Conflicts

An organization that is not experiencing change is a dying organization. In any vibrant organizations, conflict occurs when: individuals' change, personnel change, structures change, procedures change, competition and challenges change, or resources change. One of the most important reasons for management rather than avoidance of conflict is that some level of conflict drives most change that occurs in organizations. In order to manage change, we must learn, grow, and develop effective conflict management skills. The conflicts we engage in our personal lives and in the workplace are essential to personal, professional, and organizational development. However, when managed poorly, conflicts can escalate to the point where they can harm the health and vitality of individuals and organizations.

The *key to managing conflict is to expect, understand, and embrace conflict* in a manner that allows it to be beneficial to individuals and the organization. The alternative to well managed conflict is not the absence of conflict, but typically the costly loss of talented members of an organization or campus community, an unhealthy campus climate, or even formal grievance or unresolved issues leading to lawsuits. In this book, we provide approaches for one of the most recognized and useful alternative methods of managing conflicts – mediation. Further, we share important communication tools for addressing conflict and the value of using dialogue to address social and cultural differences. We challenge readers to reflect upon personal biases and beliefs that may negatively impact conflict and the mediation process.

In Chapter 2, we consider the *realities about conflict* and what is known about conflict. We discuss the perception most people have, which is that conflict is *bad* and something to be avoided and challenges the reader to reflect on the positive aspects of conflict. Further, we will discuss how

prevalent and frequent conflict is, and the potentially destructive and cata-strophic consequences of escalating conflict. Finally, we share about conflict in relationship to an individual's and an organization's overall health and stress.

REFERENCES

Adams, M., Bell, L. A., & Griffin, P. (Eds.). (2007). *Teaching for diversity and social justice*. Abington, England: Routledge.

Algert, N. E., & Froyd, J. (2002). Understanding conflict and conflict management. Retrieved from http://www.foundationcoalition.org/publications/brochures/conflict.pdf

Algert, N. E., & Watson, K. L. (2002). *Conflict management: Introductions for individuals and organizations*. Bryan, TX: Center for Change and Conflict Resolution.

Algert, N. E., & Watson, K. (2005). Systemic change in engineering education: The role of effective change agents for women in engineering. *Proceedings: Women in Engineering Advocates Network (WEPAN)/National Association of Minority Engineering Professionals Advocates (NAMEPA), Las Vegas, Nevada, 4/05*.

Blake, R. R., & Mouton, J. S. (1975). An overview of the grid. *Training and Development Journal, 29*(5), 29–37.

Metcalf, H. C., & Urwick, L. F. (1942). *Dynamic administration: The collected papers of May Parker Follet*. New York, NY: Harper & Brothers.

Kolb, D. M., & Putnam, L. L. (1992), The multiple faces of conflict in organizations. *Journal of Organizational Behavior, 13*, 311–324.

Senge, P. M. (1990). *The fifth discipline: The art and practice of the learning organization*. New York, NY: Currency Doubleday.

Satir, V., & Banmen, J. (1991). *The Satir model: Family therapy and beyond*. Palo Alto, CA: Science & Behavior Books.

Satir, V., Banmen, J., Gerber, J., & Gomori, M. (1991). *The Satir model*. Mountain View, CA: Science & Behavior Books.

Thomas, K. W., & Kilmann, R. H. (1974). *Thomas-Kilmann Conflict Mode Instrument*. Mountain View, CA: Xicom.

Watson, K. L. (2000). National Science Foundation Foundation Coalition. c

Watson, N., & Watson, K. (2011). *Conflict management: An introduction for individuals and organizations* (2nd ed.). Bryan, TX: The Center for Change and Conflict Resolution.

Windle, R., & Warren, S. (2009). Communication skills. Retrieved from http://www.derectionservice.org/cadre/section4cf

CHAPTER 2

REALITIES ABOUT CONFLICT

Every conflict we face in life is rich with positive and negative potential. It can be a source of inspiration, enlightenment, learning, transformation, and growth—or rage, fear, shame, entrapment, and resistance. The choice is not up to our opponents, but to us, and our willingness to face and work through them.

—Kenneth Cloke and Joan Goldsmith

Conflict Is Normally Perceived to Be Bad

Conflict is neither good nor bad. It is neither constructive nor destructive, nor helpful or hurtful. It is how individuals engage in conflicts as they arise that is either constructive or destructive for the individual, other people in the conflict, or an organization.

When people think about engaging in conflict, the words and phrases often used to describe their thoughts and feelings associated with conflict, include: fight, flight, anger, destructive, divisive, illness, bad changes, spawn new problems, and distress. It is therefore easy to understand why people often behave as if any conflict is viewed through this lens. Many individuals and organizations tend to avoid conflict at all cost, and think they should be avoided if possible or squashed as soon as possible. Conflict is then viewed as dangerous, worrisome, and a burden. It is assumed that an organization in conflict is broken or weak. If this is the perception, then it is no wonder that many leaders of an organization want their unit to be

---

known as having conflict. Therefore, to deny that conflicts exist is common. It is therefore important to understand some of the reasons behind the commonly held perception that conflict is negative.

First, we find that many people are socialized or have role models who foster a mental model that the correct perspective of conflict is negative. Often this is because individuals have not been taught how to manage conflicts. Unmanaged or unresolved conflict can lead to aggression, which in turn can lead to violence, thus conflicts are negative. People are not taught to frame the conflict differently from the consequences of the responses to the conflict. Furthermore, people may have learned that conflict means change, and it is very normal to resist change, even if the change is intellectually perceived to be desirable. One form of resistance is to brand what is occurring as negative. A third reason why conflicts is always perceived as negative is the intuitive as well as cognitive signals our body sends when we are under stress, or a unit is under stress, and we want relief from the stress. We will address physiological responses later, however, it is sufficient to say here that stress may lead to labeling an experience as negative.

The Positive Aspects of Conflict

Be mindful that conflict is simply defined as differences with regard to values, needs, ideas, beliefs, or goals between people, then we can understand that being aware of such differences is actually a positive step toward understanding conflict. In other words, it would be insensitive to lack a sense of awareness about social justice, or reflect on one's privilege, and assume that everyone else's perspective or experience is the same as yours. So one positive aspect of conflict, not necessarily the outcome of how the conflict is managed, is that it increases one's awareness and openness to diverse perspectives. Researchers have shown that diverse teams, particularly in their approaches to thinking about, framing, and engaging in a problem, are stronger teams than those who are not as diverse (Milem, 2003; Watson, Johnson, & Merritt, 1998).

Another positive aspect of conflict is the signals it gives to an individual about the need for, or impending initiation of, change. This awareness, although likely to trigger resistance at first, will often help people muster the proper energy for a needed change.

Conflict also helps teams tune to be high performing teams. Consider a sports analogy—when a team really shines when the competition is truly challenging. The team has to depend on each other to do their part to ensure the overall performance is at its peak. Additionally, Tuckman and Jensen (1977), from his early research which is still used today, identified four stages that commonly occur when a team is engaged in teamwork:

forming, storming, norming, performing. These stages have clear implications for thinking about how conflict can lead to positive outcomes and
enhance productivity. Tuckman and Jensen found that when a team *storms*,
it engages differences and conflicts within the team, then it can norm,
or calibrate itself on what the team is truly able to accomplish. Further,
Lencioni (2002) in his book *The Five Dysfunctions of a Team* addressed the
importance of effective teams and organizations. As shown in Figure 2.1,
which is an adaptation of his work, an organization is only successful in
accomplishing its goals and results if individuals and the organization are
willing to engage in meaningful conflicts.

Source: The five dysfunctions of teams.

Figure 2.1.   The five dysfunctions of teams.

Meaningful and productive conflict engagement can yield positive outcomes such as growth, increased cooperation, peace within the individual
and unit, creative and useful change, solutions and resolution to issues
that had been ongoing, and finally relief. The primary reason why adults
decide to engage in conflict is to experience relief; relief that the conflict is resolved, relief they will spend less energy at work in interpersonal
conflicts, and relief that there is no longer a lingering unresolved issue.
Therefore, we contend that conflict is similar to that of the *canary in the
mine*, which sends needed signals to individuals about their own beliefs,
interests, needs, and values in relation to those around them. The consequence of receiving such signals is entirely dependent on how the signaling
of the conflict is received and subsequently managed.

Conflict Frequency

Conflict is a high probability event. Twenty years ago, managers it was reported that managers spent at least 40% of their day engaged in conflict (Putnam, 1995), and 25 years, ago, it was reported that adults average five conflicts per day, and adolescents, such as undergraduate college students, average nine conflicts per day (Opotow, 1990). According to Acuna (2013), more recent overall statistics indicate that between 10 to 26% of time of managers is spent handling conflict.

A foundational tenet for this book is that organizations are strongest when (a) they are well practiced in conflict management and (b) coaching this practice becomes one of the most important leadership responsibilities in the organization. Because conflict is a high probability event addressing conflict early on is important, because there is typically a range of resolution/management options as well as the likelihood of diminished escalation.

Conflict Intensity (Escalation)

Conflict and change go hand in hand. Thus, the intensity of resistance to change can serve as a proxy for an individual's perception about the intensity of a conflict. Rick Maurer described the following three levels of resistance and motivations that occur during conflict:

Level I—I don't get it (confusion about the idea)—motivation is an intellectual lack of information or disagreement about the information.

Level II—I don't like it (an emotional reaction to the change)—motivation is a concern that some personal belief or value is being challenged or changed.

Level III—so maybe they like you, and I don't like you—motivation is rooted in historical experiences and hard to disentangle from the current situation or conflict ("What Creates Resistance," Maurer, n.d.).

With regard to Level III, Maurer said "so maybe they like you, but they don't trust you—or don't have confidence in your leadership. That's a hard pill to swallow, I know. But lack of attention to Level III is a major reason why resistance flourishes and changes fail" (para. 1)

Jordon (2000) translated and summarized Glasl's model as how conflicts escalate. When conflicts are ignored and not addressed, then the conflict typically escalates. Table 2.1. was created to summarize Glasl's steps. Further, the people involved in the conflict typically become more positional in nature. Unresolved conflict and unaddressed conflict can eventually lead to the death of a partnership and an organization.

Table 2.1.   **Conflict Escalation**

	Stage	Conflict Issues	Behavioral Norms	Threshold to Next Level
1.	Hardening	Objective	Straight arguing	Tricks in argument
2.	Debate	Relative positioning	Verbal confrontation	One-sided action
3.	Action w/o words	Self-image	Symbolic behavior	Attacks aimed at other's identity
4.	Images & Coalitions	Save reputation	Exploit gaps form coalition	Loss of face
5.	Loss of Face	Fundamental values & dignity	Attack other publicly	Ultimatum or strength test
6.	Strategic Threats	Control other	Ultimatums & binding statements	Execute ultimatum
7.	Limited "Blows"	Hurt other's survival	Attack others greater Threats	Attack core of the enemy
8.	Shatter Enemy	Annihilate other and survive	ATTACK on all levels	Sacrifice self preservation
9.	Together into ABYSS	Annihilation at any cost	WAR, Limitless violence	

Sources: Glasl, F. (1982). Konfilktmanagement.E in Handbuch fur Fuhrunfskafte, Berterinnen und erater, 5, Erweiterte Auflage, Bern: Verlag Paul Haupte. Summarized by Thomas Jordan (2000)

Resolving conflict at its lowest point of escalation is obviously beneficial. First, when a conflict is addressed between the initial disputants/parties, the maximum number of options for resolution exists. As a conflict is *passed up through the ranks*, the range of resolution options diminishes and the options often are more punitive in nature. Second, it is empowering for the disputants to resolve their own conflicts versus having a hierarchical third party mandate the resolution. Through this empowerment, individuals are more likely to follow-through on their resolution. Third, it is cost effective for conflicts to be resolved at their lowest level of escalation possible. As more parties become involved in resolving or managing conflict, each of these individuals must spend more time away from their work responsibilities.

A common mistake in managing a conflict is to ignore the intensity or escalation level of a conflict. Examples include:

- Treating a historically based mistrust of each other as a lack of information
- Treating a simple lack of information as a fundamental difference in beliefs
- Treating a debate as a war
- Treating teams working to annihilate one another as a simple position on a new issue or change

Therefore, it is clear that regardless of our mental models, whether a conflict is perceived as positive or negative, anyone wanting to manage or resolve a conflict will not likely succeed if they do not understand the nature and intensity of the conflict being considered. Glasl (1982) explained that once a conflict is escalated to a certain stage, the effort to resolve a conflict must involve deescalating it one stage at a time, rather than jumping back to Stage 1 which triggers conflict.

Personal Health and Stress Related to Conflict

Feelings accompany conflict even though people often state their conflict has nothing to do with feelings or emotions. Individuals in conflict often exhibit anger, resentment, fear, guilt, and hopelessness. Their thoughts often take the form of "they are doing it again," "they are trying to win," "they are trying to take credit for my work," "I will not tolerate this," "someone has to have standards here," "they entered my turf," "they are discriminating against me," or "they are wrong" (Algert & Watson, 2005, p. 2). The behavioral response to conflict may be "fight or flight," or as Taylor et al. (2000) indicated women may have a different response to conflict, and that is to "tend and befriend" (p. 411). These behavioral responses relate well to the conflict behavioral modes described by Thomas-Kilmann in Chapter 1. Stress always accompanies change or conflict and for some people change creates distress. When a person experiences distress with change, it is harder for the person to reason constructively and engage in the conflict.

Figure 2.2 illustrates that under distress or eustress, individuals do not perform at an optimal level, yet another reason why conflict engagement can be good. However, long durations of operating under stress, and the duration required depends on the strength of the stress, which can ultimately wear people out. When this occurs, individuals may not only have diminished abilities to help an organization, they may suffer temporary or permanent health issues.

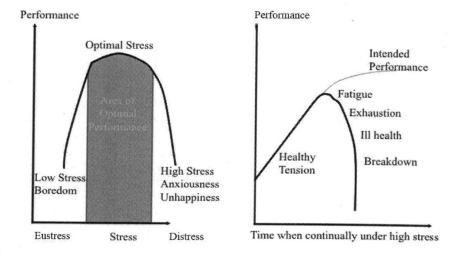

Figure 2.2. Two important aspects of stress. 1. stress is required for optimal performance and 2. long durations under stress eventually cause performance failure.

Regardless of the stress levels, performance, or behavioral instincts, an individual in conflict exhibits certain physiological responses. For example, physiological responses to conflict for many are associated with anxiety or fear, and include: sweaty palms, a shortness of breath or rapid breathing, stomach queasiness, headache, rapid eye movement, neck and shoulder tension, tingling sensation, lower back pain, and/or tightness in the jaw. On the other hand, others may feel a need to repress these feelings and work toward a heightened acuteness of adrenaline and are prepared to fight. All physiological responses can ultimately influence one's stress levels and health. Therefore, managing the causes of these reactions, through self-awareness, practice, and processes that bring relief and aid individual health and performance.

Organizational Health and Effectiveness Related to Conflict

Our fundamental philosophy is that effective conflict management practices are key for organizational effectiveness. Conflict management is having the ability to notice and address, versus solve, conflict in a constructive manner (Watson & Watson, 2011). Developing and refining individual conflict management skills are also key for institutional integrity and prosperity. It is easier to learn to manage conflicts constructively, than try to control all people, places, events, and things that create conflict. If individuals in an organization attempt to control all potential conflict situations, the

person is first unsuccessful and, second, creates an environment that lacks reflection, creativity, rich dialogue, and trust. Conflict resolution means engaging in a process to resolve or solve a dispute or disagreement whereas conflict management implies the presenting conflict issue (e.g., insufficient resources) is still present and, through productive dialogue, strong strategies are employed to effectively manage the conflict implemented (Watson & Watson, 2011). A unit well practiced and skilled in conflict management is healthier and better prepared for facing challenges and change.

In Chapter 3, we focus on the unique attributes around conflict in higher education. We discuss the core missions of higher education, including the constituencies of higher education. Further, we share structures and leadership in higher education and higher education processes and some common problems for conflict management in higher education.

REFERENCES

Acuna, A. (2013). How much time do managers spend on conflict? *Learning4Managers*. Retrieved from https://learning4managers.com/dir/conflict_management/

Algert, N. E., & Watson, K. (2005). *Systemic change in engineering education: the role of effective change agents for women in engineering*. Paper presented at the Women in Engineering Advocates Network (WEPAN)/National Association of Minority Engineering Professionals Advocates (NAMEPA) Joint Conference, Las Vegas, Nevada. Retrieved from https://journals.psu.edu/wepan/article/viewFile/58417/58105

Cloke, K., & Goldsmith, J. (2001). *Resolving conflicts at work: A complete guide for everyone on the job*. San Francisco, CA: Jossey-Bass.

Glasl, F. (1982) *Konfilktmanagement.E in Handbuch fur Fuhrunfskafte, Berterinnen und erater,* 5 , Erweiterte Auflage, Bern: Verlag Paul Haupte.

Jordon, T. (2000). Glasl's nine-stage model of conflict escalation. *Mediate.com*. Retrieved from http://www.mediate.com/articles/jordan.cfm

Lencioni, P. (2006). *The five dysfunctions of a team*. San Francisco, CA: John Wiley & Sons.

Maurer, R. (n.d.). *Resistance to change—why it matters and what to do about it*. Retrieved from http://www.rickmaurer.com/wrm/

Milem, J. F. (2003). The educational benefits of diversity: Evidence from multiple sectors. *Compelling Interest: Examining the Evidence on Racial Dynamics In Higher Education*, 126–169. Retrieved from http://www.researchgate.net/punlication/238506813

Miller, C. W. (2016). Conflict escalation. *The International Encyclopedia of Interpersonal Communication*.

Opotow, S. (1990). Moral exclusion and injustice: An introduction. *Journal of Social Issues, 46*(1), 1–20.

Putnam, L. L. (1995). Formal negotiations: The productive side of organizational conflict. In A. M. Nicoreta (Ed.), *Conflict and organizations: Communicative processes* (pp. 183–200). Albany, NY: State University of New York Press.

Taylor, S. E., Klein, L. C., Lewis, B. P., Gruenewald, T. L., Gurung, R. A., & Updegraff, J. A. (2000). Biobehavioral responses to stress in females: tend-and-befriend, not fight-or-flight. *Psychological Review, 107(3)*, 411–429.

Tuckman, B. W., & Jensen, M. A. C. (1977). Stages of small-group development revisited. *Group & Organization Management, 2(4)*, 419–427.

Watson, W. E., Johnson, L., & Merritt, D. (1998). Team orientation, self-orientation, and diversity in task groups their connection to team performance over time. *Group & Organization Management, 23(2)*, 161–188.

Watson, N., & Watson, K. (2011). *Conflict management: An introduction for individuals and organizations* (2nd ed.). Bryan, TX: The Center for Change and Conflict Resolution.

CHAPTER 3

UNIQUE ATTRIBUTES AROUND CONFLICT IN HIGHER EDUCATION

Change is possible!

—Virgina Satir

We can often measure our progress by watching the nature of our conflicts.... If a man should tell you that his chief daily conflict within himself is "shall I steal or not steal?" you would know what to think of his development ... in the same way, one test of your [organization] is not how many conflicts do you have, for conflicts are the essence of life, but what are your conflicts, and how do you deal with them?

(Mary Parker Follett, 1940, p. 45)

THE FOCUS ON CONFLICT IN HIGHER EDUCATION

In most higher education institutions, conflicts exist, and successful academic leaders or anyone in titled leadership for example, a chancellor, president, provost, dean, department chair, department head, or program chair must be able to discern and effectively manage conflicts. Conflict is a natural state of existence and the academic setting is no exception. Like many other organizations, higher education is constantly being challenged

Conflict Management and Dialogue in Higher Education: A Global Perspective, pp. 25–35
Copyright © 2016 by Information Age Publishing

with greater accountability measures for effectiveness, pressure to increase "productivity" through increased student enrollment, greater outreach activities to the public and to businesses, greater success in securing external funding, and the expectation to recruit and retain a more diverse faculty and student body, with administrative efficiency and declining resources. These pressures have ensured that the probability that an academic leader will engage in or have to resolve conflicts is similar to that of their corporate counterparts. So, if these causes and effects are not particularly unique for higher education, then why single out such enterprises? Our contention is that there is no singular attribute of higher education that makes it unique with respect to conflict management, but rather it is a combination of several attributes. The main attributes to consider are the interdependence and cultural derivatives of: (a) the core missions of higher education, (b) the people engaged in higher education, (c) the administrative structures in higher education, and leaders chosen for filling those structures, and (d) the expected processes in higher education. These attributes come together in higher education and demand similar skills in conflict management, similar to that of any organization, however, there are unique requirements in the strength and distribution of those skills throughout the organization.

Core Missions of Higher Education

In academia, the core missions of teaching, research or scholarship, and service, are anchored on maintaining individual creativity, innovation, pace, and approaches-for the interactions between experts and the novices. A vibrant university or college must constantly be in flux, even though it must also ferociously stick to tenants that stabilize the core missions to resist pop-fads that have negative long-term effects. The core missions are meant to serve students and society for centuries, not just a 4-year period of study, or even the lifetime career of a graduating student. Everyone in the organization must be fluid during periods of change, that receptiveness to change becomes natural when change is occurring. For example, instructors may be required to teach true novices century old fundamental knowledge in the same way they challenge more senior students and colleagues to push the boundaries of knowledge in a specific field. Students may be required to question and then deepen their commitment to certain core values and beliefs, and change at the same time, because all learning is a change process. Scholars are required to ground discoveries in tried and tested techniques while they innovate approaches and experiments to develop new understanding. New technologies and procedures must be seamlessly integrated into activities, without wasted experiments on new fads that actually harm student learning. All of this is not to say that higher

education does not experience its fair share of resistance to change and innovation. However, subtleties of change that occurs in higher education must be acknowledged, because the fundamental missions and tenants influence immediate and long-term impacts.

The Higher Education Community—Faculty, Students, Staff and Administrators

The college and university environment are microcosms of the society and the world. The primary constituent groups of a campus community —faculty, staff, and students—are as diverse in their needs, identities, and assumptions as are the various constituency groups in our society and world. In addition, there is diversity within and across groups, offering opportunities for growth, awareness, understanding, and of course, conflict. Conflict is essential for universities to thrive. Faculty often work independently and engage in scholarly debate and conflict as they engage in their research. They look for consistencies and differences; to gauge whether their innovations, ideas, and scholarly endeavors support and conflict existing research.

Disagreements and opposing beliefs and values are hallmarks of a thriving university campus. University staff also engage in conflict to ensure that structures and processes are effective and efficient in the workplace. One unique attribute of any educational organization is the focus on the interaction between and among two sets of people, the faculty and students, and the third set of people, the staff, who are committed to ensuring that the core interaction of faculty and students is optimized. While stereotypes of any of these groups are unproductive, we present some common attributes that are often shared within each of these three constituent groups.

Faculty. In general, especially in the United States, faculty in higher education institutions represent a group of people committed to a shared value of education and the need to discover new knowledge, create new procedures and representations of current understanding, and innovate procedures and design mechanisms. While not altruistic, many faculty have chosen this path and commitment over monetary status, political influence, or business or industry development. Faculty in higher education tend to have a high level of degree attainment, making them experts in specific areas more often than others with broader and multidisciplinary experiences. While some have a hard time understanding why the pure joy of learning is not a natural motivator for everyone, most are dedicated to the idea of finding the spark that ignites students' imagination and motivation to learn. While some may appear impatient, especially to novices in the field, they are incredibly patient, considering that they work to achieve broad and long-term impact on the development of individuals and their

fields of study. In general, faculty have a choice with respect to where and how they want to use their education and career. In general, faculty are amongst the most satisfied professionals, in large part because of their ability to work autonomously to achieve the university's core mission.

Students. Students, whether they identify as undergraduate, professional, or graduate students, have opted to be in the position as novices or apprentices, learning from the hands of experts. Some may be just emerging from adolescence, while others may have more life-experience than the experts who are there to instruct and guide them. While a few may simply be 'killing time' because seeking a degree or taking a course is required by someone, most are truly committed to learning. This means they are committed to learning for a lifetime, which requires change. They may not think of learning as a change process, but if they were never challenged with what they know, how they learn, or what will be required of them beyond graduation, then they do not understand the learning process. This is not to say that all students have the same depth of commitment to learning, or the same patience within self or around others, or the same sense of urgency and motivation for change. A highly motivated and committed student in one subject or a particular learning environment may be unengaged in another situation. Students in higher education have opted to be there, even if highly pressured by sources of influence such as parents, guardians, significant others, family members, or role models. There is no law that requires them to remain in college.

Another unique aspect about students and their contributions to the higher education organizational culture is that they are customers (consuming our services), clients (being advised and mentored by college personnel and services), and employees (while not necessarily paid, they must engage in the work of learning if we are to achieve our mission). The only descriptive word for this combination is student. They are essential to the organization in multiple dimensions, and they are often key drivers of the sources of some conflicts and the culture around how conflicts should be managed.

Staff. Staff and administrators represent a wide range of academic and service professionals. Some are committed to a career, and for others it is a job for survival with a suitable standard of living. Some are deeply committed to the organization and its mission, and for others, it is about receiving a paycheck. Most have options, and choose to work in higher education organizations because they value the mission of higher education. Many value interactions with students. Some interact with faculty, donors, and sponsors of the university or college. Their support of the core missions of the university or college is essential for it to function, and enable the institution to achieve excellence. However, universities and colleges can do more to support the professional development of staff and administrators.

While faculty are somewhat destined to remain in a unit at the institution, staff often move from unit to unit to attain professional development and advancement. With few to no formal developmental rotation opportunities, a staff member must design and execute this effort on their own.

Administrators. In addition, many administrators are selected for their position based upon their credentials and success as a faculty member. This is especially important for trustworthiness and credibility, while at the same time having little to no experiences for the actual challenges of their administrative responsibilities. Thus, support staff are often placed in the role of mentoring their supervisors in the actual demands of the administrative job. Successful administrators are often servant leaders, not control and execution leaders. They lead by serving their units and the university or college. While they can dictate very little in ensuring or changing how well the core missions are being achieved, they are essential in creating the combined collaborative, consensus oriented culture while allowing for autonomy in faculty and student work plans and schedules. Therefore, approaches to management often require looser and more adaptive administrative strategies to accomplish the institution's core mission.

Structures and Leaders in Higher Education

Generally, higher education is structured around academic fields to achieve the core mission of teaching, service and research, and around functional services to support and run the institution. Like many other complex and large organizations, various units interact and understand their interdependencies, or they may rarely interact at all. It may make sense on a certain level that the research scholar in an academic unit may never have to deal with the utilities that support their work places. Or, a faculty member in geosciences may rarely interact with a faculty member in the liberal arts. Even managers, up to the very highest administrative levels of the institution, may have little to no knowledge of other units. That is, until a conflict arises. Conflicts are the most common reasons for units to interact within an institution. Remember, these conflicts may not be negative, however, they present an opportunity for all units to improve, and are often approached by unit leaders, with a lack of understanding or experience with the other units, in a manner that is sometimes derogatory, adversarial, and territorial. The approaches to such conflicts are primarily due to a lack of leadership development in understanding the interdependence between and among the units of the institution. While structural and leadership issues exist in many organizations, the culture in higher education that fosters autonomy and specialization, often exacerbates the type, frequency, and response to structural conflicts on college and university campuses.

Processes in Higher Education

When conflicts arise, like other organizations, many universities have formal grievance processes to handle these events. For example, many of the processes are often managed through human resources, student affairs, and through designated administrators such as a dean of faculties. Several universities are creating programs to informally resolve conflicts (Klingel & Maffie, 2011). Informal conflict management programs include ombudsman services, mediation programs, and critical dialogue programs. Formal mediation programs range from having an employee mediator, to faculty, students, and staff trained peer mediators, to hiring some external to the university for mediation. Cases deemed appropriate for mediation differ across campuses as well as the content of the *mediation* services.

It can be valuable for universities, colleges, departments and other units to think about their conflict culture and the conflict intervention strategies that help them accomplish their goals for faculty, staff, and students. Two relatively unique values that affect procedures in higher education are shared governance and tenure.

Our definition of shared governance is from (Shared Governance in Colleges and Universities: A Statement by the Higher Education Program and Policy Council, http://facultysenate.tamu.edu/Quick_Links/Shared_Governance_in_Colleges_and_Universities.pdf).

Shared governance is the set of practices under which college faculty and staff participate in significant decisions concerning the operation of their institutions. Colleges and universities are very special types of institutions with a unique mission—the creation and dissemination of ideas. For that reason, they have created particular arrangements to serve that mission best. For example, academic tenure protects the status, academic freedom and independent voice of scholars and teachers. Shared governance, in turn, arose out of a recognition that:

- academic decision-making should be largely independent of short-term managerial and political considerations;
- faculty and professional staff are in the best position to shape and implement curriculum and research policy, to select academic colleagues and judge their work; and
- the perspective of all front-line personnel is invaluable in making sound decisions about allocating resources, setting goals, choosing top officers and guiding student life.

While a commitment to shared governance is often perceived by outsiders as slowing down decision making, and indeed, it can slow down initial

decisions, shared governance is crucial for achieving the decisions concerning change, including ones that have the potential to significantly move the organization forward.

In addition, universities and colleges have formal tenure guidelines. In theory, and overwhelmingly in practice, tenure is awarded to faculty who have demonstrated productivity and the ability to meet academic freedom obligations of the institution, including academic integrity. However, there are some faculty who abuse tenure, as if they have no responsibilities to the institution or others. In some instances, an institution's procedures to ensure shared governance can interfere with a managers' abilities or perceptions of their abilities to manage personnel and conflict issues in a responsible and timely manner.

This complexity alone calls for higher education institutions to pay special attention to the competencies and skills needed to manage conflict. When leading or managing very bright people, who are often trained to dissect and find every nuance of a situation or issue, it is very important that leaders or managers do not escalate conflicts by triggering outrage over process instead of over goals and long-term organizational outcomes.

Common Problems for Conflict Management in Higher Education

Given the complexities around mission, personnel, structures, procedures, and leadership development in higher education, the goal for those responsible for the management of conflict is to develop adaptive conflict competencies. The concept of conflict competence has gained visibility in recent years (Morrison, 2008). Conflict competence is the ability to effectively manage the inevitable conflicts that arise between people. At the individual level, conflict competence involves increasing our self-awareness about reactions to conflict, improving our capacity to regulate emotions, and using constructive communication behaviors to resolve issues. At an organizational level, conflict competence involves developing norms and systems for effectively managing conflict. When conflict goes awry and the retaliatory cycle causes tensions to mount, it is essential to address matters before they escalate. While some of the elements of conflict competency are aimed at dealing with conflict effectively, there will be times when things may not go as planned. In such cases, the ability to use workplace conflict intervention strategies to reach out to the parties in conflict, get them talking, and find resolutions becomes another critical element of effective conflict competency skills.

Conflict management and conflict competencies are overlooked areas of faculty, staff, and administrative leadership development efforts in higher

education. Typically, higher education institutions work to avoid or ignore conflict hoping it will go away, and most leaders hope their unit will have no conflict. Neither of these behaviors is effective. Most people only engage in conflict when it is unavoidable. This is not strategic. When striving to avoid a conflict, most units work to "get the conflict over with" as quickly as possible, which is typically a problematic strategy for the unit. Ideally, individuals and organizations that are "well practiced" in strategic conflict engagement work to systematically and strategically address conflicts at all levels. Ideally, a unit communicates the expectation that all individuals engage in conflicts as they arise. Practicing conflict engagement, particularly the easier and simpler conflicts makes an individual nimble and more effective to address the larger conflicts successfully when they occur. An effective conflict manager should understand basic and common conflict management vocabulary. This vocabulary should be understood by all, taught to new employees, used in written conflict protocols, and become part of a unit's organizational culture. In particular, a culture of conflict management and competencies should be a distributed and broadly shared set of competencies and skills, not just something that a few administrators or special employees manage.

It is important to recognize that unmanaged conflict has the potential of costing the organization (see Figure 3.1): in time, resources, energy expended, lost productivity, aggression, and violence. The reason an unmanaged conflict becomes more costly is, not only because of the potential for wasted resources in the midst of the conflict, but also the volume of resources to find a resolution typically increases as a conflict persists. This is often attributed to the escalation of the conflict. As a conflict is not managed of resolved the range of options for engaging in the particular conflict diminish.

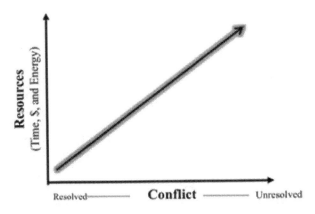

Figure 3.1.   Impact of unmanaged conflict,

The time, money, and energy that it costs to maintain unresolved conflict are tremendous for both individuals and organization. Unresolved conflicts for *individuals* can lead to distraction from work particularly in the areas of creativity and productivity. Unresolved *organizational* conflicts can lead to a climate of distrust and an overall decline in the department's productivity. In addition, the longer a conflict is left unattended the greater the time and cost, both financial and in energy, to the organization. It is clear that if individuals improve their abilities to resolve conflicts, they will save resources, and they can also expect to see improved understanding, even when parties remain in disagreement; improved communication, and; improved productivity due to better utilization of resources and relationships. Recognizing how conflicts escalate will help someone understand how a conflict may be de-escalated.

Higher education organizations must discuss how procedures and leaders think about and address conflict. However, the conflict skills that are needed to do our work are not always effective in our working relationships with one another. The culture of higher education is such that it does not easily make for a cooperative *win-win* mode (Holton, 1995; Kelso, 2005). Many on a college or university campus often think the following, "if we can just make it two more years then person Y is gone, then everything will be okay" (implying all conflict will cease in the unit). However, even if person Y appears to be the source of the conflict, conflicts are often bigger than one person or one event.

As we have discussed, conflicts are similar and also different for our administrators, faculty, staff, and students in the university setting. Below are examples of common conflicts reported across these four constituent groups that comprise higher education.

Faculty Conflicts

- Role within their Department or Unit
- Faculty-Student conflicts
- Faculty-Staff conflicts
- Tenure/Tenure Track Faculty across different ranks
- Tenure/Tenure Track-Non-Tenure Track Faculty
- Perception that conflict engagement is the responsibility of someone else to manage
- Perception of or actual inequities in the system
- Social and cultural identity conflicts

Student Conflicts

- Transition to college adjustments
- Student-Student conflicts
- Student-Faculty conflicts
- Academic-non-academic activities
- Cognitive growth and development conflicts
- Perception that conflicts are "bad" to have on campus or in relationships
- Social and cultural identity conflicts

Administrator Conflicts

- Perception of or actual limited resources
- Administrator-Administrator
- Administrator-Faculty
- Administrator-Staff
- Perception that conflicts are "bad" for the organization
- Social and cultural identity conflicts

Staff Conflicts

- Staff-Faculty conflicts
- Staff-Staff conflicts
- Perception of being a "2nd class" citizen at a university (faculty being first)
- Responding to change
- Social and cultural identity conflicts

The following section, Section II: Skills for Managing Conflict, we begin to layout skills to develop to better manage conflicts in higher education. Specifically, in Chapter 4, we discuss personal skills required to be a good conflict manager and ideas to choose conflict intervention strategies. In Chapter 5, we will discuss skills to address difficult dialogues both personally and organizationally. Finally Chapter 6 will focus on one specific area of conflict intervention—mediation.

REFERENCES

Follett, M. P. (1940). *The psychology of consent and participation. Dynamic administration: The Collected Papers of Mary Parker Follett.* New York, NY: Harper & Brothers.

Higher Education Program and Policy Council. (n.d.). Retrieved from http://facultysenate.tamu.edu/Quick_Links/Shared_Governance_in_Colleges_and_Universities.pdf

Holton, S. (1995). Conflict 101. *New Directions in Higher Education, 92,* 5–10.

Kelso, M. (2005). Nonviolent communication and ombuds work. *Conflict Management in Higher Education Report, 6*(1). Retrieved from http://www.campus-adr.org/CMHER/ReportArticles/Edition6_1/Kelso6_1a.html

Klingel, S., & Maffie, M. (2011, August/October). Conflict management systems in higher education: A look at mediation in public universities. *Dispute Resolution Journal,* 12–17.

Morrison, J. (2008). The relationship between emotional intelligence competencies and preferred conflict-handling styles. *Journal of Nursing Management, 16*(8), 974–983.

Satir, V. (1983). *Satir step by step: A guide to creating change in families.* Mountain View, CA: Science & Behavior Books.

SECTION II

SKILLS FOR MANAGING CONFLICT

CHAPTER 4

PERSONAL SKILLS REQUIRED TO BE A GOOD CONFLICT MANAGER

> *Don't let yesterday use up too much of today.*
>
> —Cherokee proverb

Regardless of the conflict behavioral modes chosen, intensity of a conflict, nature of a conflict, or choice in how to manage a conflict, there are some fundamental skills, which everyone should hone, to be more competent in managing conflict, and even managing groups or organizations in conflict. While the list of valuable competencies is potentially vast, here we will focus on seven key competencies:

- Being self-aware of your position, attitudes, and reactions to the conflict
- Being an active listener to everyone engaged in the conflict
- Being able to manage multiple perspectives on the conflict
- Being mindful
- Being able to find the best frames for understanding the nature and intensity of the conflict

- Being able to create safe dialogues concerning the conflict
- Being able to decide if your chosen behavioral style and intervention strategies are likely to be effective.

Self-Awareness

Self-awareness and the willingness to engage in self-reflection concerning your responses and biases is a key component for effectively engaging in a conflict. Conflicts exists, even if only one person perceives it. Therefore, whether you believe a conflict exists or not, when a person comes to you stating that they have a conflict, the conflict exists. Contrary to a lack of concern about a conflict, you may need to be aware, because of your own personal history and experiences, of you own hypervigilance, toward certain people or certain situations that may cause you to over react to some conflicts. If you lack the self-awareness to understand your immunity or disbelief that a true conflict exists or lack the sensitivity to certain situations where you may jump in too forcefully as if a conflict has an intensity it may not exhibit yet, then your reactions to the conflict is often to either dismiss or over dramatize the individuals who are in conflict about their beliefs, feelings, and thoughts. Too often, those who present a perceived conflict hear, "just ignore person X; he/she has behaved this way (e.g., being disrespectful to colleagues) for the past 20 years. You should just ignore him/her." Often, just as unproductive, we may let our personal experiences or emotions, inconsistently trigger reactions to eliminate a conflict so that we are perceived to have "favorites" in the organization, or even be susceptible to manipulations when others know our "hot buttons."

One effective strategy for strengthening your abilities to be more self-aware is to practice exposing your mental models (see Figure 1.1). Whenever you can, it is useful to engage in the following mental exercises:

- Consider what others observed about a situation or event that you missed, and the things you focused on, where others seemed unconcerned. Are there patterns in the kinds of things you tend to ignore? When are those patterns good? Are there patterns in the things you tend to focus on? How have your experiences shaped your ability to focus on those aspects of the situation?
- Consider the beliefs that led you to assign meaning to certain data? Beliefs are deeply held perspectives that are true for yourself and others as well. For example, do you believe that good deeds are eventually rewarded, or do you believe that no good deed goes unpunished? Do you believe that there is always calmness right

before the storm? These may be trivial examples to you personally, but they are meant to illustrate the need for you to understand how you focus your attention and interpretation of data based upon your beliefs.

- Consider the assumptions you make about a situation or individuals that may seem valuable and true, but might not have enough data present to substantiate them. This is a useful way to check your stereotypes and biases.

- Consider what you conclude about the meaning of what you have observed and how you have integrated it into your beliefs and assumptions in order to draw a conclusion. Conclusions often include decisions based on what someone's intentions are, even when only their behaviors are visible.

- Consider whether your choice of actions were the only, or even the best choice, or did you rely on habits and conclusions substantiated by the data.

The purpose of these reflections is not to say your mental model is wrong. To the contrary, mental models are necessary for us to navigate the world. The purpose of the reflections is for you to be aware of your mental models so they become more conscious.

Active Listening

Active listening is a communication procedure wherein the listener uses nonverbal behavior, such as eye contact and gestures, as well as verbal behavior, including tone of voice, open-ended questions, restatements, and summaries, to demonstrate to the speaker that he or she is being heard (Girard & Koch, 1996). Effective communication begins with effective or active listening! Practicing the active listening skills in dialogue will enhance mutual understanding of the issue. Consider the Do's and Don'ts in active listening as depicted in Table 4.1.

Body Language

People communicate in a variety of ways. They not only speak to get their messages across, but they also use their body to give signals, too. The body communicates a diverse vocabulary of gestures, postures, eye movements, twitches, grimaces, and stares. Sometimes, the body communicates a lot closer to reality than what the voice says, which is why being able to recognize and interpret body language is a valuable communication skill.

Table 4.1.   Do's and Don'ts—Active Listening Skills

DO	DON'T
Focus attention on the speaker	Talk about yourself, be critical, or give advice
Repeat back in your own words	Only say "mmm," "ah hah," or parrot other participants' words
Restate important thoughts and feelings	Ignore the facts and feelings
Reflect back so that they can hear and understand themselves	Pretend that you understand or assume that you know it all
Ask questions to make things clearer or to get more information	Be a poor listener with your voice, eyes, and body
Show listening with your voice, eyes, and body	Fill every space with your talk
Summarize facts and feelings	Fix, change, or improve what they said
Stay neutral	Take sides

Source. From Watson and Watson (2011). Reprinted with permission.

This is often referred to as, *tuning in to the vibes.* Some people are able to do it without quite knowing why or how by responding unconsciously to body language.

Body language can also communicate what we feel and think. As a participant or facilitator in a conflict, it is important not only to read other people's body language, but to also be conscious of our own body language. With the right gestures or movements, an individual can control many situations with ease. According to Watson and Watson (2011), body language can convey neutrality, confidence, and empathy—important skills for effective communication.

- Make eye contact
- Nod head to affirm the speaker
- Lean body forward and slightly toward speaker
- Keep arms unfolded
- Use appropriate facial expressions to show interest and attention.

Encouraging Others to Engage in Communication

Some individuals, in certain situations, have no reservations about communicating everything that crosses through their mind. On the other hand,

other individuals in certain situations inhibit communication. Therefore, as an active listener, individuals must work to encourage participants to stay engaged and to share. Some strategies to help encourage effective communication are:

1. Encourage the other person to keep talking. Show that you are interested in what they are saying. Example: "Can you tell us more?
2. Ask questions to get more information or to better understand the problem. Example: "Where did this happen?" "How long have you known each other?"
3. Restate in your own words the basic ideas—facts and feelings. Example: "So you were in the parking lot and he tripped you and you're feeling angry."
4. Summarize the important ideas and feelings as each person stated them. Identify the things they have in common. Example: "This seems to be what happened ... and you're feeling (or you're both feeling).... Is that right?"

Listen for Feelings Not Just Thoughts

Verbal messages in a conflict have facts, beliefs, thoughts, ideas, and feelings. Active listeners must be able to respond to both the content or facts and the feelings of the individuals in conflict. The following is a list of words that describe feelings. The list in Table 4.2. may also be helpful in identifying feelings and forming active listening responses.

Perspective Taking

Perspective taking involves working to understand another person's viewpoint, idea or belief. Perspective taking is not synonymous with agreement. Perspective taking, includes awareness of the fact that another person's *reasonable* mental model may create a completely different set of observations, trigger different beliefs and assumptions, and develop different conclusions. These differences may be equally *right*, but regardless, they are equally justified in someon e's mind.

Table 4.2.   List of Words Describing Feelings

Words Describing Feelings		
CONCERNED	ATTACKED	SURPRISED
CONFUSED	IGNORED	SCARED
ANGRY	UPSET	BLAMED
FRUSTRATED	EMBARRASSED	HATEFUL
ANNOYED	HURT	DELIGHTED
PUT DOWN	UNCOMFORTABLE	GREAT
MISUNDERSTOOD	RIPPED-OFF	BETRAYED
WORRIED	DISAPPOINTED	IRRITATED
PROUD	LEFT-OUT	IMPORTANT

Being Mindful

For a lot of people, the consequence of not keeping up with the flow of their everyday lives through online activities is a heightened sense of anxiety. They fear that if they do not keep up, they will drown in the build up of work. Mindfulness tackles this by forcing you to stop and think about which pieces of information to engage with and which to ignore. According to an interview on *ABC Radio National* in 2014 with Rasmus Hougaard (2014) of The Potential Project, in 2009 we could pay attention on an average of 13 seconds, and in 2013 it was 8 seconds—goldfish can focus for 9 seconds.

Mindfulness—taking a nonevaluative stance toward thoughts and feelings and allowing thoughts and feelings to come and go, without getting caught up in or carried away by them (Kabat-Zinn, 2003). Thus, according to Kabat-Zinn (2000), the components of mindfulness includes:

- Observing—notice
- Describing—internal
- Acting with Awareness—versus rote
- Accepting without judgment—nonconsumption with thoughts/ feelings

The Benefits of Mindfulness Are Noted As:

- Mindfulness increases productivity and decreases stress
- Help decision-makers make clearer, better quality choices
- Stronger ability to separate relevant from irrelevant information
- People who are willing to live with unwanted outcomes refrain from doing physical damage to themselves
- Practice a greater sense of self-regulation
- Decreases rumination in thinking
- Decrease stress and increase focus
- Self-compassion
- Increase perspective taking
- Increases self-reflection (Riskin, 2004),

Most people are good at considering the different perspectives involved in a conflict when they are not involved in the conflict, or none of their *hot buttons* have been pushed. The skill needed here is perspective taking when your feelings and emotions, not to mention your beliefs and values are being challenged in a situation. The fundamental principle of perspective taking is to ASSUME, that all perspectives are rational given the information and history that is presented. Thus, the goal is to understand their perspectives and do the best detective work you can to understand why their perspective is important. Conflicts are managed and conversations are more successful when the parties:

- have the ability to be self-aware (e.g., identify hidden assumptions)
- are willing to engage in self-awareness and self-reflection
- frame the/their relationship
- frame the conflict and the issue(s)
- practice mindfulness of one another
- choose to exercise perspective taking
- intentionally and strategically choose their conflict management mode(s)
- look for areas of common ground
- move from positions to interests & needs
- articulate what you want to accomplish—desired end goal
- articulate the desired end goal(s)
- use an effective communication skill set (Watson & Watson, 2011).

Understanding the Frames Involved in Conflicts

This section deepens some of the ideas presented in Chapter 2 concerning realities about conflicts. It is very important for individuals in conflicts to understand and frame the conflict well. Over simplifying a conflict will just escalate the conflict and potentially shatter trust in an organization. However, engaging every nuance and complexity of a conflict may just freeze people out of thinking there is any hope in managing a conflict.

Most conflicts have one or more of the following root causes:

- Data errors, that is, information is missing, misunderstood, or incomplete for some or all
- Interest discrepancies, that is, some people are not interested in the goals, missions, visions, or "causes" that others are interested in
- Structural issues, that is, when realities outside of the control of the parties in conflict generate conflicts, such as competition for resources or lack of resources, inaccessibility to support or access needed, external units failing to prioritize the issues in conflict
- Values, that is, when belief systems or priorities are incompatible
- Relational, that is, when historical or psychological relationships are the source of the conflict.

How an individual frames what is going on in a conflict is always complex, but Figure 4.1 illustrates many of the components that are often engaged. It is important to understand that the individual may not be conscious of the aspects of their own mental models, or external pressures that are all influencing their perception that there is a conflict, and belief in the options they have to respond. The individual may not be readily cognizant of how they have framed all of the inputs to *justify* the conflict, they may simply feel the conflict. An observer of the individual will not know all that is going on within the individual. Even the observer witnesses the same situation, event or person as the individual in conflict, and even if they know what some pressing issues are being felt by the individual in conflict, they have no way to observe how the individual is framing all of these factors and whether the perception of a conflict exists within the individual. The observer can see the behaviors, communication, and actions of the individual, and thus may begin to see that there is a conflict, but still has no information, unless the individual communicates it, how the conflict is framed for the individual.

As if the framing of one individual who perceives a conflict is not difficult enough, most organizational conflicts involve numerous people. Even though the same situations, events or people are present, and there are

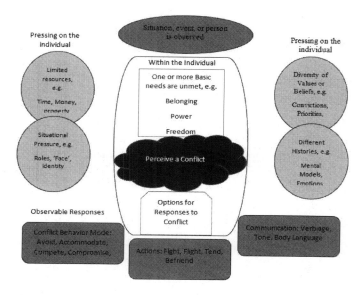

Figure 4.1. Influence on the individual that frame a conflict.

many of the same pressures, different individuals may frame a conflict entirely in different ways. For example as shown in Figure 4.2, individuals in the same conflict may perceive the root causes of the conflict to be very different.

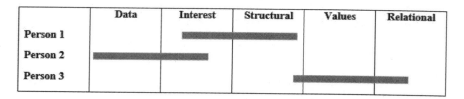

	Data	Interest	Structural	Values	Relational
Person 1		████████████			
Person 2	████████████████				
Person 3				██████████████	

Figure 4.2. Example of differences in framing of the root elements of the same conflict.

In an organization, whether it is a family unit, an academic department, or a corporation, to fully understand the framing of a conflict, it is not enough to understand how the individuals in a conflict may each frame the issues. It is also important to understand the influence the organizational culture has on the framing of the conflict. Edgar Schein's work on organizations helps in understanding the fundamental components

of an organizational culture (Schein, 1993). He described an organizational culture to be formed by its artifacts (rules, procedures, compositions, outputs), espoused values and goals, and basic underlying assumptions. For example, a university may espouse to reflect a student population that is equivalent to the region's diversity population, however, the artifacts may show great discrepancies when compared to reality. Thus, we would look for the underlying assumptions, such as *but they all must be able to pay the tuition*, or *they must all be nationally competitive in SAT scores, or this priority does not override the organization's priority to compete for national merit finalists*. To really understand an organizational culture, people must have insights into the observable artifacts and espoused values, but even more importantly they must find out the basic underlying assumptions that the employees within the organization hold, but are rarely documented or discussed. Thus, when managing conflicts within an organization, people are experiencing multiple individual framings, and simultaneously, the organizational culture around framing conflicts as depicted in Figure 4.3.

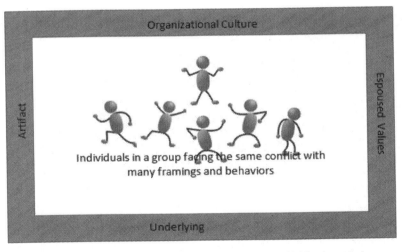

Figure 4.3.   Framing of the same conflict by multiple individuals and the organization's culture.

The skill required to *piece together* all of the individual and organizational elements, mental models, decisions, histories, cultural artifacts and goals to frame the conflict is *detective work* at its best.

Creating Dialogue

In creating dialogue, a form of communication is needed where people are asking people to suspend judgment and for them to feel safe in exposing their thoughts and feelings. Dialogue is not merely a conversation. A conversation is casual talk between two or more people during which thoughts, feelings and ideas are expressed, questions are asked and answered, or news and information are exchanged. In a conversation, there is rarely a deliberate effort made to ensure mutual understanding. Nor is a dialogue an argument or debate. In organizations and in academia, debate is often the mode of communication used. Winning, when one person convinces another that his/her ideas are right or the best, is often the goal. In debate, you listen to the other side in order to find flaws and to counter the arguments. Debate participants then affirm their point of view, defend assumptions as truth, and critique other positions. The assumption in a debate is that there is a right answer, and someone has it. The definition of dialogue is (Gergen, Gergen, & Barrett, 2004).

Dialogue (Latin: Dia: shared; Logos: meaning) involves two or more sides working toward shared meaning or common understanding. Common understanding is not synonymous with agreement. Individuals work to suspend judgment in order to listen and learn new information from others.

Figure 4.4 shows components of engaging in dialogue and if all commit to these elements then a safe place for all will be created. Absent the safety, people will hold back, protect their positions, and worst, judge who is right and who is wrong. As illustrated in Figure 4.4., from its fuzzy design, dialogue and conflict engagement, is nonlinear. There are no specific sequences or steps to creating a safe place for dialogue.

Intervention Decision

When a conflict exists between parties, individuals in the position to intervene must first decide whether intervention is advisable, and whether they should be the ones to intervene, as well as the intervention style that is needed. This consideration must take into account not only the current conflict, but also the long-term relation and interactions of the parties with each other and with the intervening party. The major factors of concern are determining the process and resolution to the current conflict, and how much influence the intervening party has on the process and resolution. Deciding if an intervention is desirable is a difficult task, because often until you dive in you have little information on the true framing of the conflict. We offer Figure 4.5 as a guide to aid in deciding if intervention is desirable.

Figure 4.4.   Attributes of a safe place for dialogue.

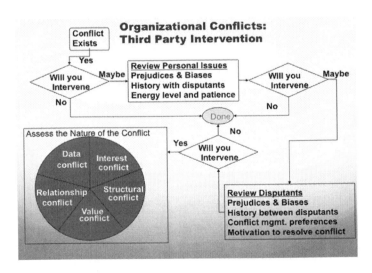

Figure 4.5.   Guide to personal intervention decision.

Other considerations in choosing an approach are how much effort, time, and resources the approach will take. Considerations when choosing an approach are:

- The long term relations and interactions of the disputants with each other and with the intervening party
- How much influence the disputants have in determining the process and resolution to the current conflict
- How much influence the intervening party has on the process and resolution
- How much effort, time and resources the approach will take
- Identify the sources of the conflict, the nature of the conflict, and determine its impact on you
- Become more aware of your own reactions and engage strategically in planning for direct and contingent actions as the conflict evolves
- Observe how others are responding to the conflict and to your approaches for managing the conflict (be aware that managing conflict is a complex dance and one where one leads and all others follow)
- Evaluate and consciously weigh the value of all approaches to the conflict and to the management styles being demonstrated by all
- Choose a conflict management style based upon your best awareness of the entire situation
- Determine if your intervention is wise and whether presenting it can manage rather than creating another attribute of the conflict.

Style of Intervention Management

If intervention is desired then there are numerous styles of intervention, as illustrated in Figure 4.6. Could we have a lead in and discussion here between this figure the faces below? I think it needs a little lead in and more explanation, Also, there are some outside the margin below. Maybe the faces need to be below the text and not intermittent. I really think we need more explanation. Like that each face grouping means.... Modeling intervener—and what is happening.

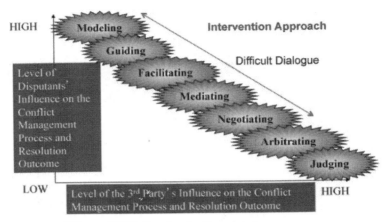

Source: Watson and Watson (2011). Reprinted with permission.

Figure 4.6.   Styles of intervention management.

To thoughtfully and intentionally model workplace behavior requires skills in:

- Self-awareness of behavior
- Managing one's emotions to demonstrate consistency.

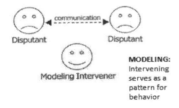

Effective guidance requires skills in:

- Active listening
- Perspective talking (seeing other's position)
- A sense of time so guidance is seen as supportive

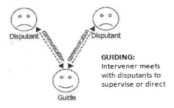

Facilitation brings disputants together to assist and support them in managing their conflict, and requires skills in:

- Active listening
- Impartiality to support all disputants

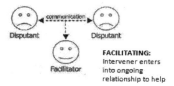

Using a formal **mediation** process to generate agreement requires skills in:

- Neutrality
- Nonthreatening confrontation
- Skills in managing people through a formal process

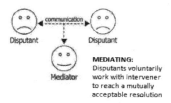

Negotiators actively help the disputants deciding the outcome of a dispute based on bringing the disputants together, and requires skills in:

- Consequence analysis
- Decision making

Arbitrators will make a decision about the outcome of the dispute if the disputants do not, and requires skills in

- Information gathering
- Consequence analysis
- Decision making

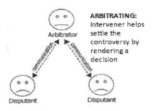

Judging requires skills in:

- Understanding and applying procedures and policies
- Clear communication
- Control of processes

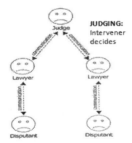

The following information is extracted from the public information provided by the U.S. government describing recognized alternative dispute resolution methods in judicial practices.

Alternative Dispute Resolution

The term "alternative dispute resolution" or "ADR" is often used to describe a wide variety of dispute resolution mechanisms that are short of, or alternatives to, full-scale court processes. The term can refer to everything from facilitated settlement negotiations in which disputants are encouraged to negotiate directly with each other prior to some other

legal process, to arbitration systems or mini-trials that look and feel very much like a courtroom process. Processes designed to manage community tension or facilitate community development issues can also be included within the rubric of ADR. ADR systems may be categorized generally as negotiation, conciliation, mediation, or arbitration systems.

Negotiation systems create a structure to encourage and facilitate direct negotiation between parties to a dispute without the intervention of a third party. Mediation and conciliation systems are very similar in that they interject a third party between the disputants, either to mediate a specific dispute or to reconcile their relationship. Mediators and conciliators may simply facilitate communication, or may help direct and structure a settlement, but they do not have the authority to decide or rule on a settlement. Arbitration systems authorize a third party to decide how a dispute should be resolved. It is important to distinguish between binding and nonbinding forms of ADR. Negotiation, mediation, and conciliation programs are nonbinding and depend on the willingness of the parties to reach a voluntary agreement. Arbitration programs may be either binding or nonbinding. Binding arbitration produces a third party decision that the disputants must follow even if they disagree with the result, much like a judicial decision. Nonbinding arbitration produces a third party decision that parties may reject. It is also important to distinguish between mandatory processes and voluntary processes. Some judicial systems require litigants to negotiate, conciliate, mediate, or arbitrate prior to court action. ADR processes may also be required as part of a prior contractual agreement between parties. In voluntary processes, submission of a dispute to an ADR process depends entirely on the will of the parties (Office of Special Counsel, U.S. Government, 2015).

Once an informed decision is made on when and how to intervene, then you can execute your decisions, evaluate new information or situations, and persevere, but not infinitely in the same mode (be prepared for contingencies and alternate approaches as the situation evolves). A conflict management plan can be an invaluable tool to effectively manage individual and organizational conflict. A Conflict Management Plan is essentially the utilization of your mental models, unless you have prepared yourself to make more conscious choices about how you want to behave in the face of a conflict. By creating awareness of different conflict management plans, prior to being involved in a conflict, a person can: (a) create an entire *toolbox* for productive intervention plans and (b) implement a conscious choice of which plan to use when in conflict. When an organization has robustly and explicitly discussed how it wants to operate in the face of conflict, and even more importantly facilitated the skills of all personnel to practice and implement the plan, then the organization can truly thrive in managing conflict.

REFERENCES

Gergen, K. J., Gergen, M. M., & Barrett, F. J. (2004). Dialogue: Life and death of the organization. In *The Sage handbook of organizational discourse* (pp. 39–59). Thousand Oaks, CA: Sage.

Girard, K., & Koch, S. J. (1996). *Conflict resolution in the schools: A manual for educators.* San Francisco, CA: Jossey-Bass.

Hougaard, R. (2014). Corporate mindfulness. Saturday Extra. *ABC Radio National.* Retrieved from http://mpegmedia.abc.net.au/rn/podcast/2014/07/sea_20140719_0850.mp3

Kabat-Zinn, J. (2003). Mindfulness-based interventions in context: past, present, and future. *Clinical Psychology: Science and Practice, 10*(2), 144–156.

Office of Special Counsel, U.S. Government. (2015). Alternative dispute resolution. Retrieved from https://osc.gov/Pages/ADR.aspx

Riskin, L. L. (2004). Mindfulness: Foundational training for dispute resolution. *J. Legal Educ., 54*, 79.

Schein, E. H. (1993). On dialogue, culture, and organizational learning. *Organizational Dynamics, 22*(2), 40–51.

Watson, N., & Watson, K. (2011). *Conflict management: An introduction for individuals and organizations* (2nd ed.). Bryan, TX: The Center for Change and Conflict Resolution.

CHAPTER 5

DIALOGUE AS A CONFLICT MANAGEMENT STRATEGY

For difficult dialogues to take place, the necessary condition is to create a **safe space** *while the sufficient condition is to create a* **courageous space** *that can allow both meaning and flow to take place. Courageous spaces are where people can reveal their authentic self.*

—Dr. Roger Worthington, Professor and
Department Chair, University of Maryland

This chapter is based upon the Difficult Dialogue Program at Texas A&M University as well as a monograph that was written by Dr. Nancy Watson and edited by Dr. Clare Gill. This chapter embodies what we have found to be useful, based on our campus climate and organizational culture, in training faculty, staff, graduate students, and undergraduate students in a 12-hour Critical Dialogues in Higher Education Program. There are many ways to engage in effective communication and conflict. One communication strategy than can be used is dialogue. Dialogue involves suspending judgment, listening for new information, and increasing one's awareness, knowledge, and skills related to the issue(s) being discussed.

Conflict Management and Dialogue in Higher Education: A Global Perspective, pp. 57–84
Copyright © 2016 by Information Age Publishing

Difficult Dialogues is a program originated by the Ford Foundation and designed to promote academic freedom and religious, cultural, and political pluralism on college and university campuses in the United States (Ford Foundation, 2005). The Critical Dialogues in Higher Education Program developed by the Office of the Vice President and Associate Provost for Diversity at Texas A&M University, serves as a campus resource for building capacity for engaging in effective communication, encouraging engagement in strategic conflict management, and supporting a skill set for managing difficult dialogues with a focus on intact work groups. This book broadens the original scope of this work, so that it can be a resource to support or augment similar programs at other organizations or academic institutions. A difficult dialogue is where at least one person internally or externally experiences some level of discomfort in engaging in a topic or issue with another. People may be unsure, unwilling, or unskilled at participating in a difficult dialogue for a variety of reasons. Therefore, many people avoid dialogues that may be difficult. For some, it might be fear of the outcome, whereas for others it could be a concern that the dialogue might get to a roadblock. Further, participants are often concerned the other person may "get upset with them" or that they may "make the situation worse" by engaging in the dialogue. In difficult dialogues, some participants are uncertain about how to proceed and so may avoid an exchange of ideas or perspectives.

A planned difficult dialogue is one where there is intentionality about calling the meeting or forum to use the communication mode called dialogue. It is anticipated that the issue or topic will be difficult for at least some of the participants. The steps of the difficult dialogue process are discussed later in this chapter. The convener of a planned difficult dialogue must be an active, skilled, dialogue facilitator and not a passive observer.

An unplanned difficult dialogue is an unforeseen meeting or other interaction with others. When this happens, the individual acting as the facilitator acknowledges the person's viewpoint, knowing that other participants may have different views. The facilitator must decide whether she/he is willing and ready to engage in this topic right away. She/he assesses, and asks, if others are willing to dialogue about this topic. To proceed with the dialogue, the next step is to follow the standard difficult dialogue process. If participants do not have the interest, willingness, or energy to engage in dialogue immediately, but it is important to the group or team, the dialogue can be scheduled for a later time. When the topic is deemed inappropriate for the current setting, the facilitator would provide an alternate organizational or campus structure, process, or forum to address the topic (adapted from Iowa State University, n.d.).

Goal of a Difficult Dialogues Program

The goal of a Difficult Dialogues Program is to make the campus/organization climate more welcoming, inclusive, and safe for the free exchange of ideas and differences in perspectives that come with building a diverse and global learning community. Accordingly, a Difficult Dialogues Program can contribute to Accountability, Climate, and Equity goals of an organization or university Climate and Diversity Plans. In particular, a Difficult Dialogues Program can contribute to fulfillment of a commitment in Climate and Diversity Plans of attending to and promoting a positive and supportive climate, which fully recognizes, values, and integrates diversity in the pursuit of organizational and academic excellence (Texas A&M University, Office of the Vice President and Associate Provost for Diversity, 2015). In this chapter we:

1. Offer a modular structure for an organization to create a cadre of dialogue facilitators for its Organizational Climate Program or Difficult Dialogues Program;
2. Provide a resource to increase skill sets and preparedness of employees, administrators, faculty, staff, and students to encounter difficult dialogues constructively both internal to their units and external to the organizational environment;
3. Provide a framework for the business organization or campus community to engage in dialogue around sensitive topics and issues, and
4. Facilitate self-awareness and recognition by individuals that their thoughts, feelings, judgments, and mental models all impact dialogue.

OVERVIEW OF MODULES

The difficult dialogue program consists of four 3-hour modules. We outline those as follows.

MODULE 1—ME WITH ME: INCREASING SELF-AWARENESS

- In this module, participants learn and assess the strength of their skills related to communication, conflict management, and dialogue.
- Effective communication begins with effective listening

- Managing conflict begins with me
- Being aware of my strengths in a difficult dialogue
- How I might get in the way in a difficult dialogue

MODULE 2—ME AND THE GROUP: MANAGING ME AS A GROUP PARTICIPANT

In this module, participants learn and discuss how they constructively or counterproductively impact group dialogue.

- My responsibilities as a participant in a difficult dialogue
- Individual and group strengths
- Mental models and decision-making
- Feelings and thoughts
- Self-management
- Making suggestions versus making judgments
- Perspective taking
- Active listening

MODULE 3—ME AS A FACILITATOR: FACILITATING A GROUP OR TEAM USING DIALOGUE

In this module, participants build their facilitation and active listening skill set.

- Effective facilitation skills
- Effectively using the difficult dialogue process with a group
- Common group behaviors

MODULE 4—REFLECTING ON ORGANIZATIONAL CLIMATE

In this module, participants increase their awareness of social and cultural diversity as well as conflicts and difficult dialogues that occur within a campus unit and/or the university as a whole.

Difficult Dialogue Process

The modules in which steps in the process will be covered are in parentheses (adapted from Group Process Consulting, n.d.).

Foundation for Dialogue

From the work from Annette Simmons (1999) *A Safe Place for Dangerous Truths: Using Dialogue to Overcome Fear & Distrust at Work,* are steps for strategically facilitating a difficult dialogue in higher education. Note that the majority of time is establishing an environment and the *right* conditions for dialogue to occur. This is similar to the mediation process described in Chapter 6.

1. Establish the dialogue environment [discussed in Module 1]
2. Identify current issues through individual pre-meetings [discussed in Module 1]
3. Define dialogue to individuals and the group [discussed in Module 1 & discussed in Module

Expectations for Dialogue

4. Individual perspective—Why and what? [discussed in Module1]
5. Facilitator—What can be expected of the facilitator? [discussed in Modules 1–4]
6. Process and commitment—Expectations for the dialogue [discussed in Module 1]

Meaning and Methods for Teams and Individuals Engaged in Dialogue

7. Team/group stages and dialogue [discussed in Module 2]
8. Awareness and adapting (e.g., pacing) [discussed in Modules 1–4]
9. Dialogue interaction is the process (how said) and content (what said). Dialogue outcome is the "how" of ending up in a different place [discussed in Module 2]
10. External and internal communication (e.g., behavior and intention) [discussed in Module 2]

Impact of Difficult Dialogue on Group or Team Over Time [discussed in Module 2]

11. Consequences of changing on the group
12. Consequences of avoiding change on the group
13. Consequences of avoiding change as an individual

14.   The ladder of inference influences your ability to change

–   Dialogue means you identify your own assumptions and you are more honest about your hidden beliefs

Engage in the Difficult Dialogue

15.   Choose the "dialogue circle" rules [discussed in Modules 2–4]
16.   Engage in dialogue [discussed in Modules 3–4]

–   ~ 2 hours using a communication skill set
–   Suspend judgment and outcomes

17.   Reflection on what next [discussed in Modules 3–4]
18.   The "so what" of the dialogue and "what's next?" [discussed in Modules 3-4]

MODULE 1—ME WITH ME: INCREASING SELF-AWARENESS

➢   Be Prepared for Conflicts

Conflict Styles

Typically, we will deal with conflict in one of two modes:

–   Fight to win, therefore there is always one or more losers
–   Flee from the situation

Furthermore, your conflict style can be impacted by factors such as gender, self-concept or confidence, skills in dealing with conflicts, communication skills, and life experiences. In addition, you will choose styles to deal with the conflict that depend on situational factors such as personal expectations and position or power. Conflict style is greatly influenced by the culture, both social and organizational, in which we operate. Numerous researchers have documented differences, in general, in how men and women, or minorities and non-minorities handle conflicts in the United States (Robbins, Finney, & O'Rourke, 2008). Learned behaviors in organizations, or units within the organization, influence the styles often chosen for managing conflicts. The key is to understand that these are learned behaviors, and they can be changed if desired (Watson & Watson, 2011).

As discussed in Chapter 1, the Thomas-Kilmann Instrument can be useful in discussing the conflict styles of behavior (avoiding, accommodating, competing, compromising, or collaborating)

Choosing Your Conflict Management Style

There are times when you have a choice to avoid or engage in a conflict. Ignoring a conflict, once it has come to your attention, is never the best decision. The following six variables should be considered when deciding if you will engage in a conflict or not: In this module the contents of Chapter 4 should be covered, especially focused on the decision to engage in a difficult dialogue and faming the dialogue to the best of your ability.

Self-Awareness

When entering a dialogue, it is an asset if you are well grounded in self-awareness and knowledge. You need to know and own your personal history. You also need to know your internal triggers. For example, do you know when you have moved to a place of arousal, vigilance, or the markers that indicate your emotions are about to escalate to anger or another strong emotion?

What are your triggers?

What words rile you up when you're tired or frustrated?

Are there events that push your buttons? (e.g., How is your physical and mental state impacted when someone glares at you?)

Minimize Conflicts by Effective Use of I-Statements

Using I-Statements is an effective way to increase clarity in communication by being specific, while simultaneously decreasing the likelihood of defensiveness on the part of the listener (Klose & Olivares, 1999).

I-Statements are the process by which:

- You construct messages that convey accurate information about your feelings and content.
- You speak so others may listen and respond in an empathetic or rational way.

Purpose of I-Statements

The purpose of I-Statements is:

- To make a clear, clean statement of your experience of an event, incident, etc., in a way that another person will hear and not need to defend.
- To use in the following situations:
  - where there is a strong emotional feeling or response
  - when you are annoyed or irritated by another person or something that has happened
  - when you want to tell another person, in a safe way, what you think of them or something about how their behavior is affecting you.

Principles for I-Statements

A listener will be much more open to listening keenly if:

1. You send feelings or perceptions, instead of solutions.

    For example, rather than saying,
    Don't ever take my (book) again. (Message: you are a thief, I don't trust you.)
    Say: *I get angry when you borrow my book without asking.*

2. You take ownership of feelings/perceptions. Blaming or evaluating and judging the other person set up a wall of anger and defensiveness.

    Instead of saying: *You are inconsiderate when you borrow my things.*
    Say: *I get annoyed when you borrow my things without asking.*

3. You are open and direct with these feelings or perceptions:

Instead of addressing the issue(s) head-on, people often avoid the issue(s) directly and say one thing while implying another. This avoidance approach will lead either to total isolation or attack and confrontation.

Use I-Statements as *openers* for the dialogue, not as statements for resolution.

FORMAT:

When you _____, I feel _____

 (Neutral description)   (No blame)

and what I would like is _____

 (Change request)

The *When* is followed by a neutral and objective description of the event or another person's behavior. It is important that it does not have any words that imply judgment or evaluation or that may provoke a defensive response, or any possibility of denial by the other person. The statement must be a statement of fact.

The *I feel* part must use a word or a few words that describe exactly your feeling response to the event or other person's behavior. People often describe how they feel by describing how they want to act (e.g., I feel like withdrawing). An important piece here is that you must own the feeling without blaming or shaming the other person.

For example:

> Instead of saying: *I feel you are being defensive.*
> Say: *I feel angry when you don't understand my feelings.*

The last part of the statement describes why you feel the way you do and/or the outcome or change desired. You need to express how you would like for something or a particular behavior to change, but it is not okay to expect or demand that it will happen. There are no guarantees that the other person will make the requested change unless you are in a position of power over the other individual and can then make a behavior change mandate. However, you have clearly communicated your expected or desired change. You should practice using I-statements when situations are not difficult or intense so they become a habit. I-statements are most effective when you have had time to formulate the I-statements before using them.

Self-Reflection of the Participants During the Module is Important

For the participants in the module it is essential that they are not simply self-aware when dealing with a conflict, but that they are reflective of the

topics and styles of dialogue that are particularly difficult for them. Thus, in the module they will spend some time reflecting and sharing on the following:

1. What dialogues are difficult for you?
2. How do you (if you do) engage in difficult dialogues?
3. What are your strengths when you participate in difficult dialogues?
4. What do you need to improve when you participate in difficult dialogues?
5. Where will you get in the way in a difficult dialogue?

Content of a Difficult Dialogue

It is important to remember that a difficult dialogue is one where at least one person feels some level of discomfort in engaging in discussion of the topic or issue. In addition, almost any topic or issue can lead to a difficult dialogue, for example, budgets, job performance, or responsibilities. Topics will be more difficult for you if you feel they relate to one of your core values, especially when the new information creates cognitive dissonance. Cognitive dissonance is when you experience a psychological conflict resulting from incongruous beliefs and attitudes held simultaneously (e.g., you like a person, but you do not like his behavior). Outside forces (e.g., current economic climate, uncertainty in the work environment) may contribute to or amplify the level of resistance to change.

Below are some ideas for organizations to reflect upon when thinking about using dialogue as a method of communication to address difficult issues.

1. There is a difference between being in a difficult dialogue and being difficult in a dialogue.
2. Most dialogues will involve an issue related to diversity (using Loden's (1996) definition of diversity as anything that makes us different from one another).
3. Organizations must develop trust (an expectation about the positive actions of other people) in order to effectively engage in dialogue.
4. There is value added in being a data driven organization to identify specific issues or concerns related to diversity.

   – Far too often organizations rely on anecdotal information as to what the "problems" are in their units. Systematic evaluation to identify prevalent and pervasive issues is important.

5. Conducting a comprehensive climate survey, regularly, can identify dimensions of an organization's climate related to diversity, as perceived and experienced by individuals in the organization.

6. In most organizations, a majority of individuals will express high levels of satisfaction with their units. However, many others may have concerns about discrimination and insensitivities.

   – Discrimination is defined as the observation of insensitive comments and actions toward an individual or group based upon individual identity attributes, and correlated with individuals' perceptions and experiences.
   – Insensitive comments are more frequently directed toward individuals and groups who are targeted and not members of the dominant group (e.g., age, class, gender, race, ethnicity, nationality, physical and learning ability, religion, sexual orientation) or those who do not hold privilege

7. Developing effective conflict management skills is critical to being an effective facilitator of dialogue around issues of diversity.

   – Individuals who perceive higher frequencies of inappropriate discriminatory practices more frequently note dissatisfaction with how leaders handle conflict.
   – In general, individuals from underrepresented racial and ethnic groups in comparison to individuals who are White, women in comparison to men, individuals with religious identities that are not Christian in comparison to those who identify as Christian, and individuals who identify as gay, lesbian, and transgender in comparison to those who identify as heterosexual, more frequently report an unwelcoming and exclusive environment.

8. It is not uncommon for individuals or groups to avoid dialogue about diversity issues. For example, when campus or unit climate assessment data results are discussed (more often debated), it is typical for the perceptions and experiences expressed by targeted group members to be judged and then discounted or minimized by those in the dominant group as the "comments of a disgruntled few."

9. Effective leaders must be willing and able to engage in difficult dialogues and have a strong communication skill set.

10. Finally, it is important to remember that engaging in a difficult dialogue involves:

- Listening for new information
- Suspending judgment
- Listening to learn (versus critique)

As we refer back to Figure 4.4 in Chapter 4, we must remember that a dialogue, or at least a safe place for a dialogue has many components. However, dialogue begins with self awareness and awareness of our inner dialogue (or mental models). Dialogue also involves awareness of how one is having an impact on others.

MODULE 2—ME AND THE GROUP: MANAGING ME AS A GROUP PARTICIPANT

In Module 1, the focus was on you, the individual, and your internal dialogue. Individuals may have over 60,000 thoughts per day. Remembering all these thoughts is impossible and probably not advisable! However, understanding what contribution you make to your 'self' is the first necessary skill and responsibility you have to be effective in difficult dialogues. For this module, visualize yourself sitting in a group entering a difficult dialogue. Think about you and the group together in a dialogue circle. A goal for this module is to be grounded in your knowledge of yourself as a participant in a group.

It is also necessary and important to know as much as you can about others in the group. Sometimes you will have no preparation time or there will be people in the dialogue who you were not expecting. This is okay, and effective engagement in a difficult dialogue can still occur. However, for an intact work group, there is greater likelihood you will know all the participants: how they prefer to be communicated to, what their hot buttons are, and their ease and willingness to engage in dialogue are important to reflect upon.

Enter the dialogue with the belief that everyone's intention is to have a productive dialogue. Choose and practice meaningfulness, and adopt a positive attitude. Even if a colleague is venting and their story is very similar to others, there is value added in sharing. Although the majority of the group may have similar narratives, each narrative is different and filtered through each person's mental model. Additionally, there are still other narratives, often unspoken, particularly early on in the difficult dialogue process. So, although there may appear to be no cognitive dissonance, there typically is some discord. All narratives may not yet have been shared, and the tendency sometimes is to consciously or unconsciously shut down these viewpoints. In this situation, you need to manage yourself and pacing of the dialogue, as others need to share. Just as you are aware of

your own triggers, be sensitive to triggers for individuals in the group. Do not stereotype and do not assume. Don Miguel Ruiz (1997) in his book *The Four Agreements* challenges people to: (a) Be impeccable with your word, (b) Do not make assumptions, (c) Do not take things personally, and (d) Always do your best. Ruiz's principles are sound when participating in a difficult dialogue. Practice mindfulness, and practice particular mindfulness when you are a member of the dominant group or in a position of privilege. What you do and say influences others, so consider whether what you say in a dialogue is valuable, productive, and making a contribution or if your words are destructive, shutting down others, and causing distrust.

Pay close attention to yourself and, simultaneously, do not become consumed with self and completely self-focused, which can be detrimental to listening and participating in the dialogue circle. Observe other people in the group in terms of tone, tempo, words being used, and body language. Know that people tend to focus only on one area (tone or body language, etc.) and interpret that behavior through their mental model. Remember too, *you can manage yourself, but you cannot alter any other person in the group*. This is the most complex area in a dialogue!

In a difficult dialogue, you and the other participants must commit to suspending judgment for the dialogue process to work. For most, this is counter to your typical mode. This is a change, and change is hard for many people! Remember, the difficult dialogue process is about acquiring: (a) new information, (b) new meaning, and (c) suspending judgment. A difficult dialogue, involving a dialogue circle, does not strive to generate an outcome, an end goal, or a solution; rather, the goal is increased learning and understanding from which additional dialogues can occur to generate solutions and solve problems.

Group/Team Patterns of Interaction

This section is discussed in Chapter 1 of the book; however, it is important to discuss leading a dialogue program. There are many models of how teams perform as they enter into difficult dialogues and move toward changing the direction they deem desirable for the organization. One model suggests the following stages in the dialogue circle: (a) Politeness and pretending, (b) Chaos, (c) Discarding and redefining, (d) Resolution and collective learning, and (e) Closure. Other Difficult Dialogues Programs use Tuckman's (1965) team development model.

Tuckman (1965) advocated that groups first come together, *Form*, and people are nice to each other because that is the social norm for interacting with people you do not know well—be on your best behavior. So when your group/team comes together, you will adhere to "traditional" expectations

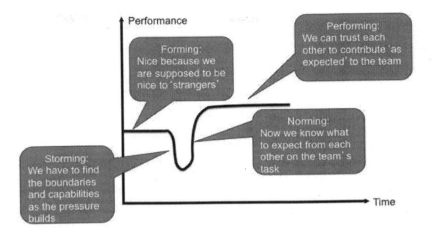

Source: Tuckman (1965). Adapted by CCCR (2004). Reprinted with permission.

Figure 5.1.   Tuckman's model of group interactions.

from the group/culture, which are unwritten and unspoken. After the group has spent some time together, you will ideally *Storm*, meaning the group will move to a deeper dialogue with one another and be willing to engage in meaningful conflict. Healthy organizations move through this process; ineffective or stuck groups never storm. After Storming, the group moves to *Norming*—the group or team has begun the process, after engaging in meaningful conflict and having the difficult dialogues, of finding its identity. The group/team establishes new norms of behavior, communication, and commitment to one another. Finally, the group or team *Performs*. In a dialogue group, performing would involve participants leading the dialogue instead of looking to the cofacilitators for guidance. You would suspend judgment, listen attentively and actively to learn new information from one another, and share new meaning as you increase your understanding of the topic, issue, or one another. At this point, your group/team typically excels and moves to a higher or stronger level of performance or commitment.

Resisting Change as an Individual

As mentioned earlier, digging in your heels and resisting change, either as an individual or as an intact work group/team, is common. You will typically resist change for several reasons whether it is known to you or not.

There will be times when you turn your opinions into facts. Therefore, when someone challenges your opinions, you resist the person because you believe your opinions really are the facts. This is common in higher education where facts and data are so important to the academy and the work we do. There will be times when other group members so strongly believe their opinions are the facts, they then believe that you are intentionally working against them.

Resisting change is also common when you make assumptions. Believing you know what a person believes, thinks, and feels are assumptive at best, and arrogant at worst. The third reason you will resist change is related to dichotomous thinking. When you believe there is only one right answer, one way of doing things (and that way, of course, is your way), then you limit opportunity for growth and further learning. Finally, you will resist change when you decide the issue being discussed is not your problem. When you distance yourself from the issue or problem, you distance yourself from the group and from making a collaborative contribution to change.

There will be resistance to change in almost every difficult dialogue.

Avoiding Change as a Group or Team

Engaging in dialogue is often related to change; you may change as you learn new information or acquire a new meaning. Common responses that occur with group members when asked to change include:

- Flight—when one or more group members want to leave the situation or encounter
- Fight—when one or more group members want to win over others
- Pairing—aligning with another group member to show force and strength by dominating others
- Dependency—when a group member expects the facilitator to take care of him or her

Self-Management With a Group

As a participant of a group, it is important to reflect on yourself. Specifically, you should reflect on the following (adapted from Watson & Watson, 2011):

- Feelings and thoughts—what you are thinking or feeling at any given moment
- Your "hot" buttons—what events, statements, behaviors trigger you to respond in a nonproductive way
- Active listening—includes encouraging others to share, restating and summarizing to check for understanding, and asking pointed, open-ended questions
- Judging—counter to the dialogue process, judging diminishes the likelihood of suspending judgment to hear and listen for new information
- Internal and external dialogue—at any given time you should be aware of your internal dialogue while simultaneously being mindful of the words shared with others
- Adding value to the team—you should reflect on what contribution you are making to the group or team with whom you are meeting, and whether it is the contribution you want to be making

Self-Reflection

What responsibilities, if any do you have to a participating group or team? Are your responsibilities different if it is an intact team (e.g. a team within your unit) as compared to a group you will encounter only one time? What responsibilities do you have to yourself when you are part of a group or team engaged in a difficult dialogue? How are your answers different if the dialogue is *not* difficult for the group/team? How aware are you of your inner dialogue when you are part of a group/team engaged in a difficult dialogue?

MODULE 3—ME AS A FACILITATOR: FACILITATING A GROUP OR TEAM USING DIALOGUE

For this Module, picture yourself and your cofacilitator as third parties to the group or team, standing outside of the dialogue circle. Your role as facilitator is to manage a process of engaging people that gives them the opportunity to lean, move, or shift within. Remember, dialogue is collaborative with two or more people working together toward common understanding. Dialogue involves a real concern for yourself and for the other people and seeks to not alienate or offend. The key to dialogue is

listening for 'new' information. As discussed by Kathy Obear (2007), facilitating dialogues can be challenging and stressful work. "Whether conscious of it or not, as a facilitator or participant you bring most, if not all, of who you are to the learning environment, including your fears, biases, stereotypes, memories of past traumas and current life experiences" (p. 25). She also said, "Many facilitators report being 'hooked' by the comments and actions of participants and feel 'triggered' emotions, including anger, fear, embarrassment, pain and sadness" (p. 26).

Facilitation is defined as to make easier; help bring about; effectively helping a group solve problems and make decisions. Facilitating a difficult dialogue is *not* about solving a problem. Instead, it is about creating an environment where people have the opportunity to be self-aware and where they can be honest and open sharing their perspective on a topic. Thus, facilitating a dialogue, or more specifically a difficult dialogue, is often a challenge for people because your primary responsibility is one of support—support to create an environment for dialogue. Participants in the dialogue must choose to self reflect, be open to new or different perspectives, be willing to suspend judgment, and be willing to change. The dialogue environment creates a growing space for change. However, as a difficult dialogue facilitator, you cannot make people change. You must have an understanding of self, have the ability to self-dialogue and self-reflect, be adaptive to change, and possess skills in conflict management.

In his book, *The Skilled Facilitator*, Roger Schwarz (2002) indicated the facilitator's main task is "to help the group increase effectiveness by improving its process and structure" (p. 40) where:

Process is how the group works together,

Structure is a stable recurring group process (e.g. group roles), and

Content refers to facilitating what the group is working on.

Facilitating Change

As a facilitator, it is important that you remember to expect resistance during a dialogue session. Participants are being asked to suspend judgment, listen actively, and not work to persuade others to their worldview. These practices are different from how they often listen and communicate; you know when you ask people to change, even during the time they are participating in the dialogue circle, resistance will often occur. Remember that resistance is not *bad*; it is an indicator that something may need to be discussed.

Facilitating people in a process of potential change means you are supporting individuals as they move from the position of there is no change that needs to occur and therefore "I have no need to change" to deciding, through increased understanding, and that they want to consciously take action to change. Following are attributes, actions, skills, and commnication needed to be a facilitator.

Attributes of an Effective Facilitator

- Manage the environment and manage yourself
- Recognize you and the group are a system

Being a Difficult Dialogues Facilitator

- You are a third party (or you should be)
- Process expert
- Content neutral (when not part of the intact group)
- Neither substantive decision-maker, nor mediator
- Help group to improve its process in a manner consistent with the core values

Facilitator Skills

- Develop effective relationships
- Work with groups
- Deal with difficult dialogues and difficult conversations
- Facilitation is impossible without trust
- Trust develops from effective and honest communication

Remember to trust yourself, choose to trust others, trust the process, and WORK THE INTENDED PROCESS.

Facilitating Effective Communication

Communication occurs with:

1. A Transmitter
2. A Receiver

The transmitter anticipates what the receiver needs to know to satisfy intellect and feelings. As a facilitator, you will aid the transmitter to present the content of the message in a format that best conveys information to the receiver. You will help the receiver to discern the information presented by the transmitter (being aware of both your and his or her mental model). Because information is always filtered through an individual's unique lens, the opportunity for miscommunication and therefore distrust (or at least not enhancing trust) are ever present. However, effective facilitation occurs when trust is present and continues to grow and develop. Typically groups and teams (and this is appropriate for a dialogue circle) "break down" at the fundamental level of **Trust** and the secondary level of **Conflict** (Algert & Watson, 2005).

A Script for Facilitating a Difficult Dialogue

Below is a brief script, aligned with the five main areas of the difficult dialogue process, for facilitating a group or team in a difficult dialogue circle. Some key phrases are embedded in the script that you may find useful when you facilitate a dialogue. The scenario is that you are one of two third party co-facilitators working with an intact work group identified as a college leadership team who wants formal support on effectively using the difficult dialogue process related to building trust (the issue for dialogue previously identified by the team).

PART I: FOUNDATION FOR DIALOGUE

We, Facilitator 1 name and Facilitator 2 name, appreciate the opportunity to support your leadership team. We would like to review with you what has occurred prior to us being together today, what you can expect from today, and then give you all the opportunity to move into dialogue.

Facilitator Note 1. In a cofacilitation model, together, you support the group by actively listening to both the verbal and nonverbal cues. You support each other by observing when to step in, to continue working the process, if one of you is triggered by behavior of individuals in the group or by the content of the dialogue.

We, Facilitator 1 and Facilitator 2, had the opportunity to meet with you individually to get your perspective of your leadership team—the team's strengths, areas to grow, and issues related to trust. We appreciate all of you taking the time to talk with

us prior to being together today. Each of you said there is value added in talking about how to increase trust among one another so that you can use more energy on accomplishing your team goals and less energy on "each other."

Remember, before we move into the process for today, that dialogue involves both individual and group responsibilities. As an individual, each of you in the group has a responsibility to be self-aware and self-reflective, to be honest, and to think about your impact on the group. Each of you is asked to work to suspend judgment and to use your active listening skills. As a group member, you are listening to understand, not to judge. You are working to be open to change and willing to reassess your viewpoint.

Group responsibilities include the commitment to work toward a common understanding, which is not necessarily agreement, realizing each of your behaviors impact the group. Your behaviors may be conscious or unconscious and verbal or nonverbal; we are not asking you to be "perfect" as this is not achievable by any of us. We ask you to be reflective and intentional. Think about you and think about your impact on the group.

We would like to share with you now what you can expect from us as your facilitators and what we expect from you. Our expectations are not about control but rather about how to create the optimum environment and process to best support you in having a productive dialogue.

PART II: EXPECTATIONS FOR DIALOGUE

As we said earlier, we had a chance to talk with each of you individually about how you saw today's dialogue. However, some time has passed since we met with each of you. So, we would like to give you the chance to share any new ideas that have arisen that are good for the group and important for you to share. Specifically, focus on "why you are here" and "what you want from today" (not stating an outcome but rather related to process).

Facilitator Note 2. You may spend just a few minutes in process here. Participants, whether an intact group or not, are typically on their "best behavior" and do not have a lot to say. Make sure you do not let one person "create an agenda" or dominate. If one person shares, get several other people's comments, and check multiple times if any one else has something they would like to share.

Thank you for sharing your comments. Let us restate what we heard you say to check for understanding. Please correct us if we misunderstood or if we miss something.

Facilitator Note 3. Restate and model effective use of active listening. Work to capture main points, be brief but thorough, and write it down for all to see if necessary.

Did we restate (or summarize) that correctly? Thank you.

What you can expect from us as your facilitators, and hopefully you have seen this thus far, is to support you in the creation of an environment where each of you has the opportunity to share your perspective. Our role is to support your process and help you fulfill your commitment to your ground rules, which you will create in a little while. Our role is not to guide, direct, or lead you in the dialogue. We commit to supporting your process and not detracting from the process. We may ask questions or point out an observation we have, and we will 'check in' periodically. As your facilitators, we are purposefully going to stand outside of the dialogue circle today because this is your dialogue. So, we encourage you to address other members of the group rather than speaking directly to either of us. It is your dialogue circle, and we respect this.

Facilitator Note 4. There are times when you will want to sit with the dialogue circle and other times that you should stand around the perimeter of the group. If you are facilitating a dialogue for a group or team and you are also a participant of the group, you will usually sit with them. If you are a third party, you will strategically decide if you will sit with the group or stand outside the group.

Are there any questions related to our role and what you can expect from us?

In our experiences of facilitating dialogues, we (names of facilitators) have found the dialogue group believes the process is far more effective when everyone is clear on what they can expect from one another related to process. So, let's take the time needed …

Facilitator Note 5. Typically takes no more than ten minutes although some groups will take more time; this usually occurs because this is their very first time together, and there is distrust or dis-ease about being with one another. Write the ground rules for all to see. Use your active listening skills here to check for understanding and for modeling.

… for you to generate the ground rules you will each commit to. Who will suggest a ground rule that will assist your dialogue process?

> Facilitator Note 6. Dialogue groups typically generate 3–7 ground rules. Get as much specificity as possible. Solicit verbal confirmation of commitment to these ground rules from the group. Common ground rules are: (a) confidentiality—what is discussed in here stays in here; (b) respect—we can disagree strongly and still be respectful; (c) there is no leader; (d) speak for yourself; (e) no decisions are being made today; (f) listen to yourself and listen to others; (g) suspend judgment; (h) acknowledge one another; (i) act as colleagues, and (j) switch off electronic devices.

You all generated these (number) of commitments/rules for today. Let us restate them one more time and get consensus that these are the dialogue circle rules you commit to.... Okay, if we observe you are not fulfilling your commitment to one another by adhering to these statements, we may "check in" with the group to help you stay focused. Are there any questions for us? Alright, well done!

> Facilitator Note 7. You spend a good deal of time in Part II of the process. Part II helps establish the foundation for the group, model what effective communication looks like, create the loose structure and parameters for difficult dialogue, aid the participants in relaxing (most people become stressed when they hear the phrase difficult dialogue), and ensure participants understand they are responsible for engaging in the process at a level of sharing and vulnerability as they are comfortable and willing.

> Facilitator Note 8. Part III should be brief. It is a time to create some additional structure for the participants. Part III consists of (a) presenting a brief explanation of group dynamics; (b) discussing the pace of the dialogue; (c) reminding them what dialogue is; and (d) mindfulness in communication.

PART III: MEANING AND METHODS

Group Dynamics

It is common for groups in dialogue to move through stages of communication and comfort. Briefly, we want to mention that often when groups form, everyone is very nice to one another. We practice the "social conventions" of nice over honest. A group then can move to "storming"—although some groups work to avoid storming at all cost, it really is a very productive time for a group. The dialogue moves from a superficial level to a clearer identification of the group and individual issues to discuss. Storming is often the most uncomfortable time a group has together but, again, it is imperative that it occurs for a group to increase communication.

A group then often moves to what Tuckman called "norming." Based upon the honest, although typically difficult, dialogue earlier, the group gets clearer in their communication, increases their commitment to one another and the team, and develops stronger "norms" of group behavior.

Finally, after effectively participating in the dialogue circle, individuals in the group experience the team excelling in a different way, often described as being more productive and consuming less energy.

Dialogue Pace

You will find the group moving at different rates throughout the two hours of dialogue. Understand this is common and expected. There will be times where there is a lot of discussion, and there will be times in your dialogue where each of you wants more time for internal reflection. We are also both very comfortable with silence if you need extra time to internally process before sharing. So, do not be surprised if the group appears to have different pacing throughout its time. We, as your facilitators, will be mindful in supporting you all in the pace of your dialogue.

Dialogue and Mindfulness

Dialogue interaction is the <u>process</u> (how something is said), and the <u>content</u> (what is said). The dialogue outcome is the <u>how</u> of ending up in a different place. There is a quote that says "we judge others by their behavior and we want to be judged by our intentions." It is important to remember that others can only observe your non-verbal communication and the words you say. Therefore, again we remind you of the importance of "you managing you" and thinking about your colleagues in the group.

PART IV: IMPACT OF DIALOGUE

Groups and teams that intentionally engage in dialogue as one process of communication in the workplace report a strong environment where diversity has greater value and the importance of engaging in discourse and conflict is understood. When the group changes through dialogue, more time and energy is spent on addressing exciting work challenges such as teaching, research, and engagement, and less energy is used in "juggling" colleagues that are "different" from you or "difficult" to you.

Schein (1993) talked about mental models. Mental models are the steps we go through, often unconsciously, that drive our decision-making and understanding of situations and people.

Facilitator Note 9. You may share the *mental model diagram* at this point if there is value added.

What is complex within a group dialogue is that each of us in the room has our own unique mental model operating. And our mental model, for most of us, has served us well, we believe. When one of our colleagues thinks from his or her own mental model, we often think our colleague is wrong, being intentionally difficult, or working against us because his or her thinking and actions may be so different from ours. Thus, we are often resistant to the ideas from another that are divergent from our own. Few of us self-reflect and work to understand our own mental model and evaluate how our colleague's mental model may be different from our own. This is not about a right or a wrong but rather a different perspective or understanding or belief.

Once we are aware of our own mental models and others, we are generally more willing to work to not personalize someone's statements, increase our ability to suspend judgment, and move to learning from our colleague. If we make this step of learning from one another, we are well on our way to be willing to change both as an individual and as a group.

Groups sometimes worry about "what will we look like if we change; I know where I fit, what is expected from me, how others behave, and changing may confuse me in regard to all of this." Once you are willing, through self-reflection and dialogue, to acknowledge change is okay (both individual change and group change), and talking about changing and the consequences of changing is valuable for the group, then exciting group opportunities can unfold.

We appreciate your willingness to listen as we briefly discussed teaming, dialogue, our mental models, and change. Hopefully, some of these thoughts will stick with you, and you see value added of participating in this dialogue today and using this skill set in other settings. Let's move now to you all entering your dialogue. We have spent ~ 20 minutes together, and we asked for a 2½ hour time commitment. The dialogue will be 2 hours in length. As we near the end of your 2 hours, we will ask you to reflect back on what you heard and to think about next steps for the group.

PART V: ENGAGING IN THE DIFFICULT DIALOGUE

Remember the ground rules you generated a bit ago. Each of you will have the opportunity to share as you are comfortable. Periodically, we will check in with those of you who have not contributed to the dialogue for some time to see if you have anything to share. You all indicated you wanted to discuss the issues related to trust. So, let's move to the dialogue. Who will begin to share your thoughts?

Additional Facilitator Notes:

1. Notice the deliberate use of "your" rather than "our" dialogue.
2. You can use a talking feather or another item to help people be deliberate in sharing.
3. Be strategic in your word choice. You can use the words "experience," "feelings," "perspective," "understanding."
4. Remember the group will be working through team stages and will be very polite and cautious initially.
5. There will be awkward silence. Be patient and wait it out. Someone will share.
6. Your role as facilitator is to support people in talking and sharing. You support the group as conflicts emerge. Your job is not to create conflict or steer the group in the direction you believe is best for them.
7. Individuals are convinced their viewpoint is right and is the real truth.
8. Manage the conflict that then arises. The group is moving to "storming;" if conflict is left unattended it usually becomes a contest.
9. Use your active listening skills (have people restate, summarize, notice nonverbal communication).
10. Dialogue allows a group to hold the conflict in view yet move to suspending the power struggle because no decision has to be made.
11. The goal during the early dialogue is to encourage exploration into the issue and resist the urge to escape uncertainty.
12. If curiosity, interest, and commitment are strong enough, a group will stay engaged in dialogue. Contrarily, if the group is pushed too rapidly into storming (from Tuckman's model) related to the issue or topic, a group will resist movement, engagement, and vulnerability.
13. If the group stays with the dialogue, a change begins to emerge— there is more silence and more pauses in speaking; the group is moving past entrenchment to more closely suspending judgment and reflecting on others; deconstruction is happening.
14. Members of the group may not agree to suddenly change, and that is okay.
15. Groups typically have the desire to rush to a consensus and to end the process. Facilitators must remind the group there is not a decision that has to be made and they have 2 hours to dialogue.
16. By finally talking about the "tough issues" and sharing "true thoughts and feelings," group members typically feel relieved.
17. Learning, often new learning, as a team has occurred, and they have a common understanding of something "new."

18. Remember, you as the cofacilitator, play an important role that is also a very small role.

19. Support the group on now moving toward the end of the time together—what occurred, what is new (if anything), so what, and what is next (if anything).

20. Wrap up the dialogue time as respectfully as you entered it. Components of wrapping up a dialogue session include:

   - Giving participants the opportunity to share what they learned, experienced, and their current reflections
   - Explaining to participants they may feel tired from the process and uncomfortable as they learned new information and challenged their existing mental model
   - Asking participants what they are going to "do next" related to the dialogue they were just a part of. Some common responses are: take a nap, listen more carefully in the future, make a specific behavioral change, and request a follow up dialogue.
   - As the cofacilitator, share the respect you have for each participant for their engagement in the process, their willingness to share, their commitment to the rules of engagement and to one another, their follow-through in suspending judgment and listening for new information, and their challenge of self to grow and learn.
   - Stating to the participants that they have now concluded their dialogue session, asking that they take care of themselves, and thanking them again. The group or team is adjourned.

Self-Reflection

What approaches will you try when you sense the group is struggling with:

   - strong emotion
   - judgment
   - managing domination by one

So what? What does dialogue mean for you, your group, and the larger external group (e.g. organization)?

What do you do after you have cofacilitated (self-care)?

MODULE 4: REFLECTING ON ORGANIZATIONAL CLIMATE

As you have seen in the Difficult Dialogues program, dialogue is one way to increase awareness and learn new perspectives about issues. Next time you enter a dialogue circle, reflect on the multiple social and cultural identities that you are aware of being represented and be intentional and open to learning about the perceptions and experiences of others. Individuals who have been historically marginalized or underrepresented in society and the academic environment fall in or among several identity groups:

- Age
- Cultural identity
- Gender identity and expression
- Nationality
- Physical and mental ability
- Political and ideological perspectives
- Racial and ethnic identity
- Religious and spiritual identity
- Sexual orientation
- Social and economic status

For additional information related to establishing a Difficult Dialogues Program contact diversity@tamu.edu.

REFERENCES

Algert, N. E., & Watson, K. (2005). Systemic change in engineering education: The role of effective change agents for women in engineering. *Proceedings: Women in Engineering Advocates Network (WEPAN)/National Association of Minority Engineering Professionals Advocates (NAMEPA), Las Vegas, Nevada, 4/05.*

Ford Foundation. (2005). New Ford Foundation program seeks to foster constructive dialogue about sensitive issues on college campuses. *Ford Foundation.* Retrieved from http://www.fordfoundation.org/newsroom/news-from-ford/151

Group Process Consulting. (n.d.). Facilitate dialogue. Retrieved from http://www.annettesimmons.com/group-process/additional-resources/listen-to-annette/

Iowa State University. (n.d.). Guidelines for facilitating difficult dialogue. Retrieved from http://www.celt.iastate.edu/teaching-resources/classroom-practice/teaching-techniques-strategies/difficult-dialogues/guidelines/

Klose, J., & Olivares, R. (1999). *Mediation program.* Bryan, TX: Bryan Independent School District.

Loden, M. (1996). *Implementing diversity.* Burr Ridge, IL: McGraw-Hill.

Obear, K. (2007). Navigating triggering events: critical skills for facilitating difficult dialogues. *The Diversity Factor* 15(3), 23–29.

Robbins, S. P., Finney, M. I., & O'Rourke, J. (2008). *The truth about winning at work.* Upper Saddle River, NJ: Pearson Education. Retrieved from https://books.google.com/books?id=45hbz7xrYsYC&printsec=frontcover&source=gbs_ge_summary_r&cad=0#v=onepage&q&f=false.

Ruiz, D. M. (1997). *The four agreements: a practical guide to personal freedom.* San Rafael, CA: Amber-Allen.

Schein, E. H. (1993). On dialogue, culture, and organizational learning. *Organizational Dynamics, 22*(2), 40–51.

Schwarz, R. (2002). *The skilled facilitator: a comprehensive resource for consultants, facilitators, managers, trainers, and coaches.* San Francisco, CA: Jossey-Bass.

Simmons, A. (1999). *A safe place for dangerous truths: Using dialogue to overcome fear & distrust at work.* AMACOM.

Texas A&M University. (2010). Diversity Plan. Texas A&M University. Retrieved from http://diversity.tamu.edu/Diversity-Plan

Tuckman, B. (1965). Developmental sequence in small groups. *Psychological Bulletin, 63*(6), 384-399.

Watson, N., & Watson, K. (2011). *Basic mediation training.* Bryan, TX: The Center for Change and Conflict Resolution.

CHAPTER 6

MEDIATION SKILLS IN MANAGING CONFLICT

Between stimulus and response, there is space. In that, space is our power to choose our response. In our response lies our growth and our freedom.

—Viktor E. Frankl

In this chapter, we present general knowledge about basic mediation, and is particularly effective for training new mediators. The chapter is best utilized in conjunction with a formal mediation training that is taught by a mediator instructor. It is designed to supplement the forty-hour training standards as recommended by the Alternative Dispute Resolution section of the State Bar of Texas. The contents of this chapter reflect areas of importance addressed in mediation training: conflict literature, alternative dispute resolution practices, the mediation format, and the skill set needed by the mediator. Readers are challenged to reflect upon their perspectives, worldviews, and biases and beliefs that may positively or negatively impact the mediation process. Self-awareness is essential for an individual to be an effective mediator. Awareness involves understanding issues related to diversity, differences, and personal strengths and weaknesses in communication. Most important, self-awareness requires that individuals know their mental, emotional, physical, spiritual, and psychological state during mediation. A knowledge base alone does not make a good mediator. The

person acting as a mediator must be neutral, ready, adaptive, and skilled if they are going to facilitate, rather than escalate conflict.

Mediate and Mediation

Mediate and mediation are words derived from the Latin word *medius*, which means "the middle". The Merriam-Webster Dictionary gives us: Mediate \me-de-at vb **–at ed; –at ing**; 1: to interpose between parties in order to reconcile them 2: to reconcile differences (Charkoudian, Ritis, Buck, & Wilson, 2009). Clearly, by definition, the action of a mediator is to place oneself in the middle of a conflict. There are many processes available to aid individuals in reconciling conflicts. However, in judicial situations in the United States, various alternatives to dispute resolution are defined. Examples include mediation, negotiation, and arbitration. This book focuses on mediation. Mediation refers to a voluntary process in which the disputants strive to find a satisfactory resolution to their dispute. The mediator serves as a facilitator for this process and helps the disputants reach an agreement. The mediator does not impose solutions, assess punishment, administer judgment, decide who is right, or persuade the parties to any side of the dispute. The mediator skill set includes anger management, strategic conflict engagement, conflict resolution and management, active listening, creativity, and a guided process to facilitate the mediation. Mediation between engaged disputants requires that the parties agree to:

- Express their feelings and points of view
- Identify their needs
- Clarify issues
- Understand the other party's view
- Explore solutions

The goal is that the disputants will be able to negotiate an agreement that is satisfactory to both parties. To enable individuals to operate as a mediator, the framework we present is that change creates conflict, which should be managed by some resolution method that may require mediation.

Change Creates Conflict

In Chapter 1, we discussed how conflict can arise when change occurs. Most of us are comfortable with change as long as it is the *other person* who has to change and not us. Sometimes, change between people has to be

mediated. We have organized this chapter to first present a brief perspective on change in the workplace and the stress and conflicts that accompany change. Then we provide a framework for understanding conflict and typical behavior patterns when individuals are dealing with conflict. With this framework in mind, the reader can begin to understand the processes and role that a mediator should use to operate in "the middle" of a conflict without getting pulled into the conflict. Several tools for the mediator to use in a mediation process are presented. Finally, aspects of a mediation program are presented for those who are striving to preempt the potential of costly conflicts by having known mediators available.

Change and the Workplace

It has been said by many that the one *constant* in life is that *change* will occur. For each individual, changes occur internally and externally. Internally, our feelings, emotions, commitments, and attitudes are examples of aspects that vary constantly. Externally, the people around us are changing constantly, as are organizations, environments, and tools. When change occurs, we are sometimes responsible for the change and at other times the change is imposed on us. We may desire to change jobs and may activate an effort to search, interview, and move into a new job; on the contrary, a change imposed on us would be a "lay-off" that forces us to leave our current job. When change occurs, whether perceived as positive or negative and whether self-imposed or a change driven by someone else, there are some common variables that always accompany change. Change is always accompanied by varying levels of resistance, stress, *conflict*, and behavior changes. Referring again to Figure 1.5, people typically do not want to change. They often feel a sense of betrayal when change is occurring and fight against the change. Only when staying "stuck" is more uncomfortable than changing do people typically change. Our common reaction to change is to have a heightened stress level. Stress is not an undesirable aspect of a job—it just needs to be managed. Stress that is above or below a certain comfort and motivational level will cause people to look for relief. We search for a resolution to the conflict that causes the uncomfortable stress

Importance of Managing Conflict

Mary Parker Follett, a social worker and organizational theorist said,

We can often measure our progress by watching the nature of our conflicts. If a man should tell you that his chief daily conflict within himself is "shall I

steal or not steal?" you would know what to think of his development ... in the same way, one test of your [organization] is not how many conflicts do you have, for conflicts are the essence of life, but what are your conflicts, and how do you deal with them? (Follett, 1996)

Conflict exists even if only one person acknowledges the struggle. Typically, people react to conflict in one of two modes: Fight to win or Flight from the situation. However, beyond the initial reaction to conflict much more complex behavioral patterns will emerge. Common examples in the workplace would be to deny, lie, cheat, argue, battle, compromise, collaborate, help, give-in, hide, or avoid. It is important to understand your own tendencies for addressing conflicts, because we tend to see our own behavior as the right behavior. In addition, if we can aid others in discerning their conflict styles, rather than assuming people's intent, we may add valuable insight to management of the conflict.

A Brief History of Alternative Dispute Resolution (ADR)

Dispute resolution outside of the courts is not new; societies the world-over have long used non-judicial, indigenous methods to resolve conflicts. What is new is the extensive promotion and proliferation of ADR models, wider use of court-connected ADR, and the increasing use of ADR as a tool to realize goals broader than the settlement of specific disputes.

The ADR movement in the United States was launched in the 1970s, beginning as a social movement to resolve community-wide civil rights disputes through mediation and as a legal movement to address increased delay and expense in litigation arising from an over-crowded court system. Ever since, the legal ADR movement in the United States has grown rapidly and has evolved from experimentation to institutionalization with the support of the American Bar Association, academics, courts, the U.S. Congress, and state governments. For example, in response to the 1990 Civil Justice Reform Act requiring all U.S. federal district courts to develop a plan to reduce cost and delay in civil litigation, most district courts have authorized or established some form of ADR. Innovations in ADR models, expansion of government-mandated, court based ADR in state and federal systems, and increased interest in ADR by disputants has made the United States the richest source of experiences in court-connected ADR.

While the court-connected ADR movement flourished in the U.S. legal community, other ADR advocates saw the use of ADR methods outside the court system as a means to generate solutions to complex problems that would better meet the needs of disputants and their communities, reduce reliance on the legal system, strengthen local civic institutions,

preserve disputants' relationships, and teach alternatives to violence or litigation for dispute settlement. In 1976, the San Francisco Community Boards program was established to further such goals. This experiment has spawned a variety of community-based ADR projects, such as school based peer mediation programs and neighborhood justice centers. In the 1980s, demand for ADR in the commercial sector began to grow as part of an effort to find more efficient and effective alternatives to litigation. Since this time, the use of private arbitration, mediation, and other forms of ADR in the business setting has risen dramatically, accompanied by an explosion in the number of private firms offering ADR services. The move from experimentation to institutionalization in the ADR field has also affected U.S. administrative rule-making and federal litigation practice. Laws now in place, authorize and encourage agencies to use negotiation and other forms of ADR in rule-making, public consultation, and administrative dispute resolution.

Internationally, the ADR movement has also taken off in both developed and developing countries. ADR models may be straight-forward imports of processes found in the United States or hybrid experiments that mix ADR models with elements of traditional dispute resolution. ADR processes are being implemented to meet a wide range of social, legal, commercial, and political goals. In the developing world, a number of countries are engaging in the ADR experiment including Argentina, Bangladesh, Bolivia, Colombia, Ecuador, the Philippines, South Africa, Sri Lanka, Ukraine, and Uruguay. The experiences with ADR in these countries provide important lessons for understanding and managing conflict in the U.S. (Barrett & Barrett, 2004).

The Characteristics of ADR Approaches

Although the characteristics of negotiated settlement, conciliation, mediation, arbitration, and other forms of community justice vary, all share a few common elements of distinction from the formal judicial structure. These elements permit them to address development objectives in a manner different from judicial systems.

1. Informality
Fundamentally, ADR processes are less formal than judicial processes. In most cases, the rules of procedure are flexible, without formal pleadings, extensive written documentation, or rules of evidence. This informality is appealing and important for increasing access to dispute resolution for parts of the population who may be intimidated by or unable to participate

in more formal systems. It is also important for reducing the delay and cost of dispute resolution. Most systems operate without formal representation.

2. Application of Equity

Equally important, ADR programs are instruments for the application of equity rather than the rule of law. Each case is decided by a third party or negotiated between disputants themselves based on principles and terms that seem equitable in the particular case, rather than on uniformly applied legal standards. ADR systems cannot be expected to establish legal precedents or implement changes in legal and social norms. ADR systems tend to achieve efficient settlements at the expense of consistent and uniform justice. In societies where large parts of the population do not receive any real measure of the overall system of justice, ADR can mitigate the problems by (a) ensuring that disputants have recourse to formal legal protections if the result of the informal system is unfair and by (b) monitoring the outcomes of the informal system to test for consistency and fairness.

3. Direct Participation and Communication Between Disputants

Other characteristics of ADR systems include more direct participation by the disputants in the process and design of settlements, more direct dialogue and opportunity for reconciliation between disputants, potentially higher levels of confidentiality because public records are not typically kept, more flexibility in designing creative settlements, less power to subpoena information, and less direct power of enforcement. Even in the United States, where ADR systems have been used and studied more extensively than in most developing countries, the impact of these characteristics is not clear. Many argue, however, that compliance and satisfaction with negotiated and mediated settlements exceed those measures for court-ordered decisions. The participation of disputants in the settlement decision, the opportunity for reconciliation, and the flexibility in settlement design seem to be important factors in the higher reported rates of compliance and satisfaction.

ACR adopted (October 10, 2011) *Model Standards for Mediator Certification Programs,* which can be found at (www.mediate.com/articles/acrcert1. cfm and Young, 2006).

What Necessitates a Mediation Process?

While there are countless possibilities of human interactions that can use a mediation process, two major categories can be identified: the need to change a basic pattern in a relationship or the need to solve a problem in the relationship. In reality, most mediations have varying combinations of these two categories. The two areas to address are: (a) wanting a change in patterns (behavior, protocols) and/or (b) problem solving. Table 6.1

illustrates goals and outcomes of what parties may be trying to adapt when in conflict with one another.

Table 6.1.   Goals and Outcomes in Mediation Process

Change in Basic Pattern	Solve a Problem
Identify the basic pattern	Identify the problem
Describe the characteristics of the basic pattern	Describe the drivers that cause the problem
Focus on parties' responsibility for characteristics	Discern controllable, influential, and unchangeable drivers
Discuss expected resistance to change	Discuss realistic constraints on solutions
Generate descriptions of desired basic patterns	Generate possible solutions
Discuss the changes required for the desired basic pattern	Evaluate the tradeoffs for the various solutions
Plan steps that 'unfreeze' resistance to change	Analyze the quality of the solutions
Plan steps that create momentum for desired change	Select a solution
Plan steps for making the change permanent	Write an agreement that describes the solution to the problem

Principles of Mediation

Mediation, which is one method of conflict intervention, has the following principles:

1. Two winners are desired rather than one winner and one loser, or two losers.
2. To have two winners there must be cooperation instead of competition.
3. To truly cooperate, the parties must have equal power in this mediation, regardless of any other status that they may have in their relationship.
4. While the past must be mutually understood, even if not agreed upon, by all parties, the future is the primary focus.
5. To focus on the future, concentration must hone in on the interests and needs of the parties and not their current positions.
6. To truly understand needs we must not only consider the facts and thoughts the parties can share, we must also consider their feelings and emotions.

7. An environment where facts, thoughts, feelings and emotions are to be shared must be based on openness and honesty.
8. To trust that this kind of environment is possible, the parties must choose to be positive rather than negative about the prospects of success.
9. Therefore, mediation must be a voluntary experience, not a mandated one.
10. The outcome must be a mutually agreed upon solution, not an order by which all must abide.

Ethical Guidelines for Mediators Model mediation training guidelines can be found at http://www.google.com/url?sa=t&rct=j&q=&esrc=s&source=web&cd=3&ved=0CCwQFjAC&url=http%3A%2F%2Fwww.imis100us2.com%2Facr%2FCMDownload.aspx%3FContentKey%3Da7f484f9-bff4-40f2-a044-1cbd6be1566e%26ContentItemKey%3D351773 6c-c49d-47cd-a228-98e5af997eb9&ei=On1rVdvzMM6yogSFk4PIBg&usg=AFQjCNHAVPS6fEgzJBfFLu0vRc3iPh0R4Q (Young, 2006).

Ethical Guidelines are intended to promote public confidence in the mediation process and to be a general guide for mediator conduct. They are not intended to be disciplinary rules or a code of conduct. Mediators should be responsible to the parties, the courts and the public, and should conduct themselves accordingly. Ethical Guidelines are intended to apply to mediators conducting mediations in connection with all conflict matters whether conducted in the workplace (e.g., such as a university) or in a civil case.

STANDARDS OF PRACTICE AND CODE OF ETHICS

PREAMBLE

In April of 1994 the ADR Section of the State Bar of Texas (the "ADR Section") adopted Ethical Guidelines for Mediators (the "Guidelines"). The Guidelines have been widely accepted in Texas as the ethical standards of practice for mediators. The TMCA Board of Directors has adopted the Guidelines, with modifications, to make them mandatory rather than suggestive or permissive, as standards of practice and a code of ethics for TMCA credentialed mediators, to be known as and referred to as the "Texas Mediator Credentialing Association Standards of Practice and Code of Ethics." In 2005, the Supreme Court of Texas adopted the Guidelines and, in 2011, the Supreme Court of Texas adopted amendments to the Guidelines that had been suggested by the State Bar ADR Section. The TMCA Standards of Practice and Code of Ethics are identical to the Guidelines and the amendments, with a few exceptions: generally, the permissive word "should" in the Guidelines is replaced with the mandatory word "shall" in every place that the word "should" appears in the Guidelines and the amendments (Texas Mediator Credentialing Association, n.d.).

The Mediation Process

The act of bringing a group of people together to work toward a common goal is the basic definition of a team. In a mediation situation, the disputants and mediator have a common goal of developing a resolution, or at least a management plan, to address a common problem for the disputants. Thus, in the mediation process, the participants must become a team. It is important to recognize that a set of team members do not have to like each other. Rather they have to acknowledge and value all members of the team, stay focused on the goals, and stay with the team process (plays or plans) so that the required interdependence of the team is used for progress instead of interference. The mediator can benefit from understanding some basics concerning how effective teams normally progress together. From Scholtes, Joiner, Streibel, Mann, and Streibel's (1998) *Handbook of Teams*, we acknowledge that, often, we must appear to move away from good performance in order to set up the team dynamics that will foster performance in the long run. The figure below is based upon Tuckman's (1977) model of teams. Recall from the previous chapter that teams do not just happen. They go through stages before they perform well (Figure 6.1).

Conflict Intervention Strategies

In Chapter 4, there are many intervention styles (Figure 4.6). When teaching conflict intervention strategies to higher education personnel the authors of this book use *mediation* as the teaching modality. Mediation is used because it is typically the most challenging conflict intervention strategy for our higher education faculty and staff to use; therefore, if our faculty and staff can hone their mediation skills then they have added to their toolkit of conflict intervention strategies. Mediation is challenging for many conflict managers because the options for resolution or management of the conflict are determined by the parties in conflict (referred to as the disputants in this chapter), and not the conflict managers (referred to as the mediators in this chapter). Most of us in higher education want to solve problems and challenge ideas and generate solutions and outcomes. Therefore, using the conflict intervention strategy of mediation feels counterintuitive to most faculty and staff in higher education.

Below is the CCCR Mediation Book that can be used to education and train mediators. The remainder of the chapter provides information on: (1) the traditional mediation process, (2) the AWS model of mediation, (3) the traditional mediation script and (4) skill sets needed to be effective conflict managers.

The Mediation Process

Mediation is a multistage process. It is important to remember that the process is flexible. The mediator must use flexibility in controlling the stages of mediation so that a suitable resolution is found. Rigidity through the stages of the process can lead to an unproductive mediation. However, each stage has important aspects that lay the groundwork for future stages. (Figure 6.1)

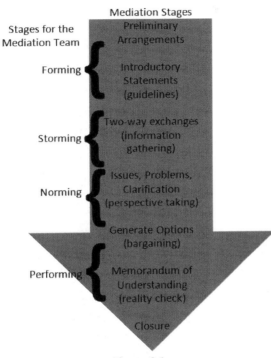

Figure 6.1.
Traditional Mediation Process Framework

Preliminary Arrangements: a stage to get ready. In this stage the disputants agree to mediation and upon a mediator (or mediators), time, place, etc. When strong emotions are involved in the conflict it is often useful for the mediator to have individual interviews with the disputants. In these interviews the mediator strives to understand the needs and interests, as well as the position of the disputant, and provides coaching on acceptable conduct during the mediation sessions.

Introductory Statements: opening of the mediation session and, even if the roles and rules of the mediation process have been presented to the disputants before, the roles and rules are presented for the disputants to agree to them in the presence of each other.

Initial Statements: each disputant has an uninterrupted opportunity to state his or her "story" of the dispute. The order of presentation is determined during the introductory statement stage.

Two-Way Exchanges: mediator helps the disputants share feelings and understand each other's viewpoints.

Issues and Problems Clarification: mediator helps the disputants understand each other's needs and interests. The disputants clarify the issues and problems that prevent both parties' needs and interests from being met.

Generating Options and Finding a Solution: disputants generate possible actions that will resolve the problems that are preventing the disputants' needs and interests from being met. The disputants agree upon a course of action to resolve the conflict.

Memorandum of Understanding (MOU) Writing: involves laying out the solution in detail to assure that it can be implemented realistically and will potentially resolve the conflict.

Closure: affirm the disputants and then close the mediation.

Goals in the Mediation Process

Each stage of the mediation process has specific goals for both the mediators and the disputants. The goals for each stage are described below.

Introductory Statement

- Mediator establishes role to parties
- Mediator establishes rapport with disputants and acceptable level of rapport among disputants
- Mediator starts building list of issues (briefly walks through process)
- Mediator eases fears and concerns of disputants and, particularly, works to eliminate stress that they are trapped or will be forced into an agreement

Introductory Statement

- Everyone is to be valued and validated as a person whose values, needs, and beliefs are respected, even if not agreed with
- Disputants share statements with other party that have not been heard before, particularly moving to understand other party's reasoning and/or reactions, again even if remaining in disagreement

Two-Way Exchange (Mediator very active)

- Disputants empowered to operate in the process and control aspects of the process
- They choose the issue they want to discuss first

- They take turns
- They engage as active listeners
- Disputants vent issues they believe drove them to the current positions
- Disputants expose minor issues that may be triggering strong responses. If these issues are truly minor, they can be acknowledged as understandable and left or linked appropriately with the major issues
- Mediator notes and exposes patterns of behavior that lack cooperation
- Avoidance in the form of: spin-offs, dead ends, diversions
- Competition in the form of: blaming, hurting, pulling on mediator to be on their side
- Disputants focus on common understanding when possible
- Mediator uses what he/she sees, hears, and feels in order to restate or summarize for other party
- Everyone hearing/looking for commonalities
- Disputants begin to focus on major or priority issues that need resolution
- Mediator notes and has disputants acknowledge differences between the two parties
- Mediator helps disputants find emerging win-win outcomes
- Mediator looks for ways to help parties save face
- Mediator begins to focus disputants on interests and needs rather than positions

Formulation of Issues and Clarification

- Disputants make issues sharp and focused
- Mediator forces parties to focus on major issues, rather than every incident
- Mediator reinforces interdependences by pushing parties to understand and validate other's perspectives
- Mediator clarifies the differences that still cause unmet needs for the disputants

Option Generating and Finding Solutions

- Mediator structures the process so options are generated before they are evaluated
- Disputants describe details of the options they propose
- Mediator formulates questions to pull option details out and cause more options to be generated
- Mediator directs the disputants toward patterns of behavior that incorporate cooperation
- Disputants collaborate to generate new options that allow optimal trade-offs for all parties
- Disputants compromise so that there is balance of wins and losses for all parties
- Disputants negotiate and adapt on issues that have less of a priority for them than the issues have for the other
- Everyone evaluates and reconciles the options
- Link; additions; seeing options in some new light by fractionalizing
- Disputants agree on options for settlement

Writing and Reality Testing of Memorandum of Understanding (MOU)

- Mediator supports the parties in determining of their MOU items/ commitments are *realistic, specific,* and *balanced.*
- Mediator pushes disputants to test long-term reality of MOU by asking questions, "What if …
- Mediator asks tough questions who, what, when, where, how
- Disputants think of issues not brought out, ones that disturb them
- Mediator exposes and clears up hidden agendas
- Mediator checks with disputants to make sure the MOU is realistic, specific, and balanced
- Mediator writes a MOU in terms demanded by parties (each sentence ~ 7 words)
- Mediator assures significant details of solution are captured in the MOU (dot I's and cross T's)

Closure

- Mediator affirms good work to help MOU "stick"
- Mediator closes the mediation with instructions and descriptions of follow-up actions

The AWS Model of Mediation

Figure 6.2.   AWS Mediation Process Framework

Watson (formerly Algert), Watson, and Stanley (AWS) modified the traditional mediation process to further support addressing conflict in higher education. Primarily components of the AWS Model include (Figure 6.2. AWS Mediation Process Framework):

1. The mediator, or one of the comediators, presents the combined narrative of the two parties (disputants).

Rationale:

- Research shows the person who shares their "narrative of the conflict first" frames the mediation.
- Disputant 2, in the traditional mediation model, spends about 50% of his/her time in rebuttal to Disputant 1 instead of sharing her/his narrative/perspective on the conflict
- Mediator models: sharing a narrative, active listening, sharing thoughts and also sharing feelings, introducing areas of common ground, clarity in issue identification, organizes the mediation in a chronological fashion
- Disputants typically: learn of new information from the other disputant sooner, have decreased positionality and therefore less defensiveness, see both the strengths and the challenges in their relationship with one another, listen for new information instead of defensive posturing

2. A shift in the mediation process moving *issue clarification* before the *two-way exchange*.

Rationale:

- the sooner the parties (disputants) can be clear on the actual issues (not their positional statements) they want to the discuss there is increased likelihood the parties can move to their underlying interests and needs related to the issue
- Parties feel a greater sense of understanding of what issue they are discussing their feelings and thoughts. Increases movement to resolve more quickly

Below is an illustration of sharing a combined narrative and a further elaboration on the AWS Model contrasted with the Traditional Mediation Process

Preliminary Arrangements

- o Setting environment of trust and comfort with what will occur
- o Understanding volunteers and commitments
- o Agreeing to commitment and confidentiality

Individual Stories With Mediators

- o Modeling an environment of active listening
- o Establishing the appreciation and valuing of the story (Cloke)
- o Mediators begin to work won self-neutralization and power neutralization for mediation (Wing)
- o Mediators must gain permission from disputants for any material from the individual stories to be presented

Joint Clarification of "True" Stories

- o Mediator's present aligned stories, looking for elements of commonality, neutral presentation, and exposure of actions, intents, beliefs, and feelings.

o Setting environment where disputants are not disempowered but are minimized in working hidden agendas (S, Hart, N. Kline, Bono —Six Hats). Let disputants' correct errors of what was presented or what was omitted now that they see aligned stories.

o See if the disputants can articulate what their story says about them—fundamental difference to traditional mediation model (storytelling, social justice literature, mental models, let D's tell us what sort means after they've heard our interpretation of stories). This may deepen the exposure of a disputant's mental model.

Synthesize Into One "True" Story

o Setting environment for understanding we are weaving stories together not judging truth or value of stories.

o Integrate (go beyond the meaning of my story to the meaning of the stories for both)

✓ Can D1 understand, not necessarily agree with, D2 perspective and

✓ What does other D's perspective mean to me

Issues and Problems Clarification

o What does the woven story reveal that needs to be resolved (what are the issues)

o Clarify issues so that we understand what is in conflict

Generating Options

o Brainstorm, nonjudgmentally, creative options to resolve or minimize conflicts

o Bargain and negotiate which options are the most likely to be effective, efficient, achievable, controllable, desirable

MEMORANDUM OF UNDERSTANDING (MOU)

- o Realistic, specific, and balanced
- o Where to disseminate

Closure

- o Notes shredded to ensure confidentiality
- o Appreciation and affirmations of disputants
- o Give information to disputants on where to go next if a problem or concern

ASSUMPTIONS FOR MEDIATION

All models assume we, as mediators, need to move the disputants higher on the cooperative axis from where they are initially presenting. Further, our goal is to keep all disputants assertive regarding their needs and interest so that one party is not accommodating on all issues. The assumption of all models is: (1) the disputants want to find a resolution and (2) their needs and interests can be met.

Traditional Mediation Model

Basic Assumptions

1. The mediator(s) can assume a neutral state.
2. History is allowed to gain understanding of the conflict issues that are the focus of the mediation.
3. Narrowing the focus will enhance the chance of success.

Process Assumptions

1. Taking equal turns and disallowing abuse assures fairness.
2. Focusing should work to narrow the information presented to the conflict issues that need and can be resolved.
3. Solution generation by the parties enhances buy in.
4. Reality, specifically, and balance will ensure fairness.

AWS Mediation Model

Basic Assumptions

1. Since no one can be absolutely neutral, the mediators must be very conscious of their own mental models concerning the disputants, the conflict, and the process.
2. History must be used to help each disputant become more conscious of their mental models concerning the other party and the conflict.
3. A narrow focus may help get a resolution, but it may not be the best resolution especially considering the ongoing relationship of the disputants.

Process Assumptions

1. Statistically, the party that gets to go first is unintentionally advantaged over 80% of the time; therefore, the mediators will strive to negate this advantage.
2. Perspective taking, including awareness of the other persons "reasonable" mental model, will enhance collaborative solution generation.
3. Rather than having one of the disputants take the first turn in the mediation, the mediators will first tell the history leading to the conflict based on the combined history of the conflict placed in a chronological format, including factors that have contributed to each disputant's mental model. Each disputant will take turn to explain, correct, or elaborate the history presented until they believe an accurate history leading to the current status of the conflict is presented.
4. Focus should be on needs for resolution for the current conflict and on the ongoing relationship of the disputants.
5. Specificity, reality, and balance are important in regard to the conflict as it fits in the context of ongoing relationship.

Example

Jess, a White, female, professor, is in conflict with Stacy, an African American female, associate professor, concerning the use of resources, specifically who will have a TA and who will not. The senior faculty member makes these assignments and has not given Stacy a TA for the semester, while another faculty member, Mike, a White, male, associate professor, has received a TA for his course.

Stacy is certain that Jess has used personal biases in making the assignment because when Mike taught the course Stacy is scheduled to teach, he was assigned a TA. Furthermore, his current course assignment has never had a TA assigned to it before. The issue is simply that Jess does not like or respect Stacy, and uses every opportunity to impede her work.

Jess is certain that her/his TA assignments are fair considering the current resources available and the departmental history. The issue is fundamentally based on algorithms for enrollment numbers and innovations proposed, as well as consideration of faculty needs to break algorithmic ties if resources are too scarce to give everyone a TA

Traditional Model Beginning

A coin is flipped and either Jess or Stacy presents their version of the issue. If Stacy goes first then Jess may spend a significant part of her time addressing the fact that she does not dislike Stacy, and that she has never impeded Stacy's work. If Jess goes first Stacy may spend a significant part of her/his time addressing the facts surrounding the algorithm for TA assignments and why it appears to be unfair.

AWS Model Beginning

After one hour interviews with each disputant, the mediators begin the mediation with the following:

	Stacy		Jess	
	Feelings	Thoughts	Feelings	Thoughts
2003			Excited to join the department, and nervous as the first woman/man	She/he was qualified but knew she/he had to make it like all the men/women had to be respected
2012	Excited to join the department because they made her/him feel valued and respected	Could contribute, make a difference, her/his passions aligned with institution's espoused values	Angry that the faculty were ignored as the normal recruiting process was not engaged to hire the first African member of the department	Diversity, specifically ethnicity and race, overrode other very important issues in the hiring of Stacy

(Table continues on next page)

(Table continues from previous page)

	Stacy		Jess	
	Feelings	Thoughts	Feelings	Thoughts
2013	Hurt and angered by hostilities, devaluing, and being ignored by Jess and others in curricula meetings	This is not much fun, may get better after tenure, why won't others who agree with her/him speak up to counter Jess's opinions	Sad and Angry because Mike almost did not get tenure because everyone compared him to Stacy	Stacy was given many more resources and opportunities than normal Asst. Profs because she/he is African American
2014	Hurt and stressed by sharp criticisms about her/his work and teaching, it is like people are watching for every little mistake	I made it (tenure), maybe it gets better now—I can start doing other things to accomplish even more work in the field	Confused and disappointed that valued colleagues did not even analyze Stacy's promotion package like they normally do	Stacy's tenure is deserved but she/he certainly has not earned it like everyone else had to
2016	Current Conflict— ignored, devalued, punished, not given same chances to contribute to the field	May need to leave, does not know how to connect so they understand her/him and her/his research. TA assignment is an indication of whether they value the time you need for research	Tired of Stacy thinking she/he deserves special treatment, and concerned for the standards Jess and others have assured exist in the department. Sympathetic to Mike.	Stacy has been treated fairly, it is her/his turn to think about the department and make some sacrifices for others. It's for her/his own good.

It is important to note that both models are strong conflict management models. It is the role of the mediator to determine which mediation model is ideal for the conflict situation they are facilitating.

The remainder of this chapter is comprised of two sections:

1. The Mediation Script—a script for beginning mediators to use in a mediation course to develop the process and skills to effectively facilitate conflicts.
2. The Mediation Skill Set—skills that are particularly important for mediators to be aware of and to hone in order to effective support individuals in conflict.

The Mediation Toolkit

Below is the mediation script used to teach people to be effective conflict managers. This script can be used for all types of conflict interventions by adapting the formality or informality of the process dependent upon the intervention method being used.

Getting Ready (Premediation): (Meeting Separately With Disputants is Optional)

Use this step to begin the mediation when disputants:

- have strong feelings
- when gathering information for a combined narrative
- to build rapport
- to explain the process
- to explain specific protocols for your setting

PURPOSE:

- Mediators meet separately with the disputants when there is high emotion such as anger.
- Mediators allow disputants to vent emotions and/or anger about the situation.
- Review mediation process and make sure that parties understand what will be happening.
- Review your role as the mediator.
- Begin to develop rapport with parties and trust in mediators and process.
- Review and get agreement to mediate and guidelines for behavior.

PROCEDURES:

1. Mediators meet separately with each of the disputants for a short meeting (10–15 minutes for traditional model; 30–45 minutes for AWS model).
2. Introduce yourselves and explain the role of the mediators.

   M: *My name is _____ and I am a mediator.*
   M: *I am here to help support you in solving your problem with*

   _____

~OR~

M: *(name of other disputant) wants to solve his/her problem with you and would like to try and resolve it with you through the process of mediation.*

M: *Mediation is voluntary. We have no power to make a decision for you. We will not take sides or decide who is right or wrong.*

3. Explain the mediation process.

M: *Mediation is a process in which we help you talk about your issue/ problem, look for possible solutions, and get a MOU that you both feel is **fair**.*

M: *Everything that is said here is confidential, except for a few things (Homicide, Suicide, and Abuse).*

4. Ask each disputant to tell his/her story.

M: *Tell me what happened and how you are feeling about it. Repeat using your own words to summarize what was said and how they are feeling about it.*

5. Get agreement to mediate.

M: *Are you ready to work to solve your conflict in mediation?*

If they say yes they are ready, prepare for the mediation. If they say no, ask them what they need in order to begin. Below are suggestions for helping the disputants agree to mediation if they are hesitant about mediating.

M: *What do you need in order to solve this conflict?*

M: *What would you like to get out of mediation?*

Find out what alternatives they have if they do not want to mediate.

M: *What will happen if you don't solve the conflict in mediation?*

Identify some of the advantages of mediation.

M: *What will happen if you don't solve the conflict in mediation?*

Identify some of the advantages of mediation.

M: *You will have a chance to express your feelings and point of view.*

M: *You will be able to talk about the conflict in a safe and neutral place.*

M: *You will be able to find a resolution to the conflict that is fair to both of you.*

M: *It's a chance to improve the situation rather than making it worse.*

6. Explain the guidelines for behavior (**RULES**).

   M: *In order for mediation to work, we need you to agree to some rules for behavior:*

   - *No name calling or put-downs*
   - *No interrupting when someone is talking*
   - *Be as honest as you can*
   - *No physical fighting or threats*
   - *Agree to try to solve the problem*

7. Ask if there are any questions.
8. Explain when and where the mediation will take place.

Introductory Statements: Roles and Rules

PURPOSE:

- Review mediation process and make sure that parties understand what will be happening.
- Review your role as mediator.
- Begin to develop rapport with parties and trust in mediators and process.
- Review and get agreement to mediate and guidelines for behavior.

PROCEDURES:

1. ROLES: Introduce yourselves and tell the role of the mediators.

   M: *Hi, my name is _____, and this is _____, we are your mediators.*

   M: *We are here to support you as you work to solve your problem.*

   M: *Mediation is* **voluntary**. *We will* **not** *decide who is right or wrong, take sides, or make decisions for you.*

M: *Each of you will have a chance to discuss ways of solving your problem so each of you gets what you need.*

M: *An agreement will be written and signed.*

M: *Everything that is said in here is confidential, except for a few things (Homicide, Suicide, and Abuse).*

2.   RULES: Explain to get agreement to guidelines for behavior.

M: *For mediation to work, we need you to agree to these rules:*

- No name-calling or put-downs
- No interrupting when someone is talking (here is some paper)
- Be as honest as you can
- No physical fights or threats
- Agree to try to solve the problem
- Speak directly to us at first, if necessary
- Clarify any time constraints
- Comfortable with us as mediators?
- No tape recordings—this is not discovery

3.   Ask if there are any questions.

Initial Statements

PURPOSE:

- FACTS and FEELINGS: To allow parties to describe their view of the situation (tell their story) and express feelings.

PROCEDURES:

1.   Decide who will talk first. Ask the **first** person to describe how they see the situation and how they are feeling about it. Get the FACTS and FEELINGS behind each issue.

M: *(name), could you tell us about the problem (what happened) and how you feel about it?*

Restate the facts and feelings using your own words.

2. Ask the **second** person to tell how they see the situation and how they are feeling about it

> **M:** *(name), could you tell us about the problem (what happened) and how you feel about it?*

Restate the facts and feelings using your own words.

Two-Way Exchanges

Below are some guidelines during two-way exchanges between disputants.

1. Ask person #1 if he/she wants to respond to what the other side said.

> **M:** *(name), would you like to respond to what (name) said?*

Restate each response using Active Listening.

2. Ask person #2 if he/she wants to respond to what the other side said.

> **M:** *(name), would you like to respond to what (name) said?*

Restate each response using Active Listening.

3. OPTIONAL: Ask questions of each disputant to help clarify and to get more information. Possible questions:

> **M:** *Can you tell us more about (name)?*
> **M:** *How long have you two known each other?*
> **M:** *How long has this problem been going on?*
> **M:** *Where or when did this happen?*

Use good teamwork if there are comediators.

Issues and Problems Clarification

PURPOSE:

- Mediators help parties to understand each other's point of view. (Understanding does not mean agreement)

PROCEDURES:

1. Ask parties to summarize each other's point of view and feelings about the problem. (Facts and feelings)

   M: *(name), would you tell us what you heard (name) say about this problem and how she/he is feeling about it?*

2. Ask the other person if the summary was correct.

   M: *(name), is that correct?*

   If the person misunderstood or didn't get all the facts and feelings, ask the other person to say it again.

3. Repeat step 1 with the other party asked to speak.
4. Repeat step 2 with the other person speaking.

   Summarize all the facts and feelings as each person said them. Find the things they have in common. For example:

   M: *(name), we heard you say that (names) used to be your friend, but it makes you angry when she/he talks with your boyfriend. Is that right?*

   M: *(name), we heard you say that you don't like it when (name) talks about you to your neighbor. You feel angry when (name) doesn't say things straight to you. Is that right?*

   ~OR~

   M: *We heard you both say that you used to be friends but now you are both angry and upset because of a problem about something that you both heard. Is that correct?*

5. Identify ISSUES and look for COMMON GROUND.
6. Make sure that both persons have said everything that they need to say.

   M: *Is there anything else that either of you needs to say before we go on to the next part?*

Generating Options and Finding a Solution

PURPOSE:

- To "brainstorm" ideas to find a fair solution to the problem.
- To encourage the parties to cooperate in order to find a solution that is one to which they both can agree.
- To help the parties evaluate the possible solution in order to get a **workable** agreement.

PROCEDURES:

1. Explain that you will support them in finding their solutions to their problem.

   M: *You now can talk about a solution to the problem that you will both feel is fair and one that you can work with.*

2. Ask the first person what he/she thinks is a fair solution to the problem.

   M: *What do you think is a fair solution to the problem?*

   ~OR~

   M: *What do you need in order to solve this problem?*

   Encourage them to come up with their own solutions. If they have difficulty thinking of something, you can say:

   M: *If this problem happened again, what would you do different to prevent it?*

   If they still cannot think of a solution to the problem remind them that they agreed to try and solve the problem. Only offer choices if necessary, for example,

   M: *In a similar situation, the people decided to …*
   M: *If (name) were willing to … what would you be willing to do?*

* You want to rarely do this, as you are "taking power" from the parties in conflict and decreasing the likelihood they will follow through with their MOU.

3. Restate what the person needs in order to solve the problem. Encourage each person to come up with more than one idea. Do not allow the other party to judge the possible solutions.

4. Ask the second party what she/he thinks is a fair solution to the problem.

M: *What do you think is a fair solution to the problem?*

~OR~

M: *What do you need in order to solve this problem?*

Encourage them to come up with their own solutions. If they have difficulty thinking of something, you can say:

M: *If this problem happened again, what would you do differently to prevent it?*

If they still cannot think of a solution to the problem remind them that they agreed to try and solve the problem. Only offer choices if necessary, e.g.,

M: *In a similar situation, the people decided to …*

M: *If (name) were willing to … what would you be willing to do?*

5. Support the parties in finding their solution they can both agree to.

6. Help the parties evaluate the solutions to make sure that they are:

- REALISTIC (it can be done)
- SPECIFIC (defines what, where, when, who, how)
- BALANCED (both parties are part of the agreement)

7. Summarize and restate all parts of the agreement. Check with the parties to make sure that it is accurate.

Writing the Agreement or Memorandum of Understanding (MOU)

PURPOSE:

- To write a MOU that states, in their language, all the issues and concerns defined by the parties.
- To determine if the MOU needs to be reviewed or evaluated after a trial period of time.
- To clearly define how the MOU will be carried out.

PROCEDURES:

1. Write the MOU on a mediation report form.

   Read the MOU and allow the parties to make changes if necessary.

2. Have each party sign the MOU.

   M: *This MOU is a record of what each of you agrees to and shows that you are serious about resolving this dispute.*

Closure

1. Ask the parties if they need to meet again to review the MOU. Ask parties if they are going to work with others (e.g., attorney in civil mediation) on the MOU.
2. Ask the parties if they are willing to come back to mediation first if their MOU breaks down.
3. (If appropriate) remind the parties about rumors. Ask them to tell their friends, families and neighbors that their conflict has been resolved.

   M: *To keep rumors from spreading, would you agree to tell your friends, families, and neighbors that your conflict is resolved?*

4. May we "check-in" with you both in the future? (pick a date)
5. Congratulate them for their hard work and for reaching an agreement.

   M: *Congratulations on working hard for resolution of your conflict.*

Go over the process as many times as needed.

Be sure to ask "What if?" questions.

RESTATE! RESTATE! RESTATE!

Example of Comediator Teamwork (abbreviated script)

Mediator #1- Opening: Roles

M: This is _____ and my name is _____. During the mediation you will both be given a chance to talk. We are not here to judge you or to take sides. We will not decide who is right or wrong or how you will solve your problem. When we finish you will come up with an agreement and everything is confidential (when break confidentiality).

Mediator #2- Rules

M: You will both need to agree to some rules before we begin the mediation.

1. No name-calling or put-downs
2. No interrupting when someone is talking
3. Be as honest as you can
4. No physical fighting or threats
5. Agree to try to solve the problem
6. Speak directly to us at first, if necessary
7. Questions?
8. Comfortable with us as mediators?
9. No tape recording of mediation
10. Time constraints

Alternate inviting disputants to speak and restate what is heard. Continue alternating invitations to disputant to share and to clarify each other's positions. Continue alternating invitations for ideas and restatement of ideas during the generation of solutions.

Mediator #1–Agreement/MOU—*Summarize Solutions and Get Verbal Agreement*

Mediator # 2–Agreement/MOU—*Write Solutions on Agreement Form*

Mediation Checklist

Introductory Statements and Items/Issues to be covered:

☐   1.   Introduction
☐   2.   Signing of any needed documentation
☐   3.   Explanation of complete process
☐   4.   Go over ground rules
☐   5.   Explanation of mediator's role, confidentiality, and neutrality
☐   6.   Get acceptance of mediator
☐   7.   Agreement and Enforceability
☐   8.   Time Constraints
☐   9.   Modification if third party present
☐   10.   Any questions
☐   11.   Comfortable with us as your Mediators

Mediator Skill Checklist

	Needs More Work			Mastered Skill	
PERSONAL AND COMMUNICATION SKILLS					
Active Listening: attention to verbal and nonverbal cues					
1. Using clear language	1	2	3	4	5
2. Asking neutral questions	1	2	3	4	5
3. Remaining patient	1	2	3	4	5
4. Remaining neutral	1	2	3	4	5
5. Working as a team	1	2	3	4	5
ROLES AND RULES: SETTING THE STAGE					
1. Explaining the role of the mediator	1	2	3	4	5
2. Explaining the mediation process	1	2	3	4	5
ROLES AND RULES: SETTING THE STAGE					
3. Creating a comfortable place for mediation to happen	1	2	3	4	5
4. Establishing rapport	1	2	3	4	5
FACTS AND FEELINGS: DEFINING THE PROBLEM					
1. Listening/note-taking skills	1	2	3	4	5
2. Ability to be objective and nonjudgmental	1	2	3	4	5
3. Using active listening	1	2	3	4	5
4. Clarifying issues	1	2	3	4	5
PERSONAL AND COMMUNICATION SKILLS					
FINDING SOLUTIONS					
1. Using active listening	1	2	3	4	5
2. Getting ideas for resolution	1	2	3	4	5
3. Using reality testing	1	2	3	4	5
4. Ability to summarize and write an agreement	1	2	3	4	5
5. Congratulating the disputants	1	2	3	4	5

Characteristics of a Successful Mediation Program

Mediation programs have been implemented in schools, businesses, and communities. The purpose of these programs is to provide resources that will improve the environment for participants by actively addressing

conflicts. Conflicts that are ignored often escalate into aggressive or even violent behavior. Therefore, the management of conflict for conscious, productive outcomes is at the core of a mediation program.

A well-designed program will benefit from the following characteristics:

- A diverse team of conflict managers, who can discern the nature of conflicts and determine the most appropriate dispute resolution strategy to use, will be available.
- Skilled mediators are available in a diversity that will accommodate different disputants biases and needs.
- People in the organization will have knowledge of the availability of the program.
- There will be widespread acceptance of the value of the program.
- Administrators, supervisors, and leaders will all support the program.
- Appropriate coordinators for the program will be supported.
- Conflict managers and coordinators will participate in ongoing training.
- The Conflict Management Program will be considered a part of the organization's improvement plans.
- External constituencies and supporters will be informed by the program and provide support as necessary.

REFERENCES

Barrett, J. T., & Barrett, J. (2004). *A history of alternative dispute resolution: The story of a political, social, and cultural movement.* New York, NY: John Wiley & Sons.

Bear, G. G. (1998). School discipline in the United States: Prevention, correction, and long-term social development. *School Psychology Review, 27*(1), 14–32.

Beck-Kritek, P. (1994). *Negotiating at an uneven table.* San Francisco, CA: Jossey-Bass.

Blake, R. R., & Mouton, J. S. (1964). *The managerial grid.* Houston, TX: Gulf.

Bodine, R. J., Crawford, D. K., & Schrumpf, F. (1994). *Creating the peaceable school: A comprehensive program for teaching conflict resolution.* Champaign, IL: Research Press.

Charkoudian, L., Ritis, C. D., Buck, R., & Wilson, C. L. (2009). Mediation by any other name would smell as sweet—or would it? The struggle to define mediation and its various approaches. *Conflict Resolution Quarterly, 26*(3), 293–316.

Consulting Psychologist Press. (2000). *Thomas Kilmann Conflict Mode Instrument.*

Cowan, D., Palomares, S., & Schilling, D. (1994). *Conflict resolution skills for teens.* Spring Valley, CA: Innerchoice.

Deturck, M. A. (1987). When communication fails: Physical aggression as a compliance-gaining strategy. *Communication Monographs, 54,* 106–112.

Duryea, M. L. (1992). *Conflict and culture: A literature review and bibliography.* Victoria, BC, Canada: University of Victoria Institute of Dispute Resolution.

Evans, S. (1991). Conflict resolution: An essential ingredient for workforce diversity. *Cultural Diversity at Work, 4*(1), 1, 14.

Fisher, R., & Ury, W. (1981). *Getting to yes: Negotiating agreement without giving in.* Boston, MA: Houghton Mifflin.

Folger, J. P., & Poole, M.S. (1984). *Working through conflict: A communication perspective.* Glenview, IL: Scott, Foresman, and Company.

Follett, M. P. (1996). *Mary Parker Follett: Prophet of management. A celebration of writings from the 1920s.* (Paulinen Graham, Ed.). Boston, MA: Harvard Business School Press.

Foreman, G. (1934). *The five civilized tribes.* Norman, OK: University of Oklahoma Press.

Gibson, J. W. (1994). *Mediation: Basic training program.* Huntsville, TX: Sam Houston State University.

Gibson, J. W. (1995). *Advanced conflict resolution training.* Huntsville, TX: Sam Houston State University.

Girard, K., & Koch, S. J. (1996). *Conflict resolution in the schools: A manual for educators.* San Francisco, CA: Jossey-Bass.

Hathaway, P. (1990). *Giving and receiving criticism: Your key to interpersonal success.* Menlo Park, CA: Crisp.

Johnson, D. W., & Johnson, R. T. (1987). *Creative conflict.* Edina, MN: Interaction Books.

Johnson, D. W., & Johnson, R. T. (1995). *Teaching students to be peacemakers.* Edina, MN: Interaction Book Company.

Opotow, S. (1989). *The risk of violence: Peer conflicts in the lives of adolescents.* Paper presented at the 97th Annual Convention American Psychological Association. New Orleans, LA.

Kabanoff, B. (1987). Predictive validity of the MODE conflict instrument. *Journal of Applied Psychology, 72,* 160–163.

Kelley, H. H. (1987). Toward a taxonomy of interpersonal conflict processes. In S. Oskamp & S. Spacapan (Eds.), *Interpersonal processes* (pp. 122–147). Newbury Park, CA: Sage.

Kilmann, K. W. (1988). The conflict-handling modes: Toward more precise theory. *Management Communication Quarterly, 1*(3), 430–435.

Klose, R., & Olivares, R. (1999). Bryan ISD peer mediation training guide. Bryan, Texas.

J. Lambert, & S. Myers. (1999). *50 activities for conflict resolution.* Pelham, MA: Human Resource Development Press

Maddus, R. B. (1995). *Successful negotiation.* San Diego, CA: Crisp.

McCormick, M. A. (1996). Confronting racism as a mediator. *Society of Professionals in Dispute Resolution, 20*(3), 1, 8.

New Mexico Center for Dispute Resolution. (1990). *Basic mediation and peer mediation training guide.* Albuquerque, NM.

Northrup, T. A. (1995). *The uneasy partnership between conflict theory and feminist theory.* (Unpublished manuscript). Syracuse, NT: Syracuse University.

Putnam, L. L. (1994). Beyond third party role: Disputes and Managerial Intervention. *Employee Responsibilities and Rights Journal, 7*(1).

Ruble, T. L., & Thomas, K. W. (1976). Support for a two-dimensional model of conflict behavior. *Organizational Behavior and Human Performance, 16,* 143–155.

Sadker, M., & Sadker, D. (1994). *Failing at fairness: How our schools cheat girls.* New York, NY: Scribner.

Satir, V., & Banmen, J. (1991). *The Satir model: Family therapy and beyond.* Mountain View, CA: Science & Behavior Books.

Scholtes, P. R., Joiner, B. L., Streibel, B., Mann, D., & Streibel, B. J. (1998). *The team handbook.* Madison, WI: Associates Inc.

Stockard, J., & ach, D. (1989). Conflict resolution: Sex and gender roles. In J.B. Gittler (Ed.), *The annual review of conflict knowledge and conflict resolution, Vol. 1* (pp. 69–99). New York, NY: Garland.

Texas Mediator Credentialling Association (n.d.). *Standards of Practice and Code of Ethics.* Retrieved from http://www.txmca.org/docs/Standards%20of%20 Practice%20and%20Code%20of%20Ethics.pdf

Thomas, K. W., & Kilmann, R. H. (1974). *Thomas-Kilmann Conflict Mode Instrument.* Tuxedo, NY: Xicom.

Tuckman, B. W., & Jensen, M. A. C. (1977). Stages of small-group development revisited. *Group & Organization Management, 2*(4), 419–427.

Watson, N.T., & Watson, K. (2011). *Basic mediation training book, 2nd edition.* Bryan, TX: The Center for Change and Conflict Resolution.

Watson, N.T., & Watson, K. (2011). *Conflict management: Introductions for individuals and organizations.* Bryan, TX: Amazon Digital Services.

Womack, D. F. (1988a). A review of conflict instruments in organizational settings. *Management Communication Quarterly, 1*(3), 437–445.

Womack, D. F. (1988b). Assessing the Thomas-Kilmann conflict MODE survey. *Management Communication Quarterly, 1*(3), 321–349.

Xicom Incorporated. (1996a). *Conflict workshop facilitator's guide.* Tuxedo, NY: Author.

Xicom, Incorporated. (1996b). *Thomas-Kilmann Conflict Mode Instrument reference guide.* Tuxedo, NY: Author.

Young, P. M. (2006). Rejoice-rejoice-rejoice, give thanks, and sing: ABA, ACR, and AAA adopt revised model standards of conduct for mediators. *Appalachian JL, 5,* 195.

SECTION III

SCHOLARSHIP ON MANAGING CONFLICT

CHAPTER 7

CONFLICT MANAGEMENT IN HIGHER EDUCATION

A Review of Selected Literature

Courage is what it takes to stand up and speak; courage is also what it takes to sit down and listen.

–Winston Churchill

Our review of literature on conflict and conflict management revealed studies that have been focused primarily on conceptual models and their effect on team performance and organizational behavior and efficiency (Alper, Tjosvold, & Law, 2000; Amason, Thompson, Hochwarter, & Harrison, 1995; Likert & Likert, 1976; Marques Santos, Uitdewilligen, & Passos, 2015; Thomas, 1992). While these researchers provided a useful and conceptual foundation for understanding conflict and conflict management, there are few selected researchers who have addressed the experiences with conflict of individuals who work and reside in public research institutions of higher education. In particular, there is a growing body of literature from researchers related to university departmental leadership (Comer, Haden, Taylor, & Thomas, 2002; Findlen, 2000; Gmelch, 1991; Hickson & McCroskey, 1991; Lumpkin, 2004; Trombly, Comer, & Villamil, 2002;

Stanley & Algert, 2007; Stevens, Williamson, & Tiger, 2013), and fewer who have focused at the level of faculty (Harrison, 2007; Olsen & Near, 1994; Reybold, 2005). Reybold (2005) engaged in a longitudinal investigation of nine faculty participants who shared disillusionment with their academic career and considered leaving higher education analyzed conflict narratives from multiple interviews. Findings indicated that personal experiences with professional conflict correspond to an individual's motivating force (source of meaningfulness) and disrupting force (interruption to meaningfulness), and the disillusioning process evolves along a continuum of expectation and disposition, resulting in differential thresholds of faculty dissatisfaction.

In a study of research university faculty in first and third years of appointment, Olsen and Near (1994) investigated the relationships among work and nonwork satisfaction, interdomain conflict, and life satisfaction. Their findings indicated that balance and conflict explained variance in life satisfaction beyond that explained by job and nonwork satisfaction. Harrison (2007) reported findings from a survey of 308 students, which revealed that student-faculty conflict is widespread, with approximately one-third of all students reporting a conflict they have pursued. These findings should come as no surprise to us, given the nature of academia and higher education institutions as discussed throughout this book. So, while we clearly see the need for more research to understand the nature of conflict that occurs at the faculty level, it might be more useful to review what we know from the literature about those who work with and lead faculty and administrative initiatives at the department level—the department chair or department head. In a 1990 survey (Gmelch, 1991) of approximately 800 department chairs from 100 research institutions, they reported a primary source of stress was confrontation with colleagues. Included in their description was conducting annual performance evaluation, making decisions that affect the lives of faculty colleagues, and resolving differences between faculty colleagues (Higgerson, 1996). Conflict is possible, if not probable, in many of the duties and responsibilities assigned to department chairs and the opportunity for conflict increases when department chairs must manage with declining human and fiscal resources, but conflict can erupt even in instances when there is (or should be) no real disagreement (American Council on Education, n.d). Sometimes department chairs must manage conflict that exists among others, including disagreements between faculty members or between faculty and students. At other times, department chairs must manage conflict between themselves and others, such as disagreements with faculty, students, or central administration. The fact that confrontation with colleagues surfaced as the second most often mentioned source of stress in a survey of some 800 chairs may be indicative of both the discomfort of managing conflict and the frequency with which department

chairs encounter conflict. Department chairs need to know how to manage conflict effectively (American Council on Education, n.d).Researchers have further elucidated departmental leaders encounter with on the job stress. Tracie Miller, a graduate student at Texas A&M University at the time of writing this book, hopes to be a department chair and eventually become a dean. In a research paper for her graduate course on conflict management and dialogue, she uncovered that Aggarwal, Rochford, and Vaidyanathan (2009) surveyed marketing department chairs from Association to Advance Collegiate Schools of Business (AACSB) accredited schools of business on the sources of department chair stress. Listed among the top 20 were handling student concerns and conflicts (ranked number 15) and resolving differences with their dean/supervisor (ranked number 16). Aggarwal et al. suggested a department chair's ability to handle conflict with peers, supervisors, and students as a way for department chairs to manage stress. Crookston (2014) discussed one of the many benefits of conflict, as a department chair, is the attainment of peace. However, peace does not mean the absence of conflict. True peace is a situation where faculty, staff, and administrators feel comfortable raising the issues that concern them. They used words such as "unity, harmony, respect, fulfillment, satisfaction, and enthusiasm" (p. 24) to describe their work environments. False peace, on the other hand, is a situation where conflicts are ignored. During false peace, faculty and staff bring issues up to their administrators and the issues are ignored, downplayed, or simply not addressed (Miller, 2015). Gmelch and Carroll (1991) argued that approaches to conflict can be organized around three time periods—the 1890–1940s, 1950–1980s, and at the time of the writing of their article, in the 1990s. They further characterized these time periods as noted in Table 7.1.

Table 7.1. Approaches to Organizational Conflict

Period	Philosophy	Nature	Prescription Strategy
1890–1940s	Traditional	Destructive	Eliminate
1950–1980s	Behavioral	Natural	Accept
Present Time	Principled	Necessary	Encourage

Source: Gmelch and Carroll (1991).

Gmelch and Carroll (1991) described the *traditionalist* approach to conflict from the late 19th century through the middle 1940s as "destructive and therefore should be eliminated. The role of the manager was to purge conflict from the organization. In higher education, this remains the predominant view" (pp. 108–109). The *behavioral* approach that was

characteristic of the 1950s is attributed to Freud's belief that aggression is a natural, independent, and instinctual. Therefore, conflict was seen as something that is natural and acceptable, and organizations by their very nature are conflict laden (Gmelch & Carroll, 1991). Departments compete for prestige…. All compete for power" (Robbins, 1974, p. 13). The *principled* approach, according to Gmelch and Carroll (1991), views conflict as "something necessary and to be encouraged in a productive organization. With this style of management, the needs of both the individual and the organization are met" (p. 109). However, our review of the current literature did not reveal any descriptors for approaches to organizational conflict since the 1990s. So, we argue, based on experience and the emerging literature that the prescription strategy that seems most prudent now in higher education that fits within the principled philosophy is to "change the organizational culture." For it is only through changing the organizational culture, where we equip individuals with the skills necessary to engage in productive conflict. For universities that have interlocking systems of assumptions, attitudes, values, communication practices, and beliefs that govern how people behave within the organization, the organizational culture is the very place, with all its innovations, challenges, and complexities to engage in large-scale change. As Barbara Sporn (1996) stated, "universities are complex social organizations with distinctive cultures. On the one hand, academic freedom and autonomy are inviolable values and, on the other hand, changing environmental conditions exert strong influence on the primary functions of universities" (p. 41). Di Virgilio and Di Pietro (2012) found that the role of organizational culture on informal conflict management illustrates that there is a relationship between culture and behavioral norms. In addition, leaders' own conflict management behaviors are associated with distinct unit conflict cultures (Gelfand, Leslie, Keller, & de Dreu, 2012). Interestingly enough, Gmelch and Carroll (1991) stated, "conflict in most complex organizations such as universities and colleges is sewn into the fabric of the institution" (p. 110). This is even more evident at institutions that are being challenged to increase enrollment and are expected to do so with declining state resources. "As the size of an organization increases, goals become less clear, interpersonal relationships become more formal, departments become more specialized and the potential for conflict intensifies" (Gmelch & Carroll, p. 110).

In 2004, we conducted a qualitative research study of 20 department heads who represented 10 academic colleges at a major public research university (Stanley & Algert, 2007). Specifically, we wanted to learn how they described their conflict management style and how this style enabled them to manage all types of conflict—faculty-faculty, faculty-staff, faculty-student, and staff-staff and whether their experiences were consistent with the existing literature. The data consisted of interview transcripts and field

notes taken during the interviews. The interviews were then transcribed. After carefully analyzing the transcripts, and as discussed in previous chapters, we relied on the Thomas-Kilmann Conflict Mode Instrument (TKI) to determine the conflict management styles of the department heads. We decided not to give them the TKI because we wanted them to describe the types of conflicts they encountered at the departmental level and their perceptions of how they handled each conflict situation. Further, we wanted to pay attention to the participants' voices and feelings to the open-ended questions we asked of them as they described how they managed conflict.

> Eleven of the department heads self-reported using the compromising mode to manage conflict in their departments (Stanley & Algert, 2007). The modes least used were "avoiding" and "accommodating," on the cooperation axis. All department heads described situations where they thought they had to "negotiate" or make concessions in order to resolve the conflict. Their management style was dependent on the nature of the conflict and the individuals involved. For example, one department head, in response to the question, *"How would you describe your conflict management style?"* attempted to describe the compromising mode of conflict management in the following manner,

> Basically, what I try to do is to first recognize that a legitimate issue exists and make sure that we have as much clarity about the issue as possible. This is what I call "discussing the un-discussible." It was so contentious between the two different faculty members who teach in this program that they would blow up from time to time and we would end up attacking each other instead of attacking the issue.... Ultimately, we created a shared position. I think that is what conflict management is all about. It is creating compromising solutions where all interests are recognized and dealt with. You may only get 60%, 70%, 80% satisfaction of all parties. Nobody gets 100% of what they want, but they get 80% and you serve the net best interest of the department. (Stanley & Algert, 2007, p. 56)

In comparison, the department heads who used the collaborative mode seemed to express a high level of confidence in recognizing and managing conflict. For example, one described these skills rather poignantly.

> I try to get people to actually come to an agreement or resolution that they can both live with. Sometimes I will propose an agreement and it just depends on what it is. If someone is really stepping out of bounds and if they really want a third person.... For example, I try to get each person to air their concerns and needs. I am more collaborating. I did a survey at mid point of my term. It was like a five-page survey. Most people filled it out because I told them that it was not going to go to the Dean, it's to be used by me but I didn't want to wait because the Dean does a survey of the faculty at the end of your term after four years.... You know if something is festering I

don't want to wait ... I gave them areas for comments and things like that so it [the feedback] was really good. (Stanley & Algert, 2007, p. 57)

The common conflicts that department heads described were "data conflicts (e.g., limited resources), inadequate personnel, [and] space issues" (Stanley & Algert, 2007, p. 58). For example, when describing a hiring decision that created conflict among faculty members, the department heads talked about other issues that impacted the conflict such as the hiring history of other faculty, belief systems held by faculty, resources, faculty retention, and diversity issues. In addition, the primary individuals involved in the majority of the conflicts seem to be faculty-faculty (Stanley & Algert, 2007). The results of the Stanley and Algert (2007) study were not unlike the work of Gmelch and Carroll (1991) where their review of the research on organizational conflicts revealed

> 10 structural conflicts which actually can create conflict among faculty and administrators, regardless of any interpersonal animosities or personality differences: (1) levels in the hierarchy; (2) rules and regulations; (3) degree of specialization; (4) staff composition; (5) nature of supervision; (6) participation in decision making; (7) sources of power; (8) rewards and recognition; (9) staff interdependence; and (10) roles and responsibilities. (p. 110)

We posed this question to the department heads. "Do you think department heads need training in conflict management? Why or why not?" Ten of the 20 department heads in the Stanley and Algert (2007) study indicated a need for more professional development opportunities for department heads and deans in the area of conflict management, and specifically to address how the university culture impacts the management of conflict. Here are two representative comments from the department heads:

> Provide professional development on a regular basis. Conflict management is a daily activity. When you go from a faculty member to a department head, even though you may have done things with the organization [department], it is not the same because now the scale of conflict is different and escalates. (Stanley & Algert, 2007, p. 61)

> I never had any training in conflict management. I have been at this university for a long time ..., but every day is a new event; and so you wrestle with it to make sure that you do all the things that I am talking about. That you are fair, that you are listening, that you make sure that to the extent you can, that parties walk away with a win-win situation. I would think that there would be a lot of value in giving somebody an opportunity to have to go through some training where conflict management issues would be sorted out, you know, maybe in terms of some scenario development situations that you would find

yourself in so that it's a little less sort of learning on the job while you are doing it. (Stanley & Algert, 2007, p. 58)

In the Stanley and Algert (2007) study, several of the department heads readily admitted that they were not particularly effective at handling conflict. In fact, 19 out of 20 department heads in that study expressed a need for learning more about conflict management. When asked, "What could the university do to further enhance departmental leadership skills in conflict management?" their responses were grouped along three very distinct themes:

1. *getting together to share best practices*
2. *understanding when and how to lead and manage people*
3. *developing a better understanding of the university's conflict culture*

Eighteen of the 20 department heads wanted more opportunities to get together to share best practices. Specifically, some suggested that conflict management training and workshops include, but not be limited to, case study scenarios through which they could learn how to identify conflict and develop appropriate strategies for managing the conflict.

When academic leaders, such as department chairs and deans, work to learn more about their conflict management styles, there is a high probability of decreased resource expenditure, improved communication, increased faculty and staff productivity, and a dynamic and resilient organizational culture. Furthermore, departmental and college communities will have a clear understanding of the university conflict culture and colleges and universities will be better equipped at responding to social and cultural change.

REFERENCES

Aggarwal, P., Rochford, L., & Vaidyanathan, R. (2009). The hot seat: Profiling the marketing department chair. *Journal of Marketing Education, 31*(1), 40–51. doi:10.1177/0273475308324089

Alper, S., Tjosvold, D., & Law, K. S. (2000). Conflict management, efficacy, and performance in organizational teams. *Personnel Psychology, 53*(3), 625–642.

Amason, A. C., Thompson, K. R., Hochwater, W. A., & Harrison, A. W. (1995). Conflict: An important dimension in successful management teams. *Organizational Dynamics, 24*(2), 20–35.

American Council on Education. (n.d). Department Leadership Project. Department chair online resource center managing conflict. Retrieved from http://www.acenet.edu/resources/chairs/

Churchill, W. (2007). Winston Churchill quotes. Retrieved March, 1, 2007, http://www.brainyquote.com/quotes/quotes/w/winstonchu161628.html

Comer, R. W., Haden, N. K., Taylor, R. L., & Thomas, D. D. (2002, April). Leadership strategies for department chairs and program directors: A case study approach. *Journal of Dental Education, 66,* 514–519.

Crookston, R. K. (2014). Using conflict to achieve true peace. *The Department Chair, 25*(2), 22–25. doi:10.1002/dch.20069

Di Virgilio, F., & Di Pietro, L. (2012). The role of organizational culture on informal conflict management. Retrieved from SSRN: http://ssrn.com/abstract=1978428

Findlen, G. L. (2000). Conflict: The skeleton in academe's closet. In D. Robillard, Jr. (Ed.), Dimensions of managing academic affairs in the community college. *New Directions for Community Colleges* (pp. 41–49, No. 109). San Francisco, CA: Jossey-Bass.

Gelfand, M. J., Leslie, L. M., Keller, K., & de Dreu, C. (2012, November). Conflict cultures in organizations: How leaders shape conflict cultures and their organizational-level consequences. *Journal of Applied Psychology, 97*(6), 1131–1147.

Gmelch, W. H., & Carroll, J. B. (1991, Winter). The three Rs of conflict management for department chairs and faculty. *Innovative Higher Education, 16*(2), 107–123.

Gmelch, W. H. (1991a, October). The creation of constructive conflict within educational administration departments. Paper presented at the Annual Meeting of the University Council for Educational Administration, Baltimore, Maryland.

Harrison, T. R. (2007, March). My professor is so unfair: Student attitudes and experiences of conflict with faculty. *Conflict Resolution Quarterly, 24*(3), 349–368.

Hickson, M., & McCroskey, J. C. (1991, October). Diagnosing communication problems of academic chairs: Applied communication in context. *ACA Bulletin, 78,* 8–13.

Higgerson, M. L. (1996). *Communication skills for department chairs.* Bolton, MA: Anke.

Likert, R., & Likert, J. G. (1976). *New ways of managing conflict.* New York, NY: McGraw-Hill.

Lumpkin, A. (2004). Enhancing the effectiveness of department chairs. *Journal of Physical Education, Recreation & Dance, 75*(9), 44–48.

Marques Santos, C., Uitdewilligen, S., & Passos, A. M. (2015). Why is your team more creative than mine? The influence of shared mental models on intragroup conflict, team creativity, and effectiveness. *Creativity & Innovation Management, 24*(4), 645–658.

Miller, T. (2015, November). *Conflict management for department chairs.* A paper presented for a conflict management course on conflict management and dialogue. College Station, TX: Texas A&M University.

Olsen, D., & Near, J. P. (1994). Role conflict and faculty life satisfaction. *Review of Higher Education, 17*(2), 179–195.

Reybold, L. E. (2005, December). Surrendering the dream. Early career conflict and faculty dissatisfaction thresholds. *Journal of Career Development, 32*(2), 107–121.

Robbins, S. P. (1974). *Managing organizational conflict.* Englewood Cliffs, NJ: Prentice-Hall.

Sporn, B. (1996). Managing university culture: An analysis of the relationship between institutional culture and management approaches. *Higher Education, 32*, 41–61.

Stanley, C. A., & Algert, N. E. (2007). An exploratory study of the conflict management styles of department heads in a university setting. *Innovative Higher Education, 32*, 49–65.

Stevens, R. E., Williamson, S., & Tiger, A. (2013). Conflict resolution strategies in an academic setting. *Feature Edition, 2013*(4), 10–21.

Thomas, K. W. (1992). Conflict and conflict management. *Journal of Organizational Behavior, 13*(3), 265–274.

Trombly, R. M., Comer, R. W., & Villamil, J. E. (2002, April). Case III: Managing conflict—The case of the faculty stuck in the middle. *Journal of Dental Education, 66*, 533–540.

SECTION IV

PERSONNEL AND PROGRAMS IN MANAGING CONFLICT

CHAPTER 8

CONFLICT MANAGEMENT FROM A PRACTITIONER PERSPECTIVE

If you believe the voice in your head, you will find yourself in an
isolated world, far away from reality

—Nissim Amon

Learning to manage conflict is integral to achieving a high-performing department, college, or university. Very few people in academia, or any organization, seek conflict, however, with any vibrant organization there will always be conflicts. More often than not, conflicts are due to inappropriate communication among the members of an organization regarding their needs, ideas, beliefs, goals, or values. The idea that we underscore the proper management of conflict is that *not* all conflicts can be resolved, but learning to manage conflicts will significantly decrease the odds of destructive escalation. Conflict management involves acquiring skills related to addressing conflict, increasing self-awareness about conflict intervention strategies, honing change management and conflict communication skills, and developing structures and protocols to address conflict in the workplace setting.

Conflict Management and Dialogue in Higher Education: A Global Perspective, pp. 135–145
Copyright © 2016 by Information Age Publishing

PREPARING FOR CONSTRUCTIVE CONFLICT ENGAGEMENT

The more you work to hone your skill set to engage in productive conflict engagement the greater are your chances of creating a high-performing work environment, where all individuals in your colleges and universities have the opportunity to thrive. The goals is to turn conflict into strategic, productive and positive outcomes for the individuals and the unit. Here we are proposing activities so organizations are better prepared for conflict engagement.

Build Trust

As discussed in Chapter 2, individuals and organizations cannot engage in meaningful conflicts if there is a lack of trust. Trust is essential for people to be willing to engage in meaningful conflict. Cruise O'Brien (2001) talked about trust as " an expectation about the positive actions of other people, without being able to influence or monitor the outcome" (p. 10). Trust involves releasing control and believing in our colleagues. Some important points Cruise O'Brien shared include:

- People award trust on the basis of fair treatment, respect and recognition for their contributions.
- People at the bottom of an organization are continuous and careful 'intuitive auditors'
- Deference to authority has been found to be based more on trust than on competence
- The durability of trust is based on integrity and consistency
- Trust builds incrementally, however, distrust is even more catastrophic.

Some leaders say, "just trust me," without realizing trust is far more complex than a simple declaration. Further, trust occurs at varying levels of occurrence. As seen from O'Brien (2001), there are five distinct levels of trust:

- Cooperation—temporary, for a specific purpose
- Participation—may evolve from instinct to cooperate, listen & offer to cooperate
- Confidence—participants' develop based on consistency of evidence

- Involvement—giving oneself on the basis of cognitive and emotional terms
- Commitment—when involvement becomes intrinsic or persistently renewable

Trust within workplace units is necessary for employees to have effective communication, including engaging in meaningful conflict, with both employees and supervisors. To build trust, especially trust when an organization is in conflict, the organization should explicitly train people to:

1. Understand common behaviors, including their own, when in conflict
2. Develop dialogue and mediation skills
3. Discuss cases of hypothetical conflicts, as table top exercises, for participants to explore options in engaging in the conflict posed.

An Example Conflict Case Study

Consider the following case study. Try to read it from the perspective of each of the participants involved and respond to the guiding questions that follow.

You are in your first year as chair of a department with 14 full-time faculty members. You have already heard some concerns about three faculty members who spend a lot of time consulting and are rarely seen on campus. You engage with one of them, Dr. Bucks, to learn about his consulting activities. He is somewhat evasive about the extent of his consulting activities but emphatically stresses the importance of professional activities to the department.

Dr. Brightlight has a national reputation. Students in her courses complain that guest speakers and videos are often used to conduct the class while she is out consulting. On the one hand, the department needs her, probably more than she needs it. On the other hand, her luminary reputation is helpful to the department's status and research activities.

Dr. Dolittle is a full professor who has been with the university for 23 years. He recently invested in a business and is spending increasing amounts of time analyzing and supervising its operations. He is frequently unavailable to students. You drop by during his office hours on three occasions, however, he is absent. When you finally get an opportunity to talk with him about his off-campus activities, he responds that the new business is really a form of

consulting, that it improves his teaching, and that his business operations are similar to other faculty members' activities.

Your executive committee suggested that absent faculty members are derailing the department's programmatic progress. Classes are not being taught or are not of the quality that they should be. These faculty members' research efforts seem to support their consultation work rather than departmental priorities. Their service to the department is nonexistent. Their attitude is having a negative impact on both faculty morale and recruitment efforts, as evidenced by students' comments to prospective students. You understand the executive committee's concerns, but you are also aware of what the impact will be on the department's reputation if all three of these faculty members explore leaving the department because of any action that you take.

Here are some guiding questions to ask, as you work through how to resolve this conflict:

1. What is the conflict?
2. Who are the disputants?
3. What are the issues?
4. Which of the conflict modes would you use and why?
5. What are the implications of using other conflict modes?
6. What is the typical response to this type of conflict?
7. What are the short-term consequences of not addressing the conflict?
8. What are the long-term consequences of not addressing the conflict?

Deepen Commitments to Diversity and Social Justice

The goal of social justice education is full and equal participation of all groups in a society that is mutually shaped to meet their needs (Adams, Bell, & Griffin, 1997). The higher education setting, which is a microcosm of our society, is no different. Faculty, staff, and administrators who are underrepresented or marginalized because of social and cultural identity characteristics such as class, race, ethnicity, gender, age, sexual orientation, political ideologies, culture, religion, nationality, and physical and learning ability bring experiences, values, and beliefs that often counter the master narrative. These counter narratives can trigger conflict. We have learned from conflict theory and mediation practice that diversity and social justice issues are important to consider when managing conflict. A basic tenet of social justice is *inclusiveness*. You cannot effectively manage conflict without ensuring that all parties involved have a voice at the table and are pro-

vided with an opportunity to tell their narrative from their seat of identity or multiple identities. Parties whose voices may not be heard or heeded in conventional forums must be given the opportunity to be heard in the conflict resolution process.

More important, the views, needs, and interests of the participants in a dispute must be given full consideration, and the "power" differences among the participants must be equalized in reaching a fair resolution of the conflict. For example, we have worked with an administrative office at a major research university that provides mediation services. Faculty members are trained to be mediators and are called on to mediate faculty conflicts when they arise. The mediators receive 40 hours of extensive training (a requirement of the State Bar where the university is located), and a large part of that training is learning about the relationship between conflict and social justice. Issues such as racial identity development, the cycle of socialization, the dynamics of oppression, and responding to triggers that can lead to conflict are important topics of discussion during the training. The mediation service is voluntary and available to all faculty members. One of the attributes of this service is that the associate provost works to assign comediators to cases to ensure that the power relations are reasonably equal, especially when it is perceived that the nature of the conflict might involve a social justice issue such as racism. For example, if there is a perceived racial conflict, the office works to find a biracial team of comediators. Mediators are never from the parties' department and college, and when more than one mediator is involved representing each of the parties, every effort is made to ensure that comediators are equally matched regarding academic rank.

Most of our colleges and universities are striving to model the diversity that is representative of our society and/or state as a whole. Regarding the goals and achievements of a diverse campus, Lee Bollinger (2007), president of Columbia University, stated,

> The experience of arriving on a campus to live and study with classmates from a diverse range of backgrounds is essential to students' training for this new world, nurturing in them an instinct to reach out instead of clinging to the comforts of what seems natural or familiar. We know that connecting with people very or even slightly-different from ourselves stimulates the imagination; and when we learn to see the world through a multiplicity of eyes, we only make ourselves more nimble in mastering and integrating— the diverse fields of knowledge awaiting us. (p. B20)

However, the learning experience that Bollinger rightly applauds when people with diverse backgrounds interact can also lead to misunderstanding and conflict. As a result, universities and academic leaders find themselves responding to and managing racial incidents or hate crimes on

their campuses. Individuals on campus are also often uncertain as to how to respond to these incidents. Still too often, we will serve on a committee or attend a meeting only to hear someone make a disparaging comment that is perceived as sexist, racist, homophobic, anti-Semitic, or Islam-phobic, and it is met with silence. We often observe and critique the conflict management skills of individuals who work to resolve these difficult conflicts.

Learning how to discern and manage racial conflicts on a college or university campus is an intellectually, emotionally, and politically challenging exercise (Bell, Love, & Roberts, 2007). For those who have engaged in discussions regarding racial conflict, they relive comments such as, "Is this really happening?" "Why is this a race issue?" "You people are so sensitive," and "They just don't get it!" Comments like these are more likely when faculty, staff, administrators, and students are not provided with opportunities to dialogue about potentially divisive racial issues in safe and supportive spaces.

Racial conflicts do not go away on their own; they usually escalate if they are not managed well. All faculty members and college administrators can become better models of diversity by learning how to facilitate difficult dialogues when racial conflicts occur. Below are some general guidelines to follow when facilitating such dialogues conflicts particularly related to diversity .

Guideline 1: Be Aware of Your Biases

Each individual holds prejudices. Prejudices may involve taking a particular point of view or perspective or reinforcing stereotypes about a group of people before facts are gathered and weighed. These prejudicial behaviors can be observed before and during conflicts. However, biases become problematic when we facilitate discussions involving racial conflicts from a subjective rather than an objective point of view. You should be open to perspective taking, including learning and unlearning information about self and others.

Guideline 2: Be Aware of Your Mental Model

Mental models are explanations in our mind of how something works in the real world. They drive our choices, actions, and behaviors. Be cognizant of the fact not everyone shares the same mental model. Each person, of course, has different life experiences, values, and beliefs that shape us as human beings. Individuals who historically have been marginalized or have been made to feel marginalized in our society might bring a differ-

ent mental model to a given situation. Racial conflicts are opportunities to uncover mental models so that there is growth and learning.

Guideline 3: Be Aware of Your Spheres of Influence

You can influence meaningful conflict dialogues by examining and understanding the mindset and assumptions of the various spheres that might collide to create areas of conflict. The first such sphere is that of self (including our own attitudes, beliefs, values, knowledge, and behavior in terms of socialization experiences, and our interactions with others). The second sphere is that of the campus itself. Does it have high expectations for behavior for all students and faculty? Does it provide a welcoming environment and support students and faculty when obstacles occur? Other spheres whose assumptions and procedures should be examined and understood, as they may influence behavior and attitudes resulting in conflicts, include those of the department, college, or school (including faculty governance and climate); community (including interactions between the campus or individual faculty members with schools, religious organizations, business and industry, and health-care agencies); and professional organizations and the assumptions and attitudes that might inform faculty scholarship and work at the local, national and international levels.

Guideline 4: Work to Listen Respectfully and Not to Judge

One of the key ingredients to facilitating discussions about racial conflict or any difficult dialogue is learning how to listen mindfully, be aware of one's own narrative and mental model, and to exercise perspective taking. Many are skilled speakers and far less proficient listeners. Additionally, the ability to suspend judgment is equally difficult for some of us. To achieve clear communication and to clarify misinformation, it is always helpful to restate and summarize what you think you heard during a conversation.

Guideline 5: Acknowledge Emotions

Difficult dialogues are difficult because human beings come to the discussion table laden with a variety of emotions-fear, disappointment, frustration, anger, confidence, courage, hate, pain, pride, vulnerability, worry, etc. These emotions often come from direct experiences with overt and covert discrimination. Emotions that ensue as a result of these experiences are natural and sustained. Avoiding dialogues under the guise of waiting until individuals appear to be "calmer" is never the best solution.

Guideline 6: Establish Ground Rules for Discussion

Ground rules are helpful in setting clear boundaries for difficult dialogues so that everyone feels reasonably safe to participate and contribute in a respectful manner. We have found that when participants in a dialogue work together to establish ground rules, there is more ownership in working to ensure that the conversation remains productive.

- Examples of useful ground rules are as follows:
- Commit to active listening.
- Agree to use "I" statements to avoid generalizations.
- Do not judge others or question their motives.
- Do not interrupt when someone is telling his or her story.
- Agree to confidentiality
- Be respectful in your contributions

Guideline 7: Establish Clear Plans for Action and Accountability

One of the questions often posed to academic leaders before and during the facilitation of discussion regarding racial conflicts is, "What is going to be done as a result of this conversation?" Effective facilitation of such discussion includes the development of clear plans of action that are realistic, specific, and goal oriented. In addition, academic leaders who are often in the best position to ensure that plans of action are developed, implemented, and assessed should be held accountable for monitoring appropriate outcomes.

CONFLICTS INVOLVING BULLYING

There is a growing body of literature (Gravois, 2006; Keashly & Neuman, 2010; Jefferson, 2007; Levine, 2006; Namie & Namie, 2000; Powers, 2007; Twale & De Luca, 2008) on bullying in academia. A majority of the authors of this literature have agreed that bullying behaviors seem to take hold when there is an imbalance of power. Keashly and Neuman (2010) underlined that related to higher education in a statement, "while the values and norms of academic freedom, collegiality, and autonomy are the foundation of the academy, the understanding and interpretation of these may vary. Such variability can lead to misunderstandings and potentially perceived or actual mistreatment" (pp. 62–63). Additionally, Houghton (2003) stated,

"Bullying thrives in situations where the perpetrators are both powerful and frightening, and those around them [are] too scared to challenge" (p. 126). In addition, these behaviors are directed at members of targeted groups in academia such as women; faculty of color; international faculty, gay, lesbian, bisexual, and transgender faculty; Muslim faculty; and Jewish faculty. Bullying can impact an individual in three ways: physiologically (illness), psychologically (anxiety, depression, fear), and behaviorally (obsession, aggression, withdrawal) (Amicus, 2005).

Academic bullies are often "older, tenured professors who are unwilling to take direction and create what many describe as a 'toxic environment' in the department" (Powers, 2007, p. 1). While bullying is often character-ized in the academic setting as powerful professors who take advantage of less powerful ones, including graduate students becoming victims, bullying can occur in any workplace. The Canadian Center for Occupational Health and Safety (2005) offered the following examples of workforce bullying:

- Spreading malicious rumors, gossip, or innuendo that is not true
- Excluding or isolating someone socially
- Intimidating a person
- Undermining or deliberately impeding a person's work
- Physically abusing or threatening abuse
- Removing areas of responsibilities without cause
- Constantly changing work guidelines
- Establishing impossible deadlines that will set the individual up to fail
- Withholding necessary information or purposefully giving the wrong information
- Making jokes that are "obviously offensive" by spoken word or e-mail
- Intruding on a person's privacy by pestering, spying, or stalking
- Assigning unreasonable duties or workload which are unfavorable to one person (in a way that creates unnecessary pressure)
- Underwork—creating a feeling of uselessness
- Yelling or using profanity
- Criticizing a person persistently or constantly
- Belittling a person's opinions
- Unwarranted (or undeserved) punishment
- Blocking applications for training, leave or promotion
- Tampering with a person's personal belongings or work equip-ment.

Academic leaders must challenge and support victims of bullying behavior. Staff, faculty, students, and administrators can bully and can be bullied. With the increase in use of social media an increase in cyberbullying has occurred. Anonymity has increased the number of people who bully and practice inappropriate behaviors towards peers, supervisors, and subordinates. These behaviors are on the rise and occurring at increasing levels of sophistication in the academy. Recognizing and responding appropriately to bullying behaviors is inherent to effective conflict management. Academic bullying is a clear example of behaviors that create conflicts, which have escalated and are not effectively addressed. Denice Denton, late chancellor of the University of California, Santa Cruz, had this to say about confronting bullying behavior, conflict, and bias in her closing address at the National Academy's Committee on Maximizing the Potential of Women in Academic Science and Engineering:

> I'm going to offer you a set of recommendations that will cost you nothing but courage. They can also be used more broadly well beyond the hallowed halls, and thus impact the "cross-institutional interlock," or as I would say as an electrical engineer, "the system." First of all, we should have zero tolerance for bullying behavior. It should not be acceptable in the workplace or anywhere else. If you are an academic leader, you should confront faculty and others who are abusive to students, staff and other faculty, particularly senior faculty. Tenure is not a license to kill. There are limits to acceptable behavior in the academy. How many of you have seen on an academic campus, senior people with tenure over and over abuse people who are lower than them in the power structure, and nobody ever does anything? Why does that happen? Why do we let that happen? It's unacceptable. If you have issues with dealing with conflict and you are an academic leader, take a class. Get help. Seek support. People don't want to confront each other. But we have to. It's our job. It's in the position description. We can learn from conflict. We do learn from conflict. Confront people's biases. When biases come out if you're an academic leader or anything else, confront people's bias. And here is another one, and this is not a popular one, but I'm just throwing it in there. Support your local senior feminist colleagues, male and female. It's lonely at the top. (Rosser, 2006, p. 23)

Within six months of delivering this address to the National Academy, Chancellor Denton committed suicide; she was a victim of bullying behavior.

REFERENCES

Adams, M., Bell, L., & Griffin, P. (1997). *Teaching for diversity and social justice* (1st ed.). New York, NY: Routledge.

Amicus (2005). *Amicus guide to tackling bullying at work.* London, England: Amicus. Retrieved from www.am.ieusthe union.org

Bell, L., Love, B. J., & Roberts, R. A. (2007). Racism and white privilege curriculum design. In M. Adams, L. Bell, & P. Griffin (Eds.), *Teaching for diversity and social justice* (pp. 125–144). New York, NY: Routledge.

Bollinger, L. (2007). Why diversity matters. *Chronicle of Higher Education, 53*(39), B20.

Canadian Center for Occupational Health and Safety. (2005). OSH Answers. *Bullying in the workplace.* Retrieved from http://www.ccohs.ca/oshanswers/psychosocial/bullying.html#_1_8

Cruise O'Brien, R. (2001). *Trust: Releasing the energy to succeed.* Chichester, England: John Wiley & Sons.

Gravois, J. (2006). Mob rule: In departmental disputes, professors can act just like animals. *Chronicle of Higher Education, 5.2*(92), 92.

Houghton, A. (2003). Bullying in medicine. *BMJ* (Clinical research ed.), *326*(7393), S125.

Jefferson, A. I. (2006). The bullying boss. *Academic Leadership Journal, 4*(4), 14–16.

Amon, N. (n.d.). Trilotherapy. Retrieved from http://trilotherapy.com/trilotherapy-by-nissim-amon/

Keashly, L., & Neuman, J. H. (2010). Facutly experiences with bullying in higher education. *Administrative Theory & Praxis, 32*(1), 48-70.

Levine, I. S. (2006, September 22). Bosses who bully. *Science Careers Forum.* Retrieved from http://sciencecareers.sciencemag.org/career_development/previous_issues/articles/2006_09_22/bosses_who_ bully/(parent)/68

Namie, G., & Namie, R. (2000). Workplace bullying: The silent epidemic. *Employee Rights Quarterly, 1*(2), 1–12.

Powers, E. (2007, July). Handling the "bad apples." News, Views and Careers for All of Higher Education. *Inside Higher Education.* Retrieved http//www.insidehighered.com/ news /2007/07/13/advance

Rosser, S. V. (2006). *Using the lenses of feminist theories to focus on women and technology.* Champaign, IL: University of Illinois Press

Twale, D. J., & De Luca, B. M. (2008). *Faculty incivility: The rise of the academic bully culture and what to do about it* (Vol. 128). New York, NY: Jossey-Bass.

CHAPTER 9

UNIT LEADERS' RESPONSIBILITIES WITH CONFLICT

Instead of suppressing conflicts, specific channels could be created to make this conflict explicit, and specific methods could be set up by which the conflict is resolved.

—Albert Low

"Conflict is a natural and inevitable part of life. It is both the constant companion and frequent trigger of change" (Aschenbrenner & Siders, 1999, p. 32). It is inherent to social interaction and common to organizational life (De Dreu & Van De Vliert, 1997). Yet many work to ignore or avoid it in our personal and professional lives. The word conflict itself is an elastic and elusive term (Ting-Toomey, 2005). As stated earlier, it is defined as "a struggle or contest between people with opposing needs, ideas, values, goals, or beliefs. It arises when one's interests or needs are perceived as being denied to them by another. Conflict, exists, even if only one person perceives it" (Watson & Watson, 2002, p. 2).

In this chapter, we dicuss the unique issues of managing conflict in the university setting from a leadership perspective. There are unique issues related to addressing faculty conflict in the university setting, particularly when one considers that *there is not a person in charge of faculty*. There are

Conflict Management and Dialogue in Higher Education: A Global Perspective, pp. 147–160
Copyright © 2016 by Information Age Publishing

department heads or department chairs who may evaluate faculty; however, they do not dictate the day-to-day work of faculty. Effective conflict engagement and strategies in college and university differ from that of business and industry. Faculty and administrators rarely assume their positions knowing how to manage conflict. However, Putnam (1988) suggested that university leaders spend over 40% of their workday engaged in conflicts. Conflict is also an overlooked area in the professional development of our faculty and administrators.

The word, conflict, conjures up a variety of images for many people. Some of us think of it as something to avoid while others think it can be healthy if managed well. Regardless of the image, management of conflict is complex (Algert & Watson, 2002). This complexity is heightened even more so in a university setting where tenure, priority of discipline, and lack of clear accountability measures limit conflict management tools available to leaders and managers. Further, unprecedented pressures such as declining public funding for higher education, increasing student enrollments, increasing external demands for accountability, and rising expectations for increased external funding require superior leadership to shape constructive responses to conflict. University leadership is critically important. Furthermore, the leadership position that often requires interaction with faculty is the department head or chair. Given the current challenges, the leadership provided by a department head to transform the faculty and the department is critical to an institution's future and mission. Furthermore, the department head, the individual in titled leadership at the center of this transformation, is often the one trying to manage all of the various sources of conflict (Stanley, Watson, & Algert, 2005).

Department leadership and management on a university or college campus are usually classified as a department chair or head. Although these titles are often used synonymously in practice, there are some clear distinctions with respect to the origin and etiology of the titles. For example, the title, "department chair," is used most often in academic settings and has a connotation of collegiality, while the title, "department head," is used most often in military and governmental settings and has a connotation of a hierarchy. For the purposes of this book and from our collective experiences, we use the term department head (Stanley & Algert, 2007).

The role of the department head is often characterized as "ambiguous," because of the differing roles and responsibilities inherent in the position. For example, McLaughlin, Montgomery, and Malpass (1975) described three roles that department heads play in colleges and universities: academic, administrative, and leadership. Academic duties include teaching, advising, facilitating research, and developing the curriculum. Administrative duties include managing the budget, managing faculty and staff, keeping records, and advocating and representing the department in

the college and the institution as a whole. Leadership duties include supporting, motivating, and developing the faculty (Wilson, 1999). Bowman (2002) argued,

> In the broadest sense, are they expected to function as managers or leaders, or both? In a narrower sense, are they expected to serve in roles as diverse as resource manager, instant problem solver, spokesperson, deep listener, motivator, enabler, meaning maker, systems designer, and cultural rainmaker? (p. 158)

After a brainstorming session with faculty in a department of education at Winona State University, Bowman (2002) noted that, "Faculty members identified more than fifty discrete roles and leadership demands central to key aspects of the department's daily operations" (p. 158). Given these daunting and comprehensive expectations, it seems safe to presume that department heads not only play a critical leadership role within the academic setting; they are also expected to fulfill a variety of responsibilities that may or may not be realistic.

Some researchers have maintained that the department head is perhaps one of if not the most challenging positions in higher education (Bennett & Figuli, 1993). Lumpkin (2004) emphasized that the position almost demands that department heads come prepared with skills necessary to manage, assist, and mediate intrapersonal as well as interpersonal conflicts. Therefore, conflict management is an important skill for a department head to have. However, most department heads are neither equipped with these skills nor aware of their conflict management style. Faculty become university and college leaders for a variety of reasons. Some department heads for example, assume this position because no one else in the department wants it; some are encouraged by their colleagues to do so because of admired accomplishments as a scholar; and others seek this leadership opportunity to learn more about administration with the hope of assuming even higher administrative responsibilities in the future (Lumpkin, 2004). Regardless of the motivation or reason for becoming a department head, it can be a lonely place to reside (Stanley & Algert, 2007).

The body of literature discussing department heads leadership skills in managing conflict in a university setting (Coffman, 2009; Comer, Haden, Taylor, & Thomas, 2002; Findlen, 2000b; Gmelch, 1995, 1991a; Gmelch & Carroll, 1991; Hickson & McCroskey, 1991; Lumpkin, 2004; Trombly, Comer, & Villamil, 2002) pointed to a common thread, which suggests that the ability to recognize and manage conflict is a skill that most chairs lack and one that is needed to enhance their effectiveness as leaders (Gmelch, 1991a; Hickson & McCroskey, 1991; Lumpkin, 2004). Furthermore, we find in the literature that department heads are practicing conflict resolution styles learned in childhood (Algert & Watson, 2002), whether adaptive

or maladaptive, unless they have made a conscious decision to reflect and evaluate their conflict management styles. It is assumed that department heads know all there is to know about being effective leaders. Yet high on the list of responsibilities of the department head is constructively resolving conflict in the department. The literature is replete with information and studies on how to recognize and resolve conflict in a variety of settings (Carmichael & Malague, 1996; Gmelch, 1995; Gmelch & Carroll, 1991). However, there are very few publications on how conflict is managed at the departmental level (Findlen, 2000b; Gmelch, 1991a, 1995; Gmelch & Carroll, 1991; Hickson & McCroskey, 1991; Trombly, Comer, & Villamil, 2002), and few of these include reported data from the individual most often managing conflict in this domain—the department head (Gmelch, 1991b; Hickson & McCroskey, 1991).

Academic departments are not unlike many organizations. Many claim to be a "community." However, a challenge that department heads face is how to create a climate where individuals who have different viewpoints can agree to disagree with each other and still feel that they are a part of the community. This is not easy. Bowman (2002) argued that the real work of the department head is learning how to "invite and orchestrate the very penetrating, perceptive, probing questions that can often give rise to the tension, dissent, and constructive stress that are absolutely essential to both defining reality and creating positive organizational change" (p. 160). For certain, "Colleges and universities are highly political institutions, but that is a statement of fact, not an indictment. The challenge for campus leadership is to understand and leverage the political realities that are present in every situation" (Bolman & Gallos, 2011, p. 72). Many faculty members assume that conflict is a negative force and has no place in a department. Despite the negative forces that are often assumed to exist around conflict, many scholars concur that, if managed properly, it can enhance working relationships and build a positive departmental climate (Bowman, 2002; Gmelch, 1995; Gmelch & Carroll, 1991; Trombly, Comer, & Villamil, 2002). Conflict, if not managed properly, "can also increase faculty antagonism, lead to interdepartment tension, disrupt normal channels of communication, and divert faculty's attention from a department's goals and mission (Gmelch, 1995, p. 35). Furthermore, if departments believe and model the concept of community, then conflict can be a positive factor. We should then come to welcome discussions, expect arguments, and tolerate challenges (Trombly, Comer, & Villamil, 2002).

Gmelch (1995) asserted that one of the first steps that a department chair must take toward a positive and constructive conflict style is "to recognize the nature and causes of conflict in the department and university setting" (p. 35). However, ultimately it is the department chair's responsibility to identify the conflict culture for that department and to equip

all employees with an understanding of the conflict culture, expectations for resolutions, and provide the necessary conflict management skills. There are several models, which are useful to our understanding of how the institutional culture influences departmental conflict and ultimately the department head's ability or inability to manage it (Baldridge, 1971; Birnbaum, 1988). First, the *bureaucratic* model assumes that conflict occurs but can be managed through bureaucratic roles and procedures. Second, the *political* model states that conflict is inevitable and is normal between and among individuals who have different needs and interests. Third, the *collegial* model views the academy as a "community of scholars" where conflict is "abnormal" and when it is identified, steps should be taken to eliminate it. The fourth and final model, *anarchical* is present in institutions that succeed in conditions of abundant resources and enter into decline when resources are limited. The latter then forces administrators to make difficult decisions, which can then lead to conflict (Gmelch, 1995, p. 36).

Gmelch (1991a), in his survey of 800 department chairs at 101 research and doctoral-granting universities, found that the development of conflict management skills can lead to a deeper self-awareness of not only one's conflict management style, but also a healthier and more productive work-life for faculty, staff, and students. Gmelch (1995) argued that, "No matter what the answer or reaction, one of the chair's main functions is to adjudicate these conflicting situations by creating a healthy web of tension. ...Chairs need to realize that regardless of the causes, it is their personal responsibility to respond to these conflict situations" (p. 40). We believe differently. This may be one role that the department head can play. More importantly, it is the department head's responsibility to discuss the department's conflict culture and to provide the skills faculty and staff need to effectively manage conflict. Department heads are tensely placed between the demands of the administration and the faculty. Many feel trapped between the pressures to perform as a faculty member and as an administrator.

Trombly, Comer, and Villamil (2002) stated that "Managing conflict is an arduous but necessary task" (p. 533). Conflict calls for the resolution of conflict, rather than managing conflict. It is easier to manage conflict than it is to control the people, places, and things that produce conflict (Algert & Watson, 2002). Within the context of the university setting we prefer to use the term, "conflict management." This term recognizes the complexity of the nature of conflict situations and, allows that some of these may result in "progressive achievements, while others do not have an ideal win-win situation".

Scholars have argued that communication is at the heart of conflict management (Hickson & McCroskey, 1991; Trombly, Comer, & Villamil, 2002). In a survey of 47 department chairs in the Southeast and Midwest to

identify communication problems, the results indicated that conflict management was one of their communication concerns (Hickson & McCroskey, 1991). Highlights from the findings of this study included the following: (a) most chairs do not like being an arbiter between faculty members, (b) most chairs do not like being an arbiter between faculty and staff, (c) most chairs find assessing faculty against one another quite difficult, (d) most chairs do not know what to do with "dead wood faculty," and (e) it is hard for most chairs to tell a faculty member, "No." We believe that department chairs need a range of options for managing interpersonal conflicts, of which one is arbitration. However, there are other options available such as modeling, coaching, facilitated dialogue, mediation, and negotiation. Tidd, McIntyre, and Friedman (2004) suggested four strategies that managers can use to deal with conflict: (a) manage perceptions and attend to context, (b) create a team environment based on trust, (c) attempt to reframe conflicts in context and address them at an appropriate time with employees, and (d) be skilled at framing the conflict by providing a social account whereby uncertainty can be addressed and understood in the work environment. These options, more than arbitration and judging, provide faculty members greater input and responsibility for managing the conflict while directly reducing the pressure placed upon the department head. This is counter to the traditional myth that faculty have to be against one another while in conflict. Further, when the parties in conflict generate a solution to their conflict, versus being told by their department head what to do, they parties are more likely (over 90% of the time) to follow through on their commitment to one another.

Conflict and Diversity

When conflict is used in concert with the word diversity, a commonly held assumption and image are that these two concepts are mutually negative forces. Universities, like many organizations, rarely consider the 'culture' for managing conflicts until the conflict overwhelms the individual or the institution. Further, we know, as stated in Chapter 5, that conflict responses are learned, led by people with the greatest longevity in the organization and driven by people in titled leadership. Also, conflict engagement styles can be changed if desired or deemed necessary (CCCR, 2002; De Dreu & Van De Vliert, 1997). Conflict is productive, and even strategic, if framed and managed well.

Conflict is an overlooked area in the professional development of academic leaders, faculty, staff and students. Engaging in meaningful conflict can enhance cultural understanding, foster creativity, and improve cross-cultural communication. A philosophy that undergirds our approach to

effective conflict engagement is that conflict, if examined critically with the simplest definition of diversity—difference—is almost always about diversity. In addition, if universities aspire to be (a) responsive learning organizations and (b) models for valuing diversity and inclusion then universities must engage and develop faculty, administrators, and staff skills in strategic conflict engagement and conflict management.

Furthermore, if universities are preparing college graduates to work and live in an increasingly diverse and global society, then it is imperative that they are equipped with the necessary cultural competency skills to engage and learn from and about difference. If conflict management is examined in a variety of cultural and international settings, much can be learned from these experiences and use them as models in the university setting.

With the increased attention given by many institutions in higher education to create a more diverse and global academic environment that reflects an educated citizenry—and as we work to develop and value individuals and groups who have different needs, values, beliefs, interests, or goals – conflicts are inevitable. Race relations theory (George, 1984; Merelman, 1995) relates that as the representation of people of color increases in an organization or community, the opportunity for conflict arises. As many universities strive to reflect the student, faculty and staff demographics of their States or the nation, very little attention is being given to how conflict can assist or work against organizational change. Even more important, there is little to no discussion about the relationship between conflict and diversity. A wrong assumption is often in place; it is a belief that people naturally know how to resolve conflicts effectively. Developing effective conflict management skills to work within the context of increasingly diverse organizations such as universities, colleges, departments and other work units will lead to long-term organizational health.

The impact of conflict on an organization's diversity culture calls for 'greater attention by scholars and practitioners on how culture influences the way individuals approach and manage instances of conflict: (Ting-Toomey et al., 1991). Every organization has a conflict culture. Within this culture, there are (a) basic underlying assumptions, (b) espoused values, interests, and goals, (c) structures or composition of the organization, and (d) rules or procedures for the organization. If the university is viewed as an organization that has a conflict culture of its own, especially in the area of diversity and globalization, we can begin to see that conflicts which confront faculty, administrators and staff are "more complex, multifaceted, and intense" (Lan, 1997, p. 29). The often-assumed state of complacency on the part of well-intentioned institutions to recruit for faculty and student diversity without thinking carefully about how diversity impacts an organizational culture, including the behavior and attitudes of the people with the organization is no longer acceptable. Closer attention needs to be

paid attention to examining the relationship between conflict and diversity and how it impacts the organizational culture. Donnellon and Kolb (1997) stated "as new social groups enter into the workplace and move up in organizations conflict rooted in class, gender, race, and ethnicity" (p. 162), along with many other dimensions have become more prominent.

Most colleges and universities are striving to model the diversity that is representative of our society and/or state as a whole. When articulating the goals and value of having a diverse college campus, Lee Bollinger, president of Columbia University (2007) stated,

> The experience of arriving on a campus to live and study with classmates from a diverse range of backgrounds is essential to students' training for this new world, nurturing in them an instinct to reach out instead of clinging to the comforts of what seems natural or familiar. We know that connecting with people very—or even slightly—different from ourselves stimulates the imagination; and when we learn to see the world through a multiplicity of eyes, we only make ourselves more nimble in mastering–and integrating–the diverse fields of knowledge awaiting us. (p. B20)

However, the learning experience that Bollinger proclaimed, occurs when people with differing backgrounds and life experiences interact can also lead to misunderstanding and conflict. As a result, universities and academic leaders often find themselves encountering racial incidents or hate crimes on their campuses. Many campus leaders are often ill-equipped to respond and manage these incidents. Still, too often, we serve on committees or attend meetings only to hear someone make a disparaging comment that is perceived as sexist, racist, homophobic, xenophobic, anti-Semitic, or Islam-phobic, and it is met with silence. We often observe and critique the conflict management skills of individuals who work to resolve these difficult conflicts. Learning how to discern and manage racial conflicts on a college or university campus is an intellectually, emotionally, and politically challenging exercise (Bell, Love, & Roberts, 2007). For those of us who have engaged in discussions regarding racial conflict, we relive comments such as, "Is this really happening?" Why is this a race issue?" "You people are so sensitive," and "They just don't get it!" Comments like these are more likely when we do not provide our faculty, staff, administrators, and students opportunities to dialogue about potentially divisive racial issues in safe and supportive spaces. In their work on racism and white privilege curriculum design, Bell et. al. (2007) made some comments that apply equally well to campus dialogues involving issues of race:

> Participants bring to a course on racism a wide range of feelings and experiences, and often misinformation, and confusion, and bias. White participants may sincerely want to learn about racism and figure out how to

play a role in making their communities, schools, and workplaces welcoming places for all, but fail to see the role white skin privilege and accumulated white advantage play in perpetuating racial inequality.

Participants of color may want to figure out how to break through the silence about racism as a historic and contemporary force that differently shapes their lives, but fear having their concerns dismissed, being viewed as too sensitive or as troublemakers, or being misunderstood by white peers and teachers. Participants from all racial groups may be reluctant to explore racism, especially in mixed groups, given the complex and often painful web of emotions that discussions about racism inevitably raise. (p. 123)

In Chapter 8, we discussed some realities and guidelines for addressing racial conflicts.

Positively Engaging in Conflict

Tjosvold (1991) argued, in his conflict-positive model, that the goal of any organization should be "not how to avoid differences but how to use them to accomplish common aspirations as effectively as possible" (p. 27). Valuing diversity and conflict involves confronting differences because these confrontations can bring out diverse views about issues that are critical for positive conflict and for the organization. Furthermore, through dialogue, employees and students, can clarify the confusions and assumptions that make them suspicious. People who confront the issues develop an understanding of each other which is one of the tenets for effective conflict management. Through dialogue, colleagues clarify assumptions, confusions, and misunderstandings; clarification moves towards trust and away from suspicion. People who confront issues, in a constructive way, gather information, identify opportunities, determine if threats are present, and determine how to move forward in their working relationship.

Deeper dialogues are important and necessary in the university environment, always, and particularly with increased diversity. Faculty and administrators will often argue convincingly that there are benefits to recruitment and retention of diversity. However, as Sonnenschein (1997) stated "Diversity's benefits are not automatic. Diversity also means challenge" and conflict. "Racism, sexism, ageism ... homophobia," and other diversity issues "can be disruptive to the workplace, preventing the unit from accomplishing its goals." Without engagement in meaningful conflict and a willingness to discuss these complex issues of diversity and identity an organization can create organizational distress. Diversity, respecting

identity, and social justice are hard work; all which bring conflicts and all which, when addressed through dialogue, can bring great success to a unit.

Implications for Faculty and Organizational Development

Managing conflict, particularly diversity conflicts, in the university setting is clearly complex. Differences in opinions, ideas, life experiences, and social and cultural attributes present formidable challenges as well as opportunities for growth, understanding, and learning. The AWS Model of conflict engagement, which is discussed in Chapter 8, is a model that has been used constructively and productively in academic environments to address such conflicts.

Sustaining a highly successful department or college, or university, is critical particularly during times of more accountability to ensure that the demographics of the faculty, staff, and student body reflect society. In addition, an integral part of sustaining the unit is to have effective strategies, protocols, and ways to address conflict. A university is dependent upon the fact that faculty are one of the keys to organizational success and that the management of conflict is critical to successful strategic planning and the success of faculty and student learning in academic settings. At the heart of mediating conflicts in the university setting is creating a climate where individuals feel welcomed and valued for not only their contributions to the academic discourse but also for who they are as human beings. The AWS Model, shared in Chapter 8, is ideal for use in mediating diversity conflicts by having positive implications for organizational and individual development around diversity and social justice. Below is some feedback gained from academic administrators (department heads and deans) and conflict managers who participated in conflict management skill set development.

Faculty Development

Faculty professional development activities such as mediation short courses and conflict management seminars can serve as catalysts to enhance faculty and administrator dialogues in understanding diversity and social justice.

1. The skills developed in the mediation short course can be used in a variety of management settings such as faculty meetings, staff training, and community meetings.
2. The use of real, problem-based case studies in conflict management and the mediation short course allow for ownership of and a

willingness by participants to engage in deeper dialogues around diversity and social justice.

3. Faculty professional development activities such as the mediation short course and conflict management seminars and critical dialogues modules can enhance cross-cultural communication skills and difference. Ultimately, the goal is improved working and collegial relationships in the academic environment.

Organizational Development

Senior academic leaders are essential to impact the organizations climate and culture related to conflict management. Leaders can impact the development of the organization as illustrated with a few examples below.

1. Senior academic leaders such as deans, presidents, chancellors, and provosts can help create a conflict-positive organizational culture by providing resources to support the professional development needs of administrators such as departments and deans in the area of conflict management and critical dialogues.
2. Senior academic leaders and administrators can help create a conflict-positive organizational culture by establishing norms stating conflict will occur with increased faculty and staff diversity and can be useful in problem-solving, creativity, visioning, recruitment, retention, and valuing difference.
3. Teaching and learning centers can play a critical role in leading the effort to enhance the professional development of faculty and administrators by sponsoring seminars and workshops on conflict management and difficult dialogues. Faculty professional development professionals can form collaborative relationships with deans and department heads to develop the content of such programs to ensure positive learning outcomes.

Conflict is inevitable and unavoidable and it is manageable. Leaders must:

*   Face that conflicts exist in organizations
*   Understand how conflicts work and be able to frame conflicts
*   Have the skills set and a variety tools to address conflicts as they arise
*   Transform destructive conflicts into opportunities
*   Be a continuous learner about conflict

- Be prepared. Leaders can address conflicts if they are prepared and well-practiced at constructively engaging in conflict
- Be patient—working through some conflicts takes time

REFERENCES

Algert, N. E., & Watson, K. L. (2002). *Conflict management: Introductions for individuals and organizations.* Bryan, TX: Center for Change and Conflict Resolution.

Aschenbrenner, C. A., & Siders, C. (1999). Managing low-mid intensity conflict in the health care setting. Retrieved from http://www.freepatentsonline.com/article/Physician-Executive/102286870.html

Baldridge, J. V. (1971). *Power and conflict in the university.* New York, NY: Wiley.

Bell, L., Love, B. J., & Roberts, R. A. (2007). Racism and white privilege curriculum design. In M. Adams, L. Bell, & P. Griffin (Eds.), *Teaching for diversity and social justice* (pp. 125–144). New York, NY: Routledge.

Birnbaum, R. (1988). *How colleges work: The cybernetics of academic organization and leadership.* San Francisco, CA: Jossey-Bass.

Bollinger, L. (2007). Why diversity matters. *Chronicle of Higher Education, 53*(39), B20.

Bolman, L. G., & Gallos, J. V. (2011). *Reframing academic leadership.* San Francisco, CA: JosseyBass

Bennett, J. B., & Figuli, D. J. (1993). *Enhancing departmental leadership: The roles of the chairperson.* Phoenix, AZ: The Oryx Press.

Bowman, R. F. (2002, January/February). The real work of department chair. *The Clearing House, 75,* 158–162.

Carmichael, G., & Malague, M. (1996, February). *How to resolve conflicts effectively.* Paper presented at the Fifth Annual International Conference for Community & Technical College Chairs, Deans, and Other Organizational Leaders. Phoenix, Arizona. (ERIC Document Reproduction Service Number ED 394 572)

Coffman, J. R. (2009). Confict management for chairs. *Department Chair, 20*(1), 18–21.

Comer, R. W., Haden, N. K., Taylor, R. L., & Thomas, D. D. (2002, April). Leadership strategies for department chairs and program directors: A case study approach. *Journal of Dental Education, 66,* 514–519.

De Dreu, C. K., & Van de Vliert, E. (Eds.). (1997). *Using conflict in organizations.* Thousand Oak, CA: Sage.

Donnellon, A., & Kolb, D. M. (1997). Constructive for whom? The fate of diversity disputes in organizations. In C. De Dreu & E. Van De Vliert (Eds.), *Using conflict in organizations* (pp. 161–176). Thousand Oaks, CA: Sage.

Findlen, G. L. (2000). The skeleton in academe's closet. In D. Robillard, Jr. (Eds.), *Dimensions of managing academic affairs in the community college: New Directions for Community Colleges* (No. 109, pp. 41–49). San Francisco, CA: Jossey-Bass.

George, H. (1984). *American race relations theory: A review of four models.* University Lantham, MD: Press of America.

Gmelch, W. H. (1991a, October). *The creation of constructive conflict within educational administration departments.* Paper presented at the Annual Meeting of the University Council for Educational Administration, Baltimore, Maryland.

Gmelch, W. W. (1991b). Paying the price for academic leadership: Department chair Tradeoffs. *Educational Record, 72*(3), 45–48.

Gmelch, W. H. (1995). Department chairs under siege: Resolving the web of conflict. In S. Holton (Ed.), *Conflict management in higher education: New directions for higher education* (No. 92, pp. 35–42). San Francisco, CA: Jossey-Bass.

Gmelch, W. H., & Carroll, J. B. (1991). The three Rs of conflict management for department chairs and faculty. *Innovative Higher Education, 16,* 107–123.

Hickson, M., & McCroskey, J. C. (1991, October). Diagnosing communication problems of academic chairs: Applied communication in context. *ACA Bulletin, 78,* 8–13.

Lan, Z. (1997). A conflict resolution approach to public administration. *Public Administration Review,* 27–35.

Low, A. (2008). *Conflict and creativity at work: Human roots of corporate life.* Long Island City, NY: Apollo Books.

Lumpkin, A. (2004). Enhancing the effectiveness of department chairs. *Journal of Physical Education, Recreation & Dance, 75*(9), 44–48.

McLaughlin, G. W., Montgomery, J. R., & Malpass, L. F. (1975). Selected characteristics, roles, goals, and satisfactions of department chairmen in state and land-grant institutions. *Research in Higher Education, 3,* 243–259.

Merelman, R. M. (1995). *Representing Black culture. Racial conflict and cultural politics in the United States.* New York, London: Routledge.

Putnam, L.L. (1988). Communication and interpersonal conflict in organizations. *Management Communication Quarterly, 1,* 293-301.

Sonnenschein, W. (1997). Defining diversity. In W. Sonnenschein (Ed.), *The diversity toolkit: How you can build and benefit from a diverse workforce* (pp. 1–12). Chicago, IL: Contemporary Books.

Stanley, C. A., Watson, K. L., & Algert, N. E. (2005, November). A faculty development model for mediating diversity conflicts in the university setting. *The Journal of Faculty Development, 20,* 129–142.

Stanley, C. A., & Algert, N. E. (2007). An exploratory study of the conflict management styles of department heads in a research university setting. *Innovative Higher Education, 32*(1), 49–66.

Tidd, S. T., McIntyre, H. H., & Friedman, R. A. (2004). The importance of role ambiguity and trust in conflict perception: Unpacking the task conflict to relationship conflict linkage. *The International Journal of Conflict Management, 15,* 364–380.

Ting-Toomey, S. (1985). *Communication, culture, and organizational process.* Beverly Hills, CA: Sage.

Ting-Toomey, S. (2005). The matrix of face: An updated face-negotiation theory. *Theorizing About Intercultural Communication,* 71–92.

Ting-Toomey, S., Gao, G., Trubisky, P., Yang, Z., Soo Kim, H., Lin, S. L., & Nishida, T. (1991). Culture, face maintenance, and styles of handling interpersonal

conflict: A study in five cultures. *International Journal of Conflict Management,* *2*(4), 275–296.

Trombly, R. M., Comer, R. W., & Villamil, J. E. (2002, April). Case III: Managing conflict—The case of the faculty stuck in the middle. *Journal of Dental Education, 66,* 533–540.

Tjosvold, D. (1991). Positive conflict: Theory and research. In D. Tjosvold (Ed.), *The conflict-positive organization: Stimulate diversity and create unity* (pp. 37–58). New York, NY: Addison-Wesley.

Watson, N.T., & Watson, K. (2002). *Basic Mediation Training Book.* Bryan, TX: The Center for Change and Conflict Resolution. (Revised 2012)

Wilson, V. (1999). *The department chair: Between a rock and a hard place.* (ERIC Document Reproduction Service No. ED 430 458).

CHAPTER 10

CONCLUSION AND
THE WAY FORWARD

*Education is the ability to listen to almost anything without losing your
temper or your self-confidence*

—Robert Frost

We conclude the book with a brief summary and discuss the "way forward"
particularly looking at the areas of conflict management and dialogue in
higher education and its implications for the future. To effectively address,
manage and resolve conflicts in an academic setting requires strategic planning, thinking, and also skillful reflection. Higher education institutions
must find a conflict management system that works for their organizational culture. In addition, leadership is essential and necessary for units
to understand the importance of having a structured conflict management
system that models the institution's commitment to conflict engagement
and dialogue.

First, this book is intended to support individuals and units to reflect
about conflict and understand conflict engagement. Second, it is intended
to offer ideas for designing and implementing conflict intervention programs, using the mediation method. Third, it is intended to provide ideas
for honing individual skill sets to engage in difficult dialogues.

Conflict Management and Dialogue in Higher Education: A Global Perspective, pp. 161–169
Copyright © 2016 by Information Age Publishing

- As you read the chapters in the book you had the opportunity to:
- Think about and understand the importance of discussing conflict, conflict engagement, and conflict management at your institution
- Understand how the decision to engage or not engage in conflict can create an environment of low morale and distrust
- Reflect on the impact of non-resolved conflicts and how they influence faculty, staff, and student recruitment and retention
- Think about effective conflict management tools that are unique to higher education
- Engage in a brief overview of the literature related to conflict engagement and dialogue in higher education
- Reflect on the roles and responsibilities of leaders to address and manage conflicts in higher education
- Learn from examples used at one institution, including those required for a State 40-hour Basic Mediation Short Course
- Learn from examples used for an institutionally based Difficult Dialogues Course
- Reflect on best practices used for engagement in Conflict Management and Dialogue

To effectively address conflicts, it is important to remember that:

- Effective conflict management begins with self
- Conflict and its impact on organizations is important for effective conflict management
- Leaders have a responsibility for strategic conflict engagement

In this chapter we will share skill sets necessary for effective and strategic conflict engagement and share programs that have been successful at institutions of higher education.

Most leaders adhere to the following: (a) they want their unit to stay together; (b) they want the people in their unit to learn to use less energy as possible related to "unproductive" and "nonaddressed" conflict, and; (c) they need to minimize the conflicts that harm people and optimize the conflicts that challenge them to move forward. There are two tenets for conflict management that are grounded in practice. Organizations that practice effective conflict management are strongest when they are (a) well-practiced in conflict management and (b) exercise coaching as one of the most important skills set within their leadership responsibilities. A

leader is ultimately responsible for determining the conflict culture of the organization. As stated in previous chapters—an organization will normally develop a dominant style or a combination of styles for dealing with conflict. We also know that:

- Conflict responses are learned and people who stay in the organization usually adapt their personal styles to the organization's conflict style over time
- The conflict culture is driven by people in titled leadership (especially at first)
- The conflict culture for the organization is driven by the majority (after time) or the "master narrative" of the unit
- The conflict culture within a unit is driven by people with the greatest longevity
- Conflict responses and conflict cultures can be changed if desired

Skill Sets for Effective Conflict Management

In order to challenge the common responses to conflict, which include: (a) paving over the conflict with superficial gestures; (b) blaming, talking, or complaining about the situation with friends or third parties (while failing to talk directly to the other party we are in disagreement with), and/or; trying to get "hired guns" to deal with the problem (they should be able to intimidate the other party) (Windle &Warren, 2013) it is important for leaders to have:

- Communication skills to reduce bias and prejudice and engage in constructive dialogue
- Negotiation skills to solve problems and settle differences
- Emotional intelligence skills to work through rage and guilt and possibly grief and loss
- Mediation skills to resolve disputes constructively
- Unit building and public dialogue skills to develop interest-based, functional groups, and collaborative leaders
- Skills to rebuild empathy and compassion and encourage forgiveness and reconciliation
- Conflict management systems designed to prevent and resolve future disputes before they become intractable (Putnam, 2004).

Factors That Contribute to Effective Conflict Management

As already mentioned in the beginning chapters of this book, certain factors must be present in order for conflict management strategies to be effective. Conflicts are managed and dialogues are more successful when the parties:

1. have the ability to be self-aware (e.g., identify hidden assumptions)
2. are willing to and engage in self-awareness and self-reflection (e.g., utlization of emotional intelligence skills)
3. are able to frame the/their relationship
4. frame the conflict and the issue(s)
5. practice mindfulness of self and others
6. choose to exercise perspective taking
7. intentionally and strategically choose their conflict management mode(s) for engaging in the conflict
8. look for areas of common ground between the parties in conflict
9. move from positions to the underlying interests and needs of the parties involved in conflict
10. have awareness of what one wants to accomplish in the dialogue/conflict management session
11. articulate the desired end goal(s) to the other party
12. use an effective communication skill set (descripted in Chapter 8)
13. use the conflict management tools Active Listening, Perspective Taking, recognizing Common Ground
14. move self, or the parties, from their Positions to underlying Interests/Needs
15. own their stuff (e.g. biases, assumptions) and let the other person(s) maintain their "stuff"
16. stay off of the Drama Triangle

Best Practices for Successful Conflict Management Programs

Our experiences show that units within a university that have successful conflict management programs have some or all of the following:

1. a common working definition of conflict and conflict management
2. an expectation for employees and students to engage effectively in meaningful conflicts when they arise
3. create opportunities to "develop" employees and students in conflict management opportunities—internal and external workshops

for example. This is based on the belief that not everyone has effective conflict management skills

4. build both individual and organizational capacity to address conflicts

5. clear modeling by university, college, and departmental leadership to engage in constructive and meaningful conflicts

6. a shared vision that conflict is not negative; in fact, constructive conflict is always present within a thriving unit

7. web presence explaining conflict and the importance of conflict engagement

8. a departmental *Code of Conduct* or *Code of Cooperation*

9. formal and informal structures to address conflict

10. structures and processes throughout the university to address conflicts at all levels; unit, department, college, and university

11. aspirant characteristics and values for each college related to dialogue, respect, and inclusion

12. a formal commitment from college and departmental leadership to lead, manage, and engage in difficult dialogues

13. briefs or white papers to formalize the college's commitment to have a culture of dialogue and productive conflict engagement. An example can be found at http://education.tamu.edu/climate-and-diversity

14. protocols for students, faculty, and staff to engage in conflicts. An example can be found at http://education.tamu.edu/sites/default/files/Climate%20Issues%20Flowcharts.pdf

15. regular and appropriate assessment of the climate and culture for diversity. An example can be found at http://diversity.tamu.edu/Diversity-Plan

16. exit interviews for staff, faculty and students when they leave a program of the college

17. mechanisms to keep leadership abreast of climate and conflict issues on a monthly or quarterly basis

18. educational resources that create learning opportunities for faculty, staff and students

19. implement formal educational programs at all levels of the institution; programs such as Ombuds Programs, Conflict Management Workshops, Difficult Dialogues Program as part of a Critical Dialogues in Higher Education Program, 1-4 day workshops to support department heads and deans in conflict management, and a 40-hour Conflict Management Short Course

20. ongoing dialogue to dispel the myth that *conflict* is negative and that conflict is an essential part of a thriving and progressive institution

21. formal programs to support all, in particular leadership for strategic conflict engagement, conflict management, and dialogue

Creating a Culture of Conflict Engagement

Higher education institutions develop and communicate expectations and protocols about issues that are important to them whether by choice or by University or System mandate. Most academic leaders espouse the importance of conflict management in their units, however, few have the structures or processes in place to address conflict. Many leaders think, "I work with smart people and therefore they should be strong conflict managers"; however, there is no correlation between being "smart" and being a "strong conflict manager." Therefore, it is important to learn, model, and communicate the conflict expectations you have for self, faculty, staff, and students in your units. Successful programs have a minimum of the following factors present in their unit.

1. An expectation and articulation that conflicts are addressed at the point of origin between the principal parties
2. They have established a common vocabulary related to conflict and dialogue
3. They work to ensure that all faculty, staff and students have effective conflict management tools and strategies
4. They provide internal and external workshops, seminars and short courses on conflict management and difficult dialogue.
5. They have developed structures and processes on how to informally or formally engage in conflicts. If this does not work what is the next step for your employee?
6. They have developed structures and process at all levels – for example, within the department, the college, and university
7. They have shared the structures for conflict engagement with all personnel; through oral and written communication.
8. They continue to revise best practices and sharing of information as new people join the unit.

Our hope is that you have found the contents of the book useful for addressing conflicts within self, with others, and when facilitating a conflict or dialogue between two or more parties. Learning or refining your conflict skill set is essential for building both individual and organizational

THE WAY FORWARD

As we know, conflict skill building is *awareness building* and also *skill building*. It is important to remember some basic assumptions related to conflict:

- it takes two or more to create conflict, it takes only one to begin the conflict resolution process
- resolving conflict in a constructive manner requires a problem-solving approach, not a "fix-it" approach
- the "best way," for a long term solution, to work out differences between parties is for the parties to talk together in an open dialogue
- People want to be *understood*, *valued*, and *respected* for who they are, and what they can contribute to the organizational culture. Everyone has basic needs related to having a sense of belonging, freedom, power, safety, and fun

It is valuable and important to engage in a reflection of your individual conflict engagement style, which entails:

- An understanding of your unit's conflict culture
- Refection if you are in a leadership role, so that all faculty, staff and students can be better equipped at conflict management

Next Steps for Leaders

Leaders need to remember that you have a responsibility to be a strong conflict manager, to model effective and constructive conflict engagement, and to communicate your expectations of conflict engagement with your faculty, staff, administrative team, and students. When conflicts arise, it is important to remember that there are always choices:

1. Consider the trade-offs in consequences
2. Frame the conflict as you and others understand it
3. Attend to the complex layers of the conflict, and look for:

   Individual patterns
   Situational patterns
   Cultural patterns

4. Select a style for addressing a conflict

5. Select a dialogue strategy
6. Learn about your mental models from the conflict
7. Establish learning opportunities for others

All conflict engagement is built on the basic concept of trust. O'Brien (2001) *referred to* trust as an expectation about the positive actions of other people, without being able to influence or monitor the outcome. People award trust on the basis of fair treatment, respect and recognition for their contributions. People at the bottom of an organization are continuous and careful "intuitive auditors." Deference to authority has been found to be based more on trust than on competence. The durability of trust is based on integrity and consistency. The development of trust builds incrementally, distrust is much more catastrophic. Although another book can be written about building trust within academic units it is important to remind academic leaders that effective leadership occurs in an environment where trust is present.

It is our hope that you are engaged in self-reflection about strategic conflict engagement and dialogue, in order to build a culture of trust within your unit. Trust leads to a willingness to engage in meaningful conflict by following structures and processes predetermined and cocreated by everyone in the organization. It can lead to a more healthy, engaging, and productive environment for all.

CONCLUSION

Our goal in this book has been to provide administrators and faculty members with conflict management information that can be beneficial both personally and professionally. Some people think that conflict is a topic that should not be discussed and that we should not engage in conflict. Productively engaging in conflict is always valuable. Most individuals are willing and interested in resolving their conflicts; they just need the appropriate skill set and opportunities to practice it. Without a conflict skill set, individuals wish to avoid conflict, hoping it will go away, or not wanting to make a "big deal out of nothing." There are times when avoiding conflict is the appropriate strategy, but avoidance is usually not the best strategy, and the implications of not acting to resolve the conflict should always be considered. Research and personal experiences show us that there are always consequences that accompany the decision to engage or not engage in conflict.

Through conflict and self-awareness you can more effectively manage your conflicts and, therefore, your professional and personal relationships. Furthermore, by discussing issues related to conflict management, aca-

demic units can establish an expected protocol to be followed by all when in conflict. All colleges, universities, and academic units have a conflict culture (the way that everyone responds or does not respond to conflict). However, most members of the campus community never discuss what the conflict culture is, leading some to make assumptions that can be counter-productive to the unit.

Practicing your conflict management skills leads to more successful engagement in conflict with outcomes of greater understanding, better communication, and increased productivity for both the individual and the unit. When you manage your conflicts more effectively, you spend more of your energy on the issues and relationships that matter most.

REFERENCES

O'Brien, R. C. (2001). *Trust: Releasing the energy to succeed.* Chichester, England: John Wiley & Sons.

Poirier, R. (1990). *Robert Frost: The work of knowing: With a new afterword* (Vol. 243). Palo Alto, CA: Stanford University Press.

Putnam, L. L. (2004). Transformations and critical moments in negotiations. *Negotiation Journal, 20*(2), 275–295.

Windle, R., & Warren, S. (2013). Collaborative problem solving: Steps in the process. *Center for Appropriate Dispute Resolution in Special Education (CADRE), Eugene, Oregon, USA.* Retrieved from http://www. directionservice.org/cadre/section5. cfm.

GLOSSARY

CHAPTER 6

Ableism: Prejudice and/or discrimination against people with mental and/or physical disabilities.

Accommodating: An individual neglects their own concerns to satisfy the concerns of the other person.

Ageism: Prejudice and/or discrimination against people because of their real or perceived age; although ageism is often assumed to be bias against older people, members of other groups, such as teens, are also targets of prejudice and/or discrimination based on their age.

Aggie Core Values: Excellence (set the bar), Integrity (character is destiny), Leadership (follow me), Loyalty (acceptance forever), Respect (we are the Aggies, the Aggies are we), Selfless Service (how can I be of service).

Anti-Oppression: Work that seeks to recognize the oppression that exists in our society and attempts to mitigate its affects and eventually equalize the power imbalance in our communities.

Anti-Semitism: Prejudice and/or discrimination against Jews; can be based on hatred against Jews because of their religious beliefs, their group

membership (ethnicity), and sometimes on the erroneous belief that Jews are a race.

Assertiveness: Includes standing up for one's rights, initiating and refusing requests, giving and receiving compliments, maintaining and terminating conversations, expressing personal opinions including disagreements, beliefs, goals, or needs, and expressing justified anger and annoyance.

Avoidance: The practice of non-engagement.

Bias: A preconceived opinion or attitude about something or someone. A bias may be favorable or unfavorable.

Body Language: Movements or positions of the body that express a person's thoughts or feelings.

Brainstorming: A storm of ideas. A group-thinking technique to create multiple options for solving a problem. Brainstorming allows all criticism and evaluation of ideas to be postponed until later.

Bullying: Behavior that harms, intimidates, offends, degrades, or humiliates a person, possibly in front of other people.

Change: To make or become different.

Civil Discourse: An engagement in conversation or dialogue intended to enhance understanding.

Classism: Prejudice and/or discrimination against people because of their real or perceived economic status.

Cognitive dissonance: Refers to stress and discomfort associated with (1) holding two or more contradictory beliefs, ideas, or values at the same time or (2) new information that conflicts with existing beliefs, ideas, or values.

Collaboration: Working with another to seek solutions that completely satisfy both parties. This involves accepting both parties' concerns as valid and digging into an issue in an attempt to find innovative possibilities. It also means being open and exploratory.

Competing: A strategy in which one pursues the satisfaction of his/her own positions or interests at the expense of others—a win-lose approach.

Compromising: Seeking an expedient settlement that only partially satisfies both people. Compromising does not dig into the underlying problem, but rather seeks a more superficial arrangement, e.g. "splitting the difference." It is based on partial concessions.

Conflict: A struggle or contest between people with opposing needs, ideas, beliefs, values, or goals.

Conflict Management Skills: Having the ability to notice and handle conflict in a proper manner.

Consensus: An agreement reached by identifying the interests of all concerned parties, and then building an integrative solution that maximizes satisfaction of as many of the interests as possible.

Consequences: A result that logically follows an action.

Conversation: Informal, interactive talk between two or more people, which is spontaneous, has largely interpersonal function, and whose purpose is to maintain and establish social relationships.

Cooperation: Associating for mutual benefit; working toward a common end or purpose; considers the interests of the other party).

Culture: The patterns of daily life learned consciously and unconsciously by a group of people; these patterns can be seen in any language, governing practices, arts, customs, holiday celebrations, food, religion, dating rituals, and clothing, to name a few.

Cyber bullying: Bullying through e-mail, instant messaging (IMing), chat room exchanges, website posts, digital messages or images sent to a cellular phone or personal digital assistant.

Debate: A formal discussion in which opposing arguments are put forward.

Dialogue: A process of exchanging views that leads to common understanding, sometimes with the purpose of finding a solution to a problem or to resolve differences.

Difficult Dialogues: A dialogue between two or more people, where at least one person experiences some level of discomfort in engaging in the topic or issue with the other people.

Discrimination: The denial of justice and fair treatment by both individuals and institutions in many areas, including employment, education, housing, banking and political rights; an action that can follow prejudicial thinking.

Discussion: The act of talking about something with another person or a group of people.

Diversity: The fact or quality of being distinct.

Empowerment: A method of balancing power in a relationship wherein the lower party acquires more power by gaining expertise, obtaining extra resources, building interpersonal linkages, and/or enhancing communication skills.

Ethics: An area of study that deals with ideas about what is good and bad behavior; a branch of philosophy dealing with what is morally right or wrong.

Equity: A justice according to natural law or right; freedom from bias or favoritism.

Facilitation: The act or process to make easier or less difficult. The use of a third party or parties to provide procedural assistance to a group attempting to reach consensus about a problem.

Heterosexism/Homophobia: Heterosexism and homophobia are prejudice and/or discrimination against people who are or who are perceived to be lesbian, gay, bisexual or transgender (LGBT). Homophobia is usually used to describe a blatant fear or hatred of LGBT people; heterosexism is a broader term used to describe attitudes and behaviors based on the belief that heterosexuality is the norm and/or that homosexuality is wrong.

Impartiality: Attitude of the third party; unbiased opinion.

Islamophobia: Prejudice and/or discrimination against people who are or who are perceived to be Muslim or of Arab descent, and a fear or dislike of Islamic culture.

Multicultural: Relating to or including many different cultures.

Myth: A traditional story, especially one that explains the early history or a cultural belief or practice of a group of people, or explains a natural event; also a commonly believed but false idea.

Neutrality: The quality or state of not supporting either side in an argument, fight, war, or dispute.

Oppression: A systemic social phenomenon based on the perceived and real differences among social groups that involve ideological domination, institutional control and the promulgation of the oppressor's ideology, logic system, and culture to the oppressed group. The result is the exploitation of one social group by another for the benefit of the oppressor group.

Perception: One's viewpoint or understanding of a situation.

Position: A point of view; a specific solution that a party proposes to meet his/her interests or needs. A position is likely to be concrete and explicit, often involving a demand or threat and leaving little room for discussion. In conflict resolution, an essential activity is for participants to move beyond positions in order to understand underlying interests and needs.

Prejudice: Prejudging or making a decision about a person or group of people without sufficient knowledge; prejudicial thinking is frequently based on stereotypes.

Racism: Prejudice and/or discrimination against people based on the social construction of race; differences in physical characteristics (e.g., skin color, hair texture, eye shape) are used to support a system of inequities.

Religious bigotry: Prejudice and/or discrimination against people based on their religious beliefs and/or practices.

Restate: To say (something) again or in a different way especially to make the meaning clearer.

Scapegoating: Blaming an individual or group for something based on that person or group's identity when, in reality, the person or group is not responsible; prejudicial thinking and discriminatory acts can lead to scapegoating.

Sexism: Prejudice and/or discrimination against people based on their real or perceived sex; based on a belief (conscious or unconscious) that there is a natural order based on sex.

Social Justice: Involves a vision of society in which distribution of resources is equitable and all members are physically and psychologically safe and secure, the goal of which is full and equal participation of all groups in society that is mutually shaped to meet their needs.

Stereotype: An oversimplified generalization about a person or group of people without regard for individual differences; even seemingly positive stereotypes that link a person or group to a specific positive trait can have negative consequences.

Summarize: To restate in a brief, concise form. Summarizing is an aspect of active listening used by both disputants and mediators to increase common understanding.

Synergy: Cooperative thoughts and/or actions of two or more people working together to achieve something neither could achieve alone.

Trust: To have confidence in or feel sure of; faith.

Value: A principle, standard, or quality considered worthwhile or desirable.

CHAPTER 6

Accommodating: An individual neglects their own concerns to satisfy the concerns of the other person.

Active Listening: A communication procedure wherein the listener uses nonverbal behavior, such as eye contact and gestures, as well as verbal behavior, including tone of voice, open-ended questions, restatements, and summaries, to demonstrate to the speaker that he or she is being heard.

Arbitration: Intervention into a dispute by an independent third party who is given authority to collect information, listens to both sides, and makes a decision as to how the conflict should be settled.

Assertiveness: To state, express, defend, or maintain your wishes, ideas, needs, beliefs or goals.

Avoidance: The practice of nonengagement.

Basic Needs: Needs that underlie all human behavior, such as survival, self-esteem, belonging, self-actualization, power, freedom, and fun. Like individuals, groups have basic needs, including the need for identity, security, vitality, and community.

Bias: A preconceived opinion or attitude about something or someone. A bias may be favorable or unfavorable.

Body Language: Nonverbal communication expressed by your body.

Brainstorming: A storm of ideas. A group thinking technique for helping disputants create multiple options for consideration in solving a problem. Brainstorming allows all criticism and evaluation of ideas to be postponed until later.

Clarify: To make clearer or to enhance understanding. With a conflict resolution style/method, open-ended questions are often used for clarification.

Collaboration: Working with the other to seek solutions that completely satisfy both parties. This involves accepting both parties' concerns as valid and digging into an issue in an attempt to find innovative possibilities. It also means being open and exploratory.

Common Interests/Common Ground: Needs and/or interests that are held jointly by the parties in a negotiation.

Community: A social group with common interests, identity, and customs.

Competing: A strategy in which one pursues the satisfaction of his/her own positions or interests at the expense of others—a win-lose approach.

Compromising: Seeking an expedient settlement that only partially satisfies both people. Compromising does not dig into the underlying problem, but rather seeks a more superficial arrangement, for example, "splitting the difference." It is based on partial concessions.

Conflict: An expressed struggle between at least two interdependent parties who perceive themselves as having incompatible goals, needs, values, ideas, and beliefs. Parties regard each other as interfering with the achievement of their own goals.

Conflict Responses/Modes: Typical styles of conflict resolution used by individuals. These styles include competing, avoiding, accommodating, and collaborating.

Conflict Resolution: A spectrum of processes that employs communication skills and creative thinking to develop solutions that are acceptable to those concerned in a dispute.

Consensus: An agreement reached by identifying the interests of all concerned parties, and then building an integrative solution that maximizes satisfaction of as many of the interests as possible.

Consequences: A result that logically follows an action.

Cooperation: Associating for mutual benefit; working toward a common end or purpose; considers the interests of the other party.

Culture: That part of human interactions and experiences that determines how one feels, acts, and thinks. It is through one's culture that one establishes standards for judging right from wrong, for determining beauty and truth, and for judging oneself and others. Culture includes one's nationality, ethnicity, race, gender, sexual orientation, socioeconomic background, age, and physical and mental ability.

Deescalate: To engage in actions that decrease the intensity of a conflict.

Disputant: One who is engaged in a disagreement or conflict.

Diversity: The fact or quality of being distinct.

Empowerment: A method of balancing power in a relationship wherein the lower party acquires more power by gaining expertise, obtaining extra resources, building interpersonal linkages, and/or enhancing communication skills.

Escalate: To engage in actions that increase the intensity of a conflict.

Facilitation: The use of a third party or parties to provide procedural assistance to a group attempting to reach consensus about a problem.

Framing: The manner in which a conflict solution or issue is conceptualized or defined.

I-Statements: three-part communication process that describes another person's behavior, your feelings, and requests a behavioral change.

Impartiality: Attitude of the third party; unbiased opinion.

Influence: Power to sway or affect.

Interest/Need: A substantive, procedural, or psychological need of a party in a conflict situation; the aspect of something that makes it significant.

Listening for Feeling: Being able to identify and differentiate facts and feelings.

Managing Emotions: Staying aware of your emotions, biases, and prejudices and realizing their impact on the conflict process.

Mediation: Intervention in a dispute by an impartial third party who can assist the disputants in negotiating an acceptable settlement.

Negotiation: An interaction between two or more parties who have an actual or perceived conflict of interest. In a negotiation, the participants join voluntarily in a dialogue to educate each other about their needs and interests, to exchange information, and to create a solution that meets the needs of both parties.

Neutrality: The statement of not favoring or biased to either side in a dispute.

Option: An alternative course of action; a possible solution that may satisfy the interests of a party to a dispute.

Peace: A process of responding to diversity and conflict with tolerance, imagination, and flexibility; fully exercising one's responsibilities to ensure that all fully enjoy human rights.

Perception: One's viewpoint or understanding of a situation

Position: A point of view; a specific solution that a party proposes to meet his/her interests or needs. A position is likely to be concrete and explicit, often involving a demand or threat and leaving little room for discussion. In conflict resolution, an essential activity is for participants to move beyond positions in order to understand underlying interests and needs.

Power: The ability to act or perform effectively; the ability to influence.

Questioning: A skill used to gather meaningful conflict information while not creating a defensive reaction by the disputant.

Reframing: The process of changing how a person or party of conflict conceptualizes his/her or another's attitudes, behaviors, issues, and interests; how a situation is defined. Reframing during conflict resolution processes help to mitigate defensiveness and deescalate tension.

Restating: Skill used to assure accurate understanding of each disputant.

Resolution: A course of action agreed upon to solve a problem.

Summarize: To restate in a brief, concise form. Summarizing is an aspect of active listening used by both disputants and mediators to increase common understanding.

Synergy: Cooperative thoughts and/or actions of two or more people working together to achieve something neither could achieve alone.

Trust: To have confidence in or feel sure of; faith.

Value: A principle, standard, or quality considered worthwhile or desirable.

Violence: Psychological or physical force exerted for the purpose of injuring, damaging, or abusing people or property.

For additional support in using Chapter 8 as part of a Mediation Course, contact:
Nancy Watson, PhD, LPC, FAPA and Nancy Hutchins, PhD
The Center for Change and Conflict Resolution
207 Sulphur Springs   Bryan, Texas 77801
T: .979.224.3638   F: 888.819.0495
email: cccrtx@gmail.com   Web: http://www.cccrtx.us

ABOUT THE AUTHORS

Nancy Watson is President of The Center for Change and Conflict Resolution (CCCR), a Clinical Associate Professor in the Department of Educational Administration and Human Resource Development, and Director for Climate Enhancement Initiatives in the Office for Diversity at Texas A&M University. She is a Licensed Professional Counselor, Licensed Mediator, TMCA Distinguished Mediator, and Fellow of the American Psychotherapy Association. As President of the CCCR, she provides counseling, consulting, and conflict management services. She works with individuals and organizations in higher education on building capacity for effective communication, conflict management and diversity, change management, and organizational development. She consults nationally and internationally on capacity building, diversity, and conflict management, and is the author of numerous publications. She teaches undergraduate and graduate courses on conflict management and dialogue, and is a member of the Board of Directors for the Difficult Dialogues National Resource Center. Her overarching professional and research interests include supporting individuals and organizations in honing their power to accomplish their personal and professional goals.

Karan L. Watson, PhD, PE, is Provost and Executive Vice President and Regents Professor of Electrical and Computer Engineering at Texas A&M University. She has held a variety of university leadership roles including associate dean for academic affairs and graduate studies in the Dwight Look College of Engineering, dean of faculties and associate provost,

vice provost, interim vice president and associate provost for diversity, and interim provost. She is a Past President of the Accreditation Board for Engineering and Technology (ABET) and an ABET Fellow. A Fellow of the Institute of Electrical and Electronic Engineers (IEEE) and the American Society for Engineering Education (ASEE), she is the recipient of numerous awards including the U.S. President's Award for Mentoring Minorities and Women in Science and Technology, the American Association for the Advancement of Science (AAAS) Mentoring Award, the IEEE International Undergraduate Teaching Medal, and two University-level Distinguished Achievement Awards from The Texas A&M University Association of Former Students—one for Student Relations and the other for Administration.

Christine A. Stanley PhD, is Vice President and Associate Provost for Diversity and Professor of Higher Education at Texas A&M University. She has held a variety of university leadership roles including associate director of the Center for Teaching Excellence, associate department head, associate dean of faculties, and executive associate dean of the College of Education and Human Development. She is a Past President of the Professional and Organizational Development (POD) Network in Higher Education. She is a recipient of numerous awards including the Spirit of POD Award, and the Mildred Garcia Award for Exemplary Scholarship from the Association for the Study of Higher Education (ASHE). The POD Network established an award in her name—the Christine A. Stanley Award for Diversity and Inclusion Research in Educational Development. A native of Jamaica, The West Indies, she served on the presidential task force to develop and write the first Standards of Professional Practice for college and university Chief Diversity Officers, commissioned by the National Association of Diversity Officers in Higher Education (NADOHE).

Made in the USA
Lexington, KY
22 March 2018